AF327148

Fallout

Fallout

Nuclear Diplomacy in an Age of Global Fracture

GRÉGOIRE MALLARD

The University of Chicago Press
Chicago and London

Grégoire Mallard is associate professor in the Department of Anthropology and Sociology of Development at the Graduate Institute of International and Development Studies in Geneva.

The University of Chicago Press, Chicago 60637
The University of Chicago Press, Ltd., London
© 2014 by The University of Chicago
All rights reserved. Published 2014.
Printed in the United States of America

23 22 21 20 19 18 17 16 15 14   1 2 3 4 5

ISBN-13: 978-0-226-15789-4 (cloth)
ISBN-13: 978-0-226-15792-4 (e-book)
DOI: 10.7208/chicago/9780226157924.001.0001

Library of Congress Cataloging-in-Publication Data

Mallard, Grégoire, 1977– author.
 Fallout : nuclear diplomacy in an age of global fracture / Grégoire Mallard.
   pages cm
  Includes bibliographical references and index.
  ISBN 978-0-226-15789-4 (cloth : alkaline paper) ISBN 978-0-226-15792-4
(e-book) 1. Nuclear nonproliferation—International cooperation—History.
2. Treaties—Interpretation and construction—History—20th century.
3. Diplomacy—History—20th century. I. Title.
  JZ5675.M35 2014
  327.1'747—dc23

                                      2014000141

CONTENTS

I finished writing this book in the hills of Tuscany, where I spent the academic year 2011–12 at the European University Institute. At the institute, unsurprisingly, I was a Jean Monnet fellow. For those who believe that the production of knowledge is situated in a social context, this will not come as a surprise: Jean Monnet, the main protagonist in the following story, was responsible for the creation of this institute; another important player, Max Kohnstamm, Monnet's assistant for many years, acted as the first president of the institute. Furthermore, in 2012, Miguel Maduro, the director of the Global Governance Programme, gave me the opportunity to invite high-level policy makers from the Middle East to meet with officials of the European Community of Atomic Energy (Euratom) and learn from the little-known story of Euratom how a regional nuclear order could be created, and with what effect. The circle seemed to come to a close.

My interest in nuclear nonproliferation policy actually started in September 2001. I had just moved to Princeton when the twin towers were hit on September 11, 2001. What was a tragedy for the United States and many parts of the world shaped my research interests for the next decade. Indeed, it was in the context of collective discussions organized on campus about the merits of the war in Afghanistan that I met some members of the Science and Global Security Program in Princeton, in particular Frank Von Hippel and Zia Mian. After this initial encounter, these nuclear scientists always welcomed the strange presence of a sociologist among them, and their weekly seminars were of tremendous help. They are the ones who consistently pushed me to relate my academic concerns with current policy-making initiatives.

September 11 mattered in another way for me: it was after this attack that US foreign policy makers started to talk about a new hybrid, "rogue states that develop nuclear weapons capabilities and harbor terrorists," which, as the "Bush doctrine" stated, required that the international community take immediate military action against them, whatever the costs, and regardless of doubts about the connections between those states, nuclear weapons, and terrorists. As a sociologist of knowledge, I was intrigued to observe that the policy makers responsible for this new doctrine had sometimes specialized in nuclear nonproliferation, the practice of which requires patience and diplomatic skills, rather than speedy action. I decided to study the sociohistorical genesis of that field of nuclear nonproliferation in the United States. Of course, my research took another direction, but some traces of that initial objective are left in this book.

So many people have helped me overcome my own limitations that I will inevitably forget some of them. But I would never have started this research if Michèle Lamont had not invited me, more than ten years ago, to join her at Princeton University. I deeply thank her as well as Bruno Latour, who had the brilliant idea to first introduce us. At Princeton, Kim Lane Scheppele, the director of the Program in Law and Public Affairs, has provided me with the intellectual shelter that I needed to develop my ideas. I had many interesting conversations with the members of the Society of Woodrow Wilson Scholars, which supported my research from 2006 to 2008. At McGill University, a Richard Tomlinson Fellowship allowed me to benefit from constructive discussions with my Canadian colleagues. And in 2009, I was extremely fortunate to join the Department of Sociology at Northwestern University: it proved to be the ideal place to exchange ideas about sociological approaches to international law. I am indebted not only to specific individuals but also to the collective culture of intellectual innovation and interdisciplinary dialogue, which my colleagues have patiently worked to create and preserve there. I want to acknowledge the support of the Weinberg College of Arts and Sciences and the Crown Family Middle East Research Awards, which made it possible to complete the research and production of this book. During the five years that I have spent in Chicago, my reflections have also been nourished by the rich conversations I have had with fellows and researchers at the American Bar Foundation.

I am also extremely grateful to Karen Alter, Yves Dezalay, Daniel Halbertsam, Terry Halliday, Gabrielle Hecht, Lucien Karpik, Michèle Lamont, Peter Lindseth, Catherine Paradeise, Kim Lane Scheppele, and Robert Wuthnow for their patience as they read and commented upon this manuscript in its different forms (from first draft to final book manuscript). I also owe many thanks to Madeleine Arenivar, Susan J. Cohan, and Andrea Saunderson, who have never grown tired of editing the many different versions of this book. Graduate students (in particular, Carolina Alvarez-Utoft, Savina Balasubramanian, Marco Bocchese, Salvatore Caserta, Anna Hanson, Diana Rodriguez-Franco, and Talia Shiff) provided great feedback on some of the chapters in the context of my Law and Globalization class at Northwestern University.

I also greatly benefited from many informal conversations on a vast array of sociological topics and international relations and international law with: Sameh Aboul Enein, Ken Adler, Alessandra Arcuri, Kai-Henrik Barth, Debbie Becher, Yael Berda, Nehal Bhuta, Pablo Boczkowski, Charles Camic, Bruce Carruthers, Miguel Centeno, Benoit Challand, Arslan Chikhaoui, Antonin Cohen, Avner Cohen, Joseph Cohen, Leo Coleman, Ariel Colonomos, Angela Creager, Paul Doty, Mitch Duneier, Wendy Espeland, Steven Epstein, Gary Fine, Paolo Foradori, Martial Foucault, Marcel and Vincent Fournier, Alexander Glaser, Michael Gordin, Neil Gross, Joshua Guetzkow, Nicolas Guilhot, Hugh Gusterson, John Hagan, John Hall, Carol Heimer, Bastien Hirondelle, Ian Hurd, James Jasper, Caroline Jorant, Alexandra Kalev, Ayman Khalil, Stephen Klement, Pierre Kremp, John Krige, Andrew Lakoff, Vincent Lepinay, Ariel Levite, Michael Loriaux, Ken Luongo, Mikael Rask Madsen, Jim Mahoney, Leslie McCall, Frédéric Mérand, Michael Merril, Vincent Mirza, Christoph Möllers, Kelly Moore, Cristina Mora, Seyed Hossein Mousavian, Mahmoud Nasreddine, Robert Nelson, Stephen Nelson, Laura Beth Nielsen, Ann Orloff, Reut Paz, Ashveen Peerbaye, Benoit Pelopidas, Alejandro Portes, Vincent Pouliot, Monica Prasad, Hassan Rahmouni, Christophe Robert, Daniel Sabbagh, Stephen Schwartz, Julien Seroussi, Jérôme Sgard, Mohamed Shaker, Graziella Silva, Augustin Simard, Patrick Simon, Anna Sodersten, Etel Solingen, Hendrik Spruyt, Laura Stark, Chana Teeger, Stamatios Tsalas, Antoine Vauchez, Pascal Vennesson, Jim Walsh, Nicholas Wheeler, Ipek Yosmaoglu, Viviana Zelizer; as well as Françoise, Pierre-Hilaire, and Antoine Mallard. The staffs of the Archives of the European Communities in Florence and Mudd Library in Princeton University have also provided me with invaluable advice and material help.

My gratitude goes to Doug Mitchell, who has successfully navigated this manuscript through the peer review process: as I claim in the following pages, the metaphor of Ulysses being tied to the mast might not be the most adequate to capture the essence of treaty-writing processes, but it might be accurate when one seeks to define the author's relationship to his or her manuscript as it moves through the waters of peer review. One can only hope that the ship has a great captain, and one cannot dream of a better one than Doug Mitchell.

As I finish writing this manuscript, I rejoice at the idea that my beloved partner in this life, Eléonore Lépinard, whose intellectual passion remains the main source of my inspiration, will finally be able to hold this book in her hands. I also hope that my two daughters, Tess and Garance, will read it one day, when they realize that not all books can rise to the level of fun provided by the adventures of Pimpa.

ABBREVIATIONS

ACRS	Arms Control and Regional Security (Middle East)
AEC	Atomic Energy Commission (US)
CEA	Commissariat à l'Energie Atomique (France)
CIA	Central Intelligence Agency
DoD	Department of Defense
ECJ	European Court of Justice
ECSC	European Coal and Steel Community
EDC	European Defense Community
EEC	European Economic Community
EPC	European Political Community
ESA	Euratom Supply Agency
EU	European Union
Euratom	European Community of Atomic Energy
FRG	Federal Republic of Germany
HEU	highly enriched uranium
IADA	International Atomic Developmental Authority
IAEA	International Atomic Energy Agency
ICBM	intercontinental ballistic missile
IRBM	intermediate-range ballistic missile
JCAE	Joint Committee on Atomic Energy (US Congress)
LTBT	Limited Test Ban Treaty
MRBM	medium-range ballistic missile

NATO	North Atlantic Treaty Organization
NNWS	non-nuclear-weapon state
NPG	Nuclear Planning Group (NATO)
NPT	Treaty on the Non-proliferation of Nuclear Weapons
NSG	Nuclear Suppliers Group
NWS	nuclear-weapon state
OECD	Organization of Economic Cooperation and Development
OEEC	Organization for European Economic Cooperation
OSRD	Office of Scientific Research and Development (US Manhattan Project)
P5+1	the permanent members of the UN Security Council and Germany
SAC	Strategic Air Command
SACEUR	supreme allied commander in Europe
TVA	Tennessee Valley Authority
WEU	Western European Union
WMD	weapons of mass destruction

ONE

Introduction

Diplomats have a complex relationship to truth. The permanent delegation of sovereign powers to diplomats was first experimented with in the Tuscan hills during the Renaissance. Since then, we have come to see the diplomat as "a man of virtue sent abroad to lie for his country,"[1] as the envoy of James I of England to the Venetian Republic put it in the early sixteenth century.

Diplomatic interactions often occur in a public space where polite half lies are expressed, and in a secret space where the true meaning of mutual pledges is negotiated. When the P5+1 (the permanent members of the UN Security Council and Germany) reached a deal with Iran in Geneva on November 24, 2013, the press revealed that President Obama had authorized at least five secret meetings between top Obama administration and Iranian officials since March 2013. These meetings were carefully hidden from the public as well as from America's closest allies. Their very existence raised some concerns among the P5+1: two weeks prior to the Geneva agreement, the draft presented by the United States was rejected by the French foreign minister, who did not appreciate that the United States and Iran had secretly drafted an agreement that imposed softer restrictions on Iran's nuclear program than those planned by the P5+1.[2]

No painter has given a better visual representation of the complex relationship diplomats have to secret truth and public space than a contemporary of James I, the Venetian painter Vittore Carpaccio. In the foreground of the painting, entitled *The Departure of the Ambassadors*, we see a Christian king from Brittany giving a letter to the ambassador from the British Isles informing him of the conditions that his daughter Ursula placed on her wedding. Behind, a member of the court dictates another letter to a scribe. The scribe is hidden from the view of the public courtiers who are watch-

Figure 1.1. Carpaccio, *The Departure of the Ambassadors* (1495)

ing the ritualized public scene. The division of the diplomatic space suggests that the second letter does not solely reiterate those words proffered by the king to the ambassador: the presence of a huge marble wall behind the scribe underlines the contrast between the insiders who have access to a hidden truth and the bystanders who are denied it.

Some may think that in the modern world, when leaders can communicate directly on secure cell phones and other "red lines" opened to avert nuclear crises, opacity and duplicity have become the norm in diplomatic transactions; for some, the exercise of sovereignty has become a form of "organized hypocrisy."[3] As Martin Jay observes, our cultural understanding of diplomacy is found in "the adjective 'diplomatic' [which] means observing the protocols of tact and decorum (as well as practicing a benign kind of hypocrisy)."[4]

Still, as the duplicity at work in the art of diplomacy has increased, calls for transparency in diplomatic negotiations have also become louder. The twentieth century began with calls for open bargaining based on the norms of publicity, clarity, and transparency in interstate negotiations. The First World War ended with the two emerging superpowers—the United States of America and the Soviet Union—asking the old European powers to stop practicing opacity in their diplomatic dealings. The first of Woodrow Wilson's Fourteen Points stated that "open covenants of peace openly arrived at, after which there shall be no private international understandings of any kind but diplomacy shall proceed always frankly and in the public view."[5] In their denunciation of opacity, the Americans were not alone: one of the first actions taken by the Bolsheviks after Lenin seized power in Russia was to open the diplomatic archives of the tsarist regime and to denounce the secret agreements that the British and French allies had reached over the future division of the territories of their enemies. When the revolutionaries published these secret wartime agreements in their new journal *Pravda*—which means "truth" in Russian—they suggested that only a transparent diplomacy could put an end to the imperialist designs of European powers.

The relative value of opacity and transparency in the making of international treaties has been debated many times since the Great War. In a world of multilateral diplomacy characterized by intense media coverage of nuclear issues, violations of the rules of transparent diplomacy rarely go unnoticed. One of the most recent examples was Secretary of State Colin Powell's 2003 attempt—and failure—to convince the UN Security Council and the International Atomic Energy Agency (IAEA) that the United States possessed credible evidence that Saddam Hussein was buying uranium from Niger, that he also imported aluminum tubes to build uranium centrifuges, and that these violations of Security Council Resolution 1441 authorized the United States to take military action against the violator.[6] Colin Powell's performance became a symbol of sovereign hypocrisy when the IAEA experts questioned the truthfulness of his claim that Iraq was about to produce enriched uranium (a particularly sensitive material that can be used as fuel for nuclear power plants when enriched at low levels, but also as the nuclear core of a "dirty bomb" or nuclear weapon when enriched at higher levels). The public display of "good faith" by the US secretary of state barely hid the secret agreement that the United States and its allies had already reached regarding military action against Iraq.[7] This duplicity led to the Anglo-American alliance being censured worldwide, proof that diplomacy based on opacity was no longer seen as legitimate.

Still, when transparency was imposed upon the inner workings of the US diplomatic service after Julian Assange's decision to publish US State Department cables on a website, few voices in the West supported the founder of WikiLeaks. Daniel Ellsberg, the nuclear strategist who had released the "Pentagon Papers," which exposed the trail of secret policy decisions that led to the US war in Vietnam, was among the few voices who spoke in support of complete transparency in diplomatic dealings. As Ellsberg wrote, even though "WikiLeaks has teased the genie of transparency out of a very opaque bottle," it was a shame that "powerful forces in America," including the Obama administration and most of its allies, "have been trying desperately to stuff the genie back in."[8] That they have consistently tried to do so shows that complete transparency is not more legitimate than exposed opacity.

Questions

Even if pressing, these debates about the acceptable relationship that diplomats should have with truth and lies, publicity and secrecy, have largely been ignored by the scholarly literature on international law and international relations.[9] Scholars of international relations pay little attention to the relationship that diplomats have with the truth when they interpret treaty rules and other legal obligations: most often, political scientists discuss treaties either as dependent variables explained by the geopolitical balance of power,[10] or as tools of policy coordination,[11] whose meaning can generally be easily identified by diplomats as well as by the social scientists who interpret them in their cozy offices in academia. Political scientists and sociologists interested in international law have generally overlooked the microlevel processes of legal interpretation; they have focused instead on macrolevel processes of normative habituation and "mimetic" socialization among political elites, which, according to them, explain the global spread of new norms of human rights and economic governance in world society.[12]

Since social and political scientists have left the terrain of legal interpretation largely untouched, most of the research on it has been produced from within the field of international law. However, this division of labor is problematic, since legal scholars tend to adopt an "internalist" reading of international legal progress (seen as an endogenous process of clarification unaffected by social or political mechanisms). Indeed, legal scholars focus mostly on legal interpretation by international courts, which they believe to be protected from the influence of politics and society.[13] Thus, legal scholars have rarely analyzed the kind of relationship that diplomats have with the truth of their legal interpretations of treaty obligations. This is highly problematic when legal interpretation concerns treaties on international security—such as nuclear nonproliferation and disarmament treaties—as the law there is produced through successive rounds of treaty negotiations in which diplomats participate, and not through jurisprudence and case law produced by international courts.[14] Thus, many questions pertaining to the study of international law are still unanswered today.

To fill this gap, this book asks the following questions: Do diplomats believe it is legitimate and effective to produce treaty rules whose interpretation is transparent? Or do they accept that the interpretation of treaty rules should remain opaque, in the sense that their public interpretation can be contradicted by privately shared understandings? How is transparency in the interpretation of treaty obligations produced in diplomatic negotiations? How are ambiguity and opacity produced? What kinds of social and political resources are needed to produce one type of interpretation instead of another?

Whereas this first set of questions seeks to explain the genesis of transparency and opacity in diplomats' interpretation of the law, a second set of questions relates to the effect that each type of interpretation has on the destiny of legal rules. This book also seeks to respond to the following questions: How do transparent and opaque treaty interpretations survive the entry into force of new treaty rules that contradict some of the interpretations of previous treaty obligations? If the truth of a treaty interpretation is opaque, who decides how legal contradictions between treaty regimes are settled? And which interpretation should prevail (the public or the private)? If diplomats generally accept opaque interpretations of treaty rules, then how can a coherent legal order be created and maintained over time?

By answering these questions and opening the interpretive practices of diplomats to scholarly analysis, this book takes part in the now well established field of studies that is concerned with analyzing the relationship that different communities of knowledge producers have entertained with the truth. Scholarly concern has grown out of the pioneering historical studies of Michel Foucault on the practices associated with various types of philosophical, psychological, and social knowledge.[15] It has also been developed by abundant studies of knowledge practices among scientific communities,[16] some comparative[17] and others not, which renewed the Foucaltian studies of knowledge production in the social sciences.[18] But never has this kind of study been applied to examine how diplomats and foreign policy elites have practiced the art of interpreting the legal rules expressed in treaties, conventions, memorandums of understandings, and other textual traces in which international law is spelled out. To open this field of study, this book focuses on how diplomats have read legal commitments in the nuclear age.

Focus

This book focuses on a wide range of interpretations of treaty obligations created by sixty years of diplomatic discussions in the "global nonproliferation regime,"[19] which can be divided into two successive periods. From the end of the Second World War to the mid-1970s, the West finally negotiated a compromise with the Soviets between the new legal obligations created by the Non-proliferation Treaty (NPT), signed in 1968, and their previous legal obligations: this moment of rules creation is the main focus of this book. But since the mid-1970s, this legal order was challenged by outsiders to the NPT regime, mostly Pakistan and its clients, which played on opaque agreements and legal ambiguities contained in the interpretation of the law in order to subvert the global regime, as I explain in the last chapter of this book.

Some clarifications are needed in order to understand the focus of this book. First, the obligations contracted within the nonproliferation regime should not be seen as isolated from obligations in adjacent global regimes: nonproliferation obligations often intersect with other commitments, such as nuclear disarmament and civilian nuclear cooperation obligations, which are all tackled by the NPT, for example. Indeed, in the NPT, the nuclear-weapon states (NWS) were committed not to help other states acquire nuclear-weapons technology, and non-nuclear-weapon states (NNWS) swore not to seek that help from the NWS (art. 1 and 2); but the NWS also recognized that NNWS have an "inalienable right" to peaceful nuclear development (art. 4), and they have pledged to offer them privileged access to international trade in civilian nuclear technologies. In addition, the NWS pledged to "pursue negotiations in good faith" on nuclear disarmament (art. 6).

Second, the legal obligations that are the object of the present analysis are not all contained in one treaty, the NPT. The comprehensive focus on the nonproliferation regime adopted here is akin to the "ecological" approach to international law in which the unit of analysis is not the interpretation of one legal rule found in one treaty but "the sea in which [the interpretation of a bundle of rules] swims,"[20] in the words of Susan Block-Lieb and Terence Halliday. The NPT is just one legal instrument in a grand bargain between the five NWS (first the United States, the Soviet Union, and the United Kingdom, and then France and China) and the NNWS, which was initially supposed to last for only twenty-five years, after which the parties would decide whether they wished to extend their obligations indefinitely—which they did during the 1995 NPT Review and Extension Conference. The global nonproliferation regime is also composed of a myriad of treaties and agreements other than the NPT: for instance, the global nonproliferation regime is made of a dense web of Safeguards Agreements that the NNWS signed with the IAEA, which the NPT charged with the "exclusive purpose of verification of [the NNWS' nonproliferation] obligation with a view to preventing diversion of nuclear energy from peaceful uses to nuclear weapons" (art. 3.1).[21] Any study of the interpretation of the nonproliferation obligations undertaken by states therefore needs to encompass the study of these other legal instruments, and the way they were arrived at.

Third and last, the range of obligations found in the global nonproliferation regime should not all be seen as coherent and fixed throughout time, as the multiplicity of legal instruments that define the true interpretation of nonproliferation obligations often leads to tension and contradictions between interpretations. This idea goes against the view developed by most analysts who presented the NPT as constituting a tightly integrated regime, which placed many preexisting treaties on nuclear trade in a coherent framework.[22] In contrast to these, I claim that the NPT created legal obligations that were coherent with other treaty rules only in some cases but not in general.

In fact, many tensions existing within the global nuclear nonproliferation regime concerned the role that the rules previously accepted in Western Europe and between the United States and Europe would continue to play after the NPT entered into force, and whether rules similar to those applied to Europe would be applied to the non-Western and decolonizing world: the strongest tensions concerned the post-NPT survival of the European system of control of nuclear activities set up by the European Community of Atomic Energy (Euratom) Treaty in 1957,[23] signed by six European states (France, West Germany, Italy, the Netherlands, Belgium, and Luxembourg), and recognized as a valid instrument of international law by the United States when it signed the United States–Euratom Treaty in 1958. The existence of the Euratom system of controls explains that, as Astrid Forland writes, "in spite of the global orientation of the negotiations and the global problem that the NPT was addressing, it [wa]s in fact striking to what extent the European context set the framework for the negotiations."[24]

This "European exceptionalism" was partly the result of the unique density of legal agreements that tied West European nations to each other (and to the United States) prior to the NPT.[25] But more generally, it can also be a reflection of the fact that European lawmakers, who have long used international law to enslave instead of empower the non-European world,[26] have wanted to preserve a zone of exception in Europe, and have created a special European order to buffer the influence of rising great powers such as the United States and the Soviet Union, whose role in promoting nonproliferation rules has far exceeded the role of Europe after the Second World War.

As a result, the harmonization of the rules of control, as requested by the NPT (art. 3), required a tremendous work of commensuration between the European and global legal organizations involved in the negotiation. The compromise was reached with the IAEA-Euratom Safeguards Agreement that was signed in 1972. Since then, the compromise has created enough coherence within the global nuclear regime that we do not speak of "fragmentation of international law,"[27] but in fact, not all countries were convinced that the result erased the fracture between Europe and the rest of the world: among the former colonized nations, India refused to enter into what it called the "nuclear apartheid"[28] that the NPT organized when it allowed Western Europe and NWS to keep special rights and privileges.

The exceptional complexity of the legal situation of Europe with regard to the NPT therefore begged a close examination of the role that European diplomats played in the making of the successive interpretations of their nonproliferation obligations.[29] This focus led me to conduct archival research in the private papers of European and American diplomats, statesmen, and specialists of international law who were particularly instrumental, first, in creating the Western nuclear regime and, second, in negotiating how Europe and the United States would find their place within the global nonproliferation regime.[30] This strategy enabled me to capture how the interpretation of key legal rules was negotiated collectively, leading sometimes to a public agreement on the true meaning of a rule (transparency), sometimes to the recognition that a disagreement existed on what the rule really meant (ambiguity), and sometimes to the acknowledgment of a private meaning that contradicted public statements (opacity).

The archival research that I conducted confirmed the exceptional role that the Frenchman Jean Monnet (1888–1979) played in negotiating most of the treaties that regulated nuclear trade between the United States and Europe before the NPT, and in defining the scope and limitation of the NPT for Western Europe. Monnet's centrality was testimony to his influence both in Europe, where he gained fame as a war planner during the First World War, and in the United States, where he acquired influence while he planned Anglo-American military preparedness efforts during World War II. In the words of Justice Felix Frankfurter, for the Americans, Monnet was a "teacher to our defense administration,"[31] and he remained so well into the Cold War. Starting with Jean Monnet, and following the paper trail that led to Western policy makers interested in foreign nuclear policy after the Second World War,[32] it was no coincidence that I soon encountered key US policy makers such as John Foster Dulles, John McCloy, and George Ball, who often adhered (for longer or shorter periods of time) to the ideal of "Eurofederalism"[33] that Monnet defended. This Eurofederalist ideal had a central nuclear component: it prescribed that West European states (and the United States, which was for some time in charge of West Germany's defense policy) delegate sovereign prerogatives in matters of defense, including nuclear defense, to a strong European Union that could face the Soviet threat on its own. In many ways, their attachment to Eurofederalist ideals explains the exceptional place from which Europe benefitted in the global nuclear nonproliferation regime set up by the NPT.

The narrative thus reveals how the "Eurofederalists" around Monnet wrote parts of the most important nuclear nonproliferation treaties proposed by the US government after the war, a story that is largely unknown to international security specialists,[34] and even to specialists of the European process of integration.[35] Consultation of their private archives, which have now been opened, enabled me to present a balanced picture of their successes and failures, in contrast to earlier studies, which Alan Milward calls the hagiographies of the "lives and teachings of the European Saints,"[36] which rely mostly on the oral testimonies of Monnet's collaborators.[37] This book shows that in many ways, Eurofederalists failed in their efforts to secure the right for the European Communities to build nuclear weapons and trade nuclear military and dual-use technologies (technologies with civilian as well as military applications) with the United States. But in many other ways, this book shows that the treaties of the earlier generation of Eurofederalists survived the creation of the NPT thanks to their sustained legal mobilization.

Organization of the Book

The book is composed of a theoretical chapter; five historical chapters, each divided into two sections; and a conclusion, which applies some lessons drawn from the European case to rethink the challenges facing the global nonproliferation regime today. In the next chapter (chapter 2), I define the terms essential to my analysis of international law, especially *transparency*, *ambiguity*, and *opacity*, and I situate my hermeneutic focus on the complexity of legal interpretation within the existing sociological theories of legal change: first, on the sociological theories that focus on the domestic mechanisms at work in the national fields of foreign policy; second, on the sociological theories that focus on the temporality of international law and more particularly on the dynamics at work in "recursive cycles" of legal change.[38] I formulate hypotheses on the role that transparency, ambiguity, and opacity play at the domestic level as well as on their effect on future cycles of treaty revision.

Then, I present the results of my historical inquiry in five chapters. The historical narrative is divided into five acts, as if they were scenes from a classical eighteenth-century tragedy. The first three of these chapters tell the story of how the Eurofederalists close to Jean Monnet successfully deceived powerful enemies as they turned their European ideals into international law. The last two of these chapters show the price paid by Monnet and other Eurofederalists for having adopted an interpretive tactic that privileged opacity over transparency: they show the fate of the European treaties of Eurofederalist inspiration when the NPT was ratified by West European states.

Negotiating Nonproliferation Obligations in the West

In the first section of chapters 3–5, I show how Monnet and the diplomats he gathered around him attempted three times (the last one successfully) to turn their ideals into binding treaty obligations. Each time, they successively adopted a different interpretive tactic to present the most controversial articles in each treaty: tactics of *transparency*, *ambiguity*, and *opacity*, in chronological order. These three chapters show how the choice of each tactic affected the outcome of treaty negotiations.

Chapter 3 explains the domestic reasons why the US diplomats, scientists, and statesmen who tabled the first nuclear nonproliferation and disarmament treaty at the United Nations immediately after the Second World War (from 1945 to 1948), privileged the search for clearly understood legal rules whose interpretation was discussed in public forums. More specifically, it shows that public and transparent diplomacy, far from being the consensual product of a Wilsonian approach to nuclear diplomacy, was imposed on the US scientists and diplomats who wanted to conclude a nuclear disarmament treaty with the Soviets by the American nationalists who opposed their goal. American nationalists imposed diplomatic transparency to make it impossible for the Soviet and Western diplomats to conclude secret deals and play on legal ambiguities that would have made treaty obligations agreeable to all parties. Not only did diplomatic transparency affect the outcome of global negotiations, but it also shifted the blame for the failure of negotiations to those "world federalists" in the US government who lobbied in favor of a comprehensive global nuclear nonproliferation and disarmament treaty by which all states would agree to permanently delegate their most important rights to nuclear development to an all-powerful UN nuclear agency. Thus, transparent diplomacy was a double-edged sword: while it gave a transnational public forum to the world federalists who defended the creation of supranational organizations dealing with nuclear research, development, and trade, transparency also eliminated the diplomatic back channels between the West and the East.

Thus, it appeared that without a dose of polysemy and/or secrecy, global treaty negotiations on nuclear nonproliferation and disarmament issues were doomed to fail at the beginning of the Cold War. In chapter 4, I focus on the role of ambiguity in the closing (or rather, postponing) of controversies between the United States and Western Europeans regarding issues of nuclear proliferation and nuclear cooperation (from 1949 to 1954). As in Molière's *Tartuffe*, the main character of this plot, Jean Monnet, does not appear before this second empirical chapter. This chapter analyzes which domestic mechanisms forced Monnet and US diplomats such as John McCloy or John Foster Dulles to choose a tactic of ambiguity when they drafted the European Defense Community Treaty (EDC Treaty). This treaty aimed at organizing the transition from the legal regime of Allied occupation, in which the United States, the United Kingdom, and France directly regulated West German nuclear activities as the occupying powers, to a European legal regime, organized like a quasi federation in the nuclear (and defense) field. As this chapter shows, their choice of ambiguity, which consisted in leaving many treaty obligations unspecified, was not without consequences, as many competing policy makers (mostly in France) denounced the ambiguity of future treaty rules as a sign of their incompetence and even of their national betrayal. As a result, France refused to ratify that EDC treaty, and this chapter explains the effect that ambiguity had on that failure. It also shows that the tactic of ambiguity paid off by accelerating the speed of treaty negotiations; but when the parliamentarians refused to postpone the clarification of treaty interpretation until after the treaty's entry into force, the publicity granted to the negotiated text allowed key national stakeholders to challenge its legitimacy in public. Thus, contrary to what many legal analysts believe, ambiguity can present some serious drawbacks as a tactic.[39]

In chapter 5, I will show that Eurofederalists (both in France and in the United States) avoided the pitfalls of ambiguity by adopting a tactic of opacity when they negotiated the Euratom Treaty and the United States–Euratom Treaty (from 1955 to 1958). Chapter 5 shows how opacity worked at the domestic level (mostly in France and in the United States): publicly, Euratom was presented (for instance, to the US senators in charge of ratifying the United States–Euratom Treaty) as a purely peaceful and supranational endeavor that easily turned Euratom into an instrument of "Cold War politics"[40] by associating closely the US and European nuclear civilian industries; but privately, Euratom was finally accepted by Europeans after it was reframed to fit with the French colonial policy, as France hoped to use Euratom to develop its military nuclear activities with West Germany (and the United States) and devote its financial resources to fight the war in Algeria. This time, Eurofederalists under Monnet's leadership were successful not only because of *who* they had formed alliances with in Washington, but also because of *how* they wrote and interpreted the future legal rules of nuclear trade in Europe. Opacity allowed Eurofederalists to postpone controversy over the European rules of control of nuclear activities until after the entry into force of new treaties instead of during the process of ratification. But then, the question of how long the secret purpose of opaque treaty interpretations could remain hidden was raised as well as the correlate question of how this secret purpose would survive geopolitical changes—in particular, the rise of new American governmental coalitions that defended a strong nuclear nonproliferation agenda in the 1960s.

Negotiating Nonproliferation Obligations in the Whole World

The opacity that characterized Europe's new legal rules affected how these obligations were interpreted when put into practice. Chapters 6 and 7 analyze how the recursive process of clarification (or rather, reinterpretation) of these obligations was affected by key dynamics at the domestic and international level.

In chapter 6, I show that opacity failed as a negotiating tactic when the time came to implement opaque rules in the nuclear trade. There is a price to opacity: namely, by providing a public interpretation of the treaty that differs from its confidential interpretation, the opaque and multileveled interpretation of a legal obligation enabled one signatory state (or more, in this case) to ignore its secret interpretation while avoiding sanctions. I show that the opaque rules contained in the Euratom Treaty and the cluster of secret European treaties signed in its background were reinterpreted after changes in the governments of two key signatory states: France and the United States (from 1958 to 1965). In the United States, young policy makers in the Kennedy administration no longer shared Monnet's Eurofederalist objectives of building a European nuclear force to balance the Soviet threat in Europe. The intergenerational change at the highest policy level in the United States produced major changes in how the legal obligations signed in the previous period were interpreted by the relevant administrations: the new US governmental officials had little training in or patience for the complexity of the international treaty rules, and they were prone to relying only on what was publicly said about these treaty obligations. They used the public interpretation of the Euratom Treaty as a nonproliferation treaty to restrict the transatlantic cooperation between the United States and Europe to the purely peaceful nuclear activity of electricity production and to exclude any cooperation in dual-use nuclear activities with Euratom. In so doing, new American governmental officials (aided by the French officials) rejected the secret goal of the drafters of the Euratom Treaty, who wanted to produce a European nuclear force. This chapter thus confirms the point already made by Hannah Arendt about the Pentagon Papers that "publicly established and accepted propositions" always win "over whatever an individual may secretly know or believe to be the truth,"[41] in the case of a legal commitment.

Chapter 7 analyzes whether opaque treaty rules survived changes in a new international legal environment, rather than in the changing domestic environment of their signatory states. In particular, this chapter explains how the direct negotiations started between the United States and the Soviets with the goal of creating a new global nonproliferation regime affected the relationships between the only two existing international organizations in charge of verifying states' legal commitments with regard to their use of traded fissile material and nuclear technologies: Euratom and the IAEA.

This focus on how international organizations negotiate the interpretation of legal obligations due to changes in the international legal environment thus complements most sociological approaches to international law, which focus almost exclusively on domestic factors (as chapter 6 also does) and thus fail to account for the coexistence of legal norms inherited from a succession of treaties with overlapping jurisdiction.[42] Here, I show how Jean Monnet and the Eurofederalists preserved the one aspect of their legal reform for which they had fought to obtain clear and public recognition from the United States: Euratom's exclusive control of nuclear activities in Europe. In this case, the public rules bargained with the Euratom Treaty superseded the soft-law regulations produced by the IAEA: not only did the IAEA sponsors fail to unilaterally abrogate key interpretations of controls in the United States–Euratom Treaty, but when NPT negotiations revealed the contradictions between the two organizations, Euratom forced the IAEA to design a new global NPT safeguards system that was based upon the Euratom system. The Euratom control system shaped how the IAEA, charged with the responsibility of ensuring compliance with the NPT, was to function in the global nonproliferation regime. As I show in chapter 7, this transfer of procedures and guidelines from Euratom to the IAEA had fateful consequences. Indeed, the verification of the nondiversion of peaceful nuclear materials for military goals had never been part of Euratom's mandate. Thus, its system of safeguards was less intrusive than that discussed in the IAEA prior to the NPT negotiation. After the NPT was signed, and the new model of IAEA safeguards agreement was put in place, some countries—Iran, in particular—exploited the loopholes resulting from this negotiation between Euratom and the IAEA.

In the concluding chapter (chapter 8), I systematize my analysis of legal opacity by comparing the evolution of Euratom's opaque rules with three other trajectories of opaque treaty rules. Indeed, the clarification of Europe's opaque rules and their harmonization with the rules of the global nonproliferation regime (as described in chapter 7) is only the first of the four possible outcomes in the evolution of opaque treaty rules. In this chapter, I describe the other three possible outcomes, based on the study of the nuclear status of the three countries that have never signed the NPT or adhered to the rules of the NPT regime: Israel, India, and Pakistan. As I show, the US and Western European governments have long kept the nuclear status of these three countries opaque, but the opacity of each of these three other cases has survived differently over time. In the case of Israel, the West's tactic of opacity has been sustained over a fifty-year period, showing that the decoupling between public and private interpretations of legal rules can effectively survive key domestic and international changes; and that in this case, opacity—conceived in Europe as a short-term emergency measure—has found legitimacy as a long-term measure to manage Israel's nuclear affairs.[43] In the case of India, the United States and Europe have long tried to maintain opacity regarding the interpretation of their obligations with respect to nuclear trade with India, in order to lessen the tensions between India's nuclear behavior and the rules of the global nuclear regime. Even though India has long criticized such duplicity,[44] it has recently come to share with the West some opaque interpretations of the rules of the global nonproliferation regime, as a sign that it was ready to harmonize its legal views with those of the rest of the world. Finally, I explain why the West's tactic of opacity with regard to Pakistan's nuclear proliferation policy has led to significantly more threatening outcomes as far as the global nonproliferation regime is concerned than the West's (un-acknowledged) exemption given to Israel, or its direct confrontation (and eventual harmonization) with India. In this case, the growing opacity has led to the silent subversion of the whole nonproliferation regime.

By comparing the evolution of opaque rules in each case, this chapter aims at addressing the question of the universalization of the NPT, and the conditions that would make it possible to include these three last outliers in a way that would emulate the harmonization between Europe's regional and global treaty rules. As chapter 8 concludes, the harmonization of each set of rules for each region with the global rules remains the most pressing challenge that policy makers need to address in order for the nuclear non-proliferation regime to survive in the new century. Otherwise, as former IAEA director general and Nobel Peace Prize laureate Mohamed ElBaradei acknowledges, the existence of "double [or triple] standards" pervading the international legal system will eventually lead us to a "state of chaos."[45] It is the challenge of our time to avoid global fractures and bring harmony to this system, and this concluding chapter shows how the story of Europe's nuclear opacity, and its evolution, can offer new lessons to deal with the issue.

TWO

Explaining Recursive Cycles of Treaty Interpretation: The Role of Transparency, Ambiguity, and Opacity

Knowing the accurate interpretation of a treaty obligation is not always simple. The layers of meanings of legal rules can be multiple and drastically different depending on whether the interpretation is performed in a public or private forum. This chapter develops hypotheses on how legal interpretation works in practice, and how the interpretive practices that diplomats follow when they negotiate new legal rules are likely to affect the survival of these new rules over time. In so doing, I accomplish three goals in this chapter. First, I propose a typology of the ways of interpreting legal obligations. I define the terms *transparency, ambiguity,* and *opacity,* which refer to three different tactics[1] that diplomats employ to interpret the nature of the legal obligations contracted by their states.

Second, I show how these interpretive practices play out in the domestic context in which foreign policy elites struggle to impose their agenda and problem-solving strategies[2] on their government. I discuss the reasons why the recent studies on foreign policy elites carried out by sociologists in the wake of Pierre Bourdieu to examine international security,[3] human rights law,[4] colonial law,[5] and European law[6] have claimed that ambiguity is a particularly efficient interpretive tactic to mobilize domestic coalitions in favor of one's preferred global agenda.[7] I also present a counterexample to this general rule: when foreign policy makers permit ambiguity in the interpretation of international rules, they can suffer from domestic attacks on their competence and ability to stabilize their state's legal and geopolitical international environment. Thus, I show that in the domestic realm, there are good reasons why transparency and opacity (two tactics that limit the polysemy of interpretation of legal obligations) can be favored over the tactic of ambiguity.

Third, I focus on how legal interpretation plays out in the international dynamics of treaty negotiation, ratification, implementation, and revision. Drawing on the recursivity approach to international law,[8] I present reasons why each kind of interpretive practice is likely to shape the outcome of future cycles of international legislation in different ways. For example, the law signed at a particular period in time can be made compatible with the law created in successive periods, or not, depending on whether past treaty obligations are interpreted clearly or not. Transparency, ambiguity, and opacity are likely to affect the process of harmonization between the legal rules created by successive and overlapping treaty regimes in different ways. More generally, I present some hypotheses about the role of each practice of interpretation in facilitating regime integration, harmonization, and fragmentation in the global system of legal rules.

Studying Legal Interpretation in Practice

Previous "law and society" scholars have focused on legal interpretation when studying how the law operates in domestic settings. Patricia Ewick and Susan Silbey call the analysis of the "commonplace of law" a study of the "legality," which operates "as persons and groups deliberately *interpret* and *invoke law's language,* authority and procedures . . . to manage their relations."[9] But the "commonplace of international law" has seldom been used to study the interpretation of international treaty rules designed by diplomats and foreign policy elites, so that we have yet to develop a complete typology of how international legal obligations are interpreted when they are invoked to manage interstate relations.

This section seeks to develop a more elaborate and complete typology of the ways in which international law is interpreted in practice than what has been proposed before. For those sociologists of law who have focused on international legal interpretation, most have assumed that the interpretation of legal instruments can be either *clear*, when their meaning is explicitly understood by everyone and in a similar way; or *ambiguous*, when no one claims to have the definitive interpretation of the meaning of vague treaty commitments.[10] Most authors thus focus on whether the interpretation of a legal rule is subject to one or many different meanings in public. But they ignore the possibility that there may be discrepancies between how legal obligations are interpreted in public and in private. To capture all possible situations, I classify interpretive tactics according to two dimensions: whether the interpretation of one obligation is understood in only one way or not (monosemy versus polysemy) or whether the interpretation of one obligation is different when interpreted in public or

Table 2.1 The typology of interpretive tactics

	Similarity of meanings in public and private interpretations	Differences of meanings in public and private interpretation
Monosemy of the interpretation in the same forum	Transparency	Opacity
Polysemy of the interpretation in the same forum	Ambiguity	—

Note: I will limit my analysis of interpretive tactics to only these three cells and ignore the fourth cell, which can be seen as an aggravated type of ambiguity. Indeed, this fourth possibility presents a case in which not only would diplomats publicly acknowledge that the interpretation of a legal obligation is open to many different meanings, but that there might even be more meanings to it when interpreted in private. Here, the interplay of secrecy and denial is less important than it is in the case of opacity, which makes it less interesting for the purpose of my argument.

in private (see table 2.1). The resulting typology allows me to distinguish between three various types of interpretive practices: transparency, ambiguity, and opacity.

These terms function as an ideal type: each type of interpretive practice might be present in the same treaty negotiation, and affect different subsets of rules of the resulting treaty. Indeed, a treaty often contains a bundle of rules that diplomats may interpret differently: while some rules can be clearly interpreted, others can be made opaque. Furthermore, it is important to note that the adjectives *transparent*, *ambiguous*, and *opaque* refer to interpretive practices that result from an intersubjective process of constructing meaning at the micro level: the interpretation of a legal text circulates in a sociolegal network made of texts, judgments, values, construction of legitimacy, and modes of ascertaining interpretive authority.[11] These adjectives are not qualities of the text of a treaty itself. For instance, an interpretive practice characterized as transparent means that the authors of specific provisions in a new treaty (or convention) seek to produce some text that circulates only in an open and public space of interpretation (rather than behind closed doors), and that they will seek to write the new rules in a way that ensures their legibility for different publics (international judges, diplomats, politicians, experts, and even the broad public). Of course, not all jurists and diplomats agree about what legibility means, depending upon who they think the future interpreters of their treaties are (and should be). Thus, transparency, ambiguity, and opacity are attached to unstable ontologies (i.e., practices of interpretation that are heavily context-dependent) rather than to sentences set in the stone of a treaty.

This focus on the hermeneutic flexibility of legal interpretation draws upon previous research in the sociology of law and literature, as developed, for instance, by Stanley Fish or Pierre Bourdieu. But in contrast to these authors, I do not claim that "polysemy" is a fact of life for any legal obligation: that it is a general property of textual interpretation to be plurivocal. Indeed, Bourdieu writes that a legal text, like any other text, "travels without its context,"[12] and thus changes in time and space because the "interpretive community,"[13] as Stanley Fish calls it, changes. This characteristic of legal artifacts whose "elasticity is extraordinary"[14] would explain how diplomats and other foreign policy elites with very different worldviews can congregate around the same ambiguous legal norms (such as human rights, nuclear security, etc.), and still differ when they interpret these norms to design concrete policies and rules—a "decoupling" between normative adherence to international law and practical interpretation that has been observed, time and again, by sociologists of the world polity such as John Meyer and his colleagues.[15] Although my theoretical framework draws upon their insights, I claim that there are some differences in the degree to which legal texts are open to multiple (and sometimes contradictory) interpretations, and that these differences reflect the various tactics adopted by diplomats during the negotiation of treaties and conventions.

Monosemy/Polysemy in the Interpretation of the Law

As shown in table 2.1, transparency in diplomacy captures two aspects of the diplomats' interpretive practices, as the latter engage in a negotiation from which a legal text (collectively authored) emerges: the singularity of meaning of the legal rule in question, and the absence of any secret circuits where unofficial (and different) interpretations of the same rule would circulate.

There are different reasons why authors of a new legal text might develop interpretive practices that emphasize transparency over indeterminacy and opacity. First, there exists some social and even cultural predisposition that favors transparency in diplomatic dealings and legal activities.[16] For instance, as Martin Jay observes, the style in which law was written in the early United States might have reflected a "quest for perfect legibility" as the "plain style" adopted to speak the law pretended that "language can be like glass, a medium without the infusion of a self."[17] Woodrow Wilson's call for transparency in diplomacy might reflect the objection of puritans to lying.

Second, what Jon Elster calls the "civilizing force of publicity"[18] and clarity (transparency) is likely to increase the overall coherence of the international legal system: clarity gives not only more legitimacy to the rule, but also more efficacy.[19] The public search for clearly understood rules usually means longer negotiations, but also more stable outcomes. If public deliberation can generate a high consensus on the diagnosis of a geopolitical problem and its solution, then, transparency as a practice of interpreting legal texts can strengthen the robustness of the rule of law.

Third, state leaders can sometimes insist on achieving transparency for cynical purposes: when they insist on accepting only clear public contracts during the negotiation stage, and when they know that the consensus needed to attain transparency is lacking, they might insist on transparency to kill the chances that some agreement might be arrived at during interstate negotiations. Why would a government do so? For instance, in order to render illegitimate some policy proposals that it does not really support, but that it cannot legitimately reject publicly. I will illustrate such a cynical use of transparency in chapter 3.

In contrast, a legal obligation is ambiguous when it can be interpreted in many different ways, and when the diplomats charged with the task of collectively writing a treaty publicly agree that they cannot arrive at a public and clear consensus about the meaning of new rules (see table 2.1). Authors such as Bruce Carruthers and Terence Halliday relate this ambiguity to the "polysemy"[20] of legal texts.

Ambiguity is a very common tactic in the field of security. For example, multilateral treaties that condemned "aggressive war" such as "the Briand-Kellogg Pact, the Covenant of the League of Nations and the Charter of the United Nations" were typically couched in ambiguous and "vague terms":[21] even though international lawyers commonly distinguish between aggressive or preventive (illegal) wars and preemptive (legal) wars by asking states to prove not only the existence of a threat but also the imminence of that threat, the question of how imminent a danger is has never been codified in these treaties.[22]

In similar ways, scholars of the global nonproliferation regime have often noticed the high polysemy in the legal interpretation of global rules set by the NPT regime: Gabrielle Hecht, for instance, writes about the type of "nuclearity" of things (natural uranium, enriched uranium, etc.) defined by the existing instruments of international law (the NPT, the IAEA Safeguards Agreements) that "the degree to which these things count as 'nuclear' can never be defined in simple, clear-cut scientific terms," and that "nuclearity is a technopolitical spectrum that shifts in time and place."[23] However, there exist different degrees of "polysemy" of the legal rules in the nuclear nonproliferation regime. Gabrielle Hecht recognizes that, although the IAEA changed its safeguards procedures various times from 1956 to 1972, the IAEA tried to eliminate much of the ambiguity of alternative definitions of safeguarded and unsafeguarded materials when it carefully avoided the "more ambiguous term 'fissionable material' [which India wanted to use] in favor of other categories: 'source materials,' 'special fissionable materials,' and uranium in the isotope 235 or 233."[24]

In practice, there can be different reasons why the writers of a treaty would opt for ambiguity in public negotiations. First, when diplomats and experts are confronted with unexpected tensions between various national "strategic cultures"[25] that prevent other consensual legal obligations from being signed, they can, then, intentionally introduce legal ambiguities in treaties to downplay those strategic differences on specific contentious points, in order to avoid deadlocking general negotiations (see table 2.2). In this sense, ambiguity is a tactic used to limit the importance of disagreements.

Second, statesmen and jurists might introduce ambiguity because they do not know the future costs and benefits of different options, or they do not know the full list of options. Typically, great powers hesitate to sign treaties that limit their freedom of action in a world of uncertainties: as far as legal texts against the act of aggressive war are concerned, the lack of clear and singular definition in these texts might be a testament to the willingness of powerful states to impose their interpretation of that term in the future (see table 2.2).[26]

Ambiguity, then, is used to prevent uncertainty from forcing inaction on the part of diplomats and other treaty writers: the new regulations form what legal scholars call "soft law," in the sense understood by Kenneth Abbott and Duncan Snidal—that is, rules that are weakened on one of the following three dimensions: their binding nature, their clarity, and the fact that contracting parties have delegated their interpretative authority to a third neutral party (in general, an international court).[27] Without committing to a clear pathway, the signing of such ambiguous soft-law regulations can provide the opportunity to define a list of objectives that have less binding force than transparent legal rules, but that are recognized as having a normative existence nonetheless. As Gregory Shaffer and Mark Pollack write, usually, "non-binding soft-law instruments help pave the way into binding hard-law instruments."[28]

Thomas Risse and Kathryn Sikkink argue that such a positive dynamic occurred in the field of human rights: the ambiguity of legal commitments

Table 2.2 The role of transparency, ambiguity, and opacity in legal change

	Transparency	Ambiguity	Opacity
Power relations in negotiation process	Increases policy makers' control over negotiators	Leaves some freedom to negotiators Exposes politicians/negotiators to being blamed for a sloppy job	Leaves some freedom to negotiators Creates some measure of deniability for politicians
Proposals in negotiation process	Limits the range of acceptable policies	Widens the range of acceptable policies	Focuses the public's attention on acceptable policy proposals and away from controversial ones
Negotiation outcome	Decreases the likelihood of success	Increases the likelihood of success	Increases the likelihood of success
Ratification process	Increases the predictability for lawmakers/public	Increases the uncertainty for lawmakers/public	Gives the appearance of predictability for lawmakers/public
Ratification outcome	Increases the likelihood of success	Decreases the likelihood of success	Increases the likelihood of success
Power relations in implementation process	Constrains the interpretation by bureaucrats, inspectors, courts	Leaves a lot of freedom in the interpretation of new rules to bureaucrats, inspectors, courts	Creates conflicts of interpretation between insiders with knowledge of private goals (politicians) and outsiders (bureaucrats, courts, etc.)
Implementation outcome	High coupling between initial goals and achieved objectives	Hazardous decoupling between initial/broad goals and achieved objectives	Decoupling between private goals and achieved objectives is unsustainable in the long term, except if bureaucrats, courts, are co-opted by insiders
Vulnerability to mechanisms of actor substitution	Low: newcomers in politics/bureaucracy are likely to keep the same rules (or they will face sanctions), except if they have a public mandate to change them	High: newcomers in politics/bureaucracy are likely to interpret the rules to fit their own policy objectives, without a public mandate	Very high: newcomers in politics/bureaucracy will likely abandon private goals if they do not share them, and claim to follow the rules as publicly interpreted (no sanction)
Vulnerability to mechanisms of actor mismatch	Low: insider powers will defend clear goal under pressure from outside power	High: insider powers will be divided under pressure from outside power	Low: insider powers will defend public goal and will deny the existence of private objective

(continued)

Table 2.2 (*continued*)

	Transparency	Ambiguity	Opacity
Vulnerability to overlaps between distinct legal regimes	Low: regime complexes likely to emerge with no clear winner and strong tensions	High: low tensions in case both regimes are equally ambiguous; and in case one regime gives ambiguous rules and the other clear ones, the latter will become hegemonic	High: if the member states situated at the point of overlap want to abandon private goals to fit with their other treaty obligations Low: if the overlap states want to pursue their private goals, despite some contradictions with other legal obligations

in the Universal Declaration of Human Rights and other regional treaties was useful to overcome the initial opposition of national governments to new global legislation promoted by transnational advocacy networks.[29] In Latin America, for instance, new transnational advocacy networks convinced national governments to adhere to vague and nonbinding international instruments; then, by mobilizing the support of foreign nongovernmental organizations (NGOs) in their campaign against human rights violations, these advocacy networks forced their governments to lift secrecy and clarify their understanding of the rules governing the protection of human rights.[30] In this story, the vagueness of international legal commitments worked as a strategic resource with constructive value: a global network of human rights activists delayed the clarification of vague legal commitments in order to engage reluctant states in a multilateral process of deliberation of their obligation to protect their own citizens.

Ambiguity, like transparency, is therefore attached to an unstable ontology—that is, a network of interpretations of various legal texts, which need not always result in ambiguous pronouncements about the true meaning of the law. In that sense, ambiguity differs from *ambivalence*,[31] a term that scholars of the global nonproliferation regime sometimes use to assert that law can *never* be based on clear-cut categories (or clear-cut dichotomies such as "security/insecurity," "war/peace," or "military/peaceful" nuclear activities), as if the law could have a stable ontology.[32]

Public/Private Interpretations of the Law

I use a second dimension to distinguish opacity from both transparency and ambiguity: an opaque treaty rule is interpreted differently by insiders, who share a clear but private understanding of the treaty behind closed doors, and by outsiders, who also believe they understand clearly what the legal obligation means. Both sets of meanings (some public, some secret) are different, and the existence of secret interpretations of the law must remain unacknowledged. Here, the difference (and the asymmetry) between the private and public meaning of the legal obligation is key. Opacity rests on the belief that (1) there should be (at least) two truths—one for the outsiders, the other for the insiders; (2) that the boundary between the two should never be crossed; (3) and that one truth (the private one) shall prevail over the other (the public one) after the treaty enters into force.

Opacity is therefore produced by a series of lies. The main lies concern the fact that (1) a treaty secretly works to accomplish some outcome that it seems to prohibit when read without the context of negotiation; and (2) some limited amount of people are aware of that secret interpretation. Thus, opacity is an intentional result rather than the product of the cacophony created when authors and interpreters of new legal rules present their meaning slightly differently as they speak to different publics (politicians, experts, bureaucrats, industrials, citizens).

Opacity, however, is produced by specific lies: indeed, an opaque interpretation of the law cannot be reduced to a simple lie about a past action, as in what John Mearsheimer calls "strategic cover-ups"—that is, situations in which "a leader bent on covering up a controversial or failed policy . . . seeks to deceive his public."[33] As Martin Jay remarks, interpreting the law and "lying [about it] is inherently future oriented."[34] Diplomats thus produce an opaque interpretation of a rule when they agree that, for them, the new rule authorizes their state to achieve some future goal and actually advances the fulfillment of that goal, whereas the public is made to believe that the new legal rules in question will prohibit this very activity. For instance, in the early 1960s, the Israelis interpreted their pledge (made to the United States) not to be "the first to introduce" nuclear weapons in the Middle East as allowing them to assemble nuclear weapons in the near future (but not to publicly claim their possession for strategic gains)— whereas the United States interpreted their pledge differently.[35] This is why, as Martin Jay adds, opacity "allows perhaps greater latitude for deception [and self-deception] than straightforward descriptive [lies]," because the production of opacity "involves a set of unarticulated assumptions about the future context in which the condition is or is not realized."[36]

In that sense, opacity cannot be reduced to a policy of deception and concealment, as it involves a policy of denial as well: opacity assumes the existence of various truths, and for that reason, it is different from pure secrecy, which does not need to create a second (public) truth about the interpretation of a treaty obligation.[37] Of course, nuclear opacity rests on secret pledges, or parallel treaties or secret protocols of application in which diplomats specify what they mean by their interpretation of a certain legal obligation contained in a public treaty.[38] But nuclear opacity consists in never acknowledging publicly that secret interpretations exist—for instance, that a nuclear program may have a military component, despite private revelations to the contrary.[39] As Avner Cohen, the main scholar of nuclear opacity, writes, "Even if a policy of [opacity] without strict secrecy is impossible, it is nonacknowledgement—not secrecy as such—that is [the] politically, culturally and socially undergirding feature of [opacity]."[40] Often, diplomats need to craft an alternative public charade to avoid acknowledging the truth of disturbing revelations about their country's secret intentions.

For Hannah Arendt, the intention to deceive that appears in the practice of opacity fundamentally changes the relationship that diplomats entertain with truth. As she writes about lying in international politics, "The efficiency of lying depends entirely upon a clear notion of the truth which the liar and deceiver wishes to hide. In this sense," Arendt adds, "even if it does not prevail in public, [the secret] truth possesses an ineradicable primacy over all [public] falsehoods."[41]

However, there is a risk that the public interpretation may gain an "ineradicable primacy" over all private interpretations of the same legal text. Indeed, the valence of private and public interpretations of the law might be reversed over time: the insiders might come to believe in the public charade, or they might be convinced to secretly abandon their private interpretations. Thus, in contrast to Arendt, we can claim that opacity is intrinsically unstable: not only is it hard to decouple the public and private interpretations of legal rules for an extended period of time (due to leaks to the press, as the Pentagon Papers and WikiLeaks demonstrate), but without intensive efforts to protect the boundary, the secret interpretation of a rule is also bound to disappear in the long term (see table 2.2). For instance, the Pentagon Papers revealed that the decision makers around US secretary of defense Robert McNamara who gradually stepped up US military involvement in Vietnam "no longer kn[e]w or remember[ed] the truth behind their concealments and their lies."[42]

Now that I have described what these three different interpretive practices mean, I will turn to the role that they are likely to play over time during various sequences through which new rules are discussed, signed, ratified, implemented, and revised (as summarized in table 2.2).

Interpretive Tactics in Domestic Fields of Foreign Policy

When they have paid attention to the interpretation of legal rules, sociologists who analyze the domestic making of international legislation stress the importance of ambiguity over its alternatives. But I show that there are also some good reasons why foreign policy makers might want to limit the polysemy in the interpretation of new legal obligations, and I list predictions about how each alternative tactic—transparency and opacity—will play out in a domestic context during the process of negotiation and ratification of new rules.

Negotiation to Ratification: The Power of Ambiguity in Domestic Fields

For sociologists, international legal change is produced by social mechanisms that go much deeper in the social fabric of domestic societies than the simple diffusion of a cognitive diagnostic from the center to the periphery by an "epistemic community,"[43] a transnational or an intergovernmental network of experts. Thus, when we study the role that transparency or ambiguity plays in the negotiation, ratification, and implementation of new treaties, we need to explain how the various professionals (politicians, diplomats, bureaucrats, judges, and lawyers) in charge of negotiating and interpreting international law can reinterpret, translate, or subvert the meaning of new rules in order to fight their domestic battles for political power.[44] As Bourdieuian sociologists Yves Dezalay and Bryant Garth have demonstrated, the social "principles of visions and divisions" that structure *symbolically* how domestic fields of power and law operate are key to understanding whether and how new international legal rules can be mobilized (and with what effects) in domestic fields of power.[45]

But most authors who study the symbolic struggles within national fields of power do not raise the question of how various interpretive tactics are used by competing groups of foreign policy makers to gain domestic approval for their most favored global agendas. Consistent with Bourdieu's claim that the meaning of legal concepts is open to many reinterpretations,[46] sociologists of international law implicitly assume (and sometimes explicitly claim) that all legal concepts are inherently ambiguous and so malleable that they can be recoded to fit with the agendas of those in power. For instance, Dezalay and Garth write about the diffusion of concepts and norms (in law and economics) that justified the passing of new trade agreements bundled under the term *Washington consensus* that are safeguarded by international organizations such as the World Bank and the International Monetary Fund, "Symbolic exports are all the more effective [during the implementation phase] as they are diverted by importers who appropriate this knowledge and recode it in accordance with the positions they occupy in national fields."[47] For them, new international rules will diffuse rapidly when their meaning is flexible enough to allow various reinterpretations: for instance, the indeterminacy of new legal rules helps powerful state administrations twist their meaning in the implementation phase.

Bourdieuian scholars believe that the ambiguity of the legal rules embedded in new treaties and agreements is not only a resource for the powerful:[48] polysemy and indeterminacy can also be resources for the outsiders in the field of foreign policy—or rather, for those who have enough social capital to compete with traditional elites and who are thus "insiders-outsiders"[49] to foreign policy. For rising elites who play on the international market of ideas to gain domestic credibility (those elites whom Dezalay and Garth call the *"compradores"*[50] of international law), support for a new global system of (ambiguous) rules represents a means to gain symbolic legitimacy for themselves. For instance, Antonin Cohen claims that ambiguity helped Jean Monnet's Eurofederalist ideas gain credibility in France among conflicting groups when Monnet was looking for support for the new policy that he introduced in Europe to regulate the coal and steel markets: the legal indeterminacy of the term *community* (as in European Community) facilitated the alliance between "modernist" policy makers such as Jean Monnet and Etienne Hirsh (Monnet's assistant at the French Commissariat Général du Plan), and traditional political forces in France. Indeed, the legal concepts of "community" and "high authority," which they borrowed from US legal and administrative traditions, betrayed an Americanophily that put Monnet and Hirsh on the side of the European and American advocates of free trade; but in France, these terms also resonated with the expectation of critics of unregulated free trade who cherished the project of building an anti-Communist "new Europe" (desired by fascists before and during the war) in the postwar context.[51]

The premium that sociologists inspired by Pierre Bourdieu place on the ambiguity of legal rules and legal concepts is not without consequence in their analysis of legal change. If ambiguity is a resource not only for the powerful but also for rising contenders, and if the law is always deemed ambiguous, then, they deduce that the interpretive practices adopted by authors and interpreters of new legal rules play no role in domestic struggles for political power. Pushed to the limit, this perspective assumes that the "social capital"[52] of policy makers is really what matters to explain legal change within domestic fields. As Dezalay and Garth write on the content of legal knowledge resources that inspire new global rules, their impact is "less dependent on their own merits than on the social and even economic and military resources deployed in the strategic game."[53] This is true not just of the role that law plays in the domestic mobilization of traditional elites (or "*notables du droit*"),[54] but also of the role that law plays in the rise of new foreign policy elites. In other words, the question of *who* the players are in foreign policy, and not the question of *how* they play on the multi-layered meanings of the law, matters during the negotiation, ratification, and implementation of new treaties.

Although these hypotheses about the role of ambiguity remain plausible, we can formulate alternative explanations about the role of legal indeterminacy in coalition-building campaigns during the phases of treaty negotiation, ratification, and implementation. Ambiguity is often associated with, and criticized as, shallowness, emptiness, and vagueness, none of which are positive terms. Rather than proving the expertise of rising elites who seek to gain political credibility by mobilizing transnational networks and foreign expertise, it can prove their incompetence and inability to arrive at a clear and workable solution (see table 2.2).

In the global nonproliferation regime, the young US negotiators were criticized many times for the indeterminacy of the "exit clause" that they included in the wording of the Limited Test Ban Treaty (LTBT) and the NPT: many of the core disarmament and nonproliferation issues tackled by these two treaties were jeopardized during the implementation by the US negotiators' choice to leave ambiguous the interpretation of the termination of agreements.[55] For instance, the NPT authorized a non-nuclear-weapon state (NNWS) to benefit from the increased civilian cooperation in nuclear-weapon states and to invest in dual-use activities to the point that it declared that "extraordinary events, related to the subject matter of [the NPT], have jeopardized the supreme interests of its country"[56] and forced it to leave the NPT (art. 10.1). The ambiguity of the "exit clause" allowed North Korea to leave the NPT on three months' notice (art. 10.2), after which it regained its ability to lawfully explode a nuclear weapon, which it did in 2003, after having benefited from the NPT regime for a long time.

Ambiguity in the interpretation of treaties can not only be seen as a sign of shallowness and general incompetence on the part of treaty negotiators, but it can also scare the national stakeholders concerned by the effects of the new global legislation during the ratification phase—especially in the case of agreements that organize the sharing of sovereignty between national and international organizations. This is particularly true of state administrations whose jurisdiction is affected by a new international legislation under negotiation. National courts and administrations can impose on treaty negotiators that they will only abide by clearly interpreted rules (supported by public statements from officials about what these rules authorize them to do and not do).[57] They are likely to criticize any ambiguity that, if power struggles work to their disadvantage in the future, would allow the future international organization created by the new treaty under discussion to expand its jurisdiction to their detriment. According to this view, in transparency, national stakeholders seek a safeguard against the tendency for international organizations to generally expand their jurisdiction by expanding their competence to tackle other issues.[58]

As far the nonproliferation regime was concerned, domestic military and atomic administrations were especially wary of ambiguous interpretations of the NPT with regard to whether the international trade in "civilian" technologies with dual-use potential (such as the enrichment of uranium for civilian purposes) would be negatively affected by the NPT or not.[59] This desire for clear and commonly understood rules explains why, for instance, West Germany refused to ratify the NPT until it signed a tripartite agreement with the United Kingdom and the Netherlands to jointly enrich uranium (Urenco Treaty), and until it agreed on the language of the Safeguards Agreement, which it signed with the IAEA. To defend themselves against the tendency of supranational organizations to expand their jurisdiction when their mandate is not clear, national stakeholders and legislators are encouraged to engage in what I call a series of "preemptive interpretations" of the future rules during the treaty ratification phase. These preemptive interpretations, which national legislators decide in a unilateral rather than coordinated manner, do not strengthen the rule of law at the international level but can instead start a chaotic cycle of treaty interpretation, as I will show in chapter 4.

The transparency rather than ambiguity of legal interpretation might therefore be a more efficient tactic for transnational coalitions in garnering the support of national stakeholders during the treaty ratification process at the domestic level (see table 2.2). The advantage of clearly interpreted rules over ambiguous ones might thus explain why, in the story of European integration, the promoters of clear and simple interstate rules have generally had more success than the Eurofederalists, who proposed to delegate some unclear amount of sovereignty to European institutions, particularly in activities related to the regulation of nuclear trade that are so central to state sovereignty.[60] Indeed, "international liberals,"[61] as historians generally call the postwar generation of pro–free trade foreign policy makers working behind Dean Acheson at the State Department, favored the design of simple interstate organizations, the mandate of which was clearly limited by government authority in the form of the veto power granted to each member state over the introduction of new legislation and/or revision of the common legal rules. As I will show in chapter 4, many European national legislators preferred clarity and transparency rather than the unknown when they were asked to contract out some of their state's sovereign rights to new international organizations.

Opacity in Domestic Contexts

There is another tactic that diplomats and foreign policy elites can use to limit the likelihood that, during the process of ratification, national stakeholders will denounce an ambiguous legal framework as a mark of incompetence and an inability to protect national sovereignty: the tactic of opacity. The decoupling between the public and private interpretations of new rules might accomplish the same goals as ambiguity while avoiding its main problems. The ability to conceal the most controversial interpretations of a new legislation can help its supporters avoid public controversy and accelerate its adoption (see table 2.2). At the same time, the ability to perform a public charade that clearly defines what the new legislation means for the national stakeholders and the general public helps its supporters escape the blame for incompetence that is often associated with vagueness and indeterminacy in domestic politics. This means that opacity can help foreign policy elites achieve quick successes that firmly establish their credibility in the domestic game. According to this view, if given the chance, foreign policy elites prefer to produce an opaque interpretation of new legislation instead of giving an ambiguous interpretation of the law, especially when they face demands for clarity from national stakeholders and legislators.

If opacity is intrinsically more efficient than ambiguity, then, why isn't opacity always preferred to ambiguity in domestic struggles over new legislation? To explain why opacity cannot always be used by treaty negotiators, we can turn to Bourdieuian explanations, which show that in international politics, only a small circle among foreign policy elites—those who can play "double games"—have the *opportunity* to speak double language to private and public audiences.[62] Still, it appears that the ability to mobilize different types of socioeconomic, legal, and political capitals, to talk to different publics in different contexts, is only a necessary (but not in itself sufficient) condition for the production of opacity. Indeed, the fact that one is being located at the intersection of various worlds (academic, legal, political, financial, etc.) does not necessarily translate into a tactical preference for opacity (over ambiguity or transparency) on the part of foreign policy elites. We must look, then, to other reasons to explain why opacity is rarely used.

An alternative explanation for why opacity might not be chosen over ambiguity in domestic struggles over new international legislation is that opacity might actually be even more risky than ambiguity. Indeed, as the new rules become implemented, the production of opacity involves the sustained mobilization of a vast amount of resources to maintain the public charade and the boundary between the private and public understandings of what the new legislation means (see table 2.2). As Avner Cohen shows in the case of Israel, those who shaped the tactic of opacity were working at the intersection of the academic (scientific), military, and political fields. But their specific nodal location did not, in and of itself, enable them to maintain the hermetic seal between the public and private meaning of Israel's commitment not "to introduce" nuclear weapons in the Middle East. To perform such a task, they had to refashion both the Israeli state and the public sphere—with the institution of censorship bureaus and surveillance mechanisms imposed on all academic, media, and political speeches on the atom. Furthermore, not only did they have to spend a lot of political capital to acquire new institutional and legal resources, but they also had to rely on the increasing willingness of the general public to be duped (and co-opted at the same time) by military authorities.[63] Otherwise, the public façade would have crumbled with terrible effects. In such cases when opacity is exposed, the political leaders who have supported contradictory interpretations of a legal rule in private and in public generally lose all credibility and political capital abroad and at home. Opacity is therefore a double-edged sword, which might cause significant damage to the reputation of its supporters, and is much harder to sustain than ambiguity in the long run.

So far, I have shown that advantages and disadvantages exist for each tactic, and that these pros and cons are different for each depending on how domestic struggles play out during the phases of adoption, ratification, and implementation of new international legislation. Whereas ambiguity might help dilute the geopolitical differences between countries at the negotiating table, it might increase the opposition of national stakeholders to the legislation's ratification in domestic contexts, as ambiguity can reflect the lack of competence and credibility of the legislation's supporters. In contrast, opacity necessitates the mobilization of various forms of expertise in different social worlds. But it is a risky tactic for two reasons: those who produce opaque interpretations of new legal rules run the risk that the public charade they enact in domestic settings will naturally impose itself over time (in case those in the know fail to sustain their secret efforts to work toward their private goals), and they run the risk of losing political, legal, and moral credibility if their secret goals are exposed.

Explaining Recursivity: Interpretive Tactics in the International Realm

Here, I focus on how various types of legal interpretation (transparency, ambiguity, and opacity) operate in the international dynamics of treaty revision and treaty change (thus after their adoption and ratification). I also formulate hypotheses on how the interpretive quality of overlapping legal rules affects how these rules are likely to survive contradictions between legal regimes.

Transparency and Ambiguity in Successive Cycles of International Lawmaking

So far, I have considered the role of transparency, ambiguity, and opacity in legal interpretation in a static way. I have only looked at the role of each tactic in domestic power struggles over a single three-pronged sequence: during the adoption, ratification, and implementation of new international legislation. But the description of domestic factors at play in the adoption of new global agendas does not tell us whether, and to what extent, the law signed in one period constrains the opportunities to change it in successive periods, or whether the interpretation of legal text adopted is likely to survive external shocks. Here, I will list a series of predictions concerning whether transparency, ambiguity, and opacity are likely to affect the process and outcome of treaty revision depending upon whether governmental changes among the signatory states of the treaty lead to demands for treaty revision (what Bruce Carruthers and Terence Halliday call "mechanisms of actor substitution"), or when a nonsignatory state to a treaty requests its annulment by force (or "mechanisms of actor mismatch"),[64] or in case of overlaps between various systems of rules.

There are good reasons to believe that transparent obligations are less likely than ambiguous or opaque obligations to be changed when geopolitical conditions change, or when the national actors in charge of interpreting treaty rules change. Even old-school realist thinkers of international law would not disagree with this prediction. Hans Morgenthau writes that "during the four hundred years of its existence, the international law" of a technical nature and expressed in clear terms (for example, the international regulations on mailing practices) "has in most instances been scrupulously observed"[65] despite many external shocks in the global balance of power.

In contrast, ambiguous interpretations of legal rules are less likely to survive the rise of new coalitions to power, or requests by outside powers to change existing rules, or the emergence of legal contradictions with overlapping treaties than ambiguous or opaque legal rules. When legal contradictions are revealed between legal regimes, the ambiguous rules signed at one time are likely to become irrelevant, or to be abrogated, if an overlapping treaty signed at another time has transparent rules (see table 2.2). For instance, the ambiguous rules protecting human rights such as the UN Declaration of Human Rights of 1947,[66] which failed to establish an international judicial system such as that protected by the European Court of Human Rights, were superseded in many non-European countries when the UN Security Council decided in September 2001 that all states should pass new laws and criminal codes on the freezing of assets of designated terrorists.[67]

When two sets of equally transparent rules conflict with each other, the outcome of such conflict is harder to predict. Two clearly understood but contradictory sets of treaty rules can coexist for a long time, creating what political scientists call a "regime complex"—that is, "partially overlapping and parallel regimes that are not hierarchically ordered."[68] In this case, some polysemy emerges from the existence of equally clear (but different) rules that coexist in the legal system: such polysemy will not easily go away, as states can engage in "forum-shopping" strategies that seek to maximize the likelihood that their behavior will be found to conform with one system of rules (but not another).[69] This happened, for instance, in the same example of counterterrorism resolutions passed by the Security Council after September 11, which contradicted clearly understood rules pertaining to the European trade regime (which protects private property against undue state expropriation).[70] As both sources of international legislation contained clear rules, the judges in charge of evaluating the soundness of public decisions to freeze assets of suspected terrorists had to strike a balance between both sets of rules, but they could not entirely ignore either set of rules.

In cases when no apparent conflict of rules emerges and when the interpretive lenses of the national actors in charge of implementing the rules at the national level do not dramatically change, "legalization" scholars[71] believe that those rules that survive over time are the initially clear rules, or the ambiguous rules that have been clarified. Halliday and Carruthers also highlight that the polysemy of a single regime of legal rules generally starts a new cycle of global lawmaking to clarify their meaning, or to harmonize their content with other overlapping and ambiguous legal rules. Thus, international law would naturally move toward clarification and harmonization; such an endogenous process of clarification often occurs because "the original crafters of law s[ought] to remedy its deficiencies in order to achieve their original purposes."[72] In the global nonproliferation regime, the IAEA or the NPT Review Conferences, which are held every five years, are supposed to facilitate this endogenous process of clarification. But we cannot assume that only transparent (or clarified) rules will survive in the long run, and that opaque rules will be clarified and harmonized with the rules of more transparent overlapping treaty regimes. We need to dig deeper.

Opaque Rules in Successive Cycles of Treaty Interpretation

There are some good reasons why we may assume that opaque rules are likely to be clarified in the long run, and when overlapping regimes of rules exist, in a manner that tends to minimize conflicts between overlapping legal rules. As I said, public interpretations often end up being adopted by everyone, even by those who initially spoke two languages in public and private. Thus, even if their lies are not revealed, those who promote opacity to attain secret goals might find themselves trapped in the public charade they enact. In fact, we shall expect that the private and public interpretations of rules will be recoupled (to the advantage of the latter) quite quickly because of governmental changes, which bring new coalitions that might oppose the secret goals among the member states of an opaque system of rules; or just because the national actors in charge of implementing opaque rules are different from those who negotiated these rules in the first place (and therefore, they do not share their interpretive lenses).

In the case of Europe's nuclear trade regime, the abandonment of private interpretations occurred as a result of new governmental coalitions that opposed the secret goal of the treaty being elected to government among the signatory states (see chapter 6). In this case, the meaning was clarified almost immediately, or rather, the secret (and higher) interpretation of the nuclear cooperation agreement signed by the United States and Euratom was abandoned almost immediately, so that only the public interpretation

Table 2.3 The evolution of opaque legal rules

Clarification of opaque rules? Conflict of legal rules?	Recoupling of public and private interpretations	Decoupling of public and private interpretations maintained over time
Easy harmonization between global and specific rules	Harmonization (Euratom)	Unacknowledged exception (Israel)
Difficult harmonization (or no harmonization) between rules	Acknowledged exception (India)	Subversion (Pakistan)

of that agreement remained legitimate. In that sense, opacity seems to be a tactic that foreign policy makers will only use as a measure of last resort (an "emergency measure") during the negotiation of treaty rules: opacity buys diplomats time before possible opponents to a treaty (or agreement) realize the difference between its supposedly real and secret purposes.

Still, the clarification of opaque rules (and their harmonization with more transparent systems of overlapping rules) is not the only possible outcome of the long-term implementation of treaties. The case of Israel's nuclear status shows that the decoupling between the private and public truths can be sustained for almost fifty years. Israel is not the only case of prolonged opacity: in Pakistan, the decoupling between private and public interpretations about the true purpose of its nuclear program has been sustained for thirty years (see table 2.3). The military forces that have administered Pakistan's nuclear program (and its nuclear exports) for the last thirty years have never worked to recouple the public and private truths about Pakistan's true nuclear regime—nor have they worked to lessen the obvious tensions that such a program creates with the global nonproliferation regime.[73] In both cases of sustained opacity, the governmental elites in charge of administering these opaque nuclear programs (and their disciples after new generations arrived in power) retained their grip over the country's nuclear policy, which suggests a strong correlation between sustained opacity and the stability of the communities of interpreters (and vice versa).

Still, even if opacity is sustained over time, two different outcomes can be found: the first, which corresponds to the case of Israel, is "unacknowledged exception," and refers to the fact that opacity is used to hide (and lessen) the existence of tensions with the global nonproliferation regime; the second, which corresponds to the case of Pakistan, is "subversion," when opacity actually increases the intensity of the conflict between a secret regime and an overlapping system of rules, without leading to any resolution (see table 2.3). The difference in outcome may stem from the difference in the intensity of the outside pressures on each country to conform, even if implicitly, to the rules of the main global regime—here the NPT.[74] Pakistan has never been held accountable for its subversion of the NPT regime, although it contracted with NPT signatory states interested in acquiring enrichment technologies in ways that violated the obligations of these NPT signatory states (such as Iran or Libya). Many powerful policy makers (such as US president Ronald Reagan) knew of Pakistan's secret sales of nuclear technologies to other Muslim states, but they let Pakistan deny its secret subversion of the NPT regime. In contrast, there were, and still are, some strong pressures on Israel not to threaten the global nonproliferation regime, for instance, by acknowledging its exceptional status in the NPT regime, or by helping allies proliferate.

There is a third possible outcome of the evolution of opaque treaty rules: a clarification without harmonization, or what I call "acknowledged exception" (table 2.3). That case corresponds to the present situation of India: under the pressure of the international community, India has recently worked together with many nuclear powers (the nuclear exporters and the IAEA) to recouple the public and private interpretations India gave of its own nuclear program. Indeed, for a long time, and until the 1998 tests, India consistently denied that its program of nuclear explosives had a "military"[75] dimension—a claim the West privately contested without officially sanctioning India for its military actions. But after the 1998 tests and a decadelong process of negotiation between India and the international community, India's opaque nuclear status has been clarified, even though India was not asked to take steps toward nuclear disarmament and toward its inclusion in the global regime as a NPT non-nuclear-weapon state (NNWS).[76] The foreign pressure helped India clarify its relationship with the global nonproliferation regime, but this clarification did not harmonize the rules of the West's nuclear engagement with India and the general rules that the West follows within the NPT regime—quite the contrary.[77]

The existence of these four possible outcomes shows that the harmonization of Euratom's rules with those of the IAEA, which resulted from strong foreign pressures that were exerted upon Europe by outside powers (the United States and the Soviet Union) during the NPT negotiation, and from domestic changes in the signatory states of two various regimes, might be the exception rather than the norm. This seems to be an optimal case, but it is only one among four. Another one—that is, "subversion," as in the case of Pakistan's nuclear trade regime—is clearly the most suboptimal, with the two other outcomes standing somewhat in the middle.

In fact, whether the opacity of rules will last over time depends on different factors—in particular, whether governmental insiders among state parties to a regime of opaque rules stay in power, and whether strong outside pressures are put on these governments so that they work to harmonize their system of rules with other systems in place.

Arguments in Favor of the Hermeneutic Approach to Global Recursivity

By highlighting the role that transparency, ambiguity, and opacity play in combination with these "external" factors (governmental changes, great power pressures, etc.), the following chapters illustrate how a hermeneutic approach to international legal change can avoid the polarization between externalist and internalist conceptions of legal change (see figure 2.1).

The externalist view is commonly found among realists and neorealists

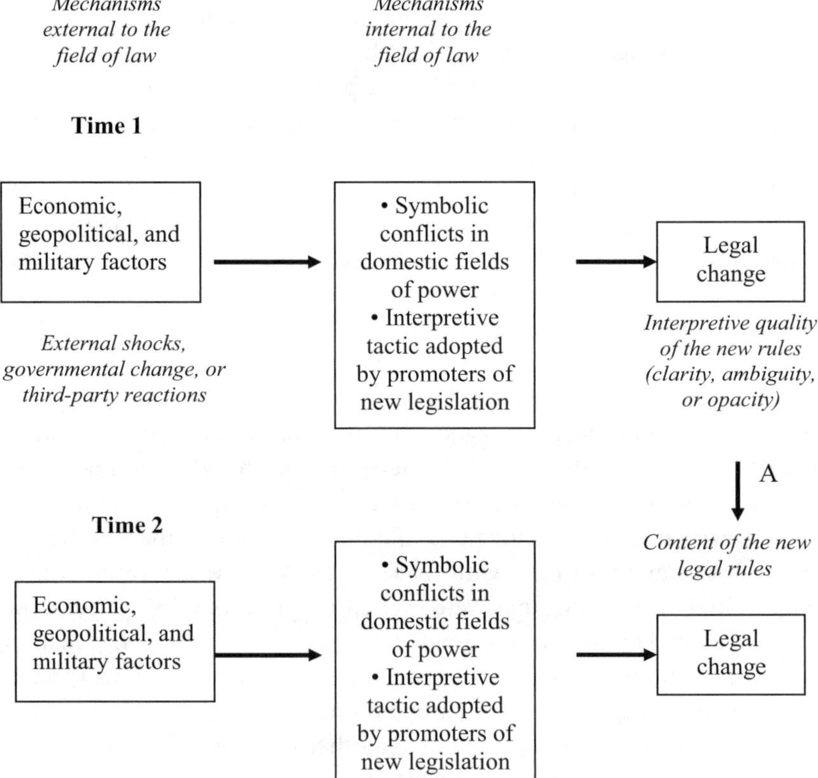

Figure 2.1. A dynamic approach of recursive cycles of global lawmaking

for whom states can make calculations outside a preexisting legal context,[78] and for whom "all those international arrangements dignified by the label regime [such as the global nonproliferation regime] are only too easily upset when either the balance of bargaining power or the perception of national interest change among those states who negotiate them."[79] This externalist conception of international law,[80] which betrays the influence of old-school German realist legal thinking on international relations theory,[81] is associated with a powerful metaphor, which many theorists use to explain why states sign legally binding treaties: the metaphor of Ulysses tying his hands to the mast. In their view, Ulysses temporarily renounced his power in order to avoid the risk of permanently submitting to the charm of the Sirens.[82]

Applied to international law, the metaphor of Ulysses and the Sirens assumes that states can make calculations outside a preexisting legal context, as if states had their hands free before signing the treaty in question. This metaphor gives an intuitive solution to the puzzle of why (supposedly) free states find it rational to self-inflict a limitation on their sovereign will in an uncertain and dangerous world. This metaphor is elegant because it offers a parsimonious and simple explanation of the reasons why, for instance, many states signed the NPT in 1968. According to the metaphor, those Ulysses-like states that renounced the possibility of trading nuclear technologies used for military purposes felt it was in their interest to freeze the number of "nuclear haves" for twenty-five years (the initial term of the NPT) in order to promote the free exchange of nuclear technologies and fissile materials for nonmilitary purposes.[83] This explanation assumes that the same interest drove all signatory states of a treaty such as the NPT, and that every state experienced the same kind of preexisting (lack of) obligations when they faced the choice of signing the NPT or not—or that if their obligations differed, they could decide to free themselves from previous obligations.

This model offers a parsimonious explanation of the genesis of a bundle of treaty rules, but it is an explanation that fails to account for the fact that most treaties propose regulating activities that are already the subject of prior treaty commitments with partially overlapping clubs of states.[84] When presented with new treaties such as the NPT, most Western European states had to choose between past and future obligations to be added on top of their prior obligations, and not between anarchy and legal order.

When we adopt a dynamic approach to law, the main question that we must answer is no longer how to explain why there is legal order and not anarchy, but how legal change occurs between successive treaty regimes, which, in contrast to domestic legislation, never completely cease to exist in a world in which overlapping clubs of states advance with different rhythms. Indeed, in contrast to domestic law, there is no doctrine of desuetude in international law; thus, when overlapping (but still different) clubs of states adopt new treaties, legal rules just pile up one onto another, and we cannot predict which ones will disappear or survive in practice. When we pay attention to conflicts of legal rules at the international level, our main concern is no longer to explain who is tied to the mast (or which states sign which treaties), but who ties the new knots and how the new knots find their place in a general pattern.

To again reference Greek mythology, scholars who adopt such an approach analyze the new treaties as new knots that Ulysses's cunning wife, Penelope, adds to her canvas in order to keep her pretendants at bay until Ulysses's return—she consistently rearranged the knots on her canvas to force them to wait—or, as far as today's international law professionals are concerned, to buy time in order to prevent challengers from subverting the rights and privileges that their state secured in past treaties. The substitution of metaphors entices us to explain in sociological terms how international legal change occurs in successive waves of treaty negotiations; who the international law professionals are who weave together successive series of treaties; how they operate at the transnational level to protect the interests of their states; and what effects legal interpretation produces in terms of the fragmentation or harmonization of international law.

THREE

Secrecy and Transparency in the Early Nuclear Age: How They Both Failed World Federalists

Diplomacy has long been conducted via agreements kept secret instead of via multilateral negotiations in the public eye. In practice, secrecy and transparency are commonly thought of as polar opposites.[1] Transparency is often viewed as a mechanism to bring policy options before the democratic public. When too much secrecy is imposed on nationals in their dealings with foreigners, they might resist and request more transparency in their foreign activities, should these take place in diplomatic conferences, scientific workshops, or simple visits to foreign countries. Secrecy, in this view, is conceived of as antithetical to that goal because secrecy keeps policy options hidden from public view and democratic debate. Sometimes, diplomatic elites contend that too much transparency hinders the working of their government, which needs to keep its forward planning within the secrecy of the cabinet.[2] From this perspective, transparency and secrecy are contradictory forces that fight each other, like good and evil.

And yet, transparency, too, may foil democratic consideration of certain policy options. Transparency does so not by hiding the policy option from public view, but by taking certain policy options entirely off the negotiating table. Transparency means both publicity and clarity. Publicity helps the national stakeholders (bureaucrats, legislators, higher officials) to know what is said in diplomatic dealings. If negotiations are public, negotiators cannot depart from their original mandate for the sake of finding an agreement. Clarity also allows national stakeholders to limit the mandate of negotiators. Seen in this light, transparency is the complement (not opposite) of secrecy: both secrecy and transparency limit access to the democratic debate by, respectively, removing knowledge from the public arena and disempowering one alternative policy in the public eye. In this sense, both secrecy and transparency may limit the democratic consideration of the entire array of options available to any given polity.

In this chapter, I argue that transparency was used as a technique of social control imposed on rising diplomats and foreign policy elites in the early nuclear age. The role that transparency played in nuclear diplomacy is not restricted to the early nuclear age. John Krige argues that the kind of scientific diplomacy performed under the aegis of the Atoms for Peace program launched by the Dwight Eisenhower administration in 1953 was also promoted by the administration for surveillance purposes. He writes about the scientific conferences in which US nuclear scientists participated in the mid-1950s, "Openness and security, sharing knowledge or technology and implementing regimes of surveillance, were two sides of the same coin."[3] In this chapter, I will show that the use of transparency as a technique of social control was at work internationally not only in scientific conferences but also in the first diplomatic conferences organized under the framework of the United Nations at the end of the Second World War.

The case under study in this chapter concerns the negotiations between the Western allies and the Soviet Union in 1945 and 1946. Negotiations were supposed to lead to a treaty that would have prevented a nuclear arms race between the Allies. The US position, known as the "Baruch plan," was based on the *Acheson-Lilienthal Report*, which, for many decades, has been a canonical reference (although almost never followed) in debates on nonproliferation and disarmament. This report was named after its authors: J. Robert Oppenheimer (1904–67), the Berkeley physicist and wartime director of the Los Alamos laboratory, where the calculations to determine the correct assembly of US nuclear weapons were done under his supervision; David Lilienthal (1899–1981), the chairman of the Tennessee Valley Authority (TVA), an expert in public administration and power development; and Dean Acheson (1893–1971), a graduate of Harvard Law School who served as undersecretary of state at the time the report was written. In this chapter, I will show how Oppenheimer's cosmopolitan position was undermined by the use of transparency in the diplomatic arena.

The chapter proceeds to demonstrate this point in two sections. The first section presents the three solutions to the problems of the nuclear age that were defended by US foreign policy elites: the nationalist, international liberal, and cosmopolitan policies. It shows how nationalists used secrecy to remove alternative policy proposals from the public debate. The second part shows how nationalists also used transparency against the policy proposals defended by international liberals and cosmopolitans. Transparent diplomacy proved effective: the publicity and clarity of negotiations of the nuclear nonproliferation treaty in the UN Committee on Atomic Energy derailed the deliberations between world federalists and the Soviets.

Secrecy as an Instrument of Social Control in Domestic Power Struggles

Power Struggles among US Foreign Policy Elites (May–August 1945)

When Harry Truman announced in his radio message on August 9, 1945, that mankind had entered the nuclear age, after the United States dropped the two nuclear bombs on Hiroshima and Nagasaki, he spelled out the broad architecture of the world nuclear order that he wanted to establish. The US president asked the nations of the world to believe in an Anglo-American atomic "trusteeship," whereby the United States and Great Britain would serve as "trustees for humanity" in atomic matters in order "to promote peace and justice in the world"[4] until proper controls could be established at the world level. By invoking the broad principles of sacred trust, Truman reinforced the right that great powers reserved for themselves to lead other nations to civilization: this time toward the post-Hiroshima civilization (see table 3.1). This concept of "sacred trusteeship" was not new. It had been used as a fundamental principle of international law through which colonial mandates had been justified since the nineteenth century. Furthermore, it was anchored in the League of Nations after the First World War, and remained a central principle in the newly founded United Nations and its Trusteeship Council.[5]

The accession of Harry Truman to the presidency after the death of President Franklin D. Roosevelt thus tilted the balance of power among foreign policy elites to the side of those whom I call the *nationalists*. Truman finally discovered the existence of the US nuclear weapons program when he replaced Roosevelt, as the former president had not included him in the circle of the trusted elites of nuclear foreign policy. Upon his arrival, Truman named James Byrnes his secretary of state, and made him integral to the planning of the postwar legal order. Truman and Byrnes's reliance on such concepts as "sacred trust" could be traced to their common sensibility, rooted in their upbringing in the small communities of the US South (Missouri for Truman, South Carolina for Byrnes), from which they inherited the white American values of the self-made men and their acceptance of the notions of the white man's burden and sacred trust.[6] In contrast, when Truman met Oppenheimer, for the first and only time, the repulsion the president felt was not only intellectual, but physical,[7] revealing a clash of

Table 3.1   US normative ideals of international law after Hiroshima

Solutions to the perils of the nuclear age	Key propositions (August–September 1945)	Key proponents (August–September 1945)
Nationalist	• Trust in Anglo-American political leadership (no trust in pledges) • US monopoly on nuclear weapons • Secrecy maintained on industrial processes discovered in Manhattan Project (enrichment of uranium, plutonium reprocessing, etc.) • Worldwide inspections of nuclear facilities and mines (uranium, thorium)	Truman, Byrnes, Groves, Bush, Conant
International liberal	• Trust in traditional interstate law based on pledges and backed by interstate inspections • Desire to criminalize atomic bombings • Destruction of all remaining US nuclear weapons components • Worldwide inspections of nuclear facilities and mines (uranium, thorium)	McCloy, Stimson, Wallace, Acheson, Shotwell
Cosmopolitan	• Trust in fraternity of the men of science • Desire to criminalize atomic bombings • Immediate sharing of all the knowledge acquired by the Manhattan Project scientists with all nations • Destruction of all remaining US nuclear weapons components	Bohr, Szilard, Frank, Oppenheimer

what Pierre Bourdieu would call the *habitus* of the southern statesmen and that of the cosmopolitan elite, in particular the Jewish scientists involved in the Manhattan Project.

Still, Truman's nationalist conception of the postwar legal order, and the central role that the United States would play in it, was also defended by the two top science administrators—that is, the wartime directors of the Office of Scientific Research and Development (OSRD) of the Allied bomb project: Vannevar Bush (1890–1974), the president of the OSRD, a former professor of electrical engineering at the Massachusetts Institute of Technology (MIT) and the president of the Carnegie Institution in Washington; and James Conant (1893–1978), the vice president of the OSRD, a chemist and the president of Harvard University for twenty years, from 1933 to 1953 (see fig. 3.1).[8] Bush and Conant had been the first to convince President Roosevelt to invest in research on the weaponization of fissionable isotopes of radioactive materials (plutonium, the most easily weaponized material, and enriched uranium), and for security purposes, to transfer the research under the authority of the Army Corps of Engineers.[9] Bush and Conant also advocated the continued trust in (Anglo-)American supremacy over nuclear matters: the same nationalistic conception defended by Truman had guided the creation of the Combined Development Trust, which Bush and Conant asked Roosevelt to create in order to ensure US access to the world's uranium and thorium mines. This cartel, which the Canadian, British, and American heads of state created in early 1944, gave the United States access to the raw radioactive materials in the British dominions (such as Canada and Australia, the biggest extractors of uranium), Belgian colonies (such as Congo), and South American states (such as Brazil). Conant and Bush strongly advocated the preservation of the Combined Trust in the postwar era, even though they agreed that its existence would be insufficient to ensure nonproliferation in the postwar era as an international inspection of Soviet territory would be necessary.[10]

Furthermore, those who defended the Anglo-American trusteeship over the atom argued against the idea that the United States should stop building nuclear weapons and destroy its nuclear weapons facilities (see table 3.1). Michael Gordin shows that before the Hiroshima and Nagasaki bombings, the military planners involved in the nuclear weapons project did not believe that Japan would surrender after two atomic bombings in early August 1945 (and the concomitant Soviet invasion of Manchuria). Before Hiroshima, they already planned to build more nuclear weapons, and they insisted that the United States should keep its nuclear war-making capacity intact.[11] In fact, Truman, Bush, and Byrnes relied on nuclear weaponry because they did not believe that the Soviets could be trusted to comply with the rules of a nonproliferation treaty. After the Nagasaki bombing, James Byrnes convinced the president that the United States could negotiate a nuclear nonproliferation and disarmament treaty with the Soviets only on the condition that the Soviets would democratize their domestic institutions and open their society to comprehensive inspections.[12] In a sense, the implementation of this policy would extend the Monroe Doctrine to the whole world, as according to the US doctrine first spelled out by

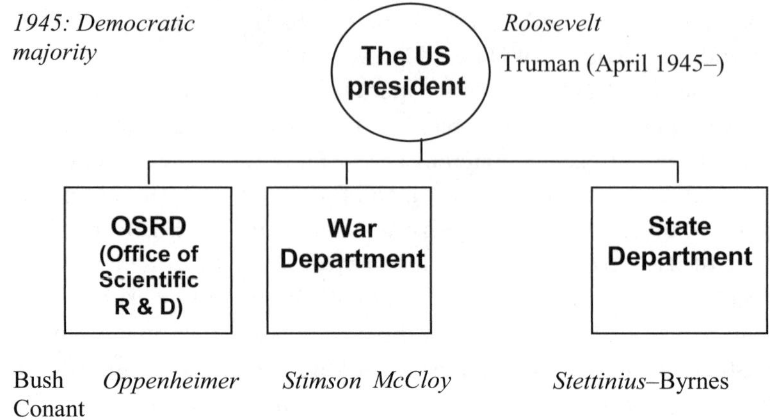

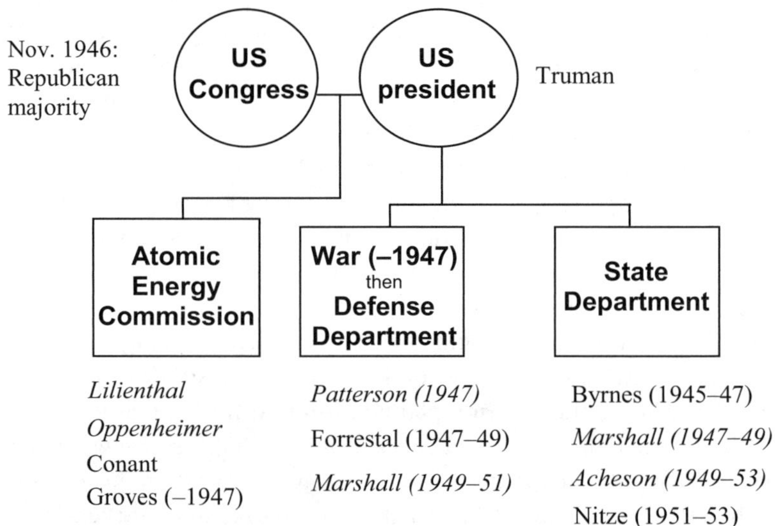

Figure 3.1. Officials in charge of US nuclear foreign policy under Truman

President James Monroe in 1823, undemocratic states could not be trusted to respect treaty commitments, which meant that the United States should avoid international legal entanglements with them.[13] Byrnes believed it was unlikely that the Soviets would agree, and then, the Americans would blame the failure of the negotiations on the Soviets, which would justify the United States building more nuclear weapons to defend the West.

And last, these officials wanted to implement their ideas and policies by ensuring continued military control over America's nuclear affairs in the postwar era. After Hiroshima, the military and scientific managers of the US nuclear weapons program, otherwise known as the "Manhattan Project," tried to preserve their jurisdiction over nuclear development: General Leslie Groves, from the Army Corps of Engineers, who oversaw the entire system of communication within the Manhattan Project (see fig. 3.1),[14] joined forces with Bush and Conant and lobbied the US Congress in favor of a promilitary domestic energy bill. Their Atomic Energy Bill (the May-Johnson Bill, Res. S179), if accepted, would have turned the US nuclear infrastructures over to the US military permanently. It planned for the military authorities to sit on the future Atomic Energy Commission (AEC). That way, General Groves would become the first chairman of the AEC.[15] With Groves in command, the nationalist hard-liners were certain that the future AEC would never exchange information on nuclear technologies with the Soviets, that the AEC would never agree to a moratorium on the production of nuclear weapons, and that the free Western states would be forced to place their trust in US nuclear leadership rather than in an international nuclear disarmament treaty.

Turning to the US Congress actually appeared to be an effective domestic strategy for Bush, Conant, and Byrnes. Senators were very receptive to their ideas. For instance, Kenneth McKellar, the Democratic senator from Tennessee, home to the uranium-enrichment plant in Oak Ridge, was firmly opposed to the idea of Soviet inspectors entering his state to inspect the nuclear operations in Oak Ridge.[16] Like Bush and Conant, Senator Arthur Vandenberg of Michigan, a highly influential Republican member of the Senate Committee on Foreign Relations, was against sharing the peaceful secrets of atomic energy as part of a deal with the Soviets, "unless and until the Soviets are prepared to be policed by the U.N.,"[17] Byrnes stipulated. Senators were reinforced in their nationalist conception of the postwar legal order as they believed that the Manhattan Project was a testament to the greatness of American development, and at the time, a poll of sixty-one congressmen showed that fifty-five opposed sharing knowledge acquired by the Manhattan Project with any country, even with the British. The American public seemed to agree with their president and with the senators: a survey conducted by the National Opinion Research Center showed that 85 percent of Americans wanted the United States to retain exclusive possession of nuclear weapons as long as possible.[18]

In contrast, I apply the term *international liberals* to those men who defended an alternative conception of the postwar legal framework in which interstate contracts would ensure stability and peace along with nuclear nonproliferation and disarmament (see table 3.1). International liberals were among Roosevelt's inner circle of foreign policy elites: Henry Stimson, the secretary of war, and a few of his associates in the Department of War whom Roosevelt consulted on nuclear matters. As far as nuclear matters were concerned, Roosevelt acted as both commander in chief and secretary of state, leaving to Secretary Harold Stettinius the organization of the UN activities.[19] But Henry Stimson, a Harvard-trained lawyer and practicing Wall Street lawyer, brought to the Department of War such kindred spirits as John McCloy (1895–1981), a graduate of Harvard Law School and Republican business lawyer, whom Stimson took as assistant secretary,[20] and whom Roosevelt trusted to keep him informed of nuclear weapons–related activities (see fig. 3.1). These men remained in the inner circle of advisors when Truman assumed the presidency, although they had to welcome newcomers such as Byrnes to the various committees in charge of planning the postwar legal order.

I label the sensibility demonstrated by these men "international liberal" partly because they advocated a classical interstate approach to diplomacy when they discussed the postwar nuclear order. They argued in favor of a disarmament treaty by which all states would pledge neither to build nor to use nuclear weapons after the war. From within the Truman administration, John McCloy in particular developed a legal argument that was close to that developed by John Foster Dulles (1888–1959), a renowned specialist in international law with whom he had worked during the interwar period:[21] from May to September 1945, John McCloy defended the old Westphalian ideal of international law—or *jus publicum europeaum*[22]—which prohibited great powers from pursuing unlimited goals in war, such as regime change, with an unlimited means of war, such as weapons of mass destruction. For instance, prior to the bombing of Hiroshima, McCloy recommended that, before the United States decided to use its nuclear weapons on Japan, it should propose that the Japanese emperor surrender and accept a transition toward a parliamentary monarchy. But, at the time, McCloy's voice was marginal among the foreign policy elites who were asked to join the special governmental group known as the "Interim

Committee," which Truman appointed in May 1945 to help him decide whether or not he should use atomic weapons against Japan and whether or not the Soviets should be informed. The Interim Committee, chaired by Byrnes, which included Vannevar Bush, James Conant, and Robert Oppenheimer, in addition to John McCloy and a few others, decided not to follow McCloy's recommendation.

McCloy's failure to convince other members of the Interim Committee to reject the surprise bombing of Japanese cities did not discourage him from advocating a classical approach to nuclear diplomacy. Well-established precedents existed in the field of international law since the Hague declarations of the late nineteenth century, which banned the use of specific weapons (such as explosive chemical weapons dropped from airplanes), whose use was deemed contrary to the principles of civilized forms of warfare (see table 3.1). In August 1945, after the bombing of the Japanese cities and Japan's unconditional surrender, McCloy criticized Byrnes's proposal that the Soviets be made to change their domestic political structures as a condition of the US moratorium on the building of more nuclear weapons. For McCloy, this idea was not only futile (as Stalin would never agree to it) but also contrary to the Westphalian tradition of noninterference in domestic matters. To convince the Soviets of America's good faith, McCloy suggested that Washington pledge to "stop work" on atomic weapons and "impound what bombs we now have."[23] In his correspondence with Henry Stimson, the secretary of war, McCloy wrote that, first, the United States should approach the Soviet Union with a plan "to control and limit the use of the bomb," and that "working with the Kremlin to control atomic weapons must take precedence over any dreams of forcing that regime to liberalize its rigidly repressed society." Stimson was persuaded, and, in turn, he tried to convince Truman that "it will not be possible" to use the atomic weapon "as a direct lever to produce change" and that Truman should drop "any demand for an internal change in Russia as a condition of sharing atomic weapons."[24]

Confronted with Truman's skepticism, officials in the Department of War tried to mobilize a broader base to win their battle against those in the State Department and White House who favored the continuation of the American atomic protectorate until Soviet approval of its own internal regime change. In August 1945, Oppenheimer, disappointed by Truman's attitude, joined forces with McCloy, after he was asked to write a report on the issue. In his report, as Kai Bird and Martin Sherwin emphasize, Oppenheimer reiterated McCloy's call for the United States to sign a disarmament treaty with the Soviet Union without conditions, as "[the] [a]ction of any international group of nations would not be taken seriously by the Soviets" otherwise.[25] Of the 300 scientists and technicians on the Manhattan Project to whom the report was circulated, 297 signed in support of it. Roosevelt's former vice president and the then secretary of commerce Henry Wallace, Truman's archenemy from the left within the Democratic Party, also gave Oppenheimer his full support, as did the secretary of war, Stimson, who widely circulated the document in the State Department and White House.

The mobilization behind the coalition of officials from the War Department and scientists in Los Alamos seemed to pay off. At the end of August 1945, McCloy and Oppenheimer even convinced the assistant secretary of state, Dean Acheson (1893–1971), a former student of Justice Felix Frankfurter at Harvard Law School, like John McCloy (see fig. 3.1). The Harvard-educated lawyers regrouped behind McCloy's classical interstate approach to geopolitical problems and attacked the nationalist approach embodied by Truman and Byrnes's proposals. It was Dean Acheson, serving as acting secretary of state in the absence of James Byrnes during a cabinet meeting in September 1945, who made the case to Truman that "the U.S. should make a direct approach to the Soviets—not through the U.N.—offering a step-by-step plan to share scientific information and adopt verifiable safeguards against the production of atomic weapons by any country."[26] Acheson also emphasized that the United States should directly and quickly approach the Soviet Union to avoid being seen as "hoarders of military secrets from our Allies, particularly this great Ally," the USSR, whose cooperation "was essential for the future peace of the world."[27]

An alternative policy proposal based on international liberal principles thus emerged around the views expressed by McCloy and Acheson, but it was still blocked by Truman's closest advisors: Byrnes, Bush, and Conant. Despite his recognition of Oppenheimer's report as being, in Bush's words, "a fine document,"[28] Vannevar Bush and James Conant believed that for any meaningful agreement to be signed with the Soviets, a system of land inspection in Soviet territory first had to be established in order to control and inspect their nuclear activities by a "U.N. corps of inspectors,"[29] and a UN agency with "the power of inspection."[30] For Conant, the United States needed to continue to pressure the USSR to impose inspections first, even if that meant that the United States should use nuclear weapons "as a lever" or a "threat" against Russia. McCloy's recommendation to avoid "threatening the world with our present power will not stand up to careful analysis," he wrote, as "you do essentially threaten or bargain if you do anything short of blandly giving away the secret."[31] James Conant declared that if Stalin did not agree to land inspection, any proposal to "outlaw atomic weapons" would fall in the "same category as the Kellogg-Briand pact"[32] of 1928, which outlawed aggressive war as an instrument of diplomacy and whose legal validity had been nullified during the Second World War.

Still, the proposal that the United States invite the British and Soviets to privately negotiate the details of a treaty banning the use of nuclear weapons and the research relevant to their development gained credibility in Washington think tanks, where McCloy's proposal appealed to renowned international law specialists. The newly created Committee on Atomic Energy of the Carnegie Endowment for International Peace, chaired by James Shotwell (1884–1965), a Canadian citizen by birth and a professor of diplomatic history at Columbia University,[33] crafted a draft of a nuclear disarmament treaty along the same international liberal lines. Shotwell staunchly believed that traditional interstate declarations signed by great powers were valid and quite effective instruments of international law,[34] especially in the field of disarmament: Shotwell had authored the "Shotwell Resolution," passed in June 1924 at the Council of the League of Nations, which declared "aggressive war" a crime,[35] and which inspired the Kellogg-Briand Declaration of 1928. In the same way, Shotwell believed that outlawing atomic weapons by a simple declaration accompanied by some form of interstate compliance mechanism would be effective because "even if covenants do not deter, they afford standards for judging state conduct."[36] As chairman of the Atomic Energy Committee of the Carnegie Endowment, in the fall of 1945, Shotwell asked his colleagues (for instance Jacob Viner, a professor of political economy at the University of Chicago)[37] to formulate a template that the US government could use if it wanted to present an interstate disarmament treaty to the Soviets.[38]

The report issued in the spring of 1946 by the Carnegie Endowment expressed the opinion that the United States should propose a treaty that only required a limited renunciation of sovereignty from its parties, rather than ask them to commit to regime change. The draft planned that most nuclear operations, such as the extraction of uranium, the reprocessing of plutonium, and nuclear research, would remain under state control, while being checked further by an international UN agency of inspectors appointed by the member states to act on their behalf—a system not unlike that adopted by the IAEA. Shotwell argued that the Soviets were likely to welcome this proposal, because they would be left free to develop their nuclear research with the limited external control of the UN agency. Furthermore, the Soviets, as permanent members of the UN Security Council, would keep a veto over the decision to sanction states found in violation of the disarmament treaty by the future UN inspection agency.[39]

In contrast, the policy coalition that comprised those whom I term *cosmopolitans* called for postwar nuclear cooperation between scientists of all the nations outside the control of nation-states, and for the establishment of a new supranational institution in charge of nuclear development. The Danish Nobel laureate in physics Niels Bohr, who came to the city of Los Alamos, was an ardent promoter of the cosmopolitan "fraternity between men of science" and wanted to convince the American authorities to communicate with the Soviets,[40] as "a preliminary approach" toward the establishment of a postwar "universal organization."[41] If Bohr's views were suspicious to Groves and even to Roosevelt,[42] his opinion on the need to reestablish open communication between all scientists of the world after the war was widely shared among the European scientists in exile who worked on the US nuclear-weapons project. As completion of the nuclear-weapons project came closer, Albert Einstein and Leo Szilard, the two European scientists in exile who first alerted Roosevelt to the possibility of building nuclear weapons, urged the US government to adopt a tactic of utmost transparency in its dealings with the Soviet leadership and the rest of the world's scientists. Szilard understood the Manhattan Project as a race against German Nazi scientists who, Szilard feared, could become the first to produce a functioning nuclear device and use it against London.

When the Third Reich capitulated in May 1945, the European scientists in exile in the United States asked for an immediate revelation of the destructiveness of the bomb, and a complete revelation of the knowledge accumulated in the development of the military application of atomic energy (see table 3.1).[43] They asked that the United States explode some atomic bombs in a desert before a panel of international observers from the United Nations to demonstrate their destructive power: such a test would be openly administered like an experiment in front of gentlemen of science. When, in May 1945, Szilard realized that he could not convince James Byrnes to pass his views to Truman, Szilard and other scientists wrote a document known as the *Franck Report*, in which they claimed that the United States put all plans for postwar nuclear disarmament in jeopardy by refusing to invite the Soviets to witness the first US test. Szilard and his colleagues reasoned, "It may be very difficult to persuade the world that a nation which was capable of secretly preparing and suddenly releasing a weapon as indiscriminate as the rocket bomb and a million times more destructive, is to be trusted in its proclaimed desire of having such weapons abolished by international agreement."[44] These views proved to be widely shared among physicists: in July 1945, a poll done by the army of 150 scientists involved in the Manhattan Project found that about three-quarters of them favored a technical demonstration before an international panel over the military use of the bomb.[45]

The scientists who adhered to the cosmopolitan and world federalist views regarded nuclear weapons as the property of the men of science rather than that of one great power, the United States. For them, the revolution in nuclear science had to be followed by a broader revolution in the international legal order. Among the scientists in Los Alamos who were inspired by Bohr's vision, Oppenheimer was initially among the most faithful of believers that the brotherhood of men of science could serve as a model for the organization of postwar international relations: before the bombs were dropped, he argued that the United States needed to accelerate the completion of the nuclear weapons,[46] because dropping the bomb represented "a way to end all wars."[47] In contrast to McCloy, who had expressed doubts about the pertinence of dropping atomic bombs on Japan,[48] Oppenheimer argued that he was "more concerned with the prevention of war" and the transformation of the structure of world society "than with the elimination of this specific weapon."[49] Finally the scientists would be able to realize Woodrow Wilson's dreams of criminalizing war as an instrument of state policy: before the scientists in Los Alamos, Oppenheimer argued that the use of nuclear weapons against Japan would enable the United States to argue for a revolutionary form of international law akin to the internal law of a world federation in which war as an instrument of diplomacy would be abolished. As one of the scientists working in Los Alamos said, Oppenheimer promised that if scientists succeeded in completing nuclear weapons to end the war with Japan, "it was the end of war as we knew it, and this was the promise that was made, that sovereignty would exist in the United Nations."[50] On the contrary, if the scientists did not finish their job and if the bombs were not used, so Oppenheimer argued in July 1945, then their work would be classified by the US military, no one would learn of the bombs' destructive power, and nuclear research and development would continue to be under the control of the military (and General Groves) after the war. Believing Oppenheimer's promise, the scientists who had initially signed the *Franck Report* redoubled their work to finish the assemblage of the US atomic weapons.

Even though charismatic leaders such as Bohr or Oppenheimer made quite popular their cosmopolitan conception of the world nuclear order, they failed to gain much credibility in policy-making circles. Their main victory in the fall of 1945 was on the domestic front: they succeeded in convincing a US senator to introduce an atomic energy bill that would be an alternative to the May-Johnson Bill sponsored by nationalists, which would have given control of domestic nuclear activities to the military. In fact, Senator Brien McMahon of Connecticut introduced a new bill in Congress to replace the May-Johnson Bill in December 1945. Scientists from the Manhattan Project from Chicago, Oak Ridge, Los Alamos, and New York, who united behind Leo Szilard and Niels Bohr in the new Federation of Atomic Scientists (FAS),[51] shaped the new legislation that McMahon introduced in Congress. The bill proposed exclusively civilian control over nuclear science. Furthermore, the US senators eventually agreed to postpone preparation of a domestic bill in order not to preempt the outcome of international negotiations that were about to start. The successful mobilization of Los Alamos scientists proved that the Federation of American Scientists could achieve some success against nationalists, even though, in the end, the new legislation (known as the McMahon Act) met their position and that of the nationalists halfway: the 1946 McMahon Act did not authorize the civilian-led AEC to develop an international cooperation agreement, even with the British.[52] This ultimate reversal showed that the nationalists had succeeded in maintaining some of their most controversial policy proposals despite intense opposition. The next subsection explores how they used secrecy to achieve their goals.

The Role of Secrecy in Domestic Power Struggles (Summer 1943–Winter 1944)

Secrecy characterized the Anglo-American nuclear weapons program from the start. Secrecy was necessary to avoid the risk that the Germans, who also attempted to weaponize the use of fissile materials, might spy on the United States. During the war, Roosevelt only consulted with Henry Stimson, the secretary of war, and a few of his associates in the Department of War on nuclear matters.[53] He kept the US Congress in the dark because of the exceptional condition of wartime and the necessity to hide American nuclear dealings from the Axis powers. The US government put in place strict security provisions that prevented foreign scientists from communicating with their governments, even if those governments were allies of the United States. Despite the fact that Roosevelt had been convinced to start the Manhattan Project by European émigré-scientists themselves,[54] he placed the scientists who worked on the Manhattan Project under strict surveillance. Scientists from defeated but allied nations such as Belgium, Poland, and France who worked in the British and American nuclear programs could not report to their governments in exile, which were headed by

Paul-Henri Spaak, General Sikorski, and General de Gaulle, respectively.[55] Instead, they were under the close scrutiny of American officers.

Secrecy was imposed not only upon the scientists who worked on the Manhattan Project and the officials in the US government who knew of its existence, but also upon the British and Canadian partners in the Manhattan Project. Indeed, three Anglo-American powers signed an agreement of nuclear cooperation in Quebec City in August 1943 (the Quebec Agreement), which greatly limited the transfer of sensitive knowledge from the United States to the United Kingdom or to Canada.[56] In the agreement, the British and Canadian prime ministers "effectively and expressly disclaim[ed] any interest in these industrial and commercial aspects beyond what may be considered by the President of the United States to be fair and just and in harmony with the economic welfare of the world"[57] (art. 4). Thus, the information on "large-scale plants," such as the uranium-enrichment plant the Americans built in Oak Ridge (Tennessee), or the plutonium-reprocessing plant that they built in Hanford (Washington), was protected from falling not only into the hands of the Nazis or even the Soviets, but also into the hands of British and Canadian allies of the United States (see table 3.2). For Bush and Conant, who were responsible for this very strict policy imposed upon America's allies, the main reason for it was that the British had signed an alliance treaty with the Soviets after the German invasion of the Soviet Union.[58] Without much choice, the British agreed to the strict conditions, and only obtained the creation of a Combined Policy Committee, chaired by Vannevar Bush, to adjudicate Anglo-American disputes (art. 5a4)[59] in case the British found that too much secrecy was imposed upon the work of US scientists.[60] Still, as Bush and Conant represented the United States on the Combined Policy Committee, they ensured that only a limited amount of knowledge circulated across the Atlantic during the war.[61]

Furthermore, the United States imposed on the United Kingdom and Canada the condition that they could not talk to their allies (France and the Soviet Union) about the Manhattan Project, at least until they obtained US approval. The Quebec Agreement barred the communication of information to any third party (art. 3) such as the Soviet Union (or France) without mutual consent—a point that violated the promise made in 1940 by the British authorities to Etienne Hirsh, who headed the armament program of Free France in London, to recognize the French contribution to the British nuclear effort in future negotiations between Anglo-American allies and the Western continent.[62] The nationalists intended to hide the

Table 3.2 The Quebec Agreement and its reinterpretation by the United States

Principles	Quebec Agreement	How it was disregarded by the United States
Nonuse	Pledge not to use the bomb against each other's territory (art. 1)	Always observed
Consultation on the use of weapons	Pledge to seek each other's consent prior to using atomic bombs outside Anglo-American territory (art. 2)	Truman did not inform *ex ante* the British or Canadian prime ministers of his decision to use two bombs against Hiroshima and Nagasaki Truman reiterated *ex post* the principle of Anglo-American trusteeship when he announced the bombings US senators rejected the need to consult the British before American use of nuclear weapons
Consultation on the sharing of information	To prohibit the communication of information to a third party without mutual consent (art. 3)	Bush convinced Truman that it barred communication on nuclear matters between Truman and Stalin at Yalta Truman authorized the publication of the *Smyth Report* without consulting his British and Canadian counterparts Truman did not authorize the British to share information with the French, even though this violated commitments made by the British
Arbitration of disputes	To establish a Combined Policy Committee to allocate materials, apparatus, and plants (art. 5a1, 5a2), and to adjudicate Anglo-American disputes (art. 5a4)	The Combined Policy Committee ceased to exist after 1947, and the United States refused to hear British complaints, while claiming that the 1946 Atomic Energy Act barred the United States from sharing any information with anybody

truth about the Manhattan Project from the Soviet Union until the end. In July 1945, Bush personally convinced Truman that the Quebec Agreement made consultation with Russia, France, and China on the bombing of Japan unnecessary and illegal. As a result, when Truman met Stalin in Potsdam in July 1945 to write the peace treaties that settled the territorial order of postwar Europe, there was no mention that the US government was about to drop two nuclear weapons on Japan. As Walter Isaacson and Evan Thomas emphasize, Truman only casually mentioned to the Soviet premier that the United States had "a new weapon of unusual destructive force,"[63] without saying that the weapon was atomic.

Secrecy was used for yet another purpose when the discussions tackled the issue of the postwar nuclear order (and the role that the Soviet Union would play in it). Those who were in charge of ensuring the secrecy in order to avoid international leaks also used their position of power to silence domestic opponents to their preferred policy. Secrecy was used by nationalists not only to prevent wartime enemies (and future enemies such as the Soviet Union) from gaining knowledge accumulated within the Manhattan Project on nuclear fuel fabrication processes (such as uranium enrichment and plutonium reprocessing) and nuclear weapons design, but also to exclude alternative policy proposals from the domestic policy debate. For instance, Bird and Sherwin note that when cosmopolitans wrote in the *Franck Report* that the German capitulation should lead to the immediate lifting of the veil over the Manhattan Project, Byrnes and Groves removed their report from the official policy circuit: the *Franck Report* was immediately confiscated and classified, and President Truman never actually saw it.[64] The American and European scientists who had signed the *Franck Report* were not invited to sit on the Interim Committee, which decided whether Soviet scientists would be invited to witness the first test. As a result of their absence, and despite Oppenheimer's proposal that the United States invite two Soviet scientists to witness their first nuclear test in Alamogordo, New Mexico, Secretary Byrnes ignored the suggestion—and Oppenheimer did not insist.

The removal of policy opinions through classification became a new tool of social control characteristic of how nuclear policy would be decided in the United States, Peter Galison argues.[65] For instance, after McCloy, Oppenheimer, and Acheson submitted their report on the international control of atomic energy in September 1945, President Truman had all of their documents classified and thus removed from public discussion. Despite his public declarations,[66] the president used secrecy to defend the policy proposals of nationalist hard-liners against alternative policy proposals. He applied this policy until the end of his tenure. For instance, in 1952, Oppenheimer continued to insist on the importance of "public candor" with the Soviets when he wrote reports for the AEC on atomic weapons and foreign policy,[67] in which he recommended "that the number of atomic weapons and bombers, a rough estimate of the rate of US fissile materials production, and [US] estimates of Soviet nuclear threat be released."[68] In 1952, Truman's cabinet similarly destroyed many copies of the report, which Oppenheimer had prepared for the newly formed UN Disarmament Committee, and it was only through informal back channels that the Republican contender in the presidential election, General Dwight Eisenhower, managed to read it.[69] This use of secrecy was widespread not only in the United States under Truman's presidency but also—and to an even greater extent—in Japan, where the censorship imposed by US general MacArthur during the Occupation (which lasted until 1951) effectively silenced any condemnation of the US decision to use nuclear weapons and any policy discussion about the US reliance on nuclear weapons.[70]

Secrecy affected not only policy recommendations but also legal commitments. The concealment of the existence of the Quebec Agreement helped nationalists gain easy acceptance of the most controversial elements of the 1946 McMahon Act on international nuclear cooperation. In the end, the McMahon Act tightened the language of article 4 of the Quebec Agreement, which already limited the sharing of information between allies on large-scale nuclear processes to information that the US president believed to "be fair" to give to the British (see table 3.2). Indeed, the Mc-Mahon Act (sec. 10) simply stated that scientific and technical information on the development of large-scale nuclear research and "industrial" reactors could not be exchanged with any other nation. Furthermore, the decision to share any "restricted data" (even data of no direct industrial relevance) with foreign nations had to be submitted to the Military Liaison Committee before final approval.[71] The future first chairman of the AEC, David Lilienthal, repeatedly mentioned that the British "blame[d] Groves for going around behind their backs and having that provision against exchange of information put into the McMahon Act, even pointing to the line which singles out 'industrial uses,' which shows on its face that whoever inserted that line had the background [in the Quebec Agreement] which only Groves and two or three others had."[72] When they voted on the 1946 McMahon Act, most senators ignored the content of the Quebec Agreement (or were unaware of its existence), so they did not know that by passing the McMahon Act, a domestic law superseded a prior international agreement (even a secret one). Actually, only Senator McMahon was privately briefed on the content of the Quebec Agreement by Vannevar Bush, who thought that "it was better to give him the story completely before the Senate started to get the situation in testimony"[73] than to have the Senate and the American public find out about the agreement during public hear-ings. When the McMahon Act was discussed in 1946, the secrecy allowed the United States to let the Quebec Agreement die a secret death rather than launch a new controversy that would inevitably pit the Republican nationalists against the Democrats.[74]

After the senators abrogated the Quebec Agreement without knowing it (and without suffering costs since the United Kingdom did not reveal the existence of this agreement until 1954),[75] they walled off the suspiciously internationalist scientists working in the United States, many of whom were scientists in exile who had not returned to their Eastern European homes (occupied by Stalin's armies), from activities involving nuclear research and development. Under the pressure of Republican congressmen, the Truman administration went so far as to pass domestic laws that expanded the surveillance of the beliefs and acts of scientists, which had been initiated on a small scale during the war by Roosevelt and Groves, to a much larger scale. In 1947, Truman signed an executive order that made it mandatory for employees of the federal government to take an "oath of loyalty." Even James Conant and others such as Michael Polanyi,[76] Robert Merton, Conant's protégé Thomas Kuhn, and Walter Lippmann[77] were unhappy with these domestic developments, which threatened the "spirit of science." In 1947, Congress wanted to pass a new law, which would have subjected recipients of an AEC fellowship for "scientific research" (and not for industrial development) to FBI investigation.[78] However, the bill was defeated by a small margin, thanks only to the efforts of the AEC insiders: David Lilienthal (the AEC chairman) and his advisors Robert Oppenheimer and James Conant (who by then found that demands for more secrecy and surveillance went beyond their initial goals).[79]

The atmosphere of suspicion, fear, and denunciation created by Senator Joseph McCarthy and Richard Nixon at the House Committee on Un-American Activities after the explosion of a Soviet A-bomb in the fall of 1949, made it finally impossible for the Truman administration to justify any progressive change to the McMahon Act toward renewed Anglo-American cooperation.[80] Though the 1946 McMahon Act had obviously failed to avoid nuclear proliferation after the Soviets exploded a nuclear weapon in 1949, nationalists became even more obstinate. For them, the Soviet explosion was due to leaks from within the AEC and the State Department, which should have been purged of their more liberal and internationalist elements. In fact, they believed they had found proof of a Communist conspiracy that spanned the Atlantic when the German-born nuclear physicist Klaus Fuchs[81] confessed in January 1950 that he had been spying for the Soviet Union since 1941. Richard Nixon promised to get rid of the "vast New Deal–Harvard–State Department conspiracy to surrender to Russia,"[82] and to find the spies in the United States.

The populist undertones of McCarthy's and Nixon's campaigns revealed that the policy debate on nuclear matters still illustrated a clash of habitus between competing US foreign policy elites, with, on one side, the Harvard-trained lawyers and cosmopolitan nuclear scientists, and on the other side, the American self-made men who distrusted anything foreign. For instance, in the AEC, Groves's demands for increased secrecy and surveillance were relayed by Commissioner Lewis Strauss (1896–1974), who was, like Byrnes and Truman, a self-made businessman and not a Harvard-trained lawyer like Lilienthal, McCloy, or Acheson. During his tenure as commissioner of the AEC (before he became chairman), Strauss successfully lobbied Truman to oppose any demand by Lilienthal or Conant to share either scientific or industrial information with British scientists, who, in the words of Strauss, "were too far to the left."[83] In 1950, David Lilienthal became the first victim of the Republicans as he was forced out of the chairmanship of the AEC by the Republican Congress.[84] Lewis Strauss understood that the removal of one's security clearance was the best way to silence opponents to Truman's policy. When he eventually acceded to the chairmanship of the AEC, after the presidential victory of General Eisenhower in November 1952, Strauss immediately put Oppenheimer on internal trial. The handful of judges whom Strauss appointed at the AEC found Oppenheimer to be a "security risk," and therefore blocked his access to classified data. Through secrecy, nationalists slowly excluded their competitors on policy from influencing the highest policy-making circles by removing knowledge from the public realm.

Transparency as Social Control

Imposing the Publicity of Negotiations with the Soviets (Fall 1945)

To block the campaign of cosmopolitan scientists and international liberals in favor of direct negotiation with the Soviets and worldwide cooperation in the development of peaceful applications of nuclear energy, nationalists not only used secrecy, they also channeled their competitors' proposals into rigid tracks that did not offer them the liberty of reaching a workable agreement with the Soviets. In other words, nationalists sponsored cosmopolitan initiatives in public forums as long as they could control scientists or foreign policy elites such as John McCloy so they could not deviate from the (very limited) mandate that was given to them.

Transparency started with a call for public diplomacy. The first step toward transparent diplomacy was taken when the successful mobilization against the May-Johnson atomic energy bill convinced Truman that he could not easily silence cosmopolitan scientists by secrecy alone. Consequently, he gave them a public forum in international negotiations with the Soviets. In November 1945, at the end of a conference with the British and Canadian prime ministers, Clement Attlee and William Lyon McKenzie King, President Truman announced that the negotiations with the Soviets on the international control of atomic energy would be held in public in a newly created UN Atomic Energy Committee. He told Attlee and King that Anglo-American wartime cooperation in the extraction of raw materials would continue in the Combined Development Trust; there was to be no exchange of "commercial" or "military" information on the later stages of development and industrial production; and all negotiation on nuclear disarmament and nonproliferation would take place at the United Nations.[85]

As Shane Maddock observes, these decisions sent a strong signal that Truman expected the negotiations of a future nuclear disarmament treaty to fail. Indeed, McCloy and Stimson had told him that Stalin would not take the US commitment to nuclear disarmament seriously if the United States refused to engage directly in bilateral talks with the Soviets: a UN conference would be seen as an instrument of propaganda directed at the lesser powers instead of a serious step toward nuclear disarmament.[86] Truman decided, in full knowledge, to ignore their advice and to listen to Bush and Conant instead.[87] After Truman's announcement, even James Conant noted with distress that the Soviets reacted with indifference or disdain. He wrote, "The Russians did not argue or talk back," except to say that they wanted the conference to report to "the Security Council rather than the Assembly,"[88] in order to keep their veto power over the final outcome of the UN Commission on Atomic Energy.

Truman gave priority to the concerns of the US senators who were reassured by the public nature of the discussions at the United Nations that the US negotiators would not secretly trade Soviet acceptance of the future American plan for the postwar control of nuclear energy against Anglo-American nuclear secrets. For the senators even the public character of the discussions at the United Nations did not go far enough to reassure them: after the Soviet acceptance of the UN commission, Senator Arthur Vandenberg requested and obtained written commitment from Secretary of State James Byrnes that no information would be given to the Soviets prior to the establishment of proper controls.[89]

Clarity: Drafting the US Position (Fall 1946)

Transparency meant not only public nuclear diplomacy but also the clarification of the US position before the beginning of the UN negotiations. After Stalin accepted the UN commission, Vannevar Bush insisted that the US president should give a very clear mandate to the US negotiator. Indeed, American diplomats observed at the conference in San Francisco in the spring of 1945 (at which the statutes of the United Nations were drawn up) that the United States gained considerable advantage over its competitors by publicly committing itself to a plan before the start of diplomatic discussions.[90] Even Oppenheimer recognized the validity of Bush's claim, as, for him, the "U.S., U.K. and Canada must have a disproportionate influence in shaping the proposal made" because of their "technical advance and scientific insight." This technical superiority did not mean that it was "desirable to avoid multilateral discussion"[91]—quite the contrary—but for Oppenheimer, America's knowledge of nuclear processes needed to be translated into political leadership.

But in this case, the clarification of the US position merely channeled the scientists' efforts into a forum that was doomed to fail, which had the positive effect for Truman of defusing domestic criticism until the scientists realized they were being duped. The tight control that the US chief executive kept on the formulation of the US policy proposal was reflected in the composition of the Board of Consultants charged with formulating the American plan: it included not only Dean Acheson and John McCloy but also Vannevar Bush and James Conant. Then, the Board of Consultants appointed five advisors, whose mandate was to develop a common diagnosis of the main problems confronting international security in the postwar era, and to formulate the principles of the US position. This other committee of five advisors, which included Oppenheimer, was chaired by the emblematic New Dealer David Lilienthal, the chairman of the TVA, another former student of Justice Frankfurter, whose ascension to the higher administrative ranks reflected the rise of progressive and secular Jews newly admitted into elite American universities and within the ranks of foreign policy advisors.[92] That Oppenheimer wrote the first draft of the report explains why the proposal reflected the cosmopolitan theses that scientists expressed at Los Alamos during the war. Still, it was quite surprising that the Board of Consultants, and especially Bush and Conant, accepted what became known as the *Acheson-Lilienthal Report*. Bush and Conant did so only because they knew that Oppenheimer would not have the opportunity to privately negotiate a deal with the Soviets on that basis.

The *Acheson-Lilienthal Report* was an ambitious attempt to create new rules of treaty writing in the field of international law and disarmament. Though legal precedents did exist, both at the domestic federal level, with the TVA, and at the international level,[93] the *Acheson-Lilienthal Report* proposed a true global law, which was not based on an Anglo-American trusteeship. It was global rather than "international" in the sense that it was not the law of states or nations, but the law of a cosmopolitan community of scientists responsible for monitoring nuclear activities around the globe on behalf of the protection of the whole of humanity (see table 3.3).[94] The International Atomic Developmental Authority (IADA), which Oppenheimer and Lilienthal proposed to establish, was supposed to form the nucleus of

Table 3.3 The *Acheson-Lilienthal Report* and its official interpretation

Principles	*Acheson-Lilienthal Report*	Baruch's additions
Condition of international security	Absolute freedom of science from states or interstate organizations by the creation of a global community of nuclear scientists, the International Atomic Developmental Authority (IADA), in charge of nuclear research and development programs	Science checked by international organization reporting to the UN Security Council
First goals	Survey of all territories where fissile materials are found in great quantities, whatever their condition (natural uranium in mines, enriched uranium, and reprocessed plutonium), and transfer of the property of these soils from nations to the IADA, in addition to a moratorium on nuclear weapons testing	Survey of all territories where fissile materials are found in great quantities, whatever their condition (natural uranium in mines, enriched uranium. and reprocessed plutonium), and transfer of the property of these soils from nations to the IADA, but against a moratorium on nuclear weapons tests and on military research and development of nuclear weapons in the United States
Ultimate goals	Clear nonproliferation and nuclear disarmament goals: the United States should destroy its nuclear stockpile and nuclear weapons laboratories in a controlled manner	Clear nonproliferation goal but ambiguous disarmament goal as the United States could produce atomic weapons for the United Nations

a world federation: this federation would be granted the responsibility to develop peaceful applications of nuclear energy and to check that they were not used for military purposes. In their report, Lilienthal and Oppenheimer proposed that the scientists in charge of the IADA would take care of all the "dangerous" atomic research and development (meaning dual-use activities), with full ownership and control of all fissionable materials (an all-encompassing term that included uranium, thorium, and other transuranic elements) at every stage of its production (from mines to separation plants and research and development on these materials). The authors of the report wrote that since peaceful, large-scale research and development comprise "80% of the work of producing nuclear weapons," and the boundary between "peaceful" and "dangerous" scientific applications shifts, only scientists "who know how"[95] could oversee these activities.[96]

Though the consensus was a surprise, chances that the report presented to Dean Acheson, Vannevar Bush, James Conant, and John McCloy by the five advisors would be accepted were slim, at best.[97] The advisors presented their conclusions to the board at the exact moment when Dean Acheson was warned not to trust the Soviets to comply with any international treaties they signed, especially in the field of nuclear disarmament:[98] the famous "Long Telegram"[99] written by George Kennan, an attaché at the US embassy in Moscow, was on Acheson's desk when Acheson received the report from the board's advisors. However, McCloy and then Acheson became staunch advocates of their report, and they won the approval of other members of the Board of Consultants initially opposed to its conclusion: Bush and Conant. To understand why Bush and Conant rallied the others, it is important to stress how they clarified the ambiguity that Lilienthal and Oppenheimer maintained over key propositions that were sacrificed in order to obtain the consensus.

On the Board of Consultants, Bush and Conant imposed important clarifications to the language of the report submitted by Lilienthal and Oppenheimer. Oppenheimer and Lilienthal planned that the delegation of sovereignty from nation-states to this new international authority would occur in two consecutive steps, the order of which remained ambiguous (see table 3.3). First, the IADA would survey the geographic dispersion of raw materials and acquire the property rights,[100] which meant that the IADA would inherit the rights that the Combined Development Trust possessed over the ores from mines controlled by the United States, in Canada, Brazil, and the Belgian Congo. It also meant that the Soviets had to agree to let international inspectors survey their vast territory in search of raw materials, as Truman, Bush, and Conant had emphasized time and again. Second, the report suggested that the IADA should then be placed in charge of the administration of the most dangerous technologies, especially uranium-enrichment and plutonium-reprocessing plants in the United States, the only ones existing being on American soil. Third, after global sovereignty was fully established, the IADA would then distribute to nation-states small quantities of radioisotopes for medical and agricultural purposes, and for university research conducted at the national level with small-scale accelerators.

Though Oppenheimer and Lilienthal suggested this order of steps, it remained unclear when each step would actually be taken. Oppenheimer initially proposed that the United States let the UN Committee on Atomic Energy set the timetable of steps toward the global control of atomic energy, which meant that the United Nations would decide the rhythm and nature of the delegation of national sovereignty to world federal sovereignty.[101] For instance, the UN committee would decide whether the second phase would start after the survey of Soviet mines ended, or shortly after such a survey had started (and before it ended). The proposal remained ambiguous on the temporal issue for a reason. Answers to these questions actually determined whether the Soviets and the United States would commit to the treaty roughly at the same time, or not.

The rejection of this ambiguity was the price that Bush and Conant imposed in exchange for their approval of the rest of the rules defined in the report. Conant and Bush fiercely opposed Oppenheimer's proposal to leave the order of steps unclear: they did not want to see the UN Committee on Atomic Energy force the United States to halt the production of nuclear weapons before the inspection of Soviet mines had finished.[102] They suggested letting the US negotiator decide the order of the steps, with the suggestion previously mentioned that the IADA would first take care of raw materials, and second take care of the processed materials and means of processing them, only after the first phase had clearly ended. Such an order of steps prolonged the declaration made in November 1945 by Truman, Attlee, and King, which proposed that Anglo-Americans first share "scientific information" along the lines of the report that Princeton professor Henry Smyth published about the scientific knowledge gained in the Manhattan Project (a step completed in August 1945), and second the "knowledge concerning raw materials."[103]

The clarification of the timetable seemed a small tactical concession granted in exchange for a much larger normative and strategic victory. The others agreed to their conditions. Oppenheimer actually agreed that there should be no further release of scientific information: he wrote, "The Smyth report is sufficient."[104] Otherwise, the Soviets would spy on the Americans, and might withdraw from the treaty before the end of the first phase, as Kennan had warned Acheson. As Oppenheimer explained to Lilienthal regarding his opposition to the immediate creation of a UN corps of inspectors, "There is pitifully little to inspect in any countries but the U.S., U.K., and Canada."[105] Furthermore, the clear order of steps made it more likely that the nationalists in the US Congress would ratify the future treaty, as it would prolong the American monopoly on the enrichment of uranium and the reprocessing of plutonium until the Soviet mines were open to inspection.

Transparency, which meant that negotiations with the Soviets would take place in public, and that the US negotiator would be given a clear mandate, from which he could not deviate (or could deviate very little), thus served two functions: it gave the appearance that Truman, Bush, and Conant had adopted a conciliatory attitude toward rising foreign policy elites; and it controlled the extent to which cosmopolitans could convince the Soviets to accept their plan. Such a tactical move seemed timely for Bush and Conant: the lost battle in Congress over the domestic atomic energy bill showed that they needed to heed the views of the European scientists such as Szilard if they wanted to avoid opposition to the future Atomic Energy Bill that was taking shape in Congress. Even though Lilienthal seemed not to have been aware that Conant and Bush were making these sorts of domestic calculations,[106] Bush and Conant bet that they would regain the trust of the scientific community by approving the Acheson-Lilienthal plan, which they did.[107]

Bush and Conant were not the only ones who needed to distance themselves from the strict policy of secrecy they had put in place in the nuclear field. In March 1946, Henry Stimson and his former assistant, Harvey Bundy, who oversaw the secrecy rules of the Manhattan Project with Leslie Groves as well as Dean Acheson, feared the devastating effect on public opinion of a public statement calling the Hiroshima and Nagasaki bombings "morally indefensible"[108] made by an influential public authority, Reinhold Niebuhr, as well as John Foster Dulles and twenty Protestant philosophers.[109] The statement directly criticized the strict rules of secrecy that Truman's circle of foreign policy advisors imposed during wartime planning. As Kai Bird reveals, Harvey Bundy, the assistant secretary of war, asked his son McGeorge Bundy to quell the controversy by exonerating key foreign policy elites for having hidden the *Franck Report*.[110] In their attempt to twist the historical narrative, US top policy makers were largely successful: American public opinion endorsed the claim made by President

Truman and Eleanor Roosevelt that Hiroshima had "saved thousands of American lives"[111]—a claim that has now been disputed by historians who showed that the Soviet entry into the war was the catalyst to the Japanese decision to sign the armistice.[112] But those who had endorsed the removal of alternatives from the policy debate, such as Byrnes or Truman, needed more than a few papers planted in the press in order to prevent critics from attacking their policy of secrecy. They could not find a better way to prove to the US public that the debate was open to diversity of opinion than by adopting the *Acheson-Lilienthal Report*, which they did in May 1946.

Is That Clear Enough? The Official US Plan (Summer 1946)

Transparency was a risky strategy. Although Truman's advisors clearly expressed the order of steps that they proposed to implement in their plan, there was a risk that the US negotiator at the United Nations would privilege the agreement with the Soviets above the clear and limited mandate he had been given. When, upon the recommendation of James Byrnes,[113] Harry Truman nominated Bernard Baruch (1870–1965) as the US representative to the UN Committee on Atomic Energy, he signaled his willingness to safeguard the clear order of steps imposed by Bush and Conant. Bernard Baruch, older than Acheson, Lilienthal, or Oppenheimer, was, like Byrnes or Truman, a self-made man from the South who had earned a fortune on Wall Street before chairing the War Industries Board during the First World War. Baruch was a renowned apostle of free trade after the First World War,[114] which made him an odd choice to negotiate a plan of worldwide regulation of nuclear industries by a global organization such as the IADA.

In fact, the authors of the *Acheson-Lilienthal Report* were deeply distressed by Baruch's appointment, especially when, upon taking his new position, Baruch completely changed the staff of advisors—among the prior advisors of the Board of Consultants, only Oppenheimer joined the team of technical experts.[115] Furthermore, Baruch immediately adopted the one recommendation made by Bush and Conant that, during the first phase of the creation of the IADA, the work of the IADA should be devoted exclusively to the survey of Soviet mines, and that, only after that survey was finished, would the United States agree to let inspectors enter its uranium-enrichment, plutonium, and reprocessing plants. Baruch actually insisted that the decision to start that second phase should not even be discussed with the Soviets: only the US Congress should have the right to decide the timing of the second step, during which the United States would turn over

American nuclear facilities such as Oak Ridge and Hanford to the IADA (see table 3.3).[116] The asymmetry of commitments could not be clearer.

Yet, to reinforce the US position, Baruch went as far as to encourage the production of nuclear weapons by the United States while negotiations at the United Nations were under way. Until the Soviets were policed by the United Nations, Baruch said that noncompliance with the future treaty would be met by "dire consequences,"[117] which could be interpreted as saying that the United States would use nuclear weapons against violators of the Baruch plan. Baruch's aides consistently emphasized that "our manufacture of bombs shall not stop until the [I]ADA is in effective operation."[118] In fact, Baruch's aides insisted that Oppenheimer's idea of a moratorium "would be only a gesture, since no inspector could verify this until the [I]ADA is operating"[119] (as if unilateral gestures could not have a positive effect on diplomatic negotiations), adding that it would also be "very dangerous because it would be the first step in the start of a general policy of appeasement, and the making of the first step would only lead to further demands."[120] It was also undesirable, from the US point of view, as Baruch believed that "the only thing that stands in the way of the over-running of Europe today is the atom bomb," so "once we outlaw that, there is nothing to stop the Russian advance"[121] in Europe (see table 3.3).[122] To avoid repeating the precedent of the "pious Kellogg-Briand Pact," Baruch therefore proposed that "the U.N. should maintain a large stockpile of bombs [which the United States could produce and control], on the theory that retaliation is a great deterrent."[123] General Groves agreed with Baruch, as he suggested to Baruch that for a long time "atomic bomb plants would remain in the larger nations."[124] These demands deeply worried Oppenheimer and Lilienthal: for Lilienthal, Baruch's insistence on the US production of nuclear weapons "would be fatal"[125] to the Acheson-Lilienthal proposal, as it reintroduced the idea of "sacred trust" in the Anglo-American atomic trusteeship.

Baruch and his team of advisors also introduced new rules whose sole purpose was to ensure that no agreement with the Soviets could be reached. For instance, they changed the mechanism of treaty compliance and sanction against future violations: Baruch recommended that the Security Council should punish states in case of treaty violations (e.g., the clandestine diversion of nuclear technologies for military purposes), and that all states with veto power in the Security Council should relinquish it since it was likely that they (and not small states) would be the ones violating the treaty (see table 3.3). Baruch knew that the Soviet Union would never agree to abandon its veto power on questions related to the inspection and assessment of its own nuclear activities, as the Soviet Union was the only noncapitalist state with a permanent seat on the Security Council. Actually, not only Lilienthal and Oppenheimer, but also the British representatives, for whom the veto was a sign of the great power and status of the United Kingdom, wanted Baruch to change his mind on this issue.[126] Baruch's friend John Foster Dulles tried (unsuccessfully) to convince him that it was counterproductive to insist on dropping the veto[127] because, in the case of a future Soviet violation of the nonproliferation treaty, it was clear that all Security Council "members so deemed to be attacked by the violator . . . would exercise the right of individual and collective self-defense as planned by article 51 of the U.N. Charter."[128] But Baruch did not compromise.[129]

Baruch's interpretation of the US position made it clear that the United States did not seek to reach an agreement with the Soviets.[130] When the negotiations opened at the UN Commission on Atomic Energy in June 1946, the Soviet representative, Andrei Gromyko, denounced Baruch's plan as a misleading strategy aimed at securing the Soviet acceptance of the Anglo-American trusteeship on nuclear weapons. Immediately after Baruch's first presentation at the United Nations, Lilienthal recorded that "the Russians stressed the point that the American proposal was designed to permit the United States to maintain its own bombs and plants almost indefinitely, 30 years, 50 years, as long as we thought necessary, whereas it wants Russia's uranium, and therefore her chance of producing materials would be taken over and controlled by the IADA at once."[131] John McCloy agreed. For him, Baruch proposed a "pact designed to prolong the U.S. monopoly."[132] Even Vannevar Bush, who believed that "any concession would be fatal" until the United States and Soviets "agree on the overall framework," thought the United States had to give something in exchange for Soviet approval of the first step, as the Soviets would be giving "a great deal" during that stage.[133] Advocates of the world federalist cause heavily criticized Baruch's interpretation of the *Acheson-Lilienthal Report* for being "myopic and impractical."[134] But Baruch was unwilling to change his plan.

The publicity of diplomatic negotiations further harmed the chances of an agreement with the Soviets. The negotiations began at the United Nations with two very different proposals. Andrei Gromyko proposed a traditional interstate treaty banning the production and use of nuclear weapons, with a compliance mechanism to be discussed later. Gromyko also let it be known that the Soviets might agree to international inspections by a UN agency, but that the question of inspection would be settled later, adding that they favored national inspections over international inspections. In fact, their proposal was very similar to the plan put forward by James Shotwell for the Carnegie Endowment,[135] or the plan initially proposed by John McCloy in September 1945. In his journal, Lilienthal wrote, "Gromyko's proposal and the Carnegie Foundation's report [were] queer bedfellows."[136] With such different proposals, it was doubtful that a compromise could be found if both parties did not make serious compromises. Instead, the publicity of the negotiations pushed each party to the treaty negotiations to proudly maintain its initial position.

Only Oppenheimer still hoped that public diplomacy would allow negotiators to broker a deal between the Soviets and the West. As he led negotiations in the Scientific and Technical Subcommittee of the UN Atomic Energy Committee, Oppenheimer believed that the US delegation should search for limited points of agreement, while postponing to a later date the points of disagreement, in order to create trust among negotiating partners. For instance, initially, Oppenheimer agreed with Baruch and others that the Soviet plan did not go far enough toward international control of nuclear activity, to the extent that the Russian proposal relied solely "on treaty engagements for the control of atomic energy rather than on the creation of a specific international agency, with free access to all nations for purposes of geological surveys and inspection and for the exercise of complete managerial control of the production of fissionable material."[137] But Oppenheimer believed that, if presented with the facts, the Soviets would come to an agreement with the Americans. After a few months of deliberation, the UN Scientific and Technical Subcommittee released its report, "which received the unanimous concurrence of the members of the subcommittee, including the Russians": Oppenheimer and the Soviets agreed that their disagreements on the system of control should not prevent deliberations from continuing, which is why their report avoided reference to any "particular system of control." Even Baruch noted that Oppenheimer scored some points, as the report of his subcommittee listed "facts that point inescapably, in our opinion, toward the U.S. proposal."[138] A clarification, at that juncture, risked threatening the whole deal, which is why Oppenheimer tried to maintain some ambiguity over controversial rules.

However, the inflexibility of the American position on halting the production of nuclear weapons derailed Oppenheimer's efforts. Without pressure from the US negotiator, there was no incentive for Truman to stop the domestic production of atomic weapons, which the army and General Groves wished to accelerate. Thus, two weeks after the UN deliberations started, Truman agreed to let the army explode its fourth atomic device close to the Bikini Atoll. Oppenheimer refused to witness the test as a sign of protest.[139] He was quite right about the deleterious effect of resumed testing on the UN negotiations: soon after the test, the *New York Times* reported that "Russia said the Bikini Test banished faith that we planned to restrict the bomb's use."[140] It doomed the success of Oppenheimer's negotiating tactic at the United Nations: after Truman made it clear that the United States would continue testing, Lilienthal denounced "the American disposition . . . to take plenty of time . . . and then [force] Russia to exercise her veto and decline to go along" with the UN report, which "will be construed by us as a demonstration of Russia's warlike intentions."[141] The logic was clear for Lilienthal: "[This tactic] will fit perfectly into the plans of that growing number who want to put the country on a war footing, first psychologically, then actually."[142]

The Soviets no longer believed that the United States bargained in "good faith"—nor did the Americans believe that the Soviets wanted to reach a compromise.[143] Oppenheimer's effort to compromise with the Soviets became a "joke," a bad one for Lilienthal, who did not appreciate Baruch's "report of progress made to the President that 'We have made great progress; the Commission is with us by a majority of 10 to 2,'"[144] when the only two Soviet countries, the Soviet Union and Poland, were the two nations abstaining from supporting Baruch's plan. As negotiations between the twelve nations of the UN committee continued during the summer of 1946, Lilienthal noted that Oppenheimer was "in deep despair about the way things are going in the negotiations in New York," as "he sees no hope of agreement, he doesn't feel that our plan is understood by the American delegation," and when "he makes suggestions, there is no real discussion," and "the subcommittees are going through motions that induce what he feels is a wholly false sense of encouragement."[145]

In the end, Baruch felt no need to compromise with the Soviets, as the president himself attacked anyone who dared to publicly challenge Baruch's authority, or any part of Baruch's proposal. For instance, in the fall of 1946, after Secretary of Commerce Henry A. Wallace, Roosevelt's former vice president before Truman, condemned Baruch's idiosyncratic interpretation of the *Acheson-Lilienthal Report*, Truman forced Wallace to resign.[146] When Republicans won the congressional elections in November 1946, Truman interpreted the new domestic political situation as unfavorable to openness toward the Soviets. At last, on December 31 of that year, before nations rotated in the UN Committee on Atomic Energy, Bernard Baruch and his aides forced the participating nations to reveal their preference by requesting a vote, even though no common strategy existed between them and the two nations of the Eastern Bloc.[147] The result was evident: the Soviet Union and Poland abstained, while the other ten countries voted to adopt Baruch's plan. Baruch told Oppenheimer that had he not forced a vote, discussions "would have gone on and on,"[148] and he resigned a week later with the air of having accomplished a mission.[149]

Conclusion

The indefinite postponement of the Baruch plan at the UN Committee on Atomic Energy and the abrogation of the Quebec Agreement left the world without any plan for a nuclear nonproliferation treaty. As a result, the nuclear arms race between great powers began, unchecked by any international legal framework. The Truman administration did not propose a new plan for nuclear disarmament and nuclear nonproliferation, and kept insisting until the end of Truman's second term that Baruch's plan still represented the official position of the United States. Great powers were stuck in this suboptimal equilibrium as policy makers on both sides of the Iron Curtain proved unable to agree on a common strategy and a legal instrument that would make their commitment to the norms of nuclear nonproliferation and disarmament credible. In this case, neither macrocultural differences in normative ideals of international law, nor national differences in strategic cultures alone, explained why the United States and the Soviets could not reach consensus on a legal instrument. Indeed, the disarmament treaty that the Soviets proposed to the UN Atomic Energy Committee came close to the draft treaty proposed by American experts from the Carnegie Endowment and the Department of War.

A Bourdieuian analysis of the US field of foreign policy demonstrates that each institution (the army and the scientists being major players, as well as the State Department and the president) proposed distinct solutions to the problems of the nuclear age, which sought to solve jurisdictional conflicts to their advantage (see fig. 3.2). The different normative and strategic conceptions of the problems and solutions also divided different groups based on what Bourdieu has called the habitus of policy makers. Whereas the nuclear disarmament treaties of cosmopolitan inspiration were all coauthored by Harvard-trained lawyers or eminent scientists, the typical American white self-made men distrusted the power of international law in coercing the Soviets and preferred protectionist solutions that relied exclusively on American sovereign power.

But a Bourdieuian approach fails to explain why each group employed different tactics to silence their adversaries, and with which effects. To win their struggle against these educated foreign policy elites, the southern

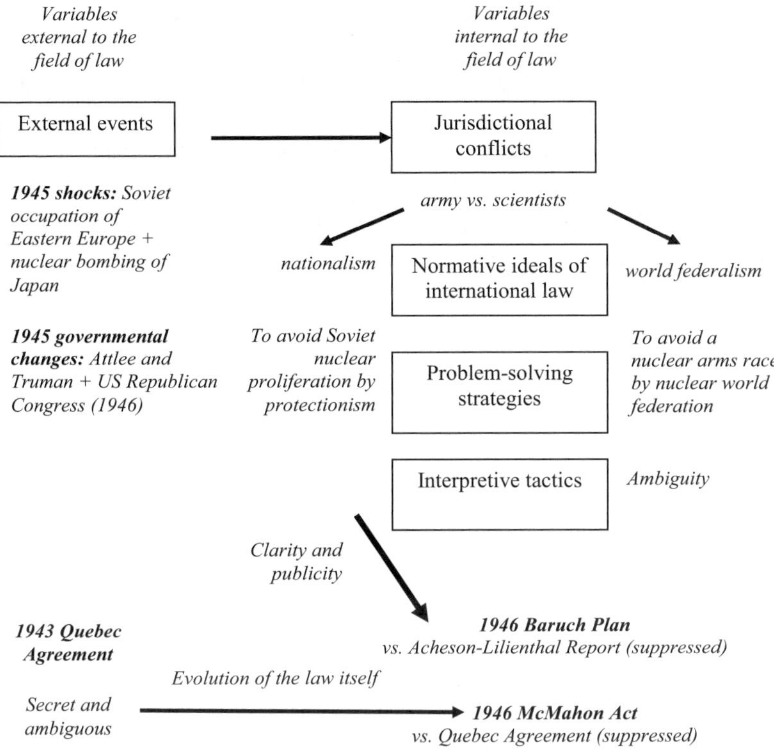

Figure 3.2. The dynamics of world federalism in the late 1940s

elites behind Truman, Byrnes, and Baruch used both secrecy and transparency to disempower their competitors in the US field of foreign policy: the publicity of diplomatic negotiations in a UN committee was used as a weapon against world federalists. When the US president mandated that deliberations with the Soviets be public in the United Nations, he made it impossible for American negotiators to bargain directly and secretly with the Soviets without risking vilification by the nationalists in Congress (see fig. 3.2). Clarity was also used by the nationalists on the UN committee to successfully disempower their competitors: negotiations with the Soviets could only fail when the top American leadership imposed, through the choice of the US negotiator at the United Nations, the requirement that the hierarchy between those goals (first nonproliferation, then disarmament) be clearly stated in the treaty under discussion at the United Nations. This hermeneutic approach to international lawmaking thus shows that transparency can start a self-fulfilling (or rather, a self-defeating) sequence of events that leads to the failure of treaty negotiations. When parties disagree on the diagnosis of the main problem at issue, and when no trust exists among parties on their ability to commit to respecting a treaty, it seems impossible for an agreement to emerge from treaty negotiations that do not allow for some ambiguity to be maintained over the meaning of the treaty. In the next chapter, I will examine whether the tactic of ambiguity was more successful in helping foreign policy elites propose a new policy that emerged from the ashes of world federalism.

FOUR

Ambiguity and Preemptive Interpretation: How Legal Indeterminacy Failed the Eurofederalists

Transparency and secrecy are two techniques of social control that a government can use to disempower competing foreign policy elites in a domestic field of power. However, in the contemporary world, short of banning access to Internet or other transnational public forums to its citizens, a government can rarely employ these two techniques to limit the range of policy proposals coming from transnational advocacy networks that promote new legal platforms (such as the protection of human rights) and that can use ambiguity as a tactic to achieve their goals. In this chapter, I focus on the role of ambiguity in explaining the outcome of a transnational mobilization for the establishment of a nuclear nonproliferation regime safeguarded by federal European institutions in the early Cold War. Through a tactic of ambiguity, members of this transnational network hoped that they could postpone the clarification of controversial rules until after the negotiated treaty entered into force.

I show that, in fact, ambiguity produced the opposite effect: the vague rules were not clarified through a multilateral process of deliberation after the treaty took effect. In fact, the ambiguity of the rules encouraged the governments involved to preempt future interpretation by advancing (rather than postponing) policy decisions. The clarification of vague legal commitments was conducted through an anarchic series of unilateral policy decisions (faits accomplis), or what I call "preemptive interpretations" of vague rules.

I demonstrate this argument based on the study of the transnational mobilization in favor of the establishment of a European legal framework that would have permanently blocked unilateral nuclear proliferation by Western European states. This mobilization was led mostly by Americans, and French and German rising foreign policy elites who drafted the European Defense Community Treaty (EDC Treaty),[1] which was signed in May 1952 by six Western European nations (France, West Germany, Italy, the Netherlands, Belgium, and Luxembourg). To explain why these "Eurofederalists" turned to a tactic of ambiguity, I will first examine the domestic situation that key members of this transnational advocacy network faced, with a specific focus on the US field of foreign policy and the position that Eurofederalists held there as "insiders-outsiders."[2] This first section describes how these insiders-outsiders produced legal ambiguity by postponing the drafting of what I call "master rules" (i.e., political rules that defined how clear technical rules, such as those rules governing nuclear trade, could be changed in the future) in the European Community in charge of military affairs to the future implementation of the EDC Treaty.

Second, I show why this tactic of ambiguity backfired when the nuclear issue suddenly moved to the top of the French policy-making agenda, and why the process of clarification of the EDC Treaty "master rules" was particularly anarchic and contentious in the case of the future European nuclear trade regime. In line with what I showed in the last chapter, I demonstrate here that the policy makers who oppose a new delegation of power to a supranational institution (here, the empowerment of the European Defense Community) can successfully use clarity as a means of social control: policy makers who opposed the EDC Treaty derailed the sequencing of negotiations that produced legal ambiguity. Indeed, they required that the EDC Treaty promoters explicate how master rules would apply to the production of nuclear energy in France *before* the ratification of that treaty rather than after its implementation. In this case, legal ambiguity persisted even after the clarification of Europe's future political master rules: after the latter became clearly defined, the ambiguity no longer concerned the meaning of the rules (interpretive ambiguity), but the identity of the subjects that agreed to conform to these rules (ontological ambiguity). This "ontological ambiguity" forced the breakdown of the ratification process, as the French government consistently insisted on maintaining vague "preemptive interpretations," by which it limited the extent of its territory where the future rules would apply.

Eurofederalists and Their Use of Ambiguity

Scholars of international regimes are prone to use the metaphor of Ulysses to explain the reasons why sovereign states agree to tie their free hands to the central mast of a binding treaty. The same metaphor underlines many narratives about the rise of the European Union institutions: like Ulysses fearing his own weakness, the postwar nation-states in Western European imposed institutional shackles upon their own regulative powers to resist the temptation of a new armament race, a new war, and some new devastation of vast proportions.[3] In particular, this metaphor seems to fit adequately with the surprising fact that proud European nation-states responded positively to the "Schuman Declaration" (named after the French minister of foreign relations) in May 1950, when the French government asked them to create a European Community to which Western European nations would delegate their power to regulate the production and exchange of steel and coal.

This metaphor, although elegant, suffers from one essential problem: it assumes that all the postwar European nations were equally free to tie their hands to a new central mast. Postwar European nations, especially the defeated powers such as West Germany, did not have a free hand they could choose to tie to a new treaty. The Americans, British, and French (the occupation powers) had already tied their hands. Before these occupation powers could agree to tie Western German (and other) hands to a new European system of rules for nuclear affairs, they needed to agree among themselves which knots they would untie in the already-existing legal tapestry. As the American and European foreign policy makers prepared the European treaties that dealt with military (and nuclear) issues in Europe, they faced various alternatives. In fact, their various proposals offered a choice between a clear transatlantic legal regime and an ambiguous European Continental regime, rather than a choice between anarchy and legal order.

The Nuclear Question in Europe after the Soviet Test

Until 1949—that is, until the Soviets first supported the North Korean invasion of South Korea and then tested their first nuclear weapon in September of that year—the nuclear question in Europe did not raise any particular difficulty for the US foreign policy makers in charge of stabilizing Western Europe. The Truman administration followed a protectionist and nationalistic policy regarding its nuclear secrets.[4] Even the United Kingdom did not benefit from American cooperation in the development of civilian applications of nuclear energy. As far as Western-occupied Germany was concerned, strong limits were placed on its indigenous nuclear development—restricted to a little research work.[5] But the Soviet nuclear test and the North Korean attack suddenly testified to the fact that the Soviets were determined to catch up to the United States in nuclear weaponry, and that

Communists would challenge the status quo not only in Europe but also in Asia. The war in Korea meant that the United States needed more troops on the Asian battlefront, and US policy makers such as Secretary of State Dean Acheson had to transfer US troops from Europe to Asia without upsetting their stabilization plans in Europe.

The stabilization plans that President Truman and the secretaries of state who succeeded James Byrnes (first George Marshall and then Dean Acheson) implemented in Europe from 1945 to 1949 strongly tied the US destiny to the fate of Western Europe, in sharp contrast with the policy recommendations of key Republican legislators, such as Senator Vandenberg or Senator McCarthy, who advocated a traditional isolationist position for the United States (a *nationalist* position that dated back to George Washington's advice that the United States should avoid European entanglements) (see table 4.1). For instance, the stabilization plan proposed by Secretary of State George Marshall in 1947 pursued in peacetime mechanisms similar to the wartime "lend-lease" program: whereas the United States had lent money to Allied nations to buy weapons during wartime, the Marshall Plan proposed lending money to European nations (not only in the West but also to Russian satellites, which nonetheless refused the proposal) during peacetime to buy civilian industrial goods and equipment from the United States.[6]

In spite of some vain attempts to include nuclear issues in the jurisdiction of the new interstate organizations charged with the stabilization of Europe, nuclear questions neither appeared in the European organization set up to implement the Marshall Plan (the Organization for European Economic Cooperation [OEEC]), nor did they initially appear in discussions that took place in the transatlantic organization set up to deal with military matters in Europe (the North Atlantic Treaty Organization [NATO]), created in 1949. It was the Frenchman Jean Monnet, then the chairman of the French Planning Commission, who killed the idea proposed by Vannevar Bush that the OEEC would serve as a conduit for peaceful nuclear cooperation across the Atlantic.[7] Instead, the OEEC served as an official forum in which European states could coordinate their economic policy to jointly present their needs for equipment to the United States, and it was organized along international liberal lines that echoed some of Acheson's own wartime thoughts.[8] Furthermore, in April 1949, when the US government participated in the creation of NATO, its main objective was to "keep the Americans in, the Soviets out, and the Germans down,"[9] in the famous words of its first secretary-general. But before 1950, no one in NATO mentioned the role that US nuclear weapons would play in the

Table 4.1 Western solutions to the problem of Europe's defense after the Korean War

Response to the Soviet threat in Europe	Key propositions (January–September 1950)	Key proponents (January–September 1950)
Nationalist	• US troops exit the Western European battlefield at some point • Allies (in particular, the United States) build up their nuclear-weapons arsenal to better defend themselves • Allies maintain strict limits upon German industries	Vandenberg, Bidault, Debré
International liberal	• US troops remain in Western Europe • West Germany integrates Western defense pacts (WEU and NATO) • West German army within the NATO chain of authority, under the command of NATO's supreme commander (a US general) • All international controls on key West German dual-use industries (such as steel) are lifted, and those industries are placed under the control of the West German chancellor	Truman, Acheson, Marshall, Bevin, Eden
Eurofederalist	• US troops remain in Western Europe • West German army within the European Defense Community chain of command, itself within NATO • All international controls on key West German dual-use industries (such as steel or nuclear energy) are lifted, and those industries are placed under the control of legislative authorities of the European Defense Community (European Council and European Commission)	Monnet, McCloy, Adenauer, Pleven, Schuman, Ball, Hirsh

defense of Europe, or the role that Europe's nuclear development would play in its future defense, or the role that the demilitarized Germany would play in the defense of the West.[10]

After the events of the summer of 1949, US foreign policy makers knew they had to reassess their options in Europe. Dean Acheson, by then the secretary of state, understood that a purely German army and armament industry was out of the question, writing that "to create a German military system complete from general staff to Ruhr munitions industry would weaken rather than strengthen European defense and repeat past errors,"[11] a point of view with which "the President agreed."[12] But West Germans could recover their international legal sovereignty and jurisdiction on limited military matters (something that their Basic Law of 1949 failed to grant them) as well as sovereignty over strategic territories such as the Saar if their rearmament was conducted exclusively within the NATO framework and under the authority of NATO's supreme commander (see table 4.1). It was clear that strict limits on West German nuclear development would continue to apply, as West German nuclear progress would be seen as an existential threat not only to the French and British but, most important, to the Soviets, who could threaten to invade Germany to prevent that prospect. Acheson's new plan meant that NATO would prepare a common doctrine in which West German forces would play a limited role as foot soldiers to ensure the defense of Western Europe. At the same time, the West German chancellor would be responsible for regulating the German war industries (including a bridled nuclear sector) to the appropriate levels under close supervision of the three occupying powers: the United States, the United Kingdom, and France.[13]

The adoption of Acheson's doctrine by Truman showed that the US president believed that the time had come for the three Western occupying powers in Western Germany (the United States, the United Kingdom, and France) to transfer part of their responsibility with respect to West German defense[14] to the shared authority of the West German chancellor and NATO's first supreme allied commander, General Eisenhower, the former commander of the Western offensive against the Nazis (see table 4.1).[15] Acheson's "one package" NATO plan, which combined "united command, increased American military force, and an armed German element,"[16] was also enthusiastically accepted by the British foreign secretary, Lord Bevin, in September 1950. However, when Acheson presented his plan to the French minister of foreign affairs, Robert Schuman, during the 1950 meetings of the Atlantic Council of NATO, the French rejected the plan put forward by the Anglo-American liberals.[17]

If Robert Schuman had accepted Acheson's plan in the fall of 1950, the European Union that we know of today might never have been created. The European Community proposed by the French government in its stead was meant to avoid the United States' maximizing its control over West German defense policy through NATO. Indeed, if NATO's supreme commander were to be responsible for deciding the armament levels of West German troops, as long as the supreme commander was an American general who took his orders directly from the US president, West Germany would be turned indefinitely into a US protectorate. Besides, France would lose its veto as one of the three Western occupying powers over German defense policy despite the fact that France was the nation most likely to be affected by West Germany's rearmament. Needless to say, the French government wanted to keep a direct say in matters of West German defense: France was Germany's closest neighbor, and their territorial disputes had led to three devastating wars (1870, 1914–18, and 1940) in less than eighty years. The French government, led during 1949 and 1950 by Georges Bidault (a Catholic and former chief of the French homeland resistance, who held strong nationalistic views about the sacredness of France's imperial sovereignty),[18] preferred to keep intact France's control over West German rearmament (see table 4.1).

Furthermore, the idea that the United States would allow the West German chancellor to regulate the coal and steel industries in the Ruhr, and to claim sovereignty over the industrial region of the Saar, which the Allies had separated from the rest of West Germany in May 1945, was absolutely anathema to Bidault and to many French politicians, including Jean Monnet.[19] Until 1949, the Allies had permitted West German industrial development in these regions only for the purposes of war reparations and the industrial reconstruction of France, according to the levels fixed by the "Monnet Plan," the 1947 five-year plan for economic recovery prepared by Monnet.[20] The French government thus wanted to prolong the Allies' strategy for reducing West German industrial capacity in the key sectors of energy and armament production, even if the Korean War and the Soviet nuclear test had created a new sense of urgency in Europe.

There was an additional reason why the French government refused Acheson's September 1950 proposal for West Germany's rearmament in NATO. In May 1950, Monnet and Hirsh had convinced then foreign minister Robert Schuman to issue the famous "Schuman Declaration" in favor of the Europeanization of the coal and steel industries as sketched out by Jean Monnet and Etienne Hirsh, Monnet's deputy at the French Planning Commission, who had long advocated that the "the coal and steel produced in Ruhr would be placed under the authority of a European institution for the benefit of all participating nations, including a demilitarized Germany."[21] In 1950, Monnet's plan no longer called for the Europeanization of the coal and steel produced in the Saar and Ruhr only,[22] but for the creation of a specific European Community, the European Coal and Steel Community (ECSC), in which all West European nations would become member states.[23] Monnet and Hirsh's new proposal presented the advantage for France that if West German industrial forces were to be placed under the authority of a European (French) high commissioner, France would increase its control of West German rearmament policy to the detriment of its Anglo-American allies. Thus, even nationalists such as Georges Bidault, General de Gaulle, or the leading Gaullist among parliamentarians and jurists, Michel Debré (1912–96), endorsed the Schuman Declaration (although they later became very critical of Monnet's Defense Community).[24] But as Jean Monnet reported, after Acheson presented his plan to other NATO foreign ministers in September, everyone agreed that "a Coal and Steel Community would have no interest in the eyes of the Germans once they would recover their full sovereignty with a national army,"[25] even if the latter would be fully integrated under the authority of NATO's supreme commander. To save Monnet's ECSC proposal, the French government had to refuse Acheson's NATO proposal.

In the fall of 1950, the French government not only rejected Acheson's NATO plan; it also drew up a new proposal that enlarged the initial ECSC proposal to include all the other European defense issues left untackled by the ECSC Treaty. The same team that Monnet had gathered to draft the ECSC Treaty, which included, among others, Etienne Hirsh,[26] prepared in haste, during the hiatus in the negotiations for the ECSC Treaty in the summer of 1950, a new treaty that would not only Europeanize the regulation of coal and steel, but that also aimed at creating a European federation with jurisdiction over all defense and energy sectors: the European Defense Community (EDC).

The EDC Treaty not only planned to create a complete chain of command running from the highest civilian authorities to the smallest military units through European generals and officers; it also planned to create new political institutions (a European Council of Ministers especially) that would be responsible for regulating all the armament industries in Western Europe. Indeed, the future Council of Ministers of this EDC was to be given the authority "to approve a joint-program of armament for the European Army" (art. 106).[27] Then, based on the armament plans approved by the European Council, the future European Defense Commissariat would oversee the execution of the "production, imports and exports of war-material to and from the member-states, control procedures of installations destined to produce war-material, as well as fabrication of prototypes and technical research on war-material" (annex 2 of art. 107). Included in the list of armament industries were not only all the conventional armament industries (those producing tanks, naval vessels, etc.) but also nuclear industries, as the treaty planned early on that this European Commissariat would be in charge of dealing with nuclear issues in Europe: the European Defense Commissariat was even entitled to license the construction of all the new plants in the defense sector, broadly defined, and it extended to the energy sector, at least as far as nuclear energy was concerned (art. 107).

That such an ambitious proposal could be presented by the French government five years after the end of the Second World War showed the advances that Eurofederalists had made in the French government, even reaching the highest position, as in the case of René Pleven (1901–93), who succeeded Georges Bidault as the head of the government in July 1950. With Pleven as head of government, and Robert Schuman (a Christian Democrat born in Luxembourg, who had fought as a German officer during World War I) as foreign minister, Jean Monnet had two close allies in charge of France's foreign policy and could therefore not only propose new ideas but also present them as the official position of the French government. Faced with two different proposals (Acheson's and Monnet's), the West German chancellor, Konrad Adenauer, had to decide which one would best advance West German interests. Both were generous offers. But whatever proposal the chancellor preferred, the ultimate decision also rested in the hands of the US president and his most important foreign policy advisors, as the West German hands were still tied by the will of the three occupying powers—with the United States as the leader.

US Foreign Policy Makers and Eurofederalism

To understand why the French proposals in favor of a European federation with jurisdiction in (conventional and nuclear) military matters moved to the top of the Allied foreign policy in Europe (over Acheson's NATO proposal), it is essential to explain how powerful US foreign policy makers enlisted Monnet's ideas in US domestic power struggles.

The key insiders in the Truman administration were at first extremely critical of Monnet's ideas. When presented with the initially vague contours of the ECSC in May 1950, Monnet reported, Acheson himself acknowledged that he "had immediate suspicions that it disguised some sort of grand cartel of steel and coal, which manifested the nostalgic desire of European industries and which would be an inexcusable sin to the eyes of the Americans who respected the law of concurrence and the freedom of trade."[28] Monnet's insistence that the ECSC be allowed to tax European economies to fund its planned public investments instead of relying on the generosity of its member states also disquieted Acheson: the federal ability to directly tax the import and export of coal and steel opened the doors to potential European protectionism at the regional level.[29] Monnet concluded that for Acheson, "the lawyer and political animal within him was instinctively repulsed."[30]

Similarly, when Monnet first briefed Acheson on the EDC Treaty in September 1950, Acheson replied that he saw no use for German rearmament within the framework of the EDC, especially if it meant that West German forces would be under the authority of a European, thus French, general.[31] George Marshall, by then Truman's secretary of defense, was even more exasperated by Monnet's proposed EDC Treaty, and in retaliation, he delayed General Eisenhower's installation as the supreme commander of NATO.[32] John Foster Dulles, by then elected senator from New York, warned his friend Monnet that "some in Washington [we]re afraid that France is trying to build a 'third force,' which will be neutral."[33] Acheson also suspected that the new plan hid an attempt by the French to delay the increase in France's contribution to the armed forces of NATO, by making that increase contingent on the unlikely creation of a European federation with jurisdiction in the military field.[34] After studying the State Department archives, Marc Trachtenberg concludes that in the Truman administration, "the prevailing view in late 1950 and early 1951 was that the Pleven plan was unrealistic" and "[it] seemed that the whole point of the proposal was to evade that basic problem of German rearmament," "to avoid provoking Russia by a decision to rearm Germany."[35]

In contrast, "insiders-outsiders,"[36] as Antonin Cohen calls these new foreign policy elites who remain central in a domestic field, but who have not yet reached the top decision-making positions, enlisted Monnet's proposals in their domestic struggles to shape US foreign policy. Most US policy makers had known of Monnet since the war, including those who did not share his views, such as Dean Acheson: in 1947, Acheson had consulted Monnet on the content of the aid the United States should send to West European nations for their reconstruction as part of the Marshall Plan, and it was Monnet who proposed that the Europeans themselves should send the list of equipment needed to the Americans, not the other way around, and that Europeans should set up a permanent organization to do so—what became the OEEC.[37] But among the US foreign policy elites with whom Monnet (as chairman of the Planning Commission from 1945 to 1951) had formed particularly strong ties, the most important man was John Mc-Cloy, who, as the president of the World Bank, had allocated the funds that France used to pay for its first Marshall Plan equipment in 1947.[38] After the end of the military occupation of Western Germany in 1947 (and the split of the unified Western zone from the Eastern zone occupied by the Soviets), John McCloy had been appointed by Harry Truman to serve as the supreme allied commissioner in West Germany, responsible for overseeing the defense and industrial policies of the three zones administered by the occupying Western powers (see fig. 4.1). This position turned McCloy into the ideal/typical insider-outsider: a Republican working in a Democratic administration, a business lawyer in charge of administering public law. McCloy could not influence the general making of US foreign policy, as he was far away from Washington, but he had the highest influence on all matters touching on Truman's Western European policy, and the position that West Germany would find in it.

Needless to say, Monnet's personal ties with McCloy and other foreign policy elites such as John Foster Dulles helped his cause.[39] These ties actually dated to before the war: in the late 1920s and early 1930s, Monnet directed the overseas investments of the bank Transamerica in Europe, which is how he met McCloy and Dulles and eventually hired them as lawyers for his business ventures in Europe. As McCloy later recalled, during the interwar period, he "went abroad to represent [his] law firm as a lawyer giving advice to a number of American investment houses that were investing abroad," and one of "the investors' representatives was Jean Monnet."[40] In fact, when he prepared the ECSC Treaty, Monnet consulted McCloy before he asked Schuman to make his May announcement, as the supreme commissioner's authorization was required before the German chancellor could be involved in negotiations leading to an international treaty.[41] René Pleven was also not a stranger to McCloy and John Foster Dulles, the strongest foreign policy voice among the Republicans. Indeed, Pleven and Dulles were hired by Jean Monnet when the latter was in charge of administering the "shock therapy" for Poland during the hyperinflation crisis of the Polish zloty in the late 1920s.[42] McCloy also knew Pleven from the time when Pleven had joined Monnet on the Allied Board of Armament in London and then in Washington during the Second World War.[43] The same was true of Etienne Hirsh, who prepared both the ECSC and EDC plans, and who had been responsible for the armament branch of Free France during the war, and as such, had negotiated on France's arms procurement deals with the

Officials in charge of US Nuclear Foreign Policy (1950-53):

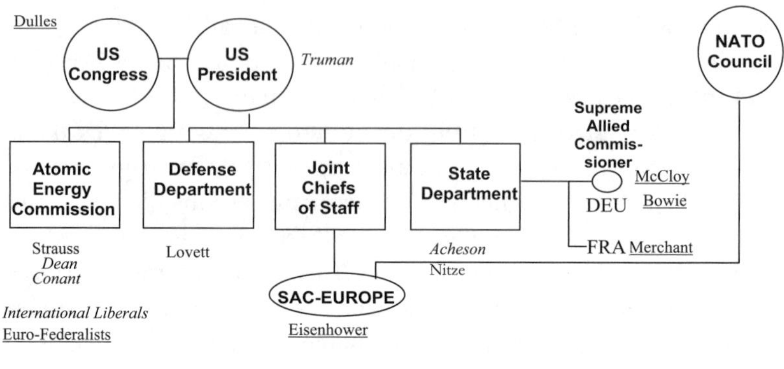

Officials in charge of US Nuclear Foreign Policy (1953-57):

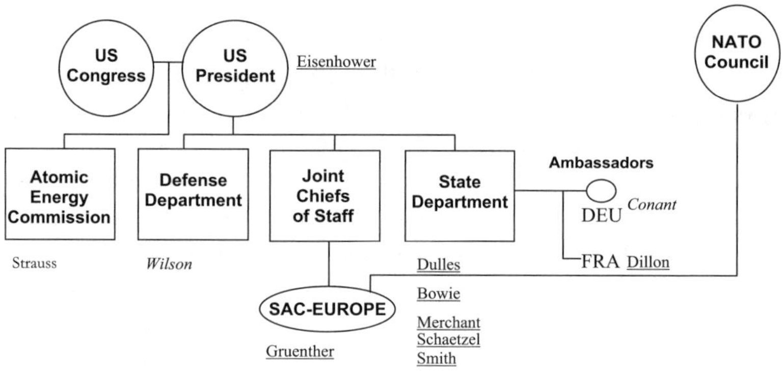

Figure 4.1. The rise and fall of international liberals in the US government

British and Americans, including the Franco-British nuclear understanding that the United Kingdom violated when it signed the Quebec Agreement with the United States and Canada in 1943 (see the previous chapter).[44] At the French Planning Commission, where he worked as Monnet's deputy, Etienne Hirsh met almost daily with other key American officials such as George Ball (1909–94), a US lawyer initially attracted by world federalist ideas, who had served during the war as the assistant to the secretary of the treasury Henry Morgenthau, in charge of the lend-lease program, and who consulted for US foreign policy makers on European issues.[45]

Through the mediation of McCloy and other American officials stationed in Europe, Eurofederalist normative ideals were introduced into the power struggles that divided the US field of foreign policy: McCloy, a Republican, was instrumental in helping key foreign policy experts in his party unite behind the plans proposed by Monnet. Through McCloy's mediation, NATO's supreme commander Dwight Eisenhower, and his assistant General Gruenther (who would replace Eisenhower as NATO's supreme commander in 1953), met Monnet shortly after the signing of the ECSC Treaty, in June 1951, so that Monnet could present to them the ideas behind the EDC treaty, which was more relevant to them than the ECSC (see fig. 4.1). Monnet later reported that the general grasped its political significance immediately.[46] After meeting Monnet, Eisenhower put all his support behind Monnet's proposal, leading some US observers of his speeches to note, "We have lost our Supreme Commander" and have found a new presidential candidate.[47] Indeed, Eisenhower bet that the Republican Party could see in Monnet's proposals not just a way to strengthen Western European democracies, but also a way to strengthen economic and political liberalism within the United States by providing a way out of Europe for US troops.[48] As Marc Trachtenberg writes, Eisenhower's objective was to convince the Republican Party that the United States should "weld France and Germany together as the core of a strong European federation that could stand up to Russia on its own, and thus make it possible for American forces to withdraw from Europe in the near future."[49]

The political capital that John McCloy, John Foster Dulles, and then general Eisenhower deployed in support of Monnet's proposals added to the ideological credibility that Monnet, Dulles, and McCloy benefited from in Wall Street, and made the criticisms against Monnet's proposals expressed by Acheson or the powerful West German minister of the economy, Ludwig Erhard, hard to sustain: even if Acheson and Erhard feared that the creation of a European public regulator, which would manage the operation of European coal and steel markets and more generally all war industries, would lead to the creation of protectionist cartels (or worse, to a socialist public authority), their fears were not shared by the Wall Street elites who knew the pro–free trade credentials of Monnet, McCloy, and Dulles. Furthermore, to answer the ideological concerns of their opponents, McCloy tapped into the academic and legal expertise provided by his alma mater's network of contacts: from 1950 to 1952, McCloy recruited Robert Bowie (1909–2010), an expert in antitrust law and the youngest law professor ever recruited by Harvard Law School, to draft the antitrust articles of the ECSC Treaty—a task he performed with such passion that British Labour politicians soon called him the "mad mullah of decartellisation."[50]

The Franco-American network of Eurofederalists had one last advantage that made the Schuman and Pleven plans credible alternatives to the proposals of direct West German integration into NATO favored by Truman, Marshall, and Acheson: the first elected German chancellor, Konrad Adenauer, was himself a staunch Eurofederalist, and he immediately applauded the Schuman Declaration of May 1950.[51] Indeed, Adenauer saw Europe as a compact of regions more important than nation-states, and as mayor of Cologne during the hyperinflation crisis of 1924, he had even sided with the French in favor of the creation of a Rhineland Republic separate from Berlin and printing its own currency.[52] After the war, he proclaimed his federalist beliefs in The Hague, when the Eurofederalist movement led by European parliamentarians created the Council of Europe in May 1949, with the task of drafting and enforcing the protection of human rights in Europe.[53] After being elected chancellor, he quickly befriended McCloy, whose wife, of German descent, was a distant cousin of Adenauer's wife.[54] Even if West German activities related to the defense sector escaped the jurisdiction of the West German chancellor (the Basic Law of 1949 was silent on these issues), as the supreme allied commander remained in control, the strong support of the West German chancellor would count in McCloy and Monnet's transatlantic campaign.

The Merits of Ambiguity in the US Field of Power (Fall 1950–Spring 1952)

With its emphasis on foreign policy makers' preexisting bonds, their mobilization of social capital, and legal expertise, the Bourdieuian perspective applied to the EDC Treaty negotiations helps us explain how Monnet's Eurofederalist proposals moved up in the agenda of US political priorities despite initial opposition by competing cliques of foreign policy makers. However, the focus on mechanisms of accumulation of social capital cannot completely explain the outcome of the battles between governmental insiders. In this case, both sides could (and did) mobilize vast amounts of legal expertise, social capital, and long-standing personal bonds that created the necessary trust among foreign policy makers, in order to impose their preferred solution for the stabilization of Europe. To understand the outcome of such conflicts, we also need to pay attention to their tactical decisions—that is, the interpretive practices they followed when presenting their plans to their allies as well as to their competitors.

Ambiguity was a tactic that Monnet, McCloy, and the supporters of the

Eurofederalist solution followed from the start and that they kept using to define the new rules of armament (both conventional and nuclear) trade and production in Western Europe and across the Atlantic. Immediately after Schuman announced his plan in May 1950, Monnet asked all future parties to the ECSC Treaty negotiations to commit in advance to "the undetailed statement he had drawn up, fortified by the prior commitment of all parties to the principle of instituting a supranational High Authority"[55] of the ECSC, when the institutional design of the European federation was still unclear. This tactic of ambiguity was also employed by Pleven when he presented the EDC Treaty for the first time to French parliamentarians. The French National Assembly voted in October 1950 in support of Pleven's vague and ambiguous proposal of a European army and armament industry rather than on a specific treaty. In the words of the leader of the French opposition to the EDC Treaty, the Gaullist parliamentarian Michel Debré, "The first parliamentary debate in October 1950 remained at the level of generalities, and the plan remained ambiguous."[56] Monnet believed that, at that point, European declarations in favor of unity, equality among future member states, and the idea of a European armament pool should not be obscured by "the legal formalism and technicism which generally goes with international treaties."[57] The details of the European treaties would be worked out after.

The recursive process that Eurofederalists followed consisted of systematically postponing the solution of complex political issues of federalism (what I call the "master rules" that defined the governance structure of the future international organization) to the negotiation of another treaty (see fig. 4.2).[58] Although the definitive political master rules of accountability for the future European Defense Community and Coal and Steel Community were supposed to have been agreed on by future EDC member states during the EDC Treaty negotiations (negotiated from October 1950 to May 1952), Eurofederalists failed to clarify in the EDC Treaty the ambiguities contained in the first European treaty on coal and steel.[59] To close the EDC Treaty negotiations and obtain the six signatures (which was done in May 1952), Jean Monnet again postponed the writing of the master rules of the future European Federation to the signing of a third treaty: the European Political Community Treaty (EPC Treaty). A structure of political accountability similar to that of the ECSC was crafted in the EDC Treaty, with the promise that a constituent assembly would be named to give the future European "federation" (or "confederation") the appropriate organization to oversee the work of both the High Authority of the ECSC and the European Defense Commissariat (art. 38 of the EDC Treaty).[60] Italian foreign min-

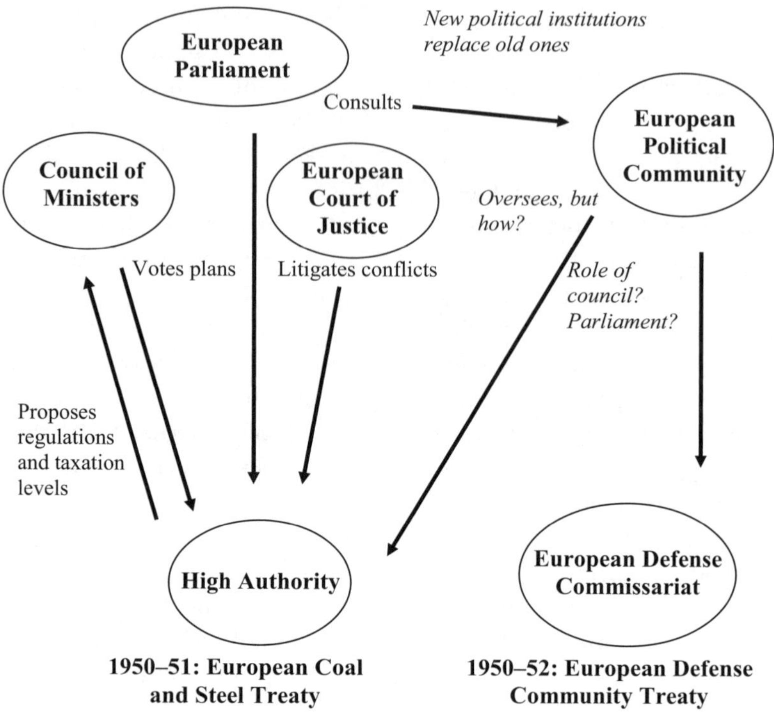

Figure 4.2. Ambiguities created by the succession of European treaties

ister Alcide de Gasperi made this suggestion, after it appeared that agreement on the final master rules of the future European Federation might be too difficult to achieve in the context of the EDC negotiations.[61]

The governance structure of the EDC was thus (for the time being) similar to the governance structure that the ECSC Treaty set up to organize the coal and steel industries: for instance, the future European Defense Commissariat would have to prepare a "scientific and technical joint-program in military activities" (art. 106)[62]—which concerned the nuclear, naval, and aircraft industries, among others—submit it to the council for approval, and then organize the competition among armament industries for the execution of the program voted in by the council.[63] These technical rules were quite clear, but provisional and subject to change in a short period of time (six months), when the future constituent assembly would finish its deliberations and define the master rules of the future European Federation.

This legal ambiguity was partly a response to the international environment that Eurofederalists faced. By proposing a comprehensive but loosely defined European federation in charge of defense matters in 1950 and 1951, the Eurofederalists sought to quickly react to Acheson's offer to integrate West German armed forces directly into NATO during the summer of 1950. As Monnet noted, after Acheson's proposal was made public in September 1950, "the French government had to buy some extra time"[64] to bring the negotiations on the first European treaty to a successful close by quickly proposing a grand bargain to West Germany covering all aspects of European defense. Indeed, with the EDC Treaty proposal, not only did France increase the gains for West Germany (in fact, if the EDC Treaty entered into force, West Germany would even gain a say on French military and nuclear policies), but it also increased the likelihood that the negotiations of the first proposal (the ECSC Treaty) would reach a successful end.

The announcement that France would open negotiations of the EDC Treaty in October 1950 also created the opportunity for France and its five European negotiating partners to postpone resolving existing disagreements over the ECSC Treaty to the future negotiations of the EDC Treaty: if the six states that negotiated the ECSC Treaty failed to agree on the final master rules of the European Federation that would oversee the Coal and Steel Community, they would get a second chance to solve their disagreements in the context of the EDC Treaty negotiations. In fact, they got a third chance to do so in the context of the EPC deliberations.

There were also strong domestic reasons for why US foreign policy makers found an interest in postponing the deliberation of future political rules in Europe. Bourdieuian scholars claim that insiders-outsiders often introduce some ambiguity to convince their government to give a chance to proposals that they would otherwise reject if they were presented as clearly understood and binding rules—as "hard law," in the language of legalization scholars.[65] In the case of the European treaties of federalist inspiration, insiders-outsiders in the US field of power, such as John McCloy, encouraged Europeans to leave contentious points unaddressed and postpone the resolution of disagreements if that meant they could quickly sign a treaty containing the other legal rules with which they agreed. Such a tactic helped them give Truman, Acheson, and Marshall the impression that Monnet's proposals found strong support among Europeans. And in fact, their tactic of ambiguity also served the interests of Truman, Acheson, and Marshall: even though Truman and his secretary of state would have preferred to force a quick acceptance of their proposal of direct West German integration into NATO, the support that insiders-outsiders such as McCloy and Eisenhower gave to Monnet's proposals (and the French opposition to their plans) made a public rejection of Monnet's plans by the Truman administration too politically costly for them.

In fact, Democrats wanted to avoid getting involved in a debate that the Republicans wanted to politicize for electoral purposes.[66] After Eisenhower condemned the British government in the summer of 1951 for having refused to sign the ECSC Treaty that April,[67] and started to publicly criticize Truman and Acheson for failing to support Monnet's effort, Monnet noticed that George Marshall's opposition to the EDC lessened, as did Acheson's expressed skepticism. The ambiguous outcome of the EDC negotiations meant that they could wait to see how the definition of Europe's political rules would shape up before attacking. Truman thus agreed to issue, along with the French and British governments, a vague declaration of support (the tripartite Declaration of Washington) in September 1951, which stated that the drafts of the EDC Treaty that were presented to them furthered the defense of Western Europe.[68]

All the US foreign policy elites therefore had an interest in postponing the clarification of the still-undefined "master rules" envisioned in the EDC Treaty to a later date: the Truman administration could avoid facing domestic opposition from Republicans, and the insiders-outsiders such as McCloy and Eisenhower could maintain their pressure on European governments to bargain harder and reach an acceptable position in favor of Monnet's approach. To the extent that the ambiguity of the EDC proposal helped hide internal disagreements in the US field of foreign policy, it helped Europeans conclude the negotiations: as Jean Monnet later wrote, "Things moved faster when Adenauer did not have to hesitate between two negotiations, one with the United States, the other with the French, after Acheson moved closer to the political line defended by McCloy."[69] The Dutch and the Belgians—who insisted that they would sign the EDC Treaty only if it was supported by the Anglo-American powers, in the form of a treaty of association among the United States, the United Kingdom, and the EDC member states[70]—also agreed to conclude the negotiations.

The Pitfalls of Ambiguity in the European Fields of Power (Fall 1950–Spring 1952)

Even though ambiguity served a useful purpose in the United States, in other contexts, the sequencing of the EDC Treaty negotiations that produced such legal indeterminacy became the specific target of criticism: it was not just the political content of Monnet's proposals that alienated some policy makers, but their ambiguous nature. In the French and British domestic contexts, the tactic of ambiguity failed to produce the same results as in the United States, contrary to what scholars who stress the merits of constructive ambiguity generally say. Indeed, in the United Kingdom and in France, the ambiguity of Monnet's proposal became one of the main reasons why politicians opposed it.

In the United Kingdom, ambiguity rhymed with shallowness, incompetence, and lack of preparation. According to Alan Milward, in May 1950, the British rejected Monnet's invitation to participate in the ECSC Treaty negotiations, not only because they were irritated that Monnet and McCloy would draw up plans for Europe without consulting them, but also because the plans did not, they believed, protect British interests, and were too vague to be preapproved by the United Kingdom.[71] For them, it would have been politically naïve to preapprove a policy that, although ambitious, reflected a lack of political thinking on the part of Monnet: initially, Monnet and Hirsh had not planned a European parliament or a Council of Ministers to check the executive power of the High Authority of the ECSC. George Ball, who was "the only American privy to the emerging draft"[72] of the European treaties, later recognized that "in its first draft, only a High Authority and some kind of judicial body were envisaged by Monnet and Schuman and neither a legislative body nor a ministerial council was contemplated."[73] The British found such a lack of political accountability appalling.[74] When Hirsh, who came with Monnet to London in May 1950 to present the plan, told British diplomats that the commissioners of the High Authority would be recruited only on the basis of technical expertise, without regard for their nationality,[75] the British government argued that it could not give an a priori agreement in good faith until a more thorough and clearer institutional design was worked out. For similar reasons, the British initially refused to participate in the negotiations of the EDC Treaty as a signatory state.

Even after the electoral victory of the conservatives in the United Kingdom in the fall of 1951, and the formation of Winston Churchill's last government, the new British foreign secretary, Anthony Eden, pursued the same policy as his predecessor, Lord Bevin: Eden, like Bevin, insisted that Monnet should propose clearly expressed political rules in the EDC Treaty if he wanted to obtain Britain's support. The British continued to ask that the Europeans clarify the relations of the European Federation with its member states and with the other NATO allies that were not EDC member states, before they would express their intention to join (or not) the ECSC and EDC Treaties. Negotiating the transition from the British Empire to the British Commonwealth, the British did not want to commit to placing their troops under the jurisdiction of a vaguely defined European authority.[76] The British government only agreed to publicly support the ECSC and EDC Treaties after Monnet agreed to let the British participate in the future deliberations of the assembly charged with writing a constitution for the European Federation—once the EDC Treaty (and its art. 38) entered into force.[77]

Adverse reactions to the tactic of ambiguity were also formulated in France, particularly in the context of the EDC Treaty negotiations. The French domestic opposition, led by the Gaullists, did not like the ambiguity of the Pleven Declaration. Later, when the EDC Treaty was finally presented to the French Parliament for ratification, the Gaullist parliamentarian Michel Debré wrote that he found the EDC Treaty to be "unreadable"[78] and almost silent on the question of its articulation with NATO. Since the articulation between NATO and the future European Federation was not clear, the Gaullists feared that the future European Defense Commissariat would take its orders from NATO's supreme commander, most likely an American general who would, in turn, take his orders from the American commander in chief, the US president (see fig. 4.3). Ultimately, all

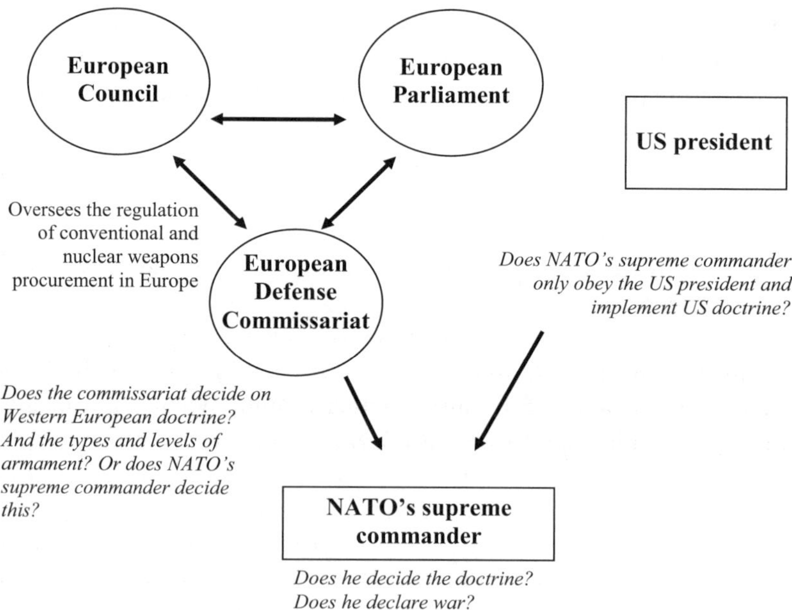

Figure 4.3. Ambiguities in the European Defense Community Treaty

European member states would be forced to accept the military budgets requested by NATO's supreme commander after a vote by the European Council.[79] Gaullist parliamentarians, such as Michel Debré, for whom the defense of the French Empire was a prime concern, feared that this plan would threaten France's ability to develop its own defense industries (in aircraft production, nuclear energy production, etc.) and to decide its military operations, at a time when decolonization movements, particularly in Indochina, demanded that France protect its imperial sovereignty.[80] Gaullists thus reduced the EDC Treaty to an instrument of "Cold War policy," by which the United States and their lackeys (Monnet and his men, in de Gaulle's view) sought to turn Western states into satellites of the United States. This viewpoint explains why, like the British imperialists, French Gaullists preferred the plan proposed by Dean Acheson, which clearly left French military policy and the conduct of its military operations in the French colonies outside the purview of NATO's supreme commander.

The French and British opponents to the EDC Treaty found it unacceptable that the rules that were left to be clarified were the political "master rules": the rules that controlled the separation of legislative powers in the community, which determined how other technical rules contained in the EDC Treaty (some of which were quite clear) could be changed in the future. Indeed, it was striking that whereas the political rules defining the future European lawmaking power of the community were left to be clarified later, other rules—especially those that concerned Europe's nuclear trade and production—were clearly expressed. For instance, the EDC Treaty specified the quality and quantity of enriched uranium allowed to be produced and possessed by future member states: it prohibited the possession by Europeans of "any nuclear fuel" enriched at a level higher than a low percentage (2.1 percent), and the quantity of nuclear fuel owned by any member state could not exceed five hundred grams (annex 2 of art. 107).

That US officials such as McCloy had been involved in the drafting of the EDC Treaty can explain why the latter contained clearly expressed commitments—for instance, regarding the level of nuclear trade and production acceptable in Western Europe: indeed, the EDC Treaty rules were directly inspired by the Allied nonproliferation approach to West Germany.[81] It was McCloy who, in March 1950 (two months before the Schuman Declaration), promulgated Law 22 in West Germany, which capped the amount of fissile material acceptable on West German soil at fifty grams,[82] and banned the operation of accelerators other than small-scale laboratory cyclotrons, to ensure that German laboratories could not produce fissile material (the material that is used to produce an uncontrolled chain reaction and explosion).[83] As compared to the occupation laws, the EDC Treaty thus only multiplied tenfold the quantities of fissile materials allowed to circulate in West Germany, and it extended these restrictions to the rest of Western Europe, which was meant to satisfy US foreign policy elites, who wanted to maintain strict nonproliferation measures in Western Germany.[84]

That France could agree to include clearly expressed limits on its nuclear development in the EDC Treaty reflected the provisional nature of these rules, which, in turn, dramatized the problem raised by the ambiguity of political rules. Indeed, France had agreed to the rules on nuclear production only to respect the federalist principle of equal renunciation of rights, which meant that France had to abide by the same strict nuclear policies as those that were applied to West Germany.[85] But in fact, these technical rules appeared unrealistic when applied to France. As Jules Guéron (a French nuclear scientist who had negotiated the wartime Franco-British agreement of nuclear cooperation in 1940 with his brother-in-law, Etienne Hirsh) remarked, the EDC Treaty authorized Germany and France to build—at most—a small nuclear pile of the size that "corresponded to the [already existing] French research pile in Saclay."[86] This meant that as soon as the future political rules of the European Federation were clarified, France would ask that the European Council vote to raise the amount of fissile materials acceptable in Western Europe (according to a procedure specified later in the EPC Treaty).[87] As Jules Guéron subsequently wrote, "The EDC treaty would have given us a real opportunity to rationally structure the development of atomic energy in Europe,"[88] but it was unclear how that political structure would work when the EDC Treaty would be implemented. Indeed, if France (or any other member state) wished to raise the numerical limits on the amount of nuclear fuel acceptable on French soil, or if it wished to start enriching uranium at higher levels, the other five European states of the EDC would need to be consulted first.

If the Western Europeans wished it, they could even, in the long term, agree to build nuclear weapons themselves, as no technical limit existed that could not be overruled by future European legislation, if all the EDC member states decided to raise such limits by a unanimous vote. But in May 1952, the procedure to make this decision, the master rules that would help states litigate conflicts of interpretation and pass new legislation, and the institutions in charge of making such a decision (the European Council or new institutions that would be part of a European Parliament) had not yet been clarified by the negotiating parties.

This relation between ambiguous master rules (to be defined at a later date) and clear technical rules (provisional but immediately enforced) became the main reasons for concern on the part of European and American policy makers. Since Europe's future political authority would be granted the right to lift the clear limits that were introduced on Europe's nuclear programs, the main problem—for Gaullist critics—was that no one knew how Europe would make those legislative changes when the EDC Treaty was signed in May 1952. At that time, few politicians actually knew that the EDC Treaty would concern France's nuclear development, as Monnet, Hirsh, and other drafters delineated these lines of the treaty in haste, without consulting the French leaders in the industries covered: Francis Perrin, the high commissioner of the Commissariat à l'Energie Atomique (CEA), in charge of France's nuclear industrial development, or the French chiefs of staff, in charge of deciding the armament levels for the defense of France's national interests.[89] None of them were informed of the content of the technical rules regarding nuclear development, even though the EDC Treaty encompassed almost all nuclear activities as falling under its jurisdiction. As a result, when the EDC Treaty was signed in May 1952, critics were shocked that no one knew how the legislative powers of the European Federation regulating nuclear trade and production, conventional arms production in general, and the organization of the European armies would be organized.

Interpretive ambiguity was therefore a tactic that served the interests of competing foreign policy elites in the US domestic field of power, but that actually harmed the legitimacy of the proposal in France and in the United Kingdom. As I will show in the next section, the sequencing of negotiations wished for by Monnet (which initially produced positive results, as the ECSC Treaty entered into force) backfired when the French and British opposition to this ambiguity triggered preemptive decisions, especially in the nuclear domain, by the French government: the latter sought to unilaterally restrict the range of acceptable future interpretation of the EDC Treaty, which was open to ratification in May 1952.

Preemptive Interpretation

I now further describe the pitfalls of ambiguity by showing its negative consequences on the ratification of the EDC Treaty. The sequencing of negotiations opened a window of opportunity for French opponents to the EDC Treaty, who used the time that elapsed between the signing of the treaty and the ratification vote to empty its content by a series of preemptive clarifications that destroyed the coherence of the legal intertextual architecture.

The British and French Faits Accomplis in the Nuclear Field (Spring–Summer 1952)

Until May 1952, the nuclear issue was not at the forefront of the political debate about the EDC Treaty. Most of the stakeholders on the nuclear issue were left uninformed of the treaty's nuclear content. In contrast, after the EDC Treaty was presented in May 1952 to the European parliamentary bodies for ratification, the nuclear issue rapidly moved to the forefront of political controversies. Critics of the EDC Treaty argued that France could not sign a treaty when it did not know whether the limits imposed on the amount of nuclear materials circulating would apply to France, or whether France would benefit from an exemption, either because the future rules would not apply to some parts of its territory, especially in Algeria but also in Corsica (what I call "ontological" ambiguity), or because a new procedure would give France a general exemption on nuclear matters (what I call "interpretive" ambiguity).

The problems that the EDC Treaty rules regarding nuclear matters raised for France were first related to Cold War logics. Since the Tripartite Declaration of September 1951, it appeared that a public consensus had emerged among allied governments in support of the EDC Treaty. However, this illusion was shattered in February 1952, after the British unilaterally decided to test their first nuclear weapon, the day after the NATO conference held in Lisbon during which Acheson introduced the first US strategic doctrine for the alliance. In fact, the British test was a direct response to the first US doctrine of nuclear weapons use that Acheson introduced for NATO: indeed, Acheson's NATO doctrine specified that US nuclear weapons would not be used to defend Western Europe, except as a last resort, only after a Russian invasion of Western Europe.[90] Then, the liberation of Western Europe would mean its destruction by US thermonuclear weapons. In the words of Marc Trachtenberg, "The victory would be Pyrrhic."[91] Most Europeans, including the British, inferred from Acheson's message that the United States intended to limit the theater of nuclear warfare to the European arena, in the hope that the Russians would not strike American cities as the United States would not strike Russian cities.[92] The British thus conducted their first nuclear test with the hope that they could convince the Russians and Americans not to include the United Kingdom as one of their European targets, a decision that signaled to the future EDC member states that, in case of a war with the Soviets, their territory would become the battlefield of a nuclear war from which the Anglo-American allies were isolated by their respective nuclear deterrents.

The British test and Acheson's strategic doctrine suddenly politicized the US policy debates about the role that nuclear weapons should play in the stabilization of Europe, and by doing so, placed the nuclear issue at the forefront of US policy debates about Europe. Indeed, these decisions revived the cleavages between Acheson and Eisenhower. Acheson's doctrine for NATO especially antagonized NATO's supreme commander, General Eisenhower, who had requested that the United States commit to an early use of nuclear weapons for the defense of Europe—a request that Western European military leaders, afraid of Soviet conventional superiority, supported.[93] Whereas Truman and Acheson defended the complete freedom of the US president over America's nuclear strategy, by supporting the use of conventional warfare first in the event of a war in Europe, Eisenhower believed it was a tragic mistake to insist on keeping nuclear weapons out of the hands of the future European army and NATO's supreme commander. In fact, Eisenhower already believed that the United States should have helped its closest allies, especially the British, acquire their own nuclear weapons—for instance, by inviting the British to test their nuclear weapon at the US nuclear test site—rather than letting them develop their nuclear weapons program on their own.[94] He even asked that the decision to use NATO's nuclear missiles be delegated from the US president to NATO's supreme commander.

The British decision also made it clear that the British would never commit to respect the rules of the EDC Treaty, whose nuclear provisions clearly subjected the production and possession of nuclear weapons to the control of the European Council (as provisionally planned by the EDC Treaty), or to the control of the future legislative powers of the European Federation (defined according to the treaty that a constituent assembly would write in the future). Ultimately, the United Kingdom showed that it did not feel bound by the outcome of the EDC Treaty negotiations. This message was accentuated after the EDC Treaty was finally signed in Bonn in May 1952, when Anthony Eden, Dean Acheson, and Georges Bidault (back to the post of foreign minister) signed another "Tripartite Declaration," which provided for the continuation of the tripartite Franco-Anglo-American sovereign powers over the military defense of West Germany, even against West Germany itself.[95] The declaration proved that neither the United Kingdom nor France was likely to consider West Germany an equal member state in the European federation. The strategic doctrine of NATO and the British nuclear test thus clarified the articulation between the future EDC and NATO, in a way that the EDC Treaty failed to do on its own. For the French military leaders, these decisions gave credence to the Gaullist claim that the institutions created by the EDC Treaty would be used by US generals to pass their orders to European industries and armies, rather than to increase consultation on their own defense and nuclear policies with their European allies.

The repercussions of the Anglo-American strategic decisions were quite dramatic for the fate of the future interpretation of the EDC rules and greatly contributed to the agonistic debates that emerged about the consequence of the EDC Treaty for France's future nuclear options. The British test convinced French leaders to create their own fait accompli in the nuclear field before the ratification of the EDC Treaty. At the very same time that the ECSC Treaty entered into force, the French National Assembly adopted in July 1952 the second five-year plan for the French Atomic Energy Commission (or CEA), presented by its administrator general, Félix Gaillard (the "Gaillard Plan"), without consulting any of the five other signatories of the EDC Treaty. The Gaillard Plan violated de facto all the nuclear commitments that France had written in the yet-to-be-ratified EDC Treaty: it proposed accelerating the production of plutonium in France up to fifty kilograms (the equivalent of eight atomic bombs), bringing French production levels of fissile materials a hundred times higher than the maximum limit authorized by the EDC Treaty.[96] As Gaillard argued, if France did not want to be relegated to the "primitive peoples of Africa,"[97] and to become the site of a nuclear war, it had to gain nuclear autonomy for the nation.[98] But as Maurice Vaïsse notes, by voting for the Gaillard Plan, the French government decided to make the implementation of the EDC Treaty impossible to respect.[99] With this new national plan, French nationalists signaled to Monnet that France would use the time remaining before the clarification of the future rules of the European Federation to preempt possible nuclear futures in a way that fitted with their conception of France's imperial grandeur. For Monnet and other Eurofederalists, it became urgent to act in order to avoid seeing the French government untie all the knots that they had patiently knitted in their complex legal construct.

The Legal Validity of the EDC Treaty in Question (May 1952–March 1953)

Although the French nuclear decision of the summer of 1952 was not a violation of the EDC Treaty, since a treaty is not considered the law of the land until it is ratified, it did violate the implicit assumption in the international community that a state that has signed (but has yet to ratify) a treaty should not breach the rules of that treaty. In fact, the French (and the British) decisions started a new cycle of dispute about the legal validity of the EDC Treaty at the very same time that it was presented to European parliamentary bodies for ratification.

The French fait accompli forced the Eurofederalists to advance the negotiation of Europe's future master rules *before* the implementation of the EDC Treaty rather than abide by the agreed-upon schedule of negotiations, under which such negotiations were planned to occur *after* the ratification of the EDC Treaty. When the ECSC Treaty entered into force in July 1952, with Jean Monnet as the first president of the High Authority of the ECSC, Monnet thus introduced in the Council of Ministers of the ECSC a resolution requesting the immediate application of article 38 of the EDC Treaty, even though the latter had only been signed and not yet ratified. The Council of the ECSC voted unanimously in favor,[100] and in September 1952, during the first meeting of the Assembly of the ECSC, its first president, the former Belgian foreign minister Paul-Henri Spaak (1899–1972), a leading supporter of the Schuman Plan since its inception, requested that the European Assembly of the ECSC (where the United Kingdom did not sit) elect some of its members to form a constituent committee and prepare the future EPC Treaty: the "ad hoc assembly"—a more neutral term than the French term "constituent assembly."[101]

This preemptive move, which Gaullists such as Michel Debré denounced as a legal "coup de force,"[102] was designed to exclude the British from the constituent assembly in charge of giving permanent political master rules to the European Coal and Steel as well as the Defense Communities. The British fait accompli had convinced Monnet, who had initially agreed to the participation of British officials in the constituent assembly of the future treaty that would institute the European Federation, that he should no longer let the British participate in these deliberations. Thanks to this maneuver, Monnet and Spaak succeeded in keeping the representatives of the Council of Europe at arm's length, and avoiding British attempts to torpedo the clarification of Europe's future master rules[103]—though they had to accept the presence of French Gaullists, such as Debré, who sat in the Assembly of the ECSC and who managed to get elected to the ad hoc assembly.[104]

During the six months of its existence, the jurists and constitutional scholars who worked in the ad hoc assembly to draw up the constitutional framework of a new European federation entertained the highest ambitions for Europe. The European treaty drafters presented themselves as modern versions of the American constitution makers who had declared independence from Europe two centuries earlier.[105] The discussions were led by Eurofederalist jurists such as Pierre-Henri Teitgen (1908–97), a French jurist and a Christian Democrat parliamentarian in the French Assembly, who occupied governmental posts as minister of justice and minister of the armed forces in the late 1940s.[106] To perfect the constitutional design, Spaak and Monnet even turned to the legal expertise of those US jurists enlisted by McCloy for the ECSC Treaty—in particular, Robert Bowie and one of his colleagues at Harvard, Carl Friedrich, a German émigré.[107] As a result of its composition, the ad hoc committee defined the future political master rules of Europe in line with their federalist conception of Europe. For example, the committee adopted the idea that all the budgets of the EDC (and the ECSC) would have to be approved by a European Lower Chamber of parliamentarians directly elected through Europe-wide elections (in proportion to the size of each country).[108] In addition, whereas the ECSC Treaty created a council that was composed of only ministers of foreign affairs, members of the future Council of the Federation (the Upper Chamber of Parliament) were to be directly elected to their office from national parliaments, with each nation having the same number of parliamentarians. When presenting the project, Spaak concluded before his fellow parliamentarians in the ECSC, "This project of a constitution subordinates the military power to a civil authority whose power emanates from people's representation . . . that of a European parliament,"[109] in line with the federalist tradition. The draft of the EPC Treaty issued in March 1953 even clarified that the powers of the future European Community would extend from the fields of defense to that of foreign policy, as it planned that member states would delegate to the federation their international legal sovereignty—for example, the sovereign authority to approve all the treaties and association agreements of its member states.[110]

This preemptive clarification (in advance of the ratification of the EDC Treaty) sought to discourage the French government from making further decisions regarding its defense without first consulting its future associates in the EDC.[111] But in fact, this preemptive clarification achieved the opposite effects, as it exacerbated the conflicts between politicians and jurists in France about the legal validity of the EDC Treaty. French nationalists found unacceptable the whole exercise of writing a political constitution for Europe in anticipation of the entry into force of a treaty that was not yet ratified. Six months after its creation, when the ad hoc assembly presented a text to the Assembly of the ECSC, which voted in its favor (with the exception of four members), Michel Debré denounced it as an "illegal text voted by an illegal Assembly."[112] Debré believed that the work of the ad hoc committee reflected the irresponsibility of the "members of the committee [who] were all jurists" rather than politicians. For him, their emphasis on technical knowledge in constitutional law led to "play[ing] with the sovereignty of states, with the legitimacy of power, and the reality of peoples, . . . by inventing a pseudo-State, a Senate and a Parliament, while they had no sense of the political realities of the time."[113] In Debré's view, their technical expertise did not give them the necessary legitimacy to invent new rules for Europe in the defense field, and the fact that the EDC Treaty defined when and how these discussions should be held (after its entry into force, per art. 38) meant that the jurists should have waited until the ratification of the EDC Treaty before holding these discussions.

Eurofederalists reduced the interpretive ambiguity of the EDC Treaty by clarifying the future master rules of the European Federation. They did so in order to guard themselves against the charge that they had asked national legislators to give carte blanche to a new supranational organization whose powers were not legally defined. But the result of their debates actually increased the confusion surrounding the legal validity of the EDC Treaty. Critics of the EDC Treaty argued that they could not delegate some authority to a supranational institution whose powers were underdefined on one side and already implemented on the other side. The French decision to jump-start the country's nuclear dual-use activities accentuated the ambiguity of the EDC Treaty, as the only clear provisions—such as the provisional rules on the regulation of nuclear trade and production in Europe—seemed obsolete. The clarification of the future legislative "master rules" of Europe performed preemptively by a handful of Eurofederalist jurists and in advance of the entry into force of the EDC Treaty increased the doubts about the legal validity of a text that seemed already partly obsolete and partly implemented.

The debates about the legal validity of the EDC Treaty, which resulted from the initial tactic of ambiguity, raised important obstacles to the ratification of the EDC Treaty in European domestic contexts as well, particularly in West Germany. Here again, the debate about the legal validity of the EDC Treaty in Germany shows the limits of the metaphor of Ulysses that has been used by scholars of European integration processes to describe the integration process as involving the delegation of sovereign power by supposedly independent nation-states to a supranational institution. Indeed, after the treaty was signed, the West German chancellor faced a strong domestic opposition that argued that the West German executive could not delegate powers it did not possess (in this case, sovereign powers to conduct foreign policy and to engage in military and/or nuclear activities) to a supranational institution whose powers were not yet clearly defined.

In fact, the threat that the highest West German judicial authorities would declare the EDC Treaty "unconstitutional" was taken very seriously by the West German and US governments. As Karl Loewenstein writes, in West Germany the process of ratification that started after Chancellor Adenauer signed the EDC Treaty in May 1952 "produced a constitutional controversy unrivaled in importance in recent German history."[114] Indeed, in June 1952, the opposition represented by the West German social democrats (who opposed the EDC Treaty on nationalist grounds)[115] convinced Germany's president, Theodor Heuss, to ask the Constitutional Court to give its opinion on the constitutional validity of the EDC Treaty. The question of its constitutional validity had serious implications, because if the court declared that this ambiguous document had "constitutional" value, then its ratification would need two-thirds of the vote of the West German parliament (a supermajority that Adenauer's government did not command) rather than the simple majority necessary to ratify a treaty. The compatibility between the new European treaties and the (quasi-constitutional) Basic Law of 1949 was not self-evident. The Basic Law of 1949 did not contain provisions on military matters, and in the absence of other legal texts on those matters, critics argued that the EDC Treaty would thus attain the status of a constitution. The opposition also claimed that the EDC Treaty contained provisions that contradicted the Basic Law: for instance, the EDC Treaty stated that the federal government of Bonn could ask the European Commissariat to place some of the European troops under its authority if "public order" was threatened (art. 12),[116] and that it affected the separation of powers between West German federal and state governments.[117] The West German opposition had a pretty good case, especially after the ad hoc assembly started working on a constitution for Europe in August 1952, implementing the EDC Treaty in advance.

In fact, in Germany (as in France),[118] the debate about the constitutional validity of the EDC Treaty was settled by a decision of the legislative branch rather than solved by the highest judicial authorities, whose legal opinion was never sought by the government in power. In West Germany, the decision to send the EDC Treaty for constitutional review convinced Chancellor Adenauer to take a series of preemptive decisions, which eventually led to the legislative (rather than judicial) declaration made in December 1953 by the chancellor's coalition in both legislative chambers, that the EDC Treaty was "constitutional." This preemptive declaration was the result of a year of legal battle that ended with a political compromise after the 1953 elections. The struggle actually started in December 1952, when Adenauer successfully got the EDC Treaty passed by the Federal Assembly (the lower chamber, composed of representatives elected by direct suffrage) with a simple majority (which was enough to ratify a treaty), before the Federal Court opened its constitutional review. The chancellor insisted on presenting the EDC Treaty for parliamentary ratification before the court made a decision for pragmatic reasons: if the court decided that the ratification of the EDC Treaty necessitated some constitutional amendments to the Basic Law (which required a majority of two-thirds in parliament), then the social democrats would be in a position to derail the ratification process, as they controlled a bit more than a third of the votes in the Federal Assembly.[119] But the assembly's vote woke up the judges in the Federal Constitutional Court, which suddenly announced that it was ready to decide on the treaty's constitutional validity, and that its decision would be binding on the Federal Council representing the West German regions (Landers), where the EDC Treaty was going to be sent for examination. This last point convinced President Heuss, himself pressured by Chancellor Adenauer, to immediately withdraw his request for advice from the court.[120] In effect, the president did not authorize the court to make a preemptive decision that would have bound the hands of the legislative branch. Thus, it was only after Chancellor Adenauer won a landslide victory in September 1953, and secured the ratification of the EDC Treaty by a majority of two-thirds in the Federal Assembly and the Federal Council, that the debate on its constitutionality was settled. As a result of this tortuous process, no one in West Germany wanted to make any change to the legal text that West Germany's parliament had declared constitutional and acceptable: the debate about the legal validity of that treaty was still boiling under the lid that West German parliamentarians had placed on top of the pan.

Penelope's Cunning: How France Untied the Knots of the EDC Treaty (Spring 1953–Summer 1954)

The anarchic process of preemptive interpretation of the EDC rules increased the vulnerability of the EDC Treaty to attacks on its legal validity and highlighted the risk of complete abandonment if all parties were to come back to the negotiating table. After the European master rules were clarified, France introduced a new type of ambiguity, which I call ontological, and which finally doomed the negotiations: indeed, the French government insisted on redefining the extent to which future rules would apply to France. When the government led by René Mayer was formed in January 1953, Michel Debré hoped that the EDC Treaty would finally be rejected by the new governmental coalition, which needed the support of Gaullists to survive. But instead of completely rejecting the EDC Treaty, in February 1953, the French government expressed its desire to open limited renegotiations with its European partners in order to abrogate article 38 (on behalf of which the ad hoc assembly had been formed) and to rewrite the nuclear provisions of the EDC Treaty in order to align the text with recent evolutions in the French thinking on nuclear affairs, and to exclude some parts of France from the jurisdiction of the future EDC.

The new negotiation produced some kind of ontological ambiguity: as far as nuclear issues were concerned, under the pressure of the highest military authorities,[121] the French government insisted on adding protocols of implementation to the instruments of ratification of the EDC Treaty, which specified that the strict qualitative and quantitative restrictions of the EDC Treaty on the nuclear activities of its signatory states only applied in the geographic zone in Europe most likely to be attacked by the Soviets. The latter included the whole of West Germany and the eastern parts of France.[122] In the "strategic zone," the future European Commissariat could conduct inspections of nuclear facilities, the licensing of new power plants would be subject to the prior approval of the commissariat, and qualitative and quantitative limits on the production of fissile materials considered "nuclear weapons" were to be enforced.[123] But outside of this strategic zone, member states would be free from the control of the European Commissariat. As most of the western and southern parts of France were outside of this zone, and since France (as well as Belgium and the Netherlands) also had departments overseas and colonies in Africa (such as Algeria), the French government hoped that this provision would allow the French to produce nuclear weapons of their own without subjecting them to the vote of the European Council.

The French demands for new negotiations of the nuclear provisions of the EDC Treaty threatened the ratification process among all the other signatory states and provoked strong negative reactions in West Germany and the United States: as Adenauer wrote, the day Mayer made his announcement in March 1953 that the French government wanted new negotiations was the "most painful day of his chancellorship,"[124] as it almost derailed his efforts to quickly end the ratification process in West Germany.

The reopening of negotiations of the EDC Treaty requested by the French government in the spring of 1953 was also forcefully opposed by the new US president, Dwight Eisenhower, elected in November 1952: his administration increased the pressure on France to quickly ratify the EDC Treaty without opening a new cycle of negotiations. This decision was not a surprise, as Eurofederalists had gained the upper hand in the State Department (see fig. 4.1). Although Eisenhower had to refrain from nominating McCloy as secretary of state because Republicans in Congress would not confirm his nomination,[125] he turned to Monnet's second closest associate, John Foster Dulles, as his second choice for secretary, a position that Dulles's grandfather and uncle had held before him. Furthermore, on McCloy's recommendation, Dulles chose Robert Bowie to succeed Paul Nitze as the director of the policy planning staff of the State Department.[126]

This sea change in the position of the US administration regarding the EDC Treaty was not without effect: as Bowie later put it mildly, "Both Dulles and Eisenhower had a personal interest" in European unity, "which probably did make a difference in the degree to which the United States made clear that it did support this movement, if compared with the times of Dean Acheson."[127] John Foster Dulles increased the pressure on the French to stop postponing parliamentary debate and to ratify the EDC Treaty as soon as possible with as few changes as possible. In October 1953, the US ambassador to France promised Max Kohnstamm (1914–2010), a Dutch diplomat who had participated in the negotiation of the ECSC Treaty and was by then Monnet's assistant at the presidency of the High Authority of the ECSC, that "unless [the] EDC is ratified soon, there will be an almost total cessation of appropriations for [foreign aid to Europe] from Congress."[128] Informed in Paris in March 1954 by Livingston Merchant, a State Department official whom Dulles later appointed assistant secretary for European affairs (see fig. 4.1), that the French might reject the EDC Treaty, the secretary of state said that the French should "put out of their mind any concept that there is an alternative or that we're considering one to the EDC."[129]

Nevertheless, threats did not work, and the ratification of the EDC Treaty by the French Parliament lagged behind the ratification process in the other five nations, which had all ratified the treaty by the spring of 1954. As France still struggled to sustain its empire overseas, the French government remained critical of the Cold War lenses that the EDC Treaty promoters had adopted when they focused almost entirely on European affairs, which as far as French interests were concerned, were much less hotly contested than France's colonial interests in Asia. Thus, after the West Germans ratified the EDC Treaty, the French government added new demands for the revision of the EDC Treaty before it would agree to submit the text to the French Parliament. In early 1954, the French government repeated its opposition to the formation of a European Federation (whose master rules were now defined by the ad hoc assembly) and said that it wanted to keep its freedom to decide how many and which type of troops it would transfer from the European army to its national army, which it needed to fight French wars outside Europe (mainly in Indochina, at the time). At a moment when the French suffered heavy losses in Dien Bien Phu, the government of René Mayer, which needed the support of Gaullist parliamentarians to remain in power, made it clear that Mayer did not want to submit the conduct of France's military affairs in the French Empire to the prior consultation, and approval, of the European Defense Commissariat. But these requests completely emptied the treaty of its federalist content: as Monnet and Dulles argued, if Washington and London agreed to these unilateral reinterpretations of the EDC Treaty by the French government, there would be no difference between the military commitment of an EDC member state such as France, which could exclude part of its territory from the rules of the EDC, and a nonsignatory state such as the United Kingdom.[130]

As they realized it was impossible to convince the French government not to reopen negotiations on the territorial extension of the jurisdiction of the future EDC institutions, Eurofederalists turned once again to the tactic of interpretive ambiguity to bargain a compromise. In March 1953, Dulles feared that if negotiations were reopened, the French government would keep adding demands:[131] it had already added demands regarding the exclusion of overseas territories from the permanent control of the European Defense Commissariat[132] and regarding France's right to stockpile nuclear weapons built on its own in its western and overseas territories.[133] Thus, Dulles proposed the following tactic: France's partners would let France ratify these protocols with the EDC Treaty, but they would not include them in their own instruments of ratification of the EDC Treaty, as they had already completed their ratification process. Indeed, Dulles said that no change could be introduced at that point that would require West Germany to go through the hardship of a ratification process again.[134] The French, for instance, should be satisfied with a guarantee that the European controls on nuclear development were not meant to prevent the growth of a French nuclear industry in the sector of electricity production.[135] The West Germans followed Dulles's tactic: they claimed that these French protocols were "interpretative texts,"[136] not signed by the European partners but circulated to inform Europeans about the French interpretation of the treaty. They also insisted that the European Court of Justice would have the power to determine its interpretation of the text of the treaty in the future.

At the same time as Dulles and Eisenhower refused to reopen the EDC

Treaty negotiations, they proposed to give the French government some concession by changing the rules of US engagement with NATO. Eisenhower proposed an overhaul of NATO's strategic doctrine that would buy the support of French generals for the EDC Treaty—but to do so, he and Monnet's US allies used the same tactic of ambiguity, adopting texts whose legal validity would be clarified at a later date by constitutional and/or legislative changes. Eisenhower's doctrine of "immediate and massive" retaliation stated that as soon as Soviet forces threatened to enter West German territory, NATO's supreme commander would annihilate the advancing Soviet forces and military reserves in Eastern Europe with tactical nuclear weapons placed under the authority of NATO's supreme commander.[137] For that new doctrine to be implemented under any circumstances (even if the US president was unreachable at the time of the emergency), NATO's supreme commander needed preapproval delegated by the US president to fire the US nuclear weapons stockpiled in Western Europe, which of course raised a constitutional problem, as the US Congress defended its constitutional prerogatives.[138] Three days before the vote on the EDC Treaty by the French National Assembly,[139] President Eisenhower and General Gruenther, his successor as NATO's supreme commander, announced that they would seek congressional authorization to give NATO's supreme commander a "permanent delegation of the power of the Alliance to launch a massive and immediate attack behind enemy lines,"[140] and that in the meantime, they implicitly agreed that NATO's supreme commander was in charge of deciding the timing of any nuclear war in Europe.[141]

But this time, the tactic of ambiguity did not convince the French to change their mind. This time, the French government did not agree to leave matters ambiguous, or to let the European Court, staffed by Eurofederalist judges, decide whether their own interpretation of the nuclear provisions of the EDC Treaty was in conformance with the treaty or not. Furthermore, Eisenhower's attempt to buy the support of the French government backfired: even though the reform of NATO's strategic doctrine he introduced in August 1954 pleased the French military professionals in NATO, it clearly antagonized the French civilian leadership, and particularly Pierre Mendès France (1907–82), a radical socialist who was elected in June 1954 with the mandate to negotiate the end of the war with the Viet Cong after the French defeat at Dien Bien Phu.[142] Indeed, the new head of the French government sought to maintain the formal prerogatives of the head of government to declare war and act accordingly: Mendès France requested that the authorization to fire US nuclear weapons, which would be stored in Europe, remain under the control of the highest civilian authorities (a tripartite political body composed of the three heads of state in France, the United States, and the United Kingdom) rather than under the authority of NATO's supreme commander.[143]

As the French refused to ratify a treaty with "interpretative texts" whose legal validity remained disputed, a new round of renegotiations on the nuclear and colonial issues at the heart of the EDC Treaty debate was imposed by Mendès France during a conference held in Brussels in August 1954. The French representatives proposed the same "protocol of application" that freed France to pursue a nuclear military outside the "strategic zone," which Paul-Henri Spaak now proposed restricting to Continental Europe, leaving French Algeria and Corsica outside the perimeter but not any part of the French metropolis. Mendès France eventually accepted this revised 1954 version of the French concept of "strategic zone."[144] To convince the Germans to recognize France's nuclear freedom in Algeria, Mendès France even proposed that the West Germans participate in the production of what were considered "nuclear weapons" (such as the enrichment of uranium) outside the "strategic area."[145] As Gunnar Skogmar writes, even though some Germans appreciated the possibility of conducting Franco-German nuclear cooperation outside the purview of the European defense institutions, no compromise was found, as the French demands were still too high: for instance, Mendès France was adamant that France would not sign the EDC Treaty if it contained article 38, as he wanted to put an end to the constitutionalist dreams of the drafters of the EPC Treaty.[146] Essentially, this concession would relegate the work of the ad hoc committee to the dustbin of history.

Reciprocally, the French failed to convince the West Germans and Americans of the legitimacy of a new round of negotiations of the EDC Treaty. When informed of the French propositions, Konrad Adenauer immediately told James Conant, who had replaced McCloy as the US representative in Germany, that he would accept no changes that required the West German ratification of new provisions to the treaty, especially if they introduced discrimination against the West Germans or if they impaired the supranational aspects of the European institutions (as the abrogation of art. 38 did). John Foster Dulles did not want to pressure Adenauer to accept the French revisions, as he "always had a lurking suspicion that the last minute modifications in the treaty [were] a cynical effort to gut the treaty in certain important respects."[147] Adenauer thus opposed the proposal of Franco-German bilateral nuclear cooperation outside the European institutions, which was a step toward the Europe of nation-states, designed according to Gaullist views.[148] Thus, in the absence of a resolution of the disagreements between the French, American, and German governments, the French Parliament voted against the ratification of the EDC Treaty in August 1954.

Closing Pandora's Box: The Constraints of Clarity

The rejection of the EDC Treaty by the French Parliament in August 1954 left pending the resolution of the problems of Western European defense. For the second time in ten years, the normative ideal of atomic federalism had failed to contribute positively to the development of international law—in this case, European law. The debate over the validity of ambiguous legal documents such as the EDC Treaty left strong traces within the West. Indeed, the ultimate solution for the stabilization of Europe was strongly influenced by the criticisms that had been expressed against the ambiguity of the rejected EDC Treaty and by the French government's demand to have a clear understanding of the future rules by which armament industries would be regulated.

Though John Foster Dulles had been a strong supporter of the EDC Treaty, as there was no plan B, he could not but advise President Eisenhower to support the British proposal that resurrected the plan first proposed by Dean Acheson in the midst of the Korean War in August 1950: the British proposed that West German rearmament be allowed within the framework of NATO, with all West German forces under the authority of NATO's supreme commander. The British proposal also resolved the question of the sovereignty of the Saar regions, which was to be safeguarded by the Western European Union (WEU) until a referendum was organized, which took place a year later.[149] Because the US Congress relentlessly requested the immediate entry of the Federal Republic of Germany into NATO, Dulles flew to Germany in September 1954, bypassing Paris,[150] and then to London, where British prime minister Eden convinced him that the British alternative to the defunct EDC Treaty was the best alternative. When the Western allies signed the final agreements in Paris in October 1954 (hereafter, Paris Agreements),[151] they granted back to the Federal Republic of Germany its international legal sovereignty, which it exercised by agreeing to enter both NATO and the West European Union in October 1954 (protocol I, art. 1 of the Paris Agreements).[152]

Eventually, the ratification of the Paris Agreements crystallized a new international legal order based on the independence of nation-states in Western Europe, in which the United Kingdom and France were engaged in a nuclear arms race, which the West Germans were free to join if the international situation required them to do so. The French Parliament only agreed to ratify these agreements after Pierre Mendès France authorized the creation of a French commission on the military applications of nuclear energy, which he did in November 1954,[153] as his active support for a French military program was "the *sine qua non* for getting enough [parliamentary] support for [the] acceptance of a German rearmament partially bridled by the Western European Union."[154]

As far as West German nuclear sovereignty was concerned, in September 1954, John Foster Dulles and his British counterpart, Anthony Eden, believed that there was no alternative to the chancellor's unilateral pledge not to produce nuclear weapons and his acceptance that the West German conventional armament industry be controlled by the only existing European organization in the field of defense (the WEU), however loose WEU controls were.[155] The only limit placed on West German nuclear development was the unilateral promise by Adenauer not to construct atomic weapons or "the constitutive elementary materials necessary to build such weapons" (protocol III).[156] But the German chancellor added the clause *sic rebus stantibus* ("everything held constant") to his promise not to produce nuclear weapons on German soil,[157] meaning that should security reasons require West Germany to relax the prohibitions on the construction of long-range ballistic missiles (which could serve for the exploration of space), as well as large naval carriers with nuclear propulsion (which could serve as tankers),[158] it would ask the Council of the WEU to relax its production limits.[159] For the time being, the WEU Arms Control Agency, which became operational only in 1957,[160] had very limited powers. Unlike the defunct European Defense Commissariat, which had to authorize the licensing of each new nuclear power plant, the WEU Agency did not create any new center for decision making that could deny ex ante the right of West Germany to build power plants or enrichment plants.[161] Furthermore, the Paris Agreements no longer mentioned the five hundred–gram limits on the production of fissile materials by which Europeans had defined the production of "nuclear weapons" in the EDC Treaty.[162] The criterion used to define nuclear weapons was now based on intention: as long as the West Germans declared that their purpose was peaceful, they could produce fissile materials in large quantities and enrich uranium on their soil.[163] Thus, the specter of West German nuclear development loomed on the horizon: as the minister of foreign affairs of the Netherlands complained, "European supranational cooperation, with the WEU as a starting-point, is bound to remain a castle in the air, only leading to disappointment."[164]

Overall, the failed ratification of the EDC Treaty and the adoption of the Paris Agreements were associated with a failure of the tactic of ambiguity that Eurofederalists had adopted since the first drafts of the EDC Treaty had been prepared in haste by Monnet, Hirsh, and their associates in the fall of 1950. By 1954, the US secretary of state took the French at their word when he chose to make US policy for Europe clearly known to America's allies. After the French had imposed a constraint of high clarity on any deal that they would accept with regard to Europe's prerogatives in the nuclear field, John Foster Dulles told them clearly how the US government understood the rules of US nuclear involvement in Europe. As Livingston Merchant, Dulles's advisor on European affairs in the State Department, wrote, the US government "could not give the French what they want[ed], so [the United States] might at least be honest about it." Indeed, Merchant insisted that "should [the US government] not agree to ambiguous language which might imply a willingness to change our position, [the] result would be to raise false hopes among the French,"[165] and further postpone the ratification of the Paris Agreements. Dulles made it clear that the United States would not coordinate its policy of transferring nuclear weapons on the European battlefields with Europeans (through the Council of the WEU, or that of NATO, as proposed by the British), as requested by Mendès France and Eden.[166] After the EDC Treaty was rejected, Dulles clearly told the British and French that such decisions would remain under the sole authority of the US commander in chief.[167] Furthermore, Dulles refused to inform the WEU Arms Control Agency, which had been created as part of the Paris Agreements to inspect West German nuclear facilities, of the number of nuclear weapons under American control in German territory.[168] With the signing of the Paris Agreements, the United States could therefore stockpile tactical weapons in Europe under US control and possession, without informing Bonn, London, or Paris of their number, exact location, or destructive power. In effect, the Paris Agreements created a US nuclear protectorate in West Germany, but they left France free to conduct the war that Algeria's Front de Libération Nationale started in November 1954.

Conclusion

The evolution of international law, from the moment the North Atlantic Treaty was signed in 1949 to the moment West Germany was integrated into NATO in 1954, was of course driven by geopolitical events such as the explosion of a Soviet nuclear weapon and the war in Korea (see fig. 4.4). But these external shocks were not the only factors explaining the outcome of five years of treaty negotiations. Indeed, various normative ideals of international law and strategies could be used to solve the difficult problem

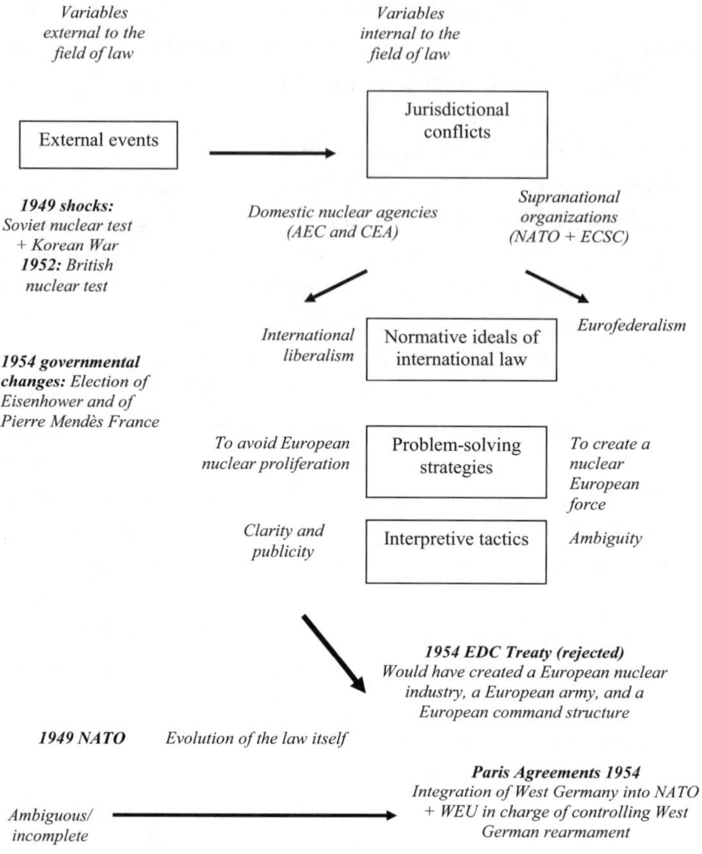

Figure 4.4. The dynamics of Eurofederalism in the early 1950s

of avoiding a new arms race between West Germany and France while allowing West German rearmament. The content of each strategy cannot explain why international liberals eventually succeeded in having the Western parliaments ratify the Paris Agreements of 1954, or why Eurofederalists failed (by a close margin) to have the EDC Treaty ratified: the two solutions adequately solved the same problem (the stabilization of Europe in a context of German rearmament), or not, depending on one's normative ideal and problem-solving strategy.

From 1949 to 1955, the nuclear issue was raised within the context of deliberations about Europe's future legal order and the role that European nation-states and empires projected for themselves. The EDC Treaty was hardly reduced to the Cold War logics followed by the United States, in contrast to what the French critics of the EDC (most notably General de Gaulle) said when they claimed that the "U.S. were the true great federators of Europe,"[169] in the sense that the United States had tried to use a European framework to turn European nations into obedient satellites. Eurofederalists among the US foreign policy elites were initially insiders-outsiders, whose efforts in favor of the EDC Treaty were initially hampered by the opposition of President Truman and his secretary of state.[170] The relative marginality of advocates of the Eurofederalist solution in the US field of foreign policy explained why the latter chose to first define a vague bundle of master rules in the EDC Treaty, which they hoped to eventually clarify at a later date (once they reached the top echelons of power in the US administration), and in a federalist sense. In fact, by using a tactic of ambiguity, Eurofederalists sought to create a flexible legal framework that would allow France to adequately address the security problems of the Cold War (the defense of Europe against the Soviet threat) but also the security problems raised by the proindependence movements in its colonies (in particular, Indochina).

But the sequencing tactic adopted by Monnet and his team bore fateful consequences. Indeed, in contrast to the beliefs of realists such as Morgenthau—and many scholars who believe in the "constructive" power of ambiguity and indeterminacy—postponing clarification of legal rules until after the signing of a treaty is not always the best way to pass new global legislation when strong normative and strategic differences exist among foreign policy elites at the international and domestic levels. The interpretive tactic that consisted of postponing the closing of disputes over the meaning of the EDC Treaty master rules until after the treaty was signed weakened the legal validity of the treaty: such an ambiguity allowed critics of the EDC to attack the incompleteness of the contract they were asked to ratify. As these critics engaged in a series of preemptive interpretations of the rules that would apply in the future community, Eurofederalists tried to ward off these attacks by defining more precisely how these master rules would operate in the future, advancing negotiations that had been planned for the period following the ratification of the EDC Treaty. But the critics were then able to attack this new strategy as legally invalid. Thus, the sequencing of negotiations, which had been announced in the EDC Treaty itself, ambushed the promoters of the treaty. Next, I will analyze whether the tactic of opacity better enabled Eurofederalists to push for the ratification of new European nuclear treaties that addressed the problems left unsolved by the Paris Agreements—in particular, the role that West Germany and France would play in the stabilization of Europe and the stabilization of the French Empire.

FIVE

Opacity in Legal Interpretation: The Transatlantic Negotiations of the Euratom Treaty

Many foreign policy elites may not want to commit to treaty rules whose meaning they do not clearly know in advance. At the same time, the desire to know clearly how future treaty rules will be interpreted can also block the adoption of a new treaty. If the only choice had been between nuclear transparency and nuclear ambiguity, it is quite possible that no new treaty regulating the global trade of nuclear materials and technologies would have been signed in the late 1950s. Here, I present a third interpretive practice that diplomats can use to present new legal rules: opacity.

Some believe that opacity may well be the inevitable price of progress in international law. As Louise Weiss wrote long ago, when the new leaders such as Woodrow Wilson "denounced the evils of secrecy, which plagued traditional national diplomacy [before World War I], [they] did not realize that public diplomacy, in order to succeed, can only progress thanks to untold bargains that were even harder to confess than the traditional secrets of nations."[1] In other words, the treaty negotiators would have to follow the principles established long ago by Niccolò Machiavelli: "The rulers who have done great things are those . . . who have been skillful in cunningly confusing men,"[2] by creating different interpretations of new rules for different publics and by making sure that their audience remains unaware that some authors privately share a different understanding of these rules.

As Weiss emphasizes, the existence of two truths (one public and one private) is what differentiates opacity from secrecy.[3] As far as nuclear matters are concerned, opacity consists in publicly revealing the existence of a nuclear program and often the existence of an international trade agreement between an importer and an exporter of nuclear technologies, but characterizing these as purely "peaceful," and hiding some of the clearest military components. Nuclear opacity consists in revealing part of the truth, but not the whole truth. The choice between what remains secret and what is revealed is made to avoid public controversy about nuclear activities with a possible military dimension: either activities that have a military component, or activities that have a dual-use component—that is, some peaceful techno-scientific activities that are nonetheless suspect in the eyes of the international community, as they could easily be redeployed to fulfill a future military need.

The production of nuclear opacity thus involves what sociologists call "struggles of classification"[4] between foreign policy elites: in effect, diplomats produce nuclear opacity when they place the cursor that separates peaceful (and legally authorized under peaceful trade agreements) from military nuclear activities differently in public and in private.[5]

This chapter explores how nuclear opacity was produced in the case of another set of treaties proposed by Eurofederalists to regulate the flows of nuclear materials and technologies across the Atlantic, and what effect it had on US domestic power struggles. The opaque rules were contained in the following series of treaties (some of which were public, others secret): the Euratom Treaty, which was signed in March 1957, and ratified by all signatory states in December 1957; and the three treaties signed by Euratom and the Anglo-American nuclear allies of the Second World War (the United States, United Kingdom, and Canada), which recognized the Euratom Treaty and its institutions as valid instruments of international law. In the case of the United States–Euratom Treaty, upon which I focus in this chapter, the ratification process ended in November 1958. Other important treaties include the secret tripartite treaty of military nuclear cooperation signed by France, West Germany, and Italy in November 1957. The drafters of these treaties produced opacity by distinguishing the public from the confidential interpretations of the boundary between peaceful and military activities.[6]

This chapter demonstrates how practices that produced opacity facilitated the adoption of these new treaty rules in two sections. The first section describes how Euratom's opacity was produced in large part as a response to the power struggles between US foreign policy elites, which pitted proponents of a global and strict nonproliferation approach to the regulation of the nuclear trade against promoters of a Western approach centered around the loose regulation of nuclear trade between the United States and a newly formed European Community in charge of the nuclear trade (Euratom). This first section shows that the opacity that the Euratom treaty negotiators created concerned not only the rules operating within the jurisdiction of Euratom, but also its jurisdictional boundaries: publicly, Euratom was presented as a purely peaceful and supranational endeavor that easily turned Euratom into an instrument of "Cold War politics," as John Krige argues;[7] privately, Euratom was finally accepted by Europeans after it was reframed to fit with the French colonial policy with regard to the Arab world, as France hoped to use Euratom to gain a "military" advantage by cooperating in the development of dual-use and military nuclear activities with West Germany (and with the United States).

The second section describes how these public and private interpretations of the Euratom Treaty rules circulated among US foreign policy elites. It shows that the boundary between the private and public interpretations of the Euratom Treaty rules and jurisdiction was maintained in the United States thanks to the complicity of the US executive branch and Euro-federalists in Europe. In particular, the White House and State Department were instrumental in denying that there was any other interpretation of the jurisdiction of Euratom than the one defended in public by Jean Monnet, despite rumors to the contrary, and that both they and Euratom negotiators agreed on the point that separated peaceful from military activities in a nation's (or group of nations') nuclear development. Their policy of denial was key to convincing Congress to pass not only the United States--Euratom Treaty but also a broader reform of the transatlantic legal order that planned additional future cooperation between the United States and Europe in military nuclear activities. Opacity was key in two different respects to convincing US skeptics to support Euratom: opacity changed the public perception of Euratom's policy objectives (as compared to its authors' private interpretation), and it increased the perceived expectation of success of Euratom Treaty negotiations. Both consequences of opacity help explain why skeptics finally agreed to give Euratom a chance.

Reforming the Transatlantic Legal Framework
to Further Nuclear Trade

After 1954, following the legal reform of West Germany's status with regard to NATO, the liberalization of nuclear trade increased the proliferation risks in Western Europe. Various plans formulated by US foreign policy elites tried to reduce these risks, including a new plan that the Eurofederalists proposed in June 1955 to reform the 1954 Paris Agreements, and institute in their place a new European nuclear order.

Competing International Agendas in the US Field
of Foreign Policy (1954–56)

In November 1954, the West reconstituted Europe's nuclear legal order on the basis of interstate exchange between sovereign nation-states. In particular, the Paris Agreements raised most of the limitations on the production of fissile materials that had been imposed on West Germany by the occupying powers and greatly expanded nuclear trade between the United States and West Germany. The US government wanted to quickly sell reactors, in particular to the West Germans, who had been frustrated for ten years in their nuclear development. For instance, James Conant, the US ambassador to West Germany, praised the American-made Brookhaven reactor model (with a capacity forty times higher than the one authorized by the defunct EDC Treaty), which the United States presented during an industrial exhibition in Berlin in the winter of 1954.[8] When the Paris Agreements entered into force in May 1955, they therefore did away with the last obstacle to the beginning of cooperation between the United States and West Germany in the peaceful exploitation of nuclear energy of vast proportion, which would be controlled only by American and German inspectors, and not by any other European nations.[9]

The expected boom in the international trade of nuclear reactors was not restricted to Europe either. In parallel to the integration of West Germany into NATO, President Eisenhower declared that he would export peaceful nuclear technologies to other nations in Asia and Africa that wished to buy them from the United States.[10] This program, which he announced under the name "Atoms for Peace" before the UN General Assembly in December 1953, was made possible by a domestic legal reform, when in 1954 the US Congress passed a revision of the 1946 Atomic Energy Act (hereafter, the 1954 McMahon Act). The 1954 McMahon Act authorized the export of nuclear power plants that were rigorously clean or "proliferation-resistant" to the rest of the world: in particular, electricity-producing power plants using low-enriched uranium as fuel, as well as the low-enriched uranium necessary to fuel those plants. The export of sensitive technologies such as uranium-enrichment technologies and plutonium-reprocessing technologies, which the US Congress labeled "military" (or "dual-use," but certainly not just peaceful), was still prohibited. The Eisenhower administration had the full support of the US Congress: despite (and in line with) a strong record in nonproliferation policy, Congress agreed to the change in the 1954 McMahon Act under pressure from other Anglo-American nations, Canada and the United Kingdom, which were trying to export their peaceful technologies abroad. The AEC and US senators of the congressional Joint Committee on Atomic Energy (JCAE), to which the AEC chairman reported its activities, reasoned that the Anglo-Canadian governments might sell less proliferation-resistant technologies than the American government, or that less stringent controls would be applied.[11] Indeed, until proper international safeguards were established, the bilateral nuclear trade agreements specified that American inspectors from the AEC would inspect how the importing nations used the newly sold reactors as well as the low-enriched uranium necessary for their operation.

In light of the proliferation risks raised by the liberalization of the global nuclear trade, especially in the European context, various plans were discussed to strengthen the controls that the Paris Agreements placed on West German nuclear development, and on West German use of future US-imported technologies and nuclear fuels, which, according to West German scientists, "could not be excluded for much longer."[12] As the main nuclear exporter in Western Europe, the US government held a large influence over any proposal for a European or global control agency to inspect Europeans' use of their nuclear technologies and nuclear fuels, all of which were imported—no uranium-enrichment plant existed at the time in Continental Europe.

The first ambitious plan of international controls was defended by Lewis Strauss, the chairman of the AEC chosen by Eisenhower to secure the support of Republican nationalists in Congress. Responsible for the downfall of Oppenheimer in 1954, Strauss had initially been suspicious of leaving the task of controlling how nuclear importers would use the power plants sold by the United States to an international organization. But as the United States was increasingly competing with the Canadians and the British to win international markets for nuclear reactor technologies, Strauss feared that the Canadians and British would convince nuclear-importing states to buy their technologies instead of American technologies because they offered more lenient control procedures. Strauss thus promoted the idea that the International Atomic Energy Agency (IAEA)—a new agency that he proposed to fashion based on a classical interstate model reporting to the UN Security Council—would set global standards for security and inspection procedures for all nuclear-exporting states in the world, including in Western Europe (see fig. 5.1).[13] If all nuclear exporters accepted placing their exports under the same IAEA safeguards, it would level the playing field, as all buyers would have to agree to the same importing conditions.[14] The promoters of the IAEA approach thus gained an important victory when, in February 1956, the United States, the United Kingdom, and Canada agreed

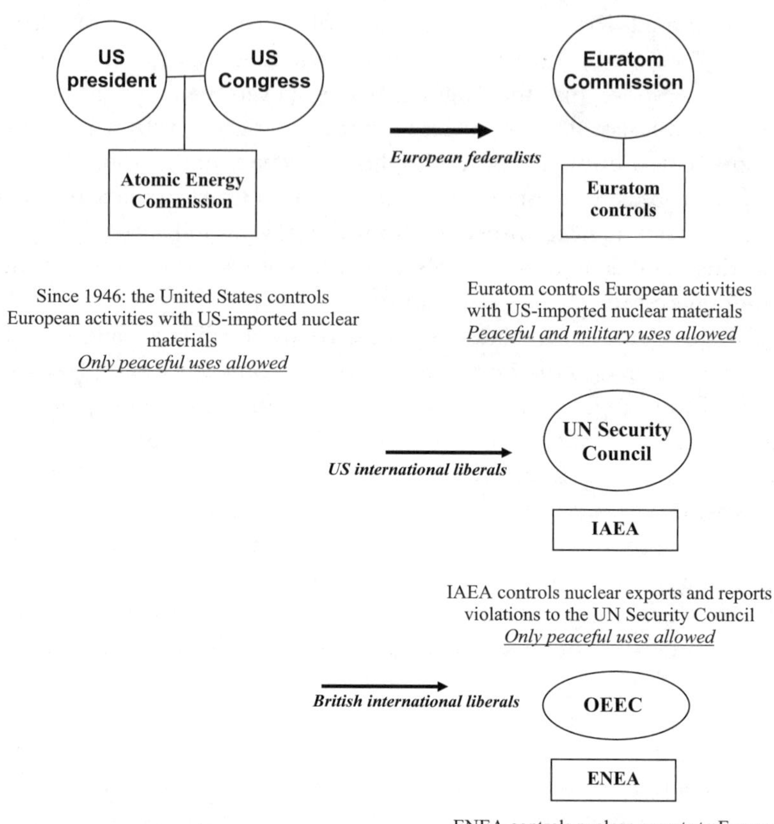

Figure 5.1. The solutions proposed for the control of European nuclear activities

to defend the same proposal for the IAEA Statute, whose function was limited to controlling how countries importing fissile materials and fuels used these materials. As Astrid Forland remarks, the IAEA Statute exempted nuclear exporters from IAEA controls, while it mandated that nuclear importers subject the construction of future power plants (such as those that the United States proposed to sell within the "Atoms for Peace" program) to being reviewed and authorized by the IAEA before their construction, as well as to being inspected after their construction.[15]

A second plan was proposed by the British government, which also hoped to control West German use of the technologies the British would sell them. The British proposed that West Germans agree to subject their use of peaceful nuclear technologies to the future control agency of a European organization rather than a global one: the OEEC, first created to administer the funds from the Marshall Plan (see fig. 5.1). With this plan, the British could hope to use one legal framework when dealing with Europe, and another one when dealing with their former colonies (such as India) and other Commonwealth member states. This proposal offered them the advantage of adopting the rules that best fitted their commercial interests in different regions rather than creating one global regime, as the Americans wished. Furthermore, in contrast to supranational European organizations such as the ECSC, the OEEC was a classical intergovernmental organization, which meant that each member state would remain free to decide the nature of its nuclear program. Thus, French Gaullists, such as Michel Debré, and the French scientists and administrators of the French CEA,[16] appreciated the flexibility offered by the British proposal.[17] The British could also count on the support of the German neoliberal followers of Ludwig Erhard, the minister of economy, who shared with the German industry the belief that the OEEC-type loose intergovernmental structure was preferable to any new plan of Eurofederalist inspiration or any global and discriminatory plan.[18] Thus, the British pursued this idea, which eventually led to the creation of a control agency in the OEEC, the European Nuclear Energy Agency (ENEA). But as neither the AEC nor the State Department had a strong interest in the OEEC approach, the US government did not plan to give its control rights over Europe's use of US-imported nuclear technologies and fuels to the OEEC, and the new organization remained peripheral in the transatlantic nuclear trade.

The third proposal for the control of Europe's nuclear activities (especially those using US-imported nuclear technologies) was put forward by the authors of the defunct EDC Treaty (see fig. 5.1). Eurofederalists close to Jean Monnet and Paul-Henri Spaak, the Belgian foreign minister who had created the ad hoc assembly in charge of writing Europe's federal constitution, felt that the fall of Pierre Mendès France's government in France in February 1955 provided a window of opportunity for the revival of the Eurofederalist ideal by applying it to regulate Europe's "peaceful" nuclear activities.[19] In the spring of 1955, they proposed a new treaty solely concerned with the regulation of atomic civilian industries (as opposed to the regulation of all armament industries and of the European armed forces): the Euratom Treaty. In May 1955, Spaak convinced the European chief executives to start immediate negotiations of both the Euratom and Common Market Treaties under his chairmanship. This negotiating body (hereafter, "the Spaak Committee") completed its work when both treaties were signed in March 1957.[20]

To make their plan appealing to the six European member states of the ECSC, Monnet had to convince the United States to sign (and ratify) a treaty of nuclear cooperation with the future Euratom Commission, in which the US Congress would agree to give Euratom the right to control European uses of US nuclear exports (see fig. 5.1). Unlike the OEEC, which Paul-Henri Spaak criticized as being "a bonus to national egoism,"[21] Euratom would have not only its own control agency but also a new supranational design ensuring the joint political control of Europe's "peaceful" nuclear development. Furthermore, Eurofederalists planed that this new community would inherit from its member states the right to contract among themselves and with Anglo-American nuclear-exporting states (legal sovereignty in the nuclear trade). Despite the anticipated opposition of French nationalists who had opposed the EDC Treaty on the grounds that it threatened France's state sovereignty, Monnet and Dulles believed that the future six Euratom member states would have a strong incentive to form this new European Community along supranational lines if the United States could be convinced to transfer its right of inspection to this European organization instead of to the IAEA.

The senators on the JCAE were not opposed to according Euratom certain rights, such as the right to control European nuclear activities, especially if Europeans defined such controls in a way similar to that of the AEC (which presently controlled how US exports were used), and if Europeans devoted their efforts to the acquisition of purely peaceful nuclear activities (and not dual-use activities, which could have a military purpose if redeployed).[22] Thus, nuclear trade with the Europeans would need to remain within the limits of a strict interpretation of the 1954 McMahon Act, according to which Congress could only allow technological cooperation with Europe that was restricted to the sale of "clean" US energy-producing power plants—that is, power plants that neither used nor produced nuclear materials that could be easily diverted for military uses (such as highly enriched uranium or plutonium).[23] They were willing to support Euratom rather than IAEA controls if and only if they could kill two birds with one stone: if they could limit the proliferation risks in Europe by ensuring that the main activity of Euratom would be the operation and maintenance of clean US power plants sold to Europe, and not the sensitive production of enriched uranium; and if they could further the commercial interests of the US nuclear industry, which would then benefit from the purchase of American reactors.[24] With these conditions, American senators would agree to respond positively to European concerns on the issue of control, and to delegate the right to control European activities to Euratom, rather than to the IAEA (whose control procedures were still under negotiation).

But the senators were under pressure from the campaign led by the AEC chairman in favor of the proposal to transfer US controls in Europe to the IAEA rather than to a highly hypothetical Euratom. Strauss repeatedly said to the senators that the AEC "assumed that there were as many doubtful characters involved in Euratom from the security standpoint as were to be found in France generally."[25] Thus, for Strauss, Euratom should not have been given any privilege in terms of controls over the IAEA, whose procedures needed to be defined for the whole world and not just for the non-European world.[26] At least, the senators should make sure of which technologies Euratom planned to acquire and develop before they agreed to transfer the control of nuclear activities on European soil to Euratom, as requested by the Europeans. Indeed, the Europeans might want to build an enrichment plant as part of Euratom, and then nothing would prevent them from enriching uranium both at low levels, to build fuel for their power plants, and at higher levels to build weapons-grade materials (especially if they had no external controls over their activities). The senators on the JCAE thus encouraged the AEC to explore the Euratom proposal, but to "propose cheap nuclear fuels [low-enriched uranium] to the Europeans in order to avoid that they produce these fuels by themselves."[27]

Fortunately for Spaak and Monnet, their Euratom proposal was immediately popular among the highest US authorities in the executive branch, especially the president and his secretary of state. Dulles appreciated the fact that Euratom would remain a Western European organization: he did not want to submit Europe's nuclear activities to the control of the IAEA (as in Strauss's plan), as a global approach would open West German nuclear sites to Soviet and East German inspectors working (and spying) on behalf of the IAEA. Dulles told Eisenhower of his dislike for using the proposed IAEA to control the use of US nuclear fuels exported to Western Europe and elsewhere: "If the Soviets matched us in money, they would have an equal voice in picking the people [e.g., inspectors], and that in this way, Soviet agents might get into neutral countries under conditions more dangerous than if they went directly as Soviet technicians instead of under cover of the United Nations."[28] For Dulles, it was of particular import that the United States chose a European agency designed according to Euro-federalist (rather than interstate) principles to replace the AEC as the legitimate organization in charge of controlling Europe's use of US-imported nuclear technologies. Dulles's support of Euratom was key in convincing

Eisenhower "that the only thing which would really be adequate would be a close political integration of the West European continental countries."[29]

When presenting the alternatives to Eisenhower, Dulles remarked that "various other institutions, like NATO and the OEEC, contribute to European cooperation but not to supranationality,"[30] whereas the Euratom Commission would be granted the exclusive right to introduce proposals for Europe's nuclear development before the Council of Ministers, which meant that the commission had a right of veto over any future legislation to be presented.[31] Also, Monnet planned that the Council of Ministers would take some decisions by qualified majority voting, which meant that future legislation on nuclear issues could result from a consensus of the three big states (France, West Germany, and Italy), or two big and two small states (Netherlands and Belgium).[32]

Quite quickly, Eisenhower agreed with Dulles that "if the six countries set up an integrated institution possessing effective control and inspection authority in the field of peaceful uses of atomic energy, control over military uses of atomic energy by these six countries would be simplified," and such a "success would bring the incalculable political and psychological advantage of tying Germany more firmly into a West European Community."[33] As John Krige writes, Dulles and other "senior officials in the administration instrumentalized America's scientific and technological advantage . . . in an attempt to build a supranational institution that embodied its foreign policy agenda in the European theater and, derivatively, to advance America's commercial opportunities in the nuclear power sector."[34]

To slow down the campaign led by Lewis Strauss in favor of the IAEA, Dulles promised Europeans that, should they sign the Euratom Treaty, the United States would then sign a bilateral treaty with Euratom, as if Euratom were a single nation-state.[35] But Jean Monnet identified the main obstacle to the advance of European negotiations of the Euratom Treaty: Strauss's proposed bilateral contracts through which he intended to sell to West European nations some electricity-producing nuclear power plants safeguarded first by the United States and then by the IAEA. Thus, Monnet urged Robert Bowie and John Foster Dulles to delay the signing of US bilateral contracts of nuclear cooperation in Europe,[36] especially with West Germany. Jean Monnet and René Mayer, the former French president of the council who succeeded Monnet as head of the High Authority after Monnet left his job at the ECSC, told John Foster Dulles that "if the Germans thought they could get a bilateral, they would prefer it to an integrated approach,"[37] and they might try to convince Dulles that proper controls should then be established within the OEEC or IAEA framework. Yet, the secretary of state told Monnet and Mayer that even though "the U.S. would like to have the six-power approach" to nuclear trade, the United States could not "be coercive," and could not "indefinitely be negative toward bilateral proposals [between the United States and individual European states] if there [wa]s no integrated proposal."[38] Indeed, in Strauss's own words, "[the] AEC objected to any U.S. foot-dragging on bilateral negotiations" with West Germans who wanted to buy American nuclear power plants under the Atoms for Peace Program.

Monnet had to help the US president delay Strauss's proposal to sell American power plants to West Germans safeguarded by the IAEA by quickly fleshing out their alternate plan. Otherwise, the negotiations would be stuck in a vicious circle: the absence of a European plan emerging from the intergovernmental negotiations led by Spaak would empower Strauss's approach to nuclear trade and nuclear nonproliferation, which would then lessen the interest of the West Germans toward the Euratom approach. To break the circle, Monnet and Spaak chose to conduct negotiations along two tracks: one public, which could rapidly give the appearance of a consensus; and one private, during which private disagreements could be addressed more slowly (and sometimes in a direction opposite to the public consensus).

Euratom in the Two Tracks of Negotiation (Summer 1955–Fall 1956)

The organization of two different European tracks of negotiation empowered the supporters of Euratom against their adversaries in the US field of foreign policy in at least two different ways: first, the public support from which Euratom benefited thanks to Monnet's public campaign increased the perceived odds that Euratom Treaty negotiations would be successful; second, Monnet's public presentation of the goals changed how Euratom was perceived by US policy makers. In that sense, the decoupling between the public and private interpretations of Euratom's objectives created a charade that made it credible that Euratom would tie all of Europe's "peaceful" nuclear development to the United States, at the same time as it allowed Europeans to secretly agree that Euratom would also further their joint cooperation in dual-use and military activities, respectively inside and outside Euratom.

Nuclear opacity was produced thanks to the creation of two negotiating tracks: while private negotiations between governments were conducted in the Spaak Committee, the public presentation of Euratom was left for Monnet to make. To that end, Monnet resigned as president of the

High Authority in 1955,[39] and in the fall of that year he created the "Action Committee for the United States of Europe" (hereafter, Action Committee), which federated the leading parliamentary representatives of the major political parties of each of the six European countries (the socialists, social democrats, liberals, and Christian democrats), and the leaders of the major trade unions.[40] Monnet benefitted from the credit of the Eurofederalist cause among US foreign policy elites: the activities of the Action Committee were funded and promoted by John McCloy, who, as chairman of the Ford Foundation, "could not become involved in political matters, but could help Monnet have a staff of research assistants, and they could do the research upon which Monnet could base some of his concepts and policies."[41]

From the rejection of the EDC Treaty, Monnet and the Eurofederalists concluded that they needed to involve European parliamentarians earlier in the private treaty negotiations. This conclusion did not mean that the Eurofederalists invested a lot of time in defending their treaty in the realm of public opinion. Rather, they only needed to lobby parliamentary opinion, as the ratification procedure was by parliamentary vote.[42] With the founding of the Action Committee, Monnet could now ensure that parliamentarians' demands for clarification of future treaty rules would not unsettle the secret compromises made during the treaty-drafting process. Monnet insisted that the resolutions passed in the Action Committee would have a binding effect on the committee participants: the European parliamentary leaders who passed resolutions in the Action Committee committed their parties to voting in favor of the same resolution in parliament. This institutional mechanism ensured that the precedent created by the EDC Treaty would not repeat itself: that a treaty signed by the French coalition in power would fail to be ratified when presented at the National Assembly.

Monnet thus turned the group of Eurofederalists into a recognizable public force, whose influence on parliamentary opinion could convince skeptics that the Euratom Treaty had a chance of being signed and ratified one day, and that it was worth waiting to see whether Europeans would agree to institute a tight system of control increasing the perceived odds of success for the new treaty negotiations. The creation of the Action Committee allowed Dulles and the State Department to convince US congressional leaders that a Euratom Treaty conforming to Eurofederalist ideals of supranationality would come out of the European negotiations, and that they should thus wait to sign a bilateral treaty between the United States and Euratom rather than immediately signing a bilateral treaty with West Germany, as Lewis Strauss proposed. To make this charade credible, Monnet introduced a first resolution in October 1955 to the members of the Action Committee. European parliamentarians voted on three questions: "Shall the new Euratom Community follow essentially peaceful goals?" the answer to which was "yes"; "Shall this new authority have a supranational character?" again "yes"; and last, "How shall this new authority contract relationships with her member-states?" the answer to which was "without any discrimination."[43] This resolution appeared to solve the Franco-German disputes over the discrimination that France's desire for nuclear weapons entailed, and it allowed Eurofederalists to give the impression to Lewis Strauss that negotiations inside the Spaak Committee were well on their way to a satisfactory solution for the tenets of a strict nonproliferation policy in Europe.

The public declarations sponsored by the Action Committee had another effect on US perception of Euratom's future goals: they gave the (wrong) impression that Euratom's main goal was to strengthen Europe's nonproliferation regime, whereas Euratom negotiators had already agreed that Euratom would do little to prevent nuclear armament in Europe, particularly in France. Indeed, at the same time as politicians in Monnet's group made these declarations, governmental officials in the Spaak Committee privately planned to leave every West European nation sovereign regarding the activities it developed on its own, without outside help. They agreed that in order to avoid repeating the same mistakes made by the EDC Treaty promoters, which had infuriated French nationalists, the Euratom Treaty should not have jurisdiction over activities that its future member states would regard as "military."

In particular, the French nuclear scientists serving as experts on the Spaak Committee made it clear that Euratom could not extend its jurisdiction to indigenous nuclear activities that France developed to further its acquisition of nuclear weapons: they opposed, from the beginning, the creation of a European common nuclear stock, which would hand over to Euratom the ownership of all of France's nuclear technologies and fissile materials (as previously planned by the EDC Treaty),[44] because such pooling of all French fissile materials under Euratom ownership would doom the creation of a French nuclear force. The new head of the French government, Guy Mollet (a socialist deeply attached to the defense of France's imperial sovereignty in Algeria), had given French experts on the Spaak Committee a clear mandate on this issue: Mollet had assured the French parliamentarians that "Euratom will not be an obstacle toward the possible decision for France . . . to build nuclear weapons."[45] As long as Euratom risked becoming such an obstacle, Mollet would not push in its favor. The French experts in the Spaak Committee thus argued that while the Euratom Commission could propose five-year plans, it was not meant to replace national planning agencies, such as the powerful CEA in France.[46] As the report of the experts on the Spaak Committee later stated, "To ease development, the Commission shall give indicative goals (rather than controlled and fixed objectives)," and "national nuclear programs will remain under the responsibility of national executives, in particular to the extent it matters for the production of energy."[47] To ensure that national governments would continue to support Euratom, in the fall of 1955, the French advisors on the Spaak Committee also ruled out the possibility that Euratom would directly tax internal nuclear trade to fund its own program, and they decided that the budgets of Euratom, unlike those of the ECSC, were to be voted on a yearly basis by the Council of Ministers.

In fact, participants in the Spaak Committee agreed that the goals of Euratom would be primarily concerned with regulating the global flow of nuclear materials between Europe and its Anglo-American allies rather than with the national production of energy generated by nuclear fission (see fig. 5.2). They agreed that the goals of Euratom should be three: to promote West European nuclear trade with Anglo-American nations; to facilitate the acquisition of fissile materials, in particular the "extraction of uranium and thorium"; and to exchange "engineering knowledge on reactor development" and "scientific knowledge"[48] among Europeans and between Europeans and Americans. Among the new powers granted to this European organization, the Americans would give the right to control nuclear activities to the future Euratom Commission and its control agency, and West European nations would give to the Euratom Commission and its supply agency—the Euratom Supply Agency (ESA)—the exclusive right to contract with the outside. In exchange, they accepted that some decisions, such as those concerning a future joint program of research and development that Euratom would conduct with third parties such as the United States, could be made by a vote of a qualified majority (art. 215). Overall, these provisions were a far cry from the supranational rules of the defunct EDC Treaty, which reflected the large influence wielded by the experts from the CEA in the Messina committee (Pierre Guillaumat, Francis Perrin, Bertrand Goldschmidt, and Jean Renou).

Still, even after Euratom's jurisdiction was limited in such a way, the deliberations in the Spaak Committee stumbled on the problem of discrimination created by the French desire to acquire nuclear weapons. The insistence that France would remain free to develop its nuclear-weapons program outside (in parallel to) Euratom created a problem for West Ger-

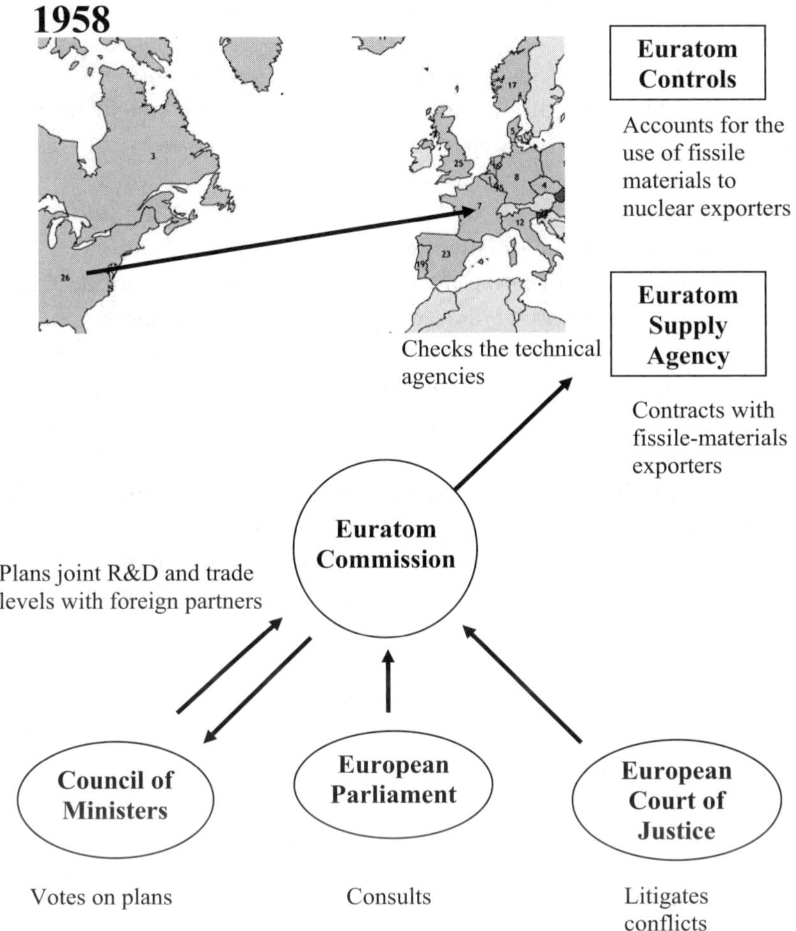

Figure 5.2. The emergence of a new European nuclear trading partner

many. On the one hand, the West Germans were only too happy to clearly limit the jurisdiction of Euratom to foreign nuclear trade, because, as the French ambassador to Bonn wrote to the French foreign minister, "The reservations and hostility that diverse German economic *milieux* express toward the new project of Euratom" proceed from the belief that "it is a bad method to subject the economy to a political logic."[49] On the other hand, the Germans believed that "it was not fair to impose unity if the . . . supranational authority does not give the same chances to all member-states"[50]—in particular, if the French were allowed to pursue a nuclear-weapons program when the West Germans had pledged not to produce nuclear weapons.

In order to avoid creating a permanent discriminatory system, the French should have either agreed to let West Germany benefit from the same liberty to conduct indigenously (with no foreign help) the nuclear activities it desired (even military ones), or agreed to renounce their own nuclear-weapons program.[51] But the French refused both conditions. As a result, Euratom would permanently leave West Germany without the national ownership of any fissile material, while it gave some to the French (those fissile materials that France declared for military purposes): indeed, Euratom promoters planned that fissile materials used for peaceful ends would remain permanently the property of and under the jurisdiction of the new Euratom Community, while the fissile materials declared for military uses would remain under the jurisdiction and property of the nation-states.[52] Chancellor Adenauer and his foreign minister found this differential treatment unacceptable, and anticipated that France would quickly declare most of its activities military in order to escape Euratom controls and ownership.[53] This disagreement plagued the negotiations of the Euratom Treaty until October 1956.

Private pressures were exercised by the State Department to bring the West Germans to compromise.[54] For instance, when Dulles was informed that "the Germans have opposed Euratom largely on grounds of economic doctrine,"[55] since Minister of the Economy Ludwig Erhard did not want to give the ownership of fissile materials to a public authority, as the provision was too reminiscent of socialism for German liberals, Dulles wrote to the US ambassador, James Conant, to ask him "to make it clear to the Europeans that the Department wants to encourage Europeans to establish federal institutions" and "to press the priority of U.S.-Euratom relationship over German-U.S. relationship and OEEC approach to Adenauer."[56] After meeting with Monnet and then with Adenauer, Conant later reported to Dulles that Adenauer had come to "agree [that] it was absurd that some Germans pretended to be against government ownership when U.S. deep commitment [to the] private enterprise system has lately reaffirmed government ownership of fissile materials." As a result of these pressures, Conant believed that the Germans were "ready to yield"[57] on this issue, but other contentious issues such as the discrimination between France and Germany remained unresolved.

As there was no agreement in sight between the French and German participants to the intergovernmental negotiations, the only thing that Spaak could do was to leave the matter privately unresolved and open to future interpretation, in the hope that West Germans would come to accept some discrimination by allowing France to conduct military activities outside Euratom. Indeed, in the spring of 1956, the Spaak Committee concluded that "a solution had to be found that did not preclude indefinitely the military uses of atomic energy," but that it was "wise not to raise the problem of military uses"[58] when discussing the impact of the treaty in public. But in the summer of 1956, more than a year after the beginning of negotiations, Adenauer still refused to give France the right to claim national ownership of nuclear materials it declared to be for military use. No solution was in sight. Therefore, despite the appearance of consensus among members of the Action Committee, most of the French participants on the Spaak Committee (such as CEA administrator Francis Perrin) believed "to the end that [Euratom] negotiations would fail, then that the treaty would not be ratified."[59]

Monnet's public campaign in favor of Euratom helped the US advocates of Euratom (in particular, President Eisenhower and his secretary of state) delay alternative solutions to the stabilization of Europe in the context of a nuclear boom (in particular, the establishment of the IAEA's system of control).[60] By raising the perceived expectation that Euratom negotiations would be successful, it bought more time for the private negotiations to finally lead to a real breakthrough, which occurred when France finally conceded that West Germany could be given almost the same liberty as France to conduct military nuclear activities in parallel to the Euratom Treaty framework. The French government abruptly changed its position in October 1956 as a result of events in Egypt that followed the forced nationalization by Egyptian president Gamal Abdel Nasser of the Suez Canal, a private company owned by French and British investors. In response, the British and French governments asked the Israelis to enter into Egyptian territory, which would then trigger the parachuting of French and British "peacekeeping" forces into the Suez Canal region. The planned two-step invasion followed Mollet's general strategic thinking about the role that France and the United Kingdom should play in the Arab world, as Mollet saw in the union between the United Kingdom and France the only way for both metropolises to save their empire (with Israel playing a role as a Western-type democracy).[61] The plan that was launched worked until Eisenhower and Dulles, shocked that they hadn't been informed, threatened to stop supporting the British pound and forced the British government to withdraw from the operation. For Eisenhower and Dulles, the secret scheme proved that old European powers would still behave in an uncontrollable and opaque manner outside the European battlefield and in their former mandates, at a time when their troops and political energy were most needed in Europe.[62]

When the episode ended with the British and French retreat, Guy Mollet and his foreign minister, Christian Pineau, observed that if France could not enlist the support of Anglo-American allies, it should now form a nuclear alliance with the West Germans and other West European nations on the Continent—as well as with Israel, whose government had followed the script prepared by Eden and Mollet with respect to the Suez invasion.[63] The Suez crisis proved to Mollet that the United Kingdom would not go as far as the French wanted in order to defeat Nasser, who was identified by the French as a key supporter of the Algerian guerrillas, and that the United Kingdom would always follow Washington against Paris. The Suez crisis thus convinced Mollet to finally deal with the West Germans (and the Israelis) as equal partners, almost, even on nuclear matters. Mollet no longer saw the nuclear association with the Germans within Euratom as an obstacle to the preservation of the French Empire, but as a way to strengthen it.[64]

The Suez crisis thus removed the obstacles that had long blocked the Spaak Committee negotiations. Indeed, for France, Euratom would no longer be only an instrument of Cold War politics, as John Krige argues, but, more important, a part of the French imperial policy with regard to the Arab world: a nuclear association with West Germany within Euratom would complement the new nuclear association that France agreed to form with Israel.[65] France intended to use the Euratom Treaty framework to indirectly develop military applications of nuclear energy in parallel, and it finally agreed to allow West Germany to do the same. In October 1956, at the height of the Suez crisis, during negotiations in the Spaak Committee, the French foreign minister told his West German counterpart, Von Brentano, and his aide Walter Hallstein, the future president of the Common Market Commission, that the French not only were considering sharing information on dual-use nuclear technologies such as enrichment technologies (which all Euratom negotiators included within the scope of "peaceful" technologies under Euratom jurisdiction, in contrast to the US Congress), but that the French government was also considering "an exchange of information about procedures and patents, including those relating to production for military purposes."[66] As Hallstein said, this was a dramatic reversal of policy on the part of France. Indeed, until now, the German minister had vainly expressed "German concerns about the possibility that some nations would use the notion of 'military secret' to arbitrarily limit the exchange of information between member-states."[67]

After Suez, the French minister of foreign affairs not only agreed to clearly limit the definition of "military activities accepted by Euratom member-states solely to the fabrication of nuclear warheads."[68] But as this definition of military activities still included a discrimination between France and West Germany (even limited to the design of the nuclear warhead), which was still "unacceptable"[69] to the German minister, the French also proposed to open to the West Germans a collaboration in such military activities (e.g., the design of such warheads) outside of Euratom. The West Germans preferred this solution to the initial proposal by the French minister to let the Euratom Commission, instead of France, delimit the boundary between peaceful and military activities.[70] The Germans had refused to let the future Euratom Commission define the line between military and peaceful nuclear activities (which would have constituted an insufferable ambiguity), as they feared that the president of the commission, a Frenchman,[71] would arbitrate in favor of France in Franco-German disputes.[72] Only the signing of this secret agreement with France, which guaranteed that France would agree to cooperate on nuclear military activities with West Germany in parallel to Euratom, reassured the Germans that France did not intend to refuse its European partners information that the French deemed military.[73]

The French promise of October 1956 was realized when, on January 17, 1957, France and West Germany signed secret agreements planning military cooperation in the nuclear field in Colomb-Béchard, in a post symbolically situated outside of Europe, in the middle of the Algerian Sahara, at a time when the war in Algeria escalated with the beginning of the battle of Algiers. The French minister of defense at the time, Maurice Bourgès-Maunoury, signed the Colomb-Béchard agreement on behalf of France at the same time as he decided to dispatch thousands of paratroopers to control Algiers.[74] The signing of this secret treaty cleared the way for the signing of the Euratom Treaty a month later: the agreement committed France to share with West Germany information on nuclear processes that could be characterized as falling within the military domain and thus outside the jurisdiction of Euratom. Its extension to Italy on November 25, 1957, a month before the Euratom Treaty was ratified by all six European nations, made it clear that France did not intend to unduly exclude its two main Euratom partners from sharing information on dual-use and military nuclear activities: the tripartite European agreements of November 1957 "concerned, in order of priority, production in aeronautics, missile technologies, and the military applications of nuclear energy," and called on the three countries "to promote a joint program of weapons production leading to the standardization of weapons, the rationalization of the joint development of R&D centers and the rationalization of industrial capabilities for their fabrication."[75] For France and West Germany, these secret treaties not only formed the beginning of a military alliance that extended to nuclear cooperation, but they were also seen as essential steps leading to the conclusion of the deliberations of the Spaak Committee and the ratification of the Euratom Treaty.

The Use of Homonyms in International Law (October 1956–March 1957)

The tactic of opacity that European negotiators adopted to define the jurisdictional boundaries of the Euratom Treaty meant that their secret deals about the definition of the rules needed to be black-boxed in the public treaty. Otherwise, the US foreign policy elites in the AEC and JCAE who insisted on applying equally strict nonproliferation policies to Europe and to the non-European world might understand that Euratom also included activities falling under the heading of what the US Congress defined as "military." The Senate would then reject the prospect of leaving to Euratom the responsibility to control the uses of US-imported technologies in Europe. As Monnet's associate Max Kohnstamm said about the definition of the proposed Euratom controls on peaceful nuclear activities, the acceptance of such European exceptionalism by Congress would constitute a "revolutionary act" for US foreign policy, and Congress would do so only if it believed that Euratom controls served nonproliferation purposes.[76]

To make this revolutionary act possible, legal expertise was mobilized inside the Spaak Committee not to clarify the meaning of the Euratom Treaty but to obscure the meaning of key rules, so that Monnet's presentation of Euratom as purely peaceful and supranational would remain credible (see table 5.1). Euratom negotiators used words such as *control* and *property*, which were perfect homonyms with the words that the US senators wanted to read in the Euratom Treaty, but whose meanings were quite different. On the divisive issue of whether all fissile materials used in Europe for peaceful purposes would be the "property" of Euratom, West Germany appeared to make a compromise by agreeing in October 1956 that "special fissionable materials shall be the property of the Community, and that this right of ownership shall extend to all special fissionable material produced by a member state" (art. 86).[77] But as Couve de Murville, the French ambassador to West Germany, noted, this notion of property was defined "as a 'property *sui generis*,' an old notion which differed from the

Table 5.1   The Euratom Treaty interpreted by insiders and outsiders

Euratom Treaty	Interpretation given to US AEC	What was left out
The function of the Euratom controls	Monnet/Kohnstamm: Commission checks that real uses are peaceful (similar to that of the AEC or IAEA)	Spaak Committee negotiations: Checks that real uses are the ones declared to the agency (be they military or peaceful)
	Euratom article 77: Commission "shall satisfy itself that provisions relating to safe-guarding obligations assumed by the Community with a third state or an international orga-nization are complied with"	Euratom article 84: "In application of safeguards, no discrimination shall be made on grounds of the use for which ores and fissile materials are intended"
The scope of Eura-tom's ownership of nuclear fuels	Monnet/Kohnstamm: Euratom ownership extends to all the nuclear materials circulating within the territory of Euratom	Spaak Committee negotiations: Euratom ownership does not extend to military materials, co-owned by the French, West Germans, and Italians
	Euratom article 86: "Special fissile materials shall be the property of the Community"	Euratom article 87: "Member-states and persons shall have the unlimited right of use and consumption of special fissile materials which have properly come into their possession"
	Euratom article 198: Euratom Treaty applies in "Eu-ropean" and "non-European" territory	
The function of the European Supply Agency	Monnet/Kohnstamm: The agency will have a mo-nopoly on the supply of fissile materials after ten years	Spaak Committee negotiations: The agency does not have a monopoly on supply
	Euratom article 52(2): The agency shall have the "right of option" and "the exclusive right to conclude contracts relating to the supply of ores of fissile materials" inside the community or with third parties	Euratom article 68: If the agency cannot deliver ores or fissile materials "in reasonable time" or at "higher prices" than those obtained by member-states, then "us-ers have the right to contract directly with the outside"
Techno-scientific program	The Three Wise Men: Euratom buys and operates US nuclear power plants	The Tripartite Agreements of November 1957 and April 1958: Research and development in nuclear dual-use activities and especially uranium enrichment
		Euratom article 215 + annex V: High-flux reactors, naval pro-pulsion, and any new program proposed by the commission and adopted by qualified ma-jority voting by the council

common notion in Roman Law, since the [ownership] of fuels by the Euratom Community granted no rights to its owner [Euratom] during normal times."[78] In normal times, private or public companies with research and development programs and industrial applications of nuclear energy could use these fissile materials as they wished (they were free to sell, store, or use them, etc.). Only if they were proved guilty of illicit activities (by the Euratom Control Agency) could the Euratom Commission reclaim its latent ownership of these fuels.[79] Euratom thus had the legal ownership of fissile materials, while in practice leaving all the property rights to the (West German, French, Italian, etc.) private companies or state institutions that used the fuels.[80]

This use of homonyms enabled the authors of the Euratom Treaty to agree privately on one interpretation of the rules of the treaty, while not acknowledging this interpretation in public. When, in January 1957, the foreign minister of France explained to the US secretary of state that had France insisted on keeping ownership of fissile materials, the French would have "found themselves in the equivocal position of being the leading proponent of Euratom's ownership of fissile material and at the same time the only country to request exception to such ownership."[81] Dulles saw the merits of the compromise reached: if Dulles did not mind that the ownership (or actual property rights) of nuclear fuels circulating in West Germany would be de facto private and national but de jure public and supranational,[82] he and other Eurofederalists feared that the US Congress would reject the future United States–Euratom Treaty if this understanding was written clearly in the treaty. Max Kohnstamm, Monnet's former assistant at the ECSC, who became the vice president of the Action Committee, wrote, "[The] fact that Euratom can institute a federal control on imported fissile materials is a weighty argument [in favor of ratification by the US Congress]; but it would significantly lose its influence if nuclear fuels were privately owned in Europe—something that neither Democrats nor Republicans have yet accepted in the U.S."[83]

The opacity of the definitions of property was related to the opacity of the notion of controls (see table 5.1). On that subject, Max Kohnstamm said, "The possible substitution of Euratom controls for American control [of imported nuclear fuels] would be in itself a revolutionary act in the foreign policy of the U.S.," and "it is not completely certain that the U.S. Congress will oppose a Euratom system of control; but if it differs from theirs, it seems next to impossible."[84] Eurofederalists anticipated that the French and German agreement on the question of controls would be problematic for Congress because the Spaak Committee defined control as a "control of conformity":[85] the Euratom control agency would have the responsibility of verifying the conformity between the "real" and "declared" uses of nuclear fuels (be they civil or military uses) of the firms and research institutions. The duty of the Euratom control agency was not to ensure that member states or firms would refrain from using fissile materials for military ends. Rather, if French (or Franco-German) installations declared that they used nuclear fuels for military ends, the control agency could only verify (up to a certain point) that these military uses were indeed the real uses.

This definition of control, as a control of conformity, therefore departed from the definition of its homonym, *control*, as adopted by the United States in its signed bilateral agreements of cooperation and import agreements with third parties. Both US controls within the Atoms for Peace program and the future IAEA controls that Lewis Strauss had in mind were indeed "controls of finality": the American AEC engineers (soon to be replaced by IAEA inspectors) were to verify that real end uses were not military in nature. To hide these differences in definition, the European negotiators in the Spaak Committee obscured the meanings of the term *control*[86] in a manner similar to how the meaning of *property* had been rendered opaque (see table 5.1). Here again, the West Germans appeared to compromise with French demands regarding controls, by accepting that all of their activities fall under the control of the Euratom Commission. But as Couve de Murville concluded, "If Germany made concessions on the question of control and property, it is because control is inevitable. Indeed, in the case of delivery of American fissile material, the right of control kept by the U.S. authority on these fuels would not disappear if another authority were not in charge of controls."[87]

Furthermore, the type of control that the West Germans accepted with Euratom was more favorable to them than either the bilateral control that the US Congress would put in place if West Germany purchased US power plants within the framework of the Atoms for Peace program or the future controls that the IAEA proposed on imported materials. For instance, in the absence of the Euratom Treaty, the United States had a "right of pursuit": the nonproliferation provisions imposed by nuclear exporters "pursued" the fissile materials wherever they might go after being first sold abroad. For instance, materials sold to one country for peaceful purposes (for instance, Italy or Germany) and then sold again to France could not be reprocessed to be used eventually in French nuclear warheads. In February 1956, when the United States, the United Kingdom, and Canada (three exporters of nuclear fuels) met to draft their proposed statute for the IAEA, they agreed to inscribe in the statute the "right of pursuit" of plutonium and other fuels in IAEA-assisted projects, which meant that the IAEA maintained the right to verify the peaceful use of the materials once sold with IAEA assistance, even after their decomposition into plutonium as waste.[88] As Astrid Forland aptly defines it, "The right of pursuit was the expression used to communicate that the safeguarding of fissile materials produced as a result of IAEA assistance (or bilateral assistance) should cover not only first-generation produced material but subsequent generations as well."[89] That constraint was exactly the one that the planned United States–Euratom bilateral agreement sought to overthrow by delegating the control of European nuclear activities to the Euratom Commission: once materials entered the territory of Euratom, they could be used as the user wished, and in the manner declared to the Euratom Commission. If France bought from Italy or Germany fissile materials originally purchased from the United States, France could use them for military purposes.

The same tactic was followed to define the Euratom rules on the procurement of nuclear fuels and fissile materials. In the end, the French agreed to let the Germans limit the jurisdiction of the Euratom Supply Agency (see table 5.1).[90] As Bertrand Goldschmidt, the French representative of the CEA interviewed by the Spaak Committee, wrote, "The French representatives, influenced by Monnet, set out the principles of Community priority in the supply of nuclear materials, with equal access to all member states, . . . with a view to possible uranium shortages in the community, . . . and in the hope that France would be able to gain access to some part of the Belgian production when the Anglo-Saxon sales contracts came to an end in 1960."[91] But the West Germans believed that Euratom member states should recover their full capacity to unilaterally buy nuclear fuels outside the community in times of crisis.[92] In October 1956, as the Suez crisis was unfolding, the West Germans won their case: the French agreed that in times of fuel supply shortages, every nation would recover the right to contract unilaterally with nuclear fuel exporters in the manner it thought best.[93] This compromise considerably watered down the supranational aspects of the future supply agency, even though the letter of the Euratom Treaty appeared to say otherwise.[94] In the end, the French and West Germans had succeeded in turning a rigid instrument of Cold War politics sponsored by promoters of Eurofederalist ideals in the US government into a flexible instrument designed to enhance France's military imperial power thanks to Franco-German cooperation in nuclear weapons development.

The Circulation of the Secret and Public Interpretations of Euratom Rules in the US Field of Foreign Policy

Private and public interpretations of the jurisdictional boundaries of the Euratom Treaty (related to the interpretation of the boundary between peaceful and military activities) circulated within different circles in the United States during the ratification of the Euratom Treaty, which coincided with the negotiation period of the United States–Euratom Treaty. It was not evident whether these public and private interpretations were consistent. In fact, they were quite different.

The Technological Content and Jurisdiction of the United States–Euratom Treaty

In 1957, it was quite clear why Eurofederalists chose not to reveal publicly that the Euratom Treaty defined rules for all peaceful and dual-use nuclear activities in Europe while military nuclear activities fell under the scope of two treaties of military cooperation, first between France and West Germany (January 1957), then extended to Italy (November 1957). Western governments feared that the public revelation of the rules and jurisdictional boundaries defined by these treaties would likely bring a very adversarial reaction from the Soviet Union and its European satellites.

By using secret trilateral defense treaties to conceal their cooperation in military nuclear research, France, Germany, and Italy countered the attack of the Soviet Union, which routinely accused the future Euratom Treaty of hiding a Franco-German military "Junktim,"[95] both in the written press and during the sessions of the General Assembly of the IAEA.[96] In October 1957, in a last-ditch effort to derail the ratification of the Euratom Treaty, the Polish minister of foreign affairs even tried to reveal the military intentions of Western states by calling for the establishment of a nuclear-free zone in central Europe (including parts of Germany, Czechoslovakia, and Poland) before the UN General Assembly, at precisely the time when the three core members of Euratom (France, West Germany, and Italy) were secretly planning military nuclear cooperation. In the spring of 1958, with the West Germans rejecting the idea that East German teams of inspectors could enter their territory in search of nuclear weapons and nuclear installations,[97] the French and West German governments rejected the "Rapacki plan" for a nuclear-free zone, arguing that it would lead to the international recognition of Eastern Germany as a separate legal entity sanctioned by international law.[98]

But there were also good reasons related to the domestic situation in the US field of foreign policy that explained why Eisenhower and Dulles were informed of the global architecture formed by the Euratom Treaty and other secret treaties while most US policy makers, especially in the AEC and Congress, were not. Not only did Euratom promoters not want to destabilize the Soviet Union, but they also did not want to threaten the ongoing negotiations with the US AEC and US Congress, which also raised doubts about the jurisdictional boundaries of Euratom and the range of nuclear activities in which Euratom would invest its resources. Indeed, at the time the Euratom Treaty negotiations were about to end, after the Suez crisis, another source of controversy existed, this time between Europeans and Americans: the Europeans wanted to commit the AEC to providing the future Euratom member states with technological help that the US Congress characterized as military. Indeed, nuclear experts on the Spaak Committee claimed that the future Euratom Commission should make it a priority to invest in peaceful nuclear activities, but it included uranium-enrichment technologies among these. In particular, French specialists defended Euratom in Parliament on the basis that France would receive financial help for its enrichment program from future Euratom partners, and technical help from the United States through the future United States–Euratom agreement.[99]

The inclusion of uranium-enrichment activities at the center of the Euratom technological program discussed in the Spaak Committee could only alarm the US authorities concerned with nuclear proliferation in Europe. It was clearly militarily important for France to build up its enrichment program, which had run into significant technical difficulty and therefore delayed the French program of H-bomb (hydrogen bomb) production. It was also hard to see how such a Euratom program would be peaceful: at the time, France had no immediate civilian use for enriched uranium, since its power plants used natural (instead of enriched) uranium. That the French government wanted to use Euratom to acquire uranium-enrichment technology, for which it had no immediate civilian use, meant only one thing: that Euratom's enrichment program would not be used to produce nuclear fuels (for which uranium is enriched at low levels), but weapons-grade materials for H-bombs (for which uranium is enriched at high levels). Jules Guéron, whom the Spaak Committee put in charge of designing Euratom's research and development program, wrote, "France's European partners entertained no illusion about the military ambitions of such a project," due to the "simultaneous pressures by the French to build nuclear power plants using natural uranium as well as a uranium enrichment plant."[100]

The risk was great that the US Congress would refuse to ratify the future United States–Euratom Treaty if the Europeans stuck to their technological program. Then, the whole deal on the Euratom definition of "controls" (as control of conformity) made in the secrecy of the Spaak Committee would be threatened, as the US government would retain its control (of finality) over fissile materials exported to Europe.

Some Europeans, however, denied publicly that the goal of the Euratom enrichment plant was to produce highly enriched uranium for French nuclear weapons. Louis Armand, an engineer by training who presided over the reorganization of the French postwar scientific and industrial landscape,[101] initially defended Euratom precisely because the technical assistance that France would receive from the United States through the future United States–Euratom Treaty would help France move toward the development of a new generation of French power plants using low-enriched uranium (rather than natural uranium) as fuel.[102] Armand argued that the construction of a Euratom enrichment plant responded to a future peaceful technological need, if not a present one. As the price of low-enriched uranium on the international market was high, the operational costs of these power plants would be too high for the Europeans to continue buying the low-enriched uranium on the international market, justifying their need for domestic production.[103]

The economic justification given by Armand for the construction of a Euratom enrichment plant was not enough to convince US senators to help Europeans develop their project. In the spring of 1956, the secretary of state made a request (which was refused) to the AEC chairman and the JCAE[104] that in the future the AEC collaborate with Euratom "beyond legal limits" (the 1954 McMahon Act prohibited American cooperation in enrichment technologies) by helping Europeans develop their uranium enrichment within the Euratom Treaty framework. John Foster Dulles had hoped that such an exceptional gift by the US Congress would facilitate Euratom negotiations, which, at the time, seemed stuck. In late 1955, Bertrand Goldschmidt, the director of foreign relations of the CEA and a French expert sitting on the Spaak Committee, also pressed Dulles to specify whether the United States would consider maritime nuclear propulsion (which could be used to propel civilian oil tankers or military nuclear submarines) "peaceful" technology that the United States could help Euratom build; Dulles maintained that it would.[105] By promising to sell to Euratom some dual-use technologies not otherwise accessible to Europeans, Dulles hoped to convince the French to compromise with the Germans. But Lewis Strauss immediately opposed Dulles's proposal to sell enrichment technologies to future Euratom member states, and the proposal was abandoned. Strauss had American law on his side, and experts in the State Department knew that Congress was not ready to relax the laws on nuclear exports in enrichment technology, especially if the justification for its peaceful nature was as shaky as in France's case. In a conversation with Dulles, Gerard Smith, assistant to the secretary of state for atomic affairs, noted that even though he personally did not object to the project of a European enrichment plant, "such a plant would be dual-use, and thus Congress would never accept it."[106]

To test the credibility of French claims that the construction of a Euratom enrichment plant was economic and peaceful, Strauss finally proposed, and Eisenhower agreed in November 1956, substantially reducing the price of the low-enriched uranium sold by the United States on the world market—as a result, decreasing it to a third of the projected price of the nuclear fuel produced by the future European enrichment plant.[107] Eisenhower hoped to send to Europeans a signal that tensions with the US government were limited to the colonial policy of the Europeans, and did not affect the will of the US government to support the goal of federating European nuclear industries, even if it meant a huge drop in the benefits to US fuel manufacturers. Indeed, as Euratom Treaty negotiations advanced much faster in the Spaak Committee, Eisenhower and Dulles recommended "joint action by the AEC and the Department of State,"[108] to make sure that American congressional opinion would be prepared to give the US rights of control over European nuclear development to Euratom when the time came to negotiate the United States–Euratom Treaty.[109] But Eisenhower's decision also required Europeans to respond favorably to the new offer. Indeed, if uranium enrichment remained the official research and development program for Euratom, it was hardly credible that its only justification could be purely economic, and that its use would be purely "peaceful," as West European national leaders had claimed. If Europeans wanted to convince the US Congress that they only wanted to develop "peaceful" uses as defined by the US Congress, they had to commit future Euratom member states to buying proliferation-resistant power plants, and low-enriched uranium to fuel those plants, in the United States (at the new price).

At this point, Jean Monnet and the Action Committee intervened in order to minimize the risk of Congress's rejecting the opaque definitions of *property* and *controls* found in the Euratom Treaty. Monnet and the Action Committee "clarified" any ambiguities in, or potential objections to, the rules contained in Euratom in a way that pleased the senators in charge of evaluating the future United States–Euratom Treaty. Indeed, after Strauss convinced Eisenhower to decrease the price of low-enriched uranium in November 1956, Monnet used the funds provided to the Action Committee by the Ford Foundation to hire three nuclear specialists (the so-called Three Wise Men)[110] to draw up a new program for the future Euratom Community (see table 5.1).[111] The choice of Louis Armand as chairman of the Three Wise Men signaled to the AEC and the Senate that the decision regarding the new technological program for Euratom would follow a purely economic logic. And after the United States substantially decreased the price of US enriched uranium, Armand immediately claimed that the construction of the Euratom enrichment plant no longer made economic sense. Announcing his visit to the United States, Armand wrote to Dulles that "tackling our problems as Europeans, we can and must embark immediately on a massive atomic power program amounting to 15 million KW in the first five years," which could be achieved through the ratification of a bilateral treaty between the United States and Euratom planning for "1) the sale of five to six U.S. nuclear power plants to Euratom member-states; 2) the organization of a joint U.S.-Euratom R&D program in nuclear technologies; 3) the sale of fissile materials (enriched uranium and plutonium) to Euratom member-states; 4) and the substitution [transfer] of the control that the AEC exercised over these materials to the Euratom Control Agency."[112] Of course, the last point was dearest to the Eurofederalists. To achieve it, Armand and the other two Wise Men worked toward translating the technological program of the future Euratom Commission into a credible, yet completely peaceful, program of electricity production that appeared to have received the agreement of the French and West German governments, when in fact it did not impose any legal commitment on the future Euratom Commission, nor its member states.

The public charade that Monnet's emissaries wrote was aptly orchestrated in the United States with the help of the State Department (see fig. 5.3). At the beginning of 1957, Monnet sent the Three Wise Men and his assistant, Max Kohnstamm, to the United States,[113] where they were welcomed by Secretary Dulles to discuss their projected program with American nuclear specialists of the AEC and members of the JCAE: Senators Pastore, Anderson, Hickenlooper, Gore, and Cole.[114] There, so Armand claimed, Europeans preferred to buy the very expensive US power plants fueled with US low-enriched uranium rather than less costly British power plants fueled with natural uranium.[115] Armand said that according to his calculations, in the long term, the production of electricity would cost less if they used American power plants. Armand also said that the Europeans

Private negotiations

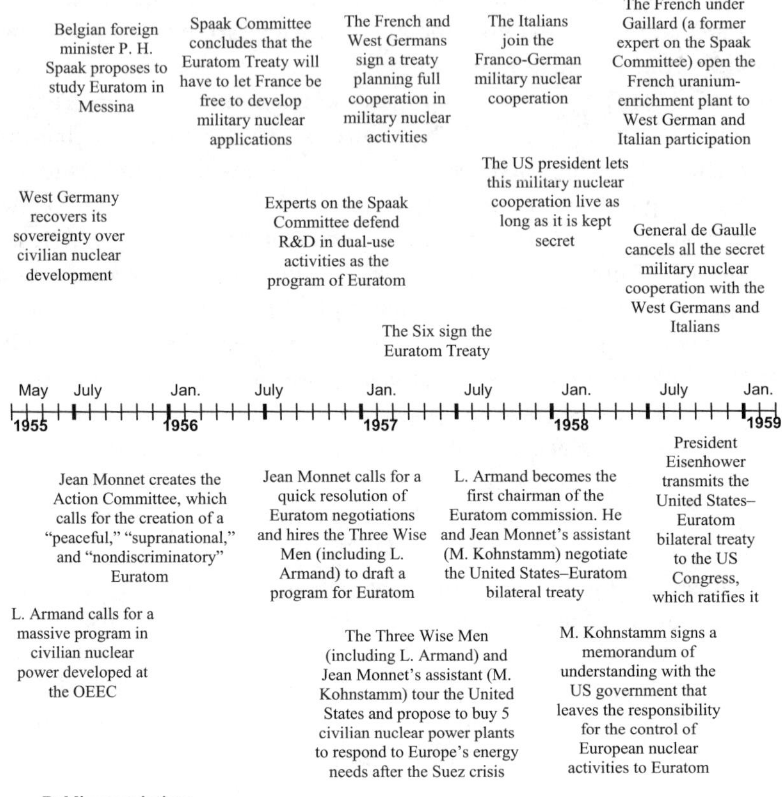

Public negotiations

Figure 5.3. History of negotiations in the Spaak Committee and Action Committee

agreed to buy the nuclear fuel for these plants from the United States if the Americans confirmed the November 1956 price of the low-enriched uranium sold by the AEC. Strauss agreed with the soundness of their plan and assured them that "the United States will be able to guarantee nuclear fuel procurement for Europe for the goal considered by the Three Wise Men."[116]

In the United States, the Three Wise Men and Monnet's assistant on the Action Committee also tried to maintain opacity over the definition of the Euratom control procedures. The Wise Men's visit to the United States coincided with the Spaak Committee secretly reaching consensus on the legal definition of Euratom control as control of conformity. This control of conformity opened the possibility for future Euratom member states to develop military applications of imported fissile materials, provided that the Euratom Commission knew about it. The Three Wise Men, led by Armand, followed Monnet and Kohnstamm's recommendations to tell the AEC that the Euratom Treaty would not change how European activities would be controlled.[117] In their letter to the secretary of state announcing their visit to the United States, the Three Wise Men wrote that "Euratom provides the essential system of control on lines closely analogous to those of the United States' AEC."[118] This was a plain lie, and Kohnstamm advised the Wise Men to avoid explaining how the system of Euratom control would work, but if pressed, to maintain the appearance of isomorphic equivalence and similarity between the AEC's and Euratom's control procedures.[119] Kohnstamm told them, "There is no doubt that the fact that Euratom does not exclude military uses of nuclear fuels will raise a sticky problem in future relations between the U.S. and Euratom. But if you are asked questions about that, just answer that so far, no bilateral treaty signed by the U.S. plans to limit the power of the importing state to own and produce nuclear weapons: the agreement between the U.S. and Euratom will not change this situation."[120] The interpretation of the Euratom controls given by Kohnstamm to the Americans was quite skewed: all American bilateral agreements signed by the United States with European nations were based on the US right of pursuit, meaning that the nuclear fuels and technologies imported from the United States should not be used to achieve military goals wherever they might go. The future United States–Euratom Treaty proposed to abrogate this right.

The Three Wise Men were instructed to systematically focus the deliberations away from the legal issues. Playing on the opacity of key notions (and their function as homonyms) in the text of the Euratom Treaty, they sought to give the impression that the Euratom Treaty set up a real federation, with exclusive "ownership" of all nuclear fuels in its territory, and with the right and duty to ensure that all nuclear fuels would be used for the exclusively peaceful program of electricity development that their projected technical program announced (see fig. 5.3). During their public meetings with Lewis Strauss and the Senate, when asked "if [the] Euratom watering-down process has not gone so far" as to make it impossible for Euratom to start a vast nuclear power program, Louis Armand replied that he and his colleagues had "seriously studied the treaty and were convinced that Euratom provided the necessary framework for joint action on the development of peaceful technologies."[121] After their meeting with the AEC, Max Kohnstamm reported to Jean Monnet that Paul-Henri Spaak's assistant told him that "we had greatly exaggerated the project, and that we prepared a great disillusion for the Americans when they see what's actually in the Treaty."[122] The idea that the Americans might become disillusioned after they signed a bilateral treaty with Euratom on Euratom's terms mattered less to Monnet and Kohnstamm than the possibility that the US Congress might refuse to ratify the United States–Euratom bilateral treaty at all, and that the AEC would retain its exclusive right of inspection in Europe.[123] To prove Euratom's peaceful character, to obfuscate its strategic consequences, and to facilitate the delegation of controls from the United States to Euratom, they focused discussions on the economic side of the arrangement and on the prospects of a financially advantageous deal for the AEC.

The interpretive tactics adopted by the Three Wise Men and the Action Committee led to the creation of opaque interpretations of the rules: rules that were interpreted in two distinct and contradictory ways depending upon the context in which the interpretation was made, and especially on whether the setting was confidential or public (see fig. 5.3). In June 1957, when the French nuclear scientist and soon-to-be first director of research and teaching for Euratom, Jules Guéron, visited the United States, he observed that Monnet's emissaries in the United States had succeeded in convincing both senators and US Atomic Energy commissioners that they "represented" Euratom in the sense of being its "spokesperson."[124] As he wrote, "Among all the Americans whom I met, three false ideas are shared by everyone: . . . the Three Wise Men represent the executive branch of Euratom [at a time when the Euratom Treaty was not ratified]; the report of the Three Wise Men is the official program of Euratom; and the Euratom Commission is comprised of the Three Wise Men."[125] The fact that the Three Wise Men were nominated to represent Euratom abroad by the parliamentary leaders of Europe represented on Monnet's Action Committee occasioned such confusion.[126]

The complicity of the White House and State Department was essential to effectively maintain the credibility of the public charade crafted by the Three Wise Men. In 1957 and 1958, as the Three Wise Men's report became the object of public scrutiny and criticism from US and European officials, John Foster Dulles and Eurofederalists in the State Department, such as Robert Schaetzel (Dulles's deputy for European affairs), helped the Europeans assert the "peacefulness" of Euratom's nuclear ambitions, after suspicions to the contrary were raised by the AEC.[127] For example, the State Department warned Monnet that proposals by European and American nuclear scientists to start with a community program of research and development on prototype reactors and naval propulsion[128] were too close to a military undertaking for the US Senate, which would then insist on keeping the AEC controls on European activities.[129]

Similarly, Schaetzel insisted that Monnet would have to hire new experts to quiet those who tried "to persuade the Commission to adopt a power prototype program."[130] Otherwise, US industrialists would lose their conviction regarding Europe's commitment to buy US nuclear power plants. In order to obtain recognition from the US Congress for Euratom controls as established by the Euratom Treaty, Dulles's associates insisted, it was of utmost importance to maintain the Euratom technological program designed by the Three Wise Men. Indeed, based on the Three Wise Men's program, there was little point in keeping American inspectors on the ground, since none of the technologies they promised to buy from the United States could be diverted for military purposes. Max Kohnstamm, who had been appointed Euratom's negotiator with the United States on the issue of Euratom controls, reported to Monnet that he had been warned by Schaetzel not to "raise the question of controls [as a separate issue],"[131] but if Strauss brought this matter up for discussion, the promoters of Euratom had to tell the AEC that the United States–Euratom Treaty would have the "immediate goal of 1,000 MW nuclear power demonstration program, with $150 million raised from industry, and $200 million that would come from Euratom (raising $100 million) and U.S. the other $100 million; fuel would be $100 million which might be leased or financed on long-term basis," as this scenario "draws directly on AEC opinion by suggesting a demonstration program which uses limited AEC money, it avoids abstract and theoretical U.S.-Euratom negotiation on control, and allows time to consider longer-range questions of U.S. relations with Euratom."[132] For Schaetzel, "the clean tangibility of the proposal eases and puts into place the other difficult questions such as safeguards, safety, insurance."[133]

As a result of this negotiating tactic, Kohnstamm and the US ambassador to the communities prepared a bilateral United States–Euratom memorandum of understanding in April 1958 (finally signed in June 1958), which clearly distinguished the rights of the Euratom Commission and those of the AEC. It was based on the memorandum of understanding on Euratom controls that Kohnstamm had signed with the British through the OEEC in December 1957, which stated, "The control will be executed by Euratom in the Euratom countries."[134] The memorandum with the United States claimed that the "Euratom control system is stricter and definitely less liberal than the IAEA's," as "under the Euratom system, nuclear materials produced within the community as well as imported will be under constant control,"[135] but it did not go into the details of how the control of conformity would be conducted. In exchange, the Euratom Commission agreed to let the United States have the right of "verification," which was distinct from the right of "control" in the sense that the United States could only verify that Euratom control procedures were "compatible" with those deemed acceptable by the United States and by the IAEA. Therefore, the distribution of rights agreed upon was a victory for Eurofederalists.

As Avner Cohen writes, it is not so much secrecy but denial that ensures the opaque character of a nuclear program (or joint program, in the case of the United States–Euratom agreement).[136] Here again, the complicity of the US president and his secretary of state with the Euratom supporters was essential to ensure the credibility of the denials that were expressed after the AEC chairman, Lewis Strauss, criticized the United States–Euratom deal on controls. Indeed, after the memorandum was signed, in June 1958, Strauss led skeptics to initiate yet another attempt to ask for closer scrutiny of the terms of the United States–Euratom Treaty. They leaked their concerns over the desirability of Euratom controls in the pages of the *New York Times*,[137] where journalists noted that "even though the issue of controls was presumably solved when the negotiators agreed that Euratom should exercise its inspection functions, with the inspection standards of meeting those followed by the U.S. and the new IAEA," the "AEC has raised last-minute objections to the proposed agreement, which center on the question of international inspection."[138] To prevent the controversy from agitating Congress, Dulles's assistant Christian Herter denied that there was any problem with the agreement reached with Euratom authorities, by writing to the chairman of the JCAE that "section 11D of the Memorandum [of understanding signed by Kohnstamm and the US ambassador to the communities] provides for frequent consultation and exchange of visits between the Parties to give assurance to both parties that the standards of the materials accountability systems of the U.S. and Euratom are kept reasonably comparable."[139] Eisenhower also took the time to assuage similar fears of leading public figures, such as Bernard Baruch, whose help the nationalists behind Strauss mobilized.[140] Dulles put maximum pressure on Lewis Strauss to remove opposition to "this joint Euratom-U.S. nuclear power program."[141] As Strauss continued to criticize the present deal, Eisenhower even fired him from the AEC chairmanship four days before the United States–Euratom Treaty was introduced to Congress for ratification. Nuclear opacity was therefore produced by private assurance, public denial, and exclusion.

The denials expressed by insiders in the US government convinced senators that it was undesirable for the United States to keep its control of Europe's nuclear activities on the ground: the sheer size of the future Euratom program of electricity production (the sale of not just one but six power plants for an astronomical 350 million dollars) made it utterly impractical. Even after the last negative campaign led by Strauss, the chairman of the JCAE, Senator Pastore, reassured Kohnstamm that "he did not expect difficulties for the program in the respect of safeguards."[142] Indeed, with the implementation of the Three Wise Men's program, tons of nuclear fuels would be delivered to the US power plants sold to Euratom, which made the maintenance of American control impractical considering the scope of the controls and inspections that would be needed if Euratom embarked on a large-scale program of power development.[143] Senator Pastore told Kohnstamm the AEC could not pretend to control European nuclear activities, especially in light of the fact that, as planned by Armand's scenarios, "the U.S. will sell 30,000 Kg of enriched uranium and plutonium to Euratom," of which "ownership and responsibility will be transferred to the Community."[144]

The US Senate eventually ratified the treaty formally recognizing the legal instruments of Euratom in August 1958,[145] and the agreement to import fissile materials signed by the president took effect in November 1958. The United Kingdom and Canada signed similar bilateral agreements with Euratom by the end of the year. Monnet's close aide, George Ball, reported to Max Kohnstamm that the architects of the United States–Euratom agreements were fortunate that the Suez crisis provided "an argument for speedy Congressional action which did not exist in such persuasive form before."[146] Robert Schaetzel wrote to Kohnstamm, a few days after the United States–Euratom agreement came into force, that he "had the pleasant surprise to meet David Lilienthal, who wanted to know more about the bilateral agreement." As Schaetzel wrote, Lilienthal was "extremely enthusiastic and he simply regretted that the political aspect of this deal had not received the place it deserved in Congressional debates."[147] However, success depended on concealing the political goals sought by the US president and his secretary of state, and on their tactic of opacity.

A Comprehensive Legal Order: Two Regimes of Nuclear Rules

Nuclear opacity helped the US executive branch and the Europeans mask the advancement of their planned nuclear-weapons program from the US Congress, in the hope that US foreign policy makers would soon agree to extend US-European cooperation to dual-use and military nuclear activities. Indeed, the United States–Euratom Treaty was ratified by Congress at the same time as Congress passed another important reform, desired by the Eisenhower administration, that liberalized nuclear trade in military technologies, which concerned many dual-use technologies, such as gaseous enrichment of uranium. Indeed, to complement the edifice created by Eurofederalists, in April 1958, Dulles's assistants proposed amendments to the Atomic Energy Act to "facilitate the use of nuclear weapons which the U.S. would furnish in the event of hostilities, . . . make available to our allies military reactors . . . and provide material for making nuclear weapons [to] those who already have built them."[148]

The 1958 revision of the McMahon Act (hereafter, 1958 McMahon Act), which entered into force in July 1958, did not immediately concern the signatory states of the Euratom Treaty, but only the United Kingdom, since only the United Kingdom had exploded a nuclear weapon at that time—what the US Congress regarded as the standard of sufficient proof of nuclear progress. Because the US Congress considered that the United Kingdom had made "sufficient progress" on the road to the acquisition of a fully functioning nuclear deterrent, it agreed to apply the 1958 McMahon Act in this case, and to let the US president sign a bilateral defense treaty of nuclear cooperation in the military field with the British, such as in the field of gaseous enrichment of uranium. But the role of Congress (and its uncertain interpretation of the selection criteria for "sufficient progress" to decide whether a nation could benefit from the 1958 McMahon Act) was one of the reasons why the British government refrained from engaging in discussions of the Euratom Treaty with its Continental allies.[149] Before the 1958 McMahon Act passed, the British believed that they could not associate themselves with the Six under the framework of the Euratom Treaty "without impairing [thei]r relations with America."[150] They did not want to see the US Congress reject their request to benefit from the 1958 McMahon Act if, for instance, Congress feared that American nuclear military secrets would fall into West German hands as a result of the United Kingdom's participation in Euratom.

The opacity of Europe's nuclear status had thus opened new rights (such as the right of "self-control") to Euratom, but the restriction imposed by Congress on the interpretation of the 1958 McMahon Act showed that, although Congress agreed to ratify the United States–Euratom Treaty, it did not want to give the US president a free hand to sign a future trade agreement with Euratom that would extend to dual-use technologies such as naval nuclear propulsion or uranium enrichment. The US Congress still had to authorize the president to help Europeans acquire dual-use nuclear technologies (such as uranium enrichment).[151] As Robert Gilpin writes, "Although in principle this act signified a major move toward nuclear sharing with America's European allies, . . . in actuality the sharing of really significant information on atomic weapons was restricted by congressional mandate."[152] The two truths that Eurofederalists had given about the meaning of the treaties and agreements they signed in 1957 and 1958 raised the question of which truth (public or private) would be accepted by the US Congress in the future, when the United States–Euratom Treaty would be first implemented. For instance, after these amendments were passed, if France exploded a rough nuclear weapon (one containing plutonium but no enriched uranium), then the US Congress might agree to help Europeans enrich uranium in France, but Congress would retain the decision-making power.

In spite of this uncertainty over the application of the 1958 McMahon Act to allow future cooperation between the United States and Euratom in the development of dual-use activities that the Congress deemed of a military nature, the Europeans quickly moved forward by agreeing to cooperate in the field of uranium enrichment. The existence of the Euratom Treaty for the regulation of Europe's peaceful activities and of the tripartite treaties for the regulation of Europe's military activities allowed Euratom supporters to include the West Germans and Italians in the enrichment of uranium produced by France while maintaining the charade presented by the Three Wise Men. For fear that the US Congress would refuse to recognize Euratom's legal instruments if senators learned of the Europeans' undertaking in the field of enrichment, in May 1958, the French government of Félix Gaillard, who had signed the European tripartite agreements of November 1957,[153] secretly agreed to open participation in the production of enriched uranium in the French plant under construction in Pierrelatte (France) to West Germans and Italians (see fig. 5.3). Their participation in this plant secured the West Germans' right to access dual-use technologies, if not on national and unilateral grounds, on collective grounds.[154] According to the French historian George-Henri Soutou, the joint participation by French, West Germans, and Italians in the enrichment of uranium was meant to produce nuclear warheads that would be owned by the three countries along supranational lines (see the chronology of the evolution of the confidential/public understandings of the Euratom Treaty in fig. 5.3).[155] This agreement revived the initial technological program for Euratom that the French and West Germans had discussed before the report of the Three Wise Men; but this time, Europeans decided to shift the cursor separating peaceful from military activities closer to where the US senators wanted it (as they declared such activities to be military and not peaceful), in order not to threaten the future deal with Euratom—but in contrast to what senators wanted, Europeans then started cooperating on military nuclear activities.

The tactic of opacity employed by Eurofederalists on the Continent did not mean that Eurofederalists in the White House and State Department were excluded from the confidential negotiations between Europeans concerning "military" joint cooperation. After the French foreign minister first told his West German counterparts, in October 1956, that France contemplated sharing military nuclear secrets with West Germany, a proposal that led to the signing of the Franco-German Agreement of January 1957, John Foster Dulles was informed by his aides on the ground[156] that in the minds of Eurofederalists on the Continent, "Euratom itself could produce atomic weapons [at least, the components of the nuclear warhead] for the use of France and other member countries (including [the] Federal Republic), if it might need them in the future."[157] Dulles even proclaimed that such a proposal had been in Monnet's and Spaak's minds "for a long time."[158] The German chancellor also told Dulles of the tripartite agreements in December 1957, and Dulles is reported to have expressed his support for the project as long as cooperation with Europe's Anglo-American nuclear partners (United States, United Kingdom, and Canada) was not ruled out.[159] Not only the Germans but also the French observed that commitment, as the day after the French signed the tripartite agreements in November 1957, they told the British prime minister that "they insisted on sharing the fabrication, the knowledge and research in all nuclear matters"[160] with their Euratom partners.[161] President Eisenhower, when informed of the tripartite agreements during the NATO meetings of December 1957, told his European informants that he did not see any problem with them "as long as work [on nuclear weapons] would go along within the Atlantic framework."[162]

For the US chief executive, there were good strategic reasons why the Europeans should start a covert nuclear-weapons program on the European Continent, and why the United States should complement the transatlantic legal order started by the United States–Euratom Treaty with a set of legal rules concerning nuclear military cooperation. Not only had Eisenhower long supported the creation of a European (Franco-German-Italian) nuclear-weapons program, but the Soviet launching of the first satellite, "Sputnik," in October 1957 also reaffirmed his ambition to hasten the creation of an autonomous and strong Western Europe. As the State Department deputy on European affairs, Robert Schaetzel, told Kohnstamm after Sputnik, "The Russian satellite showed the need for closer European-U.S. connections and faster pace for European integration."[163] Indeed, the signs of an imminent threat were harder to detect in the missile age than in the age of bombers and thus plagued the US doctrine of massive preemption. Only if Europeans constructed their own missiles with American help, and built their own warheads, could the United States accelerate its exit from the European Continent. Therefore, during the NATO meeting of December 1957, John Foster Dulles expressed the desire "to initiate in Europe a coordinated program of R&D and evaluation and production of a NATO family of weapons,"[164] including the building of atomic submarines, for which he pledged to seek legislative authority to cooperate.[165] Dulles thus intended the Euratom Treaty and the tripartite agreements of November 1957 to initiate the basis for an Atlantic nuclear authority, which could later undertake the joint (American-European) fabrication of an Atlantic nuclear deterrent.[166] Dulles's assistant for atomic affairs declared that under Robert Bowie's chairmanship as director of the policy planning staff in the State Department, "in 1957, we developed a concept that we called NACNA in the Policy Planning Staff—which stood for North Atlantic Nuclear Authority—and that would have been a very ambitious project where on a joint basis the North Atlantic Nations would have manufactured nuclear weapons, held them jointly in custody, jointly operated nuclear weapons systems," a project that "Dulles and Adenauer had approved."[167]

The European round of negotiations achieved with Euratom was therefore a preliminary step toward a broader reform of the legal rules regulating both peaceful and military transatlantic nuclear cooperation, whose public revelation needed to be postponed until Congress came to accept the strategic reasons for a qualitative jump in the kind of nuclear technologies traded across the Atlantic. For instance, Eisenhower foresaw the time when NATO'S supreme commander would be a European general with responsibility for using a European-made nuclear deterrent on his own in times of emergency, but he was aware that a commitment by the US president to let NATO's supreme commander (especially if he was a European general) decide when to start nuclear warfare in Europe would never be ratified by the Democratic Congress elected in 1956.[168] Similarly, when Dulles proposed to his NATO allies the creation of a "NATO stockpile"[169] of nuclear weapons co-owned and cobuilt by the West, he admitted that the United States could not do so by treaty in the sense that these "arrangements made with NATO-SACEUR" (NATO's supreme allied commander) would not be ratified by the US Congress, not just because NATO was not a sovereign entity legally able to sign treaties (unlike Euratom), but because many in the US Congress disagreed with Dulles about the desirability of such an agreement. Thus, Eisenhower and Dulles planned that they should start cooperating with Europeans on the joint construction of the missiles to carry nuclear weapons rather than on the fabrication of nuclear-weapons components, as only the latter would have required congressional approval.[170] During the December 1957 NATO meetings, NATO's supreme commander, Lauris Norstad, even told European allies that the United States would "promote coordination of research, development and manufacture of MRBMs,"[171] because, as Dulles told the French foreign minister, "it would be absurd" for Europeans "to engage in costly and difficult research whereas we have already done important work."[172] But future cooperation with Euratom member states on nuclear activities that the US Congress deemed military needed to wait.

Conclusion

Opacity in the case of Europe's nuclear program was produced by a specific circulation of interpretations about what European treaties and agreements meant, which allowed Europeans to agree secretly on which activities they would deem peaceful (and therefore under the jurisdiction of the Euratom Treaty) and which ones military (and therefore under the jurisdiction of secret military agreements). The existence of this legal iceberg, with the public text of the Euratom Treaty as its tip, allowed them to calibrate their definition of the jurisdictional boundary separating peaceful and military activities so that it fit (at least publicly) with US senators' definition of peaceful nuclear activities. It also increased the odds that Euratom Treaty negotiations would be brought to a successful end, which made it desirable for US skeptics to wait for the outcome of such negotiations—to see whether that outcome was preferable to other alternatives, such as the future control of nuclear activities in Europe by the IAEA. Andrew Moravcsik cites the observed difference between the final text of the Euratom Treaty signed by the intergovernmental Spaak Committee and Monnet's interpretation of the treaty's purpose as proof of the futility of Monnet's efforts at influencing the outcome of negotiations.[173] But the decoupling of the intergovernmental confidential interpretation and the public interpretation given by Monnet's transnational network was the condition for their recognition as instruments of international law by the US Congress—a recognition without which these legal instruments would have been worthless.

The Euratom Treaty and the United States–Euratom Treaty introduced for the first time the principles of atomic federalism to the reality of international law. After fifteen years, the promoters of the normative ideals of atomic federalism who had gathered behind John McCloy in 1945 finally convinced Western states to employ the legal instruments they had developed. To pass this legal reform, Eurofederalists had to shift positions at two levels: strategic and tactical. First, they abandoned the goal of pursuing nuclear disarmament in Western Germany: the Euratom Treaty and the secret tripartite treaties of November 1957 gave France an incentive to build nuclear weapons on a collective European basis, with the help of West Germans and Italians, who were thus enrolled in France's imperial ambitions. Second, federalists abandoned the tactics of transparency and ambiguity and instead employed the tactic of opacity to define both the rules and jurisdictional boundaries of the Euratom Treaty (see fig. 5.4).

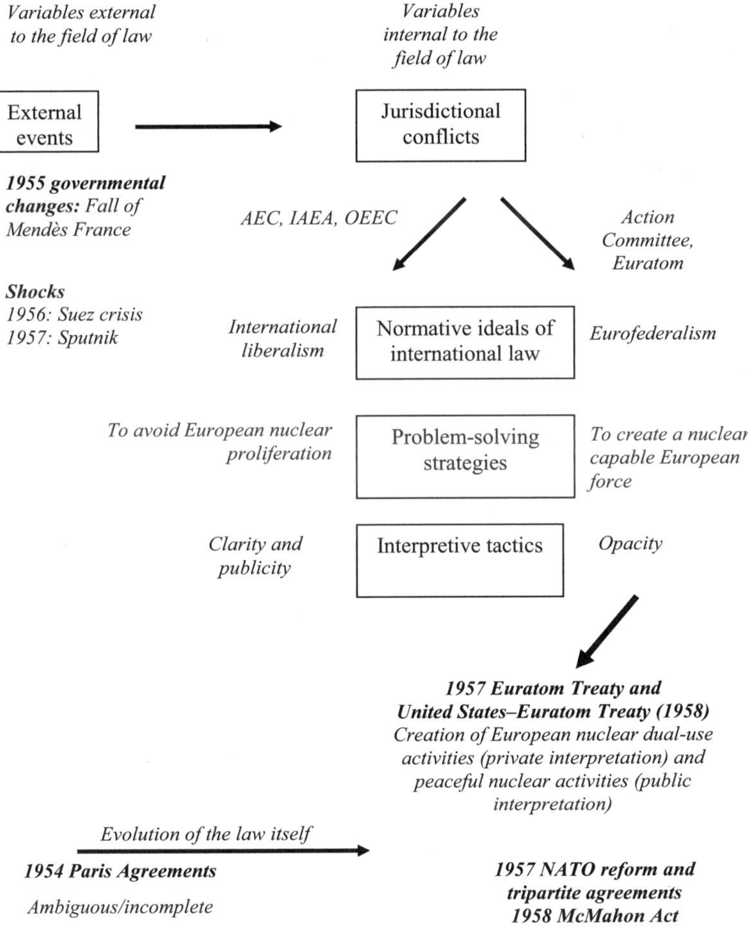

Figure 5.4. The dynamics of Eurofederalism in the late 1950s

Here, Eurofederalists succeeded in giving the impression to potential opponents of Eurofederalism that their public interpretation of these complicated rules was the valid interpretation, whereas the drafters of the treaty secretly agreed on a different interpretation of the same words, operating as homonyms, in the Euratom Treaties and in other agreements such as the IAEA procedures that were under discussion at the same time. While not in itself a sufficient condition to explain the success of the Euratom Treaty negotiations, opacity helped Eurofederalists defeat the plans of promoters of a global approach to nuclear trade through the IAEA. By means of these shifts at the tactical and strategic level, Eurofederalists were able to produce legal change. In the following chapters, I will describe the effects this choice of interpretative tactics had on the life cycle of these legal instruments once they were put into practice, and once France's imperial policy changed.

SIX

The Price of Opacity: How New Leaders Clarify Opaque Treaty Rules

As far as opacity allows states to overcome domestic and international obstacles to new global rules, we could conclude that opaque treaty rules might be more common than we usually believe. But the proliferation of opaque legal agreements may threaten the coherence of the international legal system as well as its stability. Thus, we need to ask: is the interpretation of opaque treaty rules likely to change when governmental changes among state parties to the legal regime occur? Do new domestic coalitions find in the opacity enough flexibility to impose *their* truth on the interpretation of past treaty obligations? While the next chapter analyzes how opaque rules are likely to change when the international legal context changes, this chapter focuses on the effect of direct demands for treaty reinterpretation initiated by signatory states of a treaty.

The opaque nuclear trade regime that was set up by the United States and Europe in 1958 offers a particularly interesting case to observe how opaque treaty rules and jurisdiction evolve as governmental changes occur among the parties to the treaty regime. Here, governmental changes occurred in the two main countries responsible for the signing of the treaties of Eurofederalist inspiration (France and the United States) at the very same time as the Euratom and tripartite treaties were to be implemented. Indeed, in May 1958 in France, a coup fomented by pro-French-Algeria activists brought not only a new government coalition but also a new regime led by General de Gaulle, whose opposition to Eurofederalist ideals was well known. In the United States, congressional elections in 1956 followed by the presidential election in 1960 successively brought into the legislative and executive branches new Democratic foreign policy elites who opposed Eisenhower's Eurofederalist ideals.

Using the regime of transatlantic nuclear trade as a case study, I show that the opacity of the legal rules and jurisdiction of treaties comes at a price: namely, that by providing a public interpretation of a treaty's jurisdictional boundary that differs from its confidential interpretation, an opaque truth allows new policy elites in one member state (or more) to unilaterally redefine the rules of the game and limit their scope while avoiding sanctions and other law-enforcing mechanisms. Indeed, as these interpretive struggles take place in the interstices of the law (in diplomatic conferences or intergovernmental exchanges as well as in networks of national technical agencies in charge of implementing treaties) rather than in international courts, opacity, then, allows new interpreters of the rules to privately subvert their secret purpose. This chapter demonstrates this thesis in three sections.

In the first section, I develop a Bourdieuian approach to the US field of foreign policy from 1958 to 1964. I show that in contrast to other periods during which new generations arrived in power without challenging the positions in the field, with Kennedy, intergenerational changes shifted the balance of power between US policy elites, with nationalists gaining the upper hand over the promoters of Eurofederalism. These changes internal to the field of US foreign policy were thus likely to restrict nuclear trade with Europe to the export of proliferation-resistant US power plants, and to prohibit the sale of military nuclear technologies to either France or an integrated Europe with France as its nuclear leader. But whether these new foreign policy elites would easily impose their views on their European allies remained an open question.

Second, I show how the polysemy of legal rules affected their implementation by the new policy elites in the Kennedy administration. Here, I show that the latter not only reinterpreted ambiguous domestic rules to fit with their new nuclear nonproliferation agenda, but they also abandoned the private interpretation of opaque rules. In the case of the interpretation of multilateral treaties, the existence of a public truth that supported the United States' new interpretation allowed the United States to claim that it complied with these rules, as publicly presented. Opacity allowed the Kennedy administration to change the rules of the nuclear trade with Europe without acknowledging that such a policy change had taken place. Nonacknowledgment, which Avner Cohen associates with nuclear opacity,[1] was a key resource provided to new national coalitions in charge of implementing these rules to ignore past interpretations they disliked.

Third, I show why the new foreign policy elites around Kennedy also benefitted from the Eurofederalists' refusal to acknowledge their defeat. Older Eurofederalists whose creation unraveled before their eyes clung to the belief that the US government had not renounced the larger goal of helping a united Europe acquire nuclear weapons, even though they now understood that the United States no longer wished to use the United States–Euratom Treaty to accomplish this objective. Eurofederalists hoped that the United States would agree to sign a new treaty of military nuclear cooperation with European countries. Their campaign in favor of this new arrangement (known as the Multilateral Force Treaty) was a desperate attempt to maintain the illusion that they still had influence at the highest level of government in the United States and France, despite evidence to the contrary. I show that such an illusion was produced by the opacity of the previous transatlantic nuclear regime, as well as by the deceptive tactics that the United States employed when it encouraged Eurofederalists to believe that they had only suffered a temporary reversal of fortune. Not until after the end of the Democrats' first term in power did Eurofederalists realize that the US administration had engaged in new negotiations only to buy time, before it abruptly made its policy preference for the Nonproliferation Treaty (NPT) known publicly.

Internal Changes among Foreign Policy Elites in the United States (1958–62)

Intergenerational changes in the US field of foreign policy threatened the legal architecture crafted by the Eisenhower administration in 1958 to regulate "peaceful" and "military" nuclear cooperation with Europe. Among the new US foreign policy elites, we can schematize the policy debate over the desirability of liberalizing US nuclear cooperation with Europe by distinguishing between three main positions in the field: the Eurofederalist, international liberal, and nationalist positions. The balance of power among these positions affected the definition of the boundaries separating peaceful (authorized) from military (strictly controlled) cooperation, and thus, how the United States–Euratom Treaty would be implemented.

Eurofederalists (1958–62)

Until the end of his tenure as president, Eisenhower maintained his support for enhanced cooperation in both peaceful and military applications of nuclear energy with a united Europe. As I said in the previous chapter, the passage of the United States–Euratom Treaty and the 1958 McMahon Act were the two pillars that would support future transatlantic cooperation.

Regarding peaceful nuclear cooperation, Eisenhower and key advisors

Table 6.1   Western solutions to the problem of Europe's defense after Sputnik

Response to the Soviet threat	Key propositions (1958–62)	Key proponents (1958–62)
Nationalist	• The United States centralizes the command and control of all nuclear weapons in the West • The United States ensures the invulnerability of its second-strike capability • The United States maintains strict nonproliferation policy, even toward the United Kingdom, which is pressed to integrate its nuclear deterrent under NATO's (American) authority	McNamara, Nitze, Wohlstetter, Caysen
International liberal	• The United States centralizes the command and control of all US nuclear weapons in Europe under the authority of the US president • The United States tolerates the existence of other Western national deterrents, even extends to other nations (such as France) the 1958 McMahon Act after their first nuclear test, and accepts a nonbinding coordination mechanism between nuclear powers • The United States can propose to European nonnuclear powers (including West Germany) some cooperation in the nonnuclear aspects of the construction of a nuclear deterrent (missile construction) • The United States adopts a strict nonproliferation policy with regard to European nonnuclear powers	Kennedy, Rusk, Herter, Acheson
Eurofederalist	• The United States delegates to a supranational NATO commander the command and control of Western nuclear weapons in Europe (the US as well as British and French nuclear warheads) • The United States can extend the 1958 McMahon Act to a tightly integrated European authority in charge of developing all dual-use and military nuclear activities (supranational proliferation) but not to individual European nations (such as France)	Eisenhower, Norstad, Ball, Monnet, McCloy, Adenauer

in the State Department hoped that the technological program covered by the United States–Euratom Treaty could be revised to include cooperation in the development of technologies that the US Congress might consider military (or at least dual-use), such as naval nuclear propulsion. According to the Eurofederalists' private interpretation of the United States–Euratom Treaty, nothing prevented the United States from helping Euratom develop other research activities than those publicly defined in 1958 as long as Europeans justified their technological demands as being for peaceful purposes. Experts in the State Department wanted to develop the joint program beyond the original expectations that Euratom would buy power plants and the nuclear fuels for these plants. For instance, the assistant secretary of state for European affairs, Robert Schaetzel, who had led the confidential negotiations of the United States–Euratom Treaty with Max Kohnstamm,[2] advised Euratom officials in 1959 to meet with Lilienthal, Oppenheimer, and other scientists to see whether and how the United States–Euratom joint research and development program could be used to develop new enrichment technologies such as centrifugation.[3] Monnet's protégés, Max Kohnstamm, Jules Guéron, and Etienne Hirsh, met with scientists and State Department officials in June 1959 at Oppenheimer's offices in the Princeton Institute of Advanced Studies to discuss promising joint research and development "concerning reprocessing and isotopic separation (testing other methods than gaseous diffusion)."[4] If the AEC agreed, it meant that the United States and a united Europe could immediately start cooperating on jointly producing these sensitive technologies, without waiting until France conducted a nuclear test (an event that would have triggered the extension of the 1958 McMahon Act to France, or rather, to a European compact made of France, West Germany, and Italy).

Regarding military cooperation between the United States and Europe, Eurofederalists in the State Department, such as Robert Bowie, Gerard Smith, and Livingston Merchant, sketched the contours of a new proposal for immediate transatlantic cooperation in the nonnuclear aspects (e.g., missile development) of a program aimed at creating a modern NATO nuclear deterrent along Eurofederalist lines.[5] A panel appointed by the president endorsed a report written by Bowie in August 1959, which proposed to help a united Europe build Polaris medium-range ballistic missiles (MRBMs), to be placed into a sea-based nuclear force under the authority of NATO's supreme commander (see table 6.1).[6] The old guard of Eurofederalists hoped to convince the French to accept the plan by adding a nuclear component in the military cooperation agreement, as the movable sea-based fleet of submarines (instead of a land-based force) would be propelled by nuclear reactors. This plan meant that France would have access to naval nuclear propulsion technologies that the US Congress had long considered as falling under the heading of "military" nuclear technologies (although some claimed they could also be used for tankers). However, the plan proposed by Bowie was quite revolutionary: it assumed that Congress would agree to extend the 1958 McMahon Act to a compact of European nations, which explained why "the State Department, DoD and the AEC . . . are not in agreement on the plan," and why the Eisenhower administration still waited until after the elections before discussing it with "the relevant committees of the Congress."[7] In fact, as soon as Kennedy was elected, he was made aware of the difficulties in Bowie's plans by Admiral H. G. Rickover, who headed naval-reactor development in the AEC and navy, and who warned the new president that any plan to share submarine technology with NATO allies would be killed by the US Congress, "not so much due to the use of the Polaris weapon in submarines but to the nuclear propulsion in the submarines" manned by foreigners.[8]

After Kennedy was elected, Eurofederalism was represented by a new generation of Democrats who entered the State Department behind Jean Monnet's former right-hand man, George Ball, who first became the assistant secretary for European affairs after Kennedy's election, and at the end of 1961, the undersecretary (the number-two position) in the State Department. George Ball was a close friend of the former Democratic presidential contender Adlai Stevenson (they had met while both were practicing law in Chicago),[9] who had encouraged Kennedy to think along the lines of Eurofederalism before his election. Ball and Stevenson were not opposed to the designs formulated at the end of the Eisenhower administration by Bowie, McCloy, and other older Eurofederalists, but they opposed their legal tactics. Stevenson and Ball wanted to end Eisenhower's deliberate tactic of opacity, which consisted of formulating "proposals [that] appear to be intentionally obscure as to whether or not they contemplate a transfer of the warheads to NATO, along with the delivery systems, thus abandoning the 'two key' principle."[10] For instance, they did not oppose the sale of naval nuclear propulsion technologies and missile construction technologies to a European compact of nations, nor did they reject the supranational responsibility of NATO's supreme commander. Rather, they asked the president to clearly tell the US Congress that it should approve supranational proliferation from the United States to a federal Europe; that it should oppose national proliferation in European nation-states such as France; and that it should approve "the United States['] . . . agree[ment] in advance not to employ its veto in the North Atlantic Council to the use of the NATO strategic deterrent in the event of a nuclear attack on the NATO area or in other situations to be defined by the NATO Council."[11]

In that sense, these younger Eurofederalists wanted to normalize and clarify their elders' concepts. As Ball brought Henry Owen and Walt Rostow, two strong advocates of Eurofederalist ideas,[12] to the State Department in early 1962, it was no surprise that the State Department often entered into open conflicts on foreign nuclear policy with the newcomers at the National Security Council (NSC), headed by McGeorge Bundy, and at the Department of Defense, led by Robert McNamara, or with the members of the President's Science Advisory Committee (PSAC) (see fig. 6.1).

International Liberals (1958–62)

If Eurofederalists still represented a powerful coalition in the years following the Sputnik crisis, they clearly had lost some ground to their competitors in the US field of foreign policy. In particular, proponents of an alternative conception of transatlantic nuclear trade (in both its peaceful and military dimensions) started to gain a stronger voice after the sudden death of John Foster Dulles in the spring of 1959. Dulles's death left his undersecretary, Christian Herter, to succeed him as the new secretary of state. In contrast to Dulles, Herter was a close friend of Paul Nitze (1907–2004), the former director of the policy-planning staff of the State Department under Acheson's tenure,[13] with whom he shared many ideas on nuclear foreign policy. Herter and Nitze had founded the school of policy at John Hopkins University during the Second World War, and neither of them shared Dulles's Eurofederalist commitment to nuclear integration.[14] Rather, they privileged direct bilateral relations between the United States and strong European nation-states—for instance, with the United Kingdom and even with France (see table 6.1).

In fact, Herter almost shared de Gaulle's conception of NATO as a purely intergovernmental organization, led by three nuclear-weapon states—that is, the United States, the United Kingdom, and France after 1960—which would coordinate their nuclear doctrine and which might cooperate in military nuclear research and development on a bilateral basis. Regarding the start of a nuclear military cooperation between France and the United States, Herter told France's foreign minister in May 1959 that the AEC would help the French build their uranium-enrichment plant in France (Pierrelatte), if France exploded only one atomic bomb.[15] This statement contradicted the stance of Dulles, who had warned de Gaulle in July 1958 that the United States might not cooperate with France to the same ex-

<u>Officials in charge of US nuclear foreign policy (1959–61):</u>

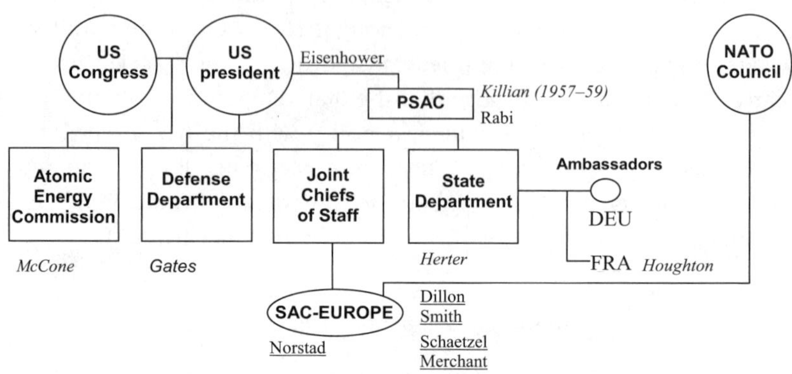

<u>Officials in charge of US nuclear foreign policy (1961–63):</u>

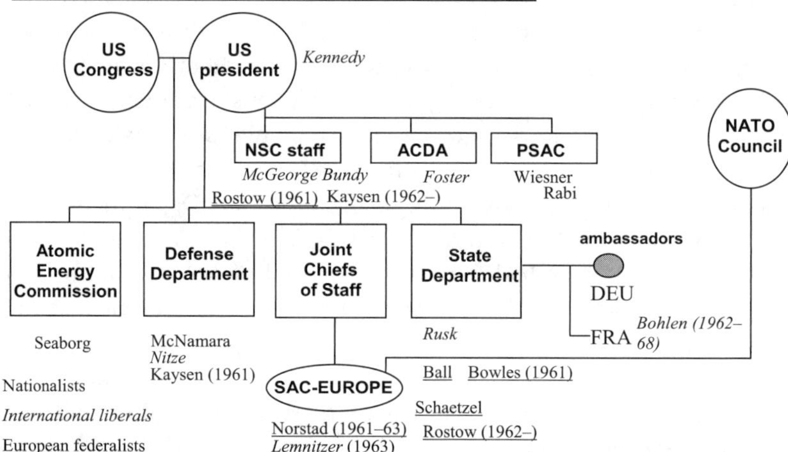

Figure 6.1. The fall of Eurofederalists in the Kennedy administration

tent as it did with the United Kingdom even after the French explosion of a nuclear weapon, especially if de Gaulle tried to challenge the European integration effort in the nuclear domain. Herter also authorized tripartite discussions among the United States, the United Kingdom, and France, as requested by de Gaulle, to discuss security problems outside of Europe (in this case, problems in the Near East and Africa) in March and April 1959.[16]

International liberals found a new opportunity to shape US foreign policy when Kennedy won the Democratic presidential primary and turned to Dean Acheson to review Eisenhower's proposals for transatlantic nuclear and nonnuclear military cooperation. Acheson and his former assistant Paul Nitze believed that NATO member states could cooperate to produce a multinational force loosely combining the American, British, and French nuclear deterrents. In March 1961, Acheson opposed the development of land-based MRBMs in Europe, which NATO's supreme commander (or SACEUR), Lauris Norstad, continued to regard as essential.[17] Acheson's plan sought to "secure control of nuclear weapons in NATO Europe" against national uses, and to "subject the use of nuclear weapons by the forces of other powers in Europe to U.S. veto and control."[18] After he was elected, Kennedy thus announced in April 1961 that he was abandoning Eisenhower's proposal to create an Atlantic force of nuclear submarines under the authority of a supranational NATO commander, a decision that was applauded by Dean Rusk, who served as the new secretary of state appointed by Kennedy on the advice of Dean Acheson (see fig. 6.1).[19]

The ascent to power of the old guard of Democrats who had served under Truman thus signaled a return to the more traditional form of alliance management, coupled with a strict nonproliferation policy oriented toward the non–nuclear-weapon states in NATO (such as West Germany). Dean Acheson, Dean Rusk (who was Acheson's former deputy for South Asia during the Korean War), and Paul Nitze (who was Acheson's director of the policy-planning staff during the Korean War and who was named undersecretary of defense after Kennedy's election) all advocated the same position as they traveled with Kennedy during his first European tour in May 1961. They were not opposed to de Gaulle's idea of a loose tripartite NATO concert of great powers with the French, British, and Americans in charge of discussing most aspects of nuclear military cooperation.[20]

Nationalists (1958–62)

A third group of younger experts with a more nationalistic viewpoint on global nuclear relations, and the role the United States should play in the new order, emerged after the launching of Sputnik in the fall of 1957. Sputnik was the catalyst that gave the Democratic majority in the US Congress a pretext to mount a criticism of the president's nuclear cooperation with Europe, in both its peaceful and military aspects. Regarding the military aspects, some leading Democrats gathered around a nationalist platform promoted by a congressional committee, the "Gaither Committee" (named after its chairman, H. Rowan Gaither), which was created to assess the military preparedness of the United States in the age of missiles. Among its key recommendations, the Gaither report called for a major increase in the military budget; the acceleration of funding for the production of nuclear submarines equipped with intercontinental ballistic missiles (ICBMs); and the relocation of the nuclear decision-making process from the office of NATO's supreme commander to the Pentagon (see table 6.1).[21]

Although Paul Nitze held more liberal views on the role that France could play in the Western nuclear deterrent than the new nuclear strategists who served on the committee, Nitze was particularly instrumental in giving a public platform to this new generation of experts.[22] As Andrew May and Fred Kaplan emphasized, most experts consulted by the committee came from the RAND Corporation, a think tank that provided the air force with studies on the cost-effectiveness of nuclear targeting plans against the Soviet Union.[23] These RAND experts, such as Albert Wohlstetter and Herman Kahn,[24] asserted that a "missile gap" existed between the number of American and Soviet missiles, which worked to the disadvantage of the United States. In their view, the number of US nuclear weapons and missiles needed to ensure deterrence after a hypothesized Soviet preemptive strike (what Wohlstetter called the "second strike capability") was "relative" to the number of Soviet missiles, which meant that this number needed to be much higher than what was deemed necessary by the Eisenhower administration, as the latter did not base its policy recommendation on the scenario of a massive Soviet first strike.[25] But as the RANDites argued, even though the United States led the race in terms of the absolute number of nuclear weapons, Sputnik proved that most US nuclear weapons and delivery vehicles (bombers or future missiles) would be eradicated if the Soviets initiated a first strike against the United States and Europe in a single blow of ICBMs. As they saw it, the United States should prepare its nuclear policy for this worst-case scenario.

This doctrine of "relative deterrence" rendered irrelevant the planned military cooperation that Eisenhower proposed to initiate in nuclear (as far as the naval propulsion mechanism was concerned) and nonnuclear (as far as missile construction was concerned) technologies (see table 6.1).[26] It also rendered irrelevant the network of NATO nuclear-sharing treaties that Eisenhower had signed in the spring of 1958 with NATO allies that agreed to host NATO missiles equipped with US-made nuclear warheads jointly controlled by the United States and the host nation. Because the nuclear warheads and the land-based missiles (which Eisenhower proposed to help Europeans build) would be located close to the Soviet border, easily spotted, and not easily transportable before an imminent attack, they would not survive a preemptive first strike by Soviet missiles.[27] The RAND-ites also rejected Eisenhower's doctrine that NATO's supreme commander could and should act independently to launch a massive preemptive strike in the event that he identified a Soviet threat in Western Europe and could not reach the US president.[28]

The strategic thinking of the experts mobilized by the Gaither Committee reflected major changes in the US field of nuclear strategy, changes that were brought about by inner transformations in the RAND Corporation itself and in the US field of foreign policy in general (see fig. 6.2). In the late 1940s, RAND strategists such as Bernard Brodie and Jacob Viner[29] had developed a doctrine of "absolute and limited deterrence"[30] with which Eisenhower (as well as de Gaulle, among others) agreed in many respects: atomic weapons were the most cost-effective weapons because, in the words of Viner, "small countries" needed to build only a few atomic weapons in order "to make their conquest cost too much"[31] for great powers. But when Eisenhower became president in 1953, former insiders in the Truman administration such as Nitze helped newcomers such as Wohlstetter and Kahn impose their doctrine of "relative deterrence" at RAND.[32] They promoted their careers in new institutions of higher learning such as the Harvard Department of Government, which gained prominence in the field while the institutions that had been central in the production of the first generation of nuclear strategists (Harvard Law School) lost their relevance (see fig. 6.2).[33]

This intergenerational shift was paradoxically an effect of Senator Joseph McCarthy's witch hunt in foreign policy–making institutions (from the State Department to the AEC), which lessened the legitimacy of traditional foreign policy makers, whom populists criticized for their elitist recruitment, characterized by social endogamy within a Harvard-trained elite of lawyers. The use of numbers and abstract rules by the RAND experts and then in Harvard's Department of Government restored their legitimacy. In fact, these young strategists distinguished themselves from their elders not by having a background in international law, least of all European law, but instead by developing statistical and "scientific" methods of geopolitical analysis. Being trained in computational techniques in the United States, their habitus, as Pierre Bourdieu would say, was much more American-centered than the more cosmopolitan Harvard-trained lawyers of the generation of McCloy or Dulles who had long practiced law for Wall Street firms investing in Europe.

The appeal of nationalist ideas to the Democratic congressional majority turned strategic disputes that had been arcane discussions in the US

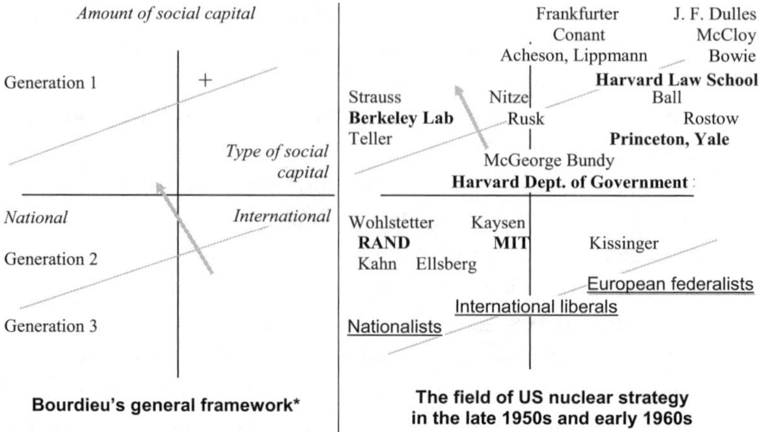

* Bourdieu represents a specific field as a plane, whose vertical axis measures the amount of social capital accumulated by its practitioners, and the horizontal axis measures the type of social capital accumulated (opposing, the capital accumulated strictly in the national institutions on the left, and the capital accumulated in international markets on the right). When represented on a plane, the avant-garde of young Turks gives the movement its direction: it generally instigates intergenerational turnover as it pushes the older generation to the upper-left corner of the plane.

Figure 6.2. Intergenerational change in the field of nuclear strategy in the early 1960s

field of nuclear strategy into debates of national importance. The Democrats, who had held the congressional majority since 1956, took advantage of these intergenerational changes in the US field of nuclear strategy to battle against Eisenhower's philosophy of fiscal conservatism and his commitment to Eurofederalism.[34] Although Eisenhower and John Foster Dulles found that "the Gaither report was 'far-fetched,'"[35] it impressed Senator Lyndon Johnson, the Senate majority leader, who supported its conclusions. From then until the presidential election of November 1960, Senator Johnson and the young Massachusetts senator John F. Kennedy relentlessly campaigned on the theme of the "missile gap" and the need for the United States to reduce that gap by centralizing the Western nuclear deterrent in the hands of the US president.[36]

The "missile gap" theme helped Kennedy defeat Eisenhower's former vice president Richard Nixon in the 1960 presidential election. As a result, President Kennedy brought the new generation of US nuclear experts to power (see fig. 6.1). Paul Nitze became the new undersecretary of defense, and Robert McNamara (1916–2009) the new secretary of defense. McNamara was an economist by training, the youngest assistant professor at Harvard Business School in 1940, who had worked under Paul Nitze and

George Ball on assessing the cost-effectiveness of US bombing during the Second World War, before managing the Ford Company in 1946, where he "rationalized" production by introducing modern methods of cost-benefit analysis.[37]

After Kennedy's election, Nitze convinced McNamara to hire the men whose careers McGeorge Bundy (1919–1996), the youngest dean of arts and science at Harvard and the son-in-law of Dean Acheson, had advanced at Harvard in governmental studies and economics (rather than in the Harvard Law School),[38] and those RAND analysts who were Nitze's protégés.[39] Among these men were Carl Kaysen, a Harvard-trained economist, professor at MIT, and longtime RAND consultant, who first worked at the DoD under Nitze and then under Bundy at the NSC; and Walt Rostow, an MIT economist who was Bundy's assistant at the NSC until he became the director of the policy-planning staff at the State Department in 1961.[40] They organized a parallel State Department to advise the president on all nuclear policy negotiations, which had traditionally been administered by specialists in international law within the State Department. In contrast to traditional State Department diplomats, none of these new hires had any knowledge of the existing European treaties, or international law in general. For instance, McGeorge Bundy later wrote that "the European Community is an institution which I chose to admire, partly with a willing suspension of disbelief but also with a necessary confession of ignorance."[41] But the fact that their careers had been sheltered at Harvard by McGeorge Bundy, the ultimate insider (recall that McGeorge's father was Harvey Bundy, Henry Stimson's undersecretary of state, and his father-in-law was Dean Acheson),[42] and that they had provided Kennedy with a ready-made theory of nuclear deterrence that the young senator from Massachusetts relentlessly used to attack President Eisenhower (the general who won the Western campaign against Hitler) on issues of defense, were sufficient reasons for them to get the jobs.

Compared to traditional diplomats such as Rusk, the RANDites shared with Bundy a more nationalistic conception of the role that the United States should play in the West, which translated to a reluctance to extend to France the terms of the 1958 McMahon Act (in contrast to older men such as Acheson), and a greater willingness to apply a strict nonproliferation policy even to the United Kingdom (see table 6.1). As the issue of nuclear military cooperation with France was debated in the new administration, the nationalists gained ground in many interadministrative struggles. For instance, Bundy convinced Kennedy to write to de Gaulle at the end of 1961 that, even though France had successfully tested a nuclear weapon, the US government has "not been able to believe that a national nuclear force for France is something we should assist."[43] Most of these newcomers in the US field of foreign policy agreed with the statement that McNamara made during the NATO meetings in Athens in May 1962, that "it [was] essential that we [the United States] centralize the decision to use our nuclear weapons to the greatest extent possible."[44] This position was shared by the new chairman of the AEC, Glenn Seaborg, whom Kennedy appointed and who, for the first time, was not a lawyer by training but a nuclear scientist who shared the same insistence as the RAND analysts that the United States should apply a strict nonproliferation policy with regard to Europe in general, and France in particular.[45]

The clash between nationalists and Eurofederalists was not just one of ideas, but also an intergenerational fight reflecting deep differences in the habitus of key US foreign policy makers, opposing skilled American civilians with no experience in the conduct of military operations and older military professionals, experienced in the art of war, who knew that formal models did not fit its reality. Even after Nitze and McNamara also realized that the "missile gap" did not exist, or rather, that it was in favor of the United States, and that American intelligence was sufficient for NATO's supreme commander to recognize an imminent threat of Soviet invasion in Europe,[46] they still supported these models because the latter helped them impose their legitimacy on older military men.[47]

The younger experts (most of whom had no fighting experience) were determined to end the monopoly of the older generation of military professionals, such as Eisenhower and Norstad, over the transatlantic military issues. For instance, alerted by RAND expert Daniel Ellsberg (who worked at the DoD) and McGeorge Bundy that executive orders signed in secret by Eisenhower stated, "If faced with a substantial Russian military action," NATO's supreme commander would have the right to "start the thermonuclear holocaust on his own initiative if he could not reach you,"[48] Kennedy immediately canceled these secret executive orders, to the dismay of NATO's supreme commander, Lauris Norstad, who protested that he could not "be a mere puppet of the American president," as "he represented the alliance in its entirety."[49] When Kennedy visited Europe in May 1961, he also forced Norstad to declare at the NATO meetings that his command would depend upon the president's orders and not upon the decision of the Atlantic Council.[50] That same month, McNamara and Nitze further cornered Norstad, having him declare that the new theory of "gradual" and "flexible response" developed at RAND by Wohlstetter would be the official strategy adopted by the US president.[51] Norstad protested, arguing that if Western Europe was attacked, including with "anti-force" nuclear weapons, "there would be no 'pause,' no 'steps,' but just total war," and that RAND's doctrine of flexible response, which created degrees and steps in nuclear warfare, reflected only "the arrogance of civilians—McNamara above all—who sought to impose policies rooted in abstract and academic theorizing, and who showed little regard or understanding for operational realities."[52] Eventually, as McNamara officially introduced the new US doctrine for NATO in June 1962, Kennedy fired General Lauris Norstad under pressure from nationalists in the DoD who criticized the general for acting like "a proconsul in Outer Gaul."[53] His replacement by General Lyman Lemnitzer, the infamous chairman of the Joint Chiefs of Staff during the Bay of Pigs operation, made it clear to Europeans that NATO's supreme commander would be simply a US general obeying the US president and lacking any political authority.[54]

The Bourdieuian perspective that I have used here to describe the differences in the habitus of two generations of foreign policy makers can also explain strategic differences across the Atlantic, as the habitus of the young US civilians around McNamara and Nitze also clashed with that of European civilians and military professionals on the Continent. As Eugene Rostow (the brother of Walt Rostow and the dean of the Yale Law School) told his good friend George Ball, Europeans disliked the conception of geopolitics and diplomacy of the RAND experts. Europeans did not believe in the primacy of numbers or in the abstractness of the rules of nuclear war designed by RANDites, which McNamara used to justify the new US policy of centralized control.[55] In the summer of 1962, McNamara's insistence on the US central command turned all the Europeans (both Gaullists and Eurofederalists) against the United States: even British prime minister Harold Macmillan described McNamara's speeches in Athens, Greece, and Ann Arbor, Michigan, as an "ill-disguised attack upon the determination of Britain."[56] Old Eurofederalists in Europe, such as Dirk Stikker, Paul-Henri Spaak's successor as the secretary-general of NATO, complained bitterly that the "American policy of taking care of all targets of the Alliance was showing evidence of a desire by the U.S. to interfere with and dominate Europe politically."[57] Thus, the intergenerational shifts in the US field of foreign policy (and the delayed intergenerational change in Europe) were likely to bring frictions and tensions to the transatlantic alliance, especially as the newcomers wished to impose their interpretation of existing legal instruments.

The Efficacy of Ambiguity and Opacity for Those in Power (1958–62)

The Bourdieuian approach to international law is helpful to visualize the positions of various schools in one domestic field of power at one particular point in time. Still, because it focuses on one domestic field only (or a series of domestic fields, taken separately), it cannot provide an explanation for how the policy changes that new coalitions announce when they campaign are received once these coalitions are in power; whether these policy changes will be successfully adopted; and if so, whether they will be perceived as violations of prior agreements, stir controversy, and impose costs on their government. Only a hermeneutic approach to international law can identify which interpretive constraints Kennedy's advisors faced regarding nuclear cooperation with Europe and whether the polysemy of the rules of the transatlantic nuclear trade crafted by the Eisenhower administration helped them change the meaning of prior obligations.

New Interpretations of Ambiguous Rules (1958–62)

Changes in the US field of foreign policy had a direct impact on the interpretation that the United States gave to the possibility that it would cooperate with Western European governments (other than the United Kingdom) in the development of military applications of nuclear energy. This impact was not surprising, as the legal basis for US military nuclear cooperation was US domestic legislation only, and not any treaty or agreement (as was the case with the regulation of peaceful nuclear cooperation). Indeed, as far as nuclear "military" cooperation was concerned, the 1958 McMahon Act established the legal basis for future cooperation between France (or a European compact led by France) and the United States, after France could prove that it had made "sufficient progress" in its nuclear-weapons program.

Furthermore, the domestic law ruling these exchanges was ambiguous enough to be interpreted different ways. Nations had to have made "sufficient progress" on the road toward a nuclear deterrent before they could receive US military help, but no clear interpretation existed of the meaning of "sufficient progress." While in 1958 Dulles warned the new French president, Charles de Gaulle, that the geopolitical context in which the French test would take place would be among the criteria used to make the decision to start military cooperation with France, his successor, Christian Herter, told de Gaulle that a successful nuclear test would be deemed "sufficient" by the State Department.[58] Still, the final responsibility to decide to extend the 1958 McMahon Act to another country was in the hands of the US senators, and as the Gaither report controversy illustrated, most senators did not espouse the goal of helping either a European or a French nuclear-weapons program get off the ground.

This ambiguity deeply affected the nuclear choices made by the new government led by de Gaulle. The entry into force of the 1958 McMahon Act one month after de Gaulle returned to power incited de Gaulle to accelerate the French nuclear military program on a purely national basis, so that France could join the Anglo-American exchange circuit of trust, from which it had been, from his perspective, unduly excluded since the Quebec Agreement.[59] In June 1958, de Gaulle's first act as the new head of government was to abrogate the tripartite nuclear agreements signed in November 1957 with Germany and Italy.[60] He also cancelled the tripartite organization of uranium enrichment for the joint production of nuclear weapons (with the West Germans and the Italians), one month after the agreements had been signed.[61] In July of 1958, this decision was relayed to the West German minister of defense, Frantz Strauss, by the new French minister of the armies and former administrator of the CEA and president of Electricité de France (EDF), Pierre Guillaumat (1909–91). Confronted with the fury of the West German minister, some French officials as well as John Foster Dulles, the US secretary of state at the time, tried to intercede: for instance, Dulles asked the West Germans to temper their anger, hoping that the general could be made to change his mind by other means. But Dulles's death and the absence of sanction from the United States—but not from the Germans[62]—convinced de Gaulle that he should further dissociate the French nuclear-weapons program from the other Europeans on the Continent (as the British had done).

De Gaulle's belief that all US decision makers agreed that one nuclear test would constitute "sufficient progress," enabling the start of US-French military cooperation, triggered a series of key decisions.[63] From 1958 to 1960, the French government was convinced that by reclaiming sovereignty over its nuclear affairs, France increased the odds that the State Department and Congress (and the future president) would reward France with US help in the development of the nuclear (uranium-enrichment and naval nuclear propulsion) and nonnuclear (missile) technologies involved in the creation of a modern nuclear deterrent. Because de Gaulle perceived Eisenhower and the Eurofederalists as losing ground on nuclear policy, he refused Eisenhower and Norstad's proposal, during the meetings of the NATO Council of December 1958, for cooperation on the nonnuclear aspects involved in the creation of a NATO nuclear deterrent (based on the American "Polaris" land-based design) with a European consortium including the West Germans. Even though the minister of armed forces, Guillaumat, thought that France should participate,[64] de Gaulle rejected the US offer, arguing that the range of the missiles (fifteen hundred miles) was too limited to allow France to strike Russian territory,[65] and that West German participation contradicted the new bilateral relation that de Gaulle hoped to form with the United States (and with the United Kingdom).[66]

In parallel, the French government proposed new, clear terms for a future nuclear military alliance. De Gaulle proposed to Eisenhower in September 1958 (and then to Kennedy when the latter came to power) not only to disentangle France's nuclear program from West Germany's in order to form a stronger association among the three former occupying powers in Europe (France, the United States, and the United Kingdom), but also to consider a grand reform of NATO's statutes, which would provide for the three former occupying powers to fully cooperate on nuclear military matters; for the democratically elected heads of government to consult one another often on matters of strategy throughout the globe (and not just in Europe);[67] and for each head of government to have a veto power over the preemptive use of nuclear force by any of the three nations.[68] De Gaulle, when he claimed that the "job of SACEUR should disappear,"[69] not only challenged the galaxy of Eurofederalist ideas supporting European nuclear integration (with Franco-German cooperation as a building block), but he also responded to the strategic uncertainty and legal indeterminacy that prevailed in the US field of foreign policy after Sputnik. Indeed, in March 1959, Guillaumat explained de Gaulle's *démarche* to the US secretary of defense, Thomas Gates, by arguing that "General de Gaulle wanted to avoid the French government slipping into a nuclear war because of a decision he did not take."[70] If the United States struck first,[71] the French nuclear strategist General Pierre Marie Gallois, whose theses influenced de Gaulle, feared that French entanglement with the United States through NATO would lead to a nuclear holocaust in Europe, while the United States would turn its territory into a "safe haven."[72]

Despite de Gaulle's best efforts, the ambiguity of the rules guiding the future transatlantic cooperation in military nuclear affairs remained intact. Eisenhower ignored the NATO reform proposed by de Gaulle, along with most smaller NATO powers, which were shocked that de Gaulle would dare exclude them from the government of the alliance.[73] Despite this negative reaction, de Gaulle continued to pursue clearer guidelines, ultimately deciding to proceed swiftly and unilaterally with his desired clarification:

de Gaulle wrote to Eisenhower in May 1959, announcing that he would remove the French forces stationed in the Mediterranean Sea from the integrated command of NATO and would create two French posts to command the French forces in that area.[74] France's unilateral move was not a violation of the obligations contracted under the North Atlantic Treaty in 1949—as France remained in the alliance—but it was a radical change in France's interpretation of NATO and its integrated structure. In many ways, this policy change anticipated the changes that Kennedy would make to NATO's command structure when he abrogated the (predelegated) right to start a nuclear war in Europe that Eisenhower had secretly granted to NATO's supreme commander.[75] But the fact that these changes were introduced in a unilateral manner rather than by a concerted effort to clarify key rules eventually worked against de Gaulle's proposed reform.

In fact, General de Gaulle's reading of the power balance among competing schools in the US field of foreign policy was based on a misperception, which had deep consequences for the success of the reform that he sought to attain with regard to US-French nuclear cooperation. De Gaulle overestimated the dominance of international liberals in the US field of power. Instead of responding positively to de Gaulle's unilateral reinterpretation of NATO and the role that France should play in it, nationalists in the US Congress gained the upper hand and moved to punish France by restricting the extent to which it allowed the AEC to cooperate with the French on nuclear matters of strategic importance. In May 1959, the US Congress pressured the secretary of state, Christian Herter, into announcing that de Gaulle's unilateral decision with regard to NATO led them "to suspend the negotiations, which had been nearly completed, for a nuclear submarine agreement with France,"[76] an agreement that John Foster Dulles had promised in November 1957 to the former French president of the council as a reward for the Europeanization of the French nuclear deterrent. In May 1959, the bilateral defense treaty signed by the French and American governments offered US aid in constructing a prototype submarine reactor and the highly enriched uranium needed for its operation, on the condition that the prototype had to be built on land: the US Congress distinguished between a land-based reactor, considered "peaceful," and a prototype reactor actually placed in a submarine, considered "military," hence classified.[77] This decision was a blow for France, and it increased the costs of building submarines propelled by nuclear energy.[78]

More important, the US foreign policy makers used the ambiguity of the 1958 McMahon Act to further punish France for the unilateral manner in which de Gaulle had brought some clarification to the goals of the alliance regarding nuclear matters: after the French government finally exploded its first nuclear weapon in the Algerian desert in February 1960, the French government hoped that its unilateral actions would force Anglo-American powers to review France's role in NATO, and that it would trigger nuclear military cooperation on a bilateral (or trilateral) basis. But the series of unilateral moves imposed by de Gaulle, and the ascent of RAND-ites in the corridors of the US Congress, led senators to decide against the extension of the 1958 McMahon Act to the French government, despite Herter's promises. The ambiguity of that notion of "sufficient progress" allowed US senators to argue that one explosion was not enough to qualify the French for American cooperation in dual-use activities, which Congress deemed military.[79] Besides, the senators did not clarify what further steps would be needed before France could benefit from US help: they protected their monopoly over the interpretation of their domestic law.

Still, this reinterpretation was not without costs for the United States. The US decision to refuse to extend the terms of the 1958 McMahon Act to France created the same catalyst as the US refusal to support the Franco-British Suez operation in the case of the Euratom Treaty negotiations. Indeed, seeing that they could not trust the United States to keep its word, de Gaulle and Adenauer started a process of Franco-German rapprochement. First, in July 1960, de Gaulle proposed to the West German chancellor a closer military cooperation, in which France would give protection to the West Germans in exchange for their political support for the reform of the Atlantic Alliance and of the European Communities along the lines sought by de Gaulle. Second, in October 1960, President de Gaulle and Chancellor Adenauer signed bilateral agreements that planned Franco-German cooperation in the development of missile technology, the nonnuclear part of the nuclear deterrent in which West Germans had long had a unique mastery of technological processes. These agreements revived some aspects of the defunct Franco-German Agreement of January 1957. General de Gaulle still excluded the West Germans from cooperation in military nuclear activities, but the bilateral agreement institutionalized Franco-German consultation on nuclear strategy, which highlighted that the two nations agreed on the principles of "forward defense" and "early and massive use" of nuclear weapons against Soviet forces and cities, which put them at odds with the new doctrine of flexible and centralized response defended by the incoming Kennedy administration.[80] That de Gaulle could convince the West German chancellor to strengthen their bilateral relation outside of NATO proved that West Europeans had started to doubt the ability of the United States to lead the alliance and to honor its commitments to strengthen Europe's defense.

The Force of Publicity: The Limited Jurisdiction of the United States–Euratom Treaty

If ambiguous domestic legislation could be interpreted differently when new groups of US foreign policy elites with different strategic concepts came to dominate the US government, it was less clear how the same domestic changes would affect the implementation of multilateral instruments such as the United States–Euratom Treaty (1958). The rise of Democrats to power did not affect the public interpretation of the United States–Euratom Treaty, but rather the ambitions that Eurofederalists had kept private during its negotiation. The new foreign policy elites wanted to use the United States–Euratom Treaty to sell peaceful US nuclear technologies to Europe. Indeed, according to the public interpretation of the treaty, the Europeans had committed to buy peaceful power plants and the amount of fissile materials necessary to fuel them; in exchange, the AEC had agreed to give Euratom the exclusive right to control how Europeans used the fuels. A Euratom official noted that the "Americans were ready to send large quantities of enriched uranium and plutonium to Euratom," but that the "Americans would send these quantities on the basis of the reports of advancement of our projects in power development, that the [European] supply agency could routinely send them."[81] In effect, the AEC and the JCAE blamed the Euratom Commission for failing to live up to what it perceived as its treaty obligations: in early 1960, "the only power station to be built in the framework of the agreement was the plant ordered in southern Italy"[82] by an Italian public utility, against the six to eight power plants that the Three Wise Men had promised to buy from the United States. Though the responsibility was shared by the French government,[83] which insisted on developing French-designed power reactors that used natural uranium, the AEC blamed the Euratom Commission and its new president, Etienne Hirsh,[84] for failing to fulfill its promise.

At the same time, the rise of nationalists in the US government brought an end to the Eurofederalist dreams of using the United States–Euratom Treaty to expand the treaty's initial technoscientific program, and to create an integrated European nuclear industry with jurisdiction in essential fields for the production of a European nuclear deterrent (such as uranium-enrichment, naval propulsion, and plutonium-reprocessing activities). In contrast to the Euratom Commission, which encouraged its member states—in particular, the Dutch—to develop new uranium-enrichment technologies such as centrifugation technologies within the framework of Euratom, and to seek help from the United States within the framework of the United States–Euratom Treaty, the United States incited the Dutch to avoid sharing their results with other nations, even with Euratom member states.[85] As the French director of the CEA's foreign policy noted, "In 1960, the U.S. even obtained from [West Germany and the Netherlands] a promise that their work would remain strictly secret, should it prove successful, as the method could be used by any industrialized country for the annual manufacture of one or two nuclear weapons."[86] Furthermore, despite attempts by the Euratom Commission and the State Department to forge direct cooperation in uranium-enrichment activities with American scientists and engineers outside the purview of the AEC, "the AEC insisted on excluding all contributions [to Euratom] from [university laboratories and] national laboratories," and "on first screening all of the proposals from the U.S."[87] The AEC insisted on strictly limiting the United States–Euratom collaboration in research and development to the study of how the US power plants sold to Euratom could be optimized.[88] As Max Kohnstamm, Etienne Hirsh, and Jules Guéron summarized their visit to the United States in June 1959: Eurofederalists such as "Schaetzel know about this situation,"[89] but were unable to turn the tide in the AEC,[90] because "changes in personnel in the AEC have driven away the 'driving spirits' in charge of Euratom collaboration," and "the new ones . . . are not aware of the capital import of Euratom for the Europe of Six and for the U.S."[91]

Ultimately, the US Congress and the AEC stuck to the public interpretation of the jurisdictional boundaries of Euratom and United States–Euratom relationships that had been given to them in 1958 by the Three Wise Men. This public interpretation excluded the production of special fissionable materials (by centrifugation techniques, for instance) from the range of peaceful activities covered by the treaty. When the Euratom Commission objected to the limitations the AEC placed on its cooperation in September 1959,[92] the chairman of the JCAE commissioned a report on the progress of both the IAEA and Euratom. The report's authors were sympathetic to Eurofederalist views, and advised the AEC to develop joint cooperation with Euratom's research and development program, including in "atomic ship propulsion" and "low-cost methods of isotope separation to secure both industrial and military support," rather than remaining within the confines of "power generation."[93] But the JCAE rejected their conclusion, and opposed the idea that the United States might help Euratom develop new uranium-enrichment techniques.[94]

Based on their interpretation of the United States–Euratom Treaty, the US authorities even rejected the attempt by the Euratom Commission to convince the AEC to export sensitive materials, such as highly enriched uranium, to France via Euratom. As reported by Bertrand Goldschmidt, when the president of the Euratom Commission, Etienne Hirsh, "made a personal approach to the American authorities . . . to supply all the enriched uranium fuel for the first French breeder reactor, Rapsodie, which was built in successful collaboration with Euratom,"[95] the US authorities refused, as the fuel would not be used in the power plants that the Three Wise Men had promised to buy from the United States. The AEC chairman actually publicly criticized Hirsh's initiative in 1960,[96] even if Hirsh was right to say that the commission could very well include "French demands for plutonium and highly enriched uranium from the U.S. . . . to the demands presented by the Commission to the U.S.,"[97] as the United States–Euratom Treaty included the guarantee that the United States would "transfer fuel for up to ten years for the needs of the Euratom Community at a reasonable price."[98] As Jules Guéron, then director of Euratom research and teaching, wrote, "It [wa]s possible that [the AEC chairman] did not understand these treaty provisions, but the French official who knew about Euratom . . . should have rectified [the chairman's] mistake."[99]

The US Congress reinforced the French interpretation of Euratom's jurisdiction, which, in the words of de Gaulle, remained limited to advancing "intergovernmental cooperation for research and development"[100] in exclusively peaceful nuclear activities concerned with power plant operation or research in new peaceful fields holding long-term promise, such as peaceful applications of nuclear fusion. The limitations that the United States placed on Euratom also helped de Gaulle convince other Euratom member states to conduct their enrichment and reprocessing projects outside the Euratom Treaty framework, on a purely intergovernmental basis.[101] For example, European cooperation in uranium enrichment took place outside Euratom, as part of a multinational joint venture called "Eurodif" in French territory, with France as the main nation owning the technology, and the other nations participating in the Eurodif project receiving a guaranteed fuel supply from France. As Guéron noted, "Eurodif was a European project in enrichment which carefully avoided the Euratom Commission, whereas the legal statutes of 'Community Enterprise' had been specifically conceived to allow this kind of venture."[102] Projects in the field of plutonium reprocess-

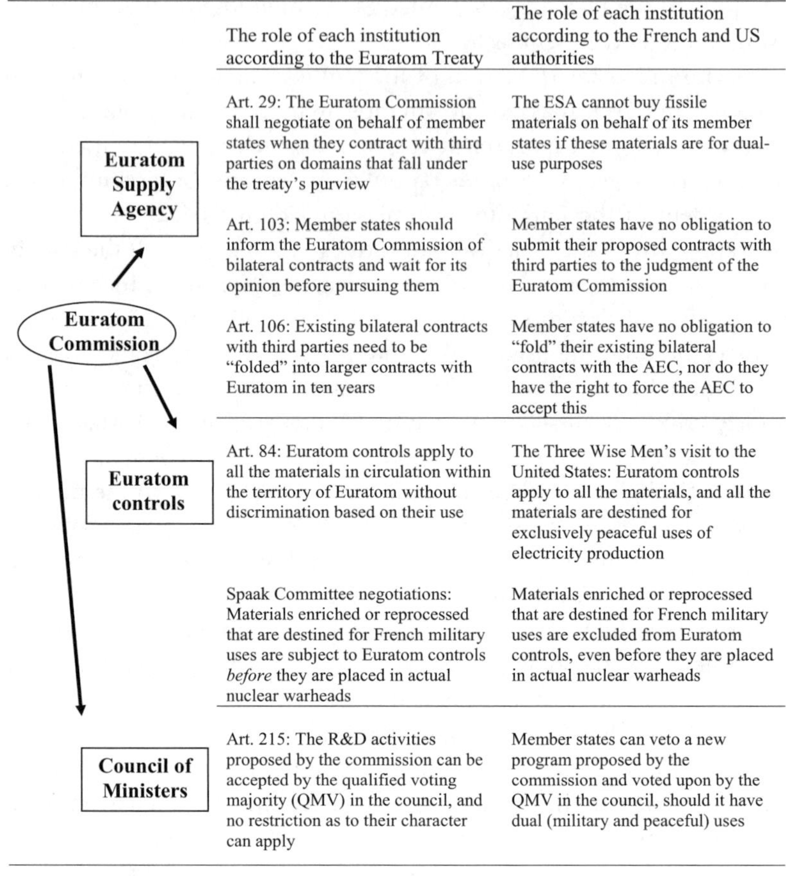

	The role of each institution according to the Euratom Treaty	The role of each institution according to the French and US authorities
Euratom Supply Agency	Art. 29: The Euratom Commission shall negotiate on behalf of member states when they contract with third parties on domains that fall under the treaty's purview	The ESA cannot buy fissile materials on behalf of its member states if these materials are for dual-use purposes
	Art. 103: Member states should inform the Euratom Commission of bilateral contracts and wait for its opinion before pursuing them	Member states have no obligation to submit their proposed contracts with third parties to the judgment of the Euratom Commission
Euratom Commission	Art. 106: Existing bilateral contracts with third parties need to be "folded" into larger contracts with Euratom in ten years	Member states have no obligation to "fold" their existing bilateral contracts with the AEC, nor do they have the right to force the AEC to accept this
Euratom controls	Art. 84: Euratom controls apply to all the materials in circulation within the territory of Euratom without discrimination based on their use	The Three Wise Men's visit to the United States: Euratom controls apply to all the materials, and all the materials are destined for exclusively peaceful uses of electricity production
	Spaak Committee negotiations: Materials enriched or reprocessed that are destined for French military uses are subject to Euratom controls *before* they are placed in actual nuclear warheads	Materials enriched or reprocessed that are destined for French military uses are excluded from Euratom controls, even before they are placed in actual nuclear warheads
Council of Ministers	Art. 215: The R&D activities proposed by the commission can be accepted by the qualified voting majority (QMV) in the council, and no restriction as to their character can apply	Member states can veto a new program proposed by the commission and voted upon by the QMV in the council, should it have dual (military and peaceful) uses

Figure 6.3. The conflicting interpretations of the Euratom Treaty

ing for Euratom put forth by Etienne Hirsh also collapsed, especially when de Gaulle developed cooperation in plutonium-reprocessing technologies (in the Eurochemic fuel reprocessing plant at Mol, in Belgium) under the framework of the European Nuclear Energy Agency (ENEA), part of the OEEC (transformed into the OECD in 1960). Later, after Hirsh's tenure as president of Euratom, each time technoscientific proposals emanated from the office of Jules Guéron, "France refused the Euratom framework, and proposed to realize [the projects] with Germany on a bilateral basis."[103]

Eurofederalists paid the price for opacity: because the US government rejected the private definition that the Euratom Commission gave of its jurisdictional boundaries (by excluding many dual-use technologies from the range of peaceful technologies that it could develop jointly with Euratom), it helped France do the same: in September 1958, during meetings in de Gaulle's private home in Colombey, de Gaulle announced to Adenauer that he would faithfully apply the Rome Treaties,[104] and he consistently claimed to do so in public, even after he changed the interpretation of key rules of the Euratom Treaty (see fig. 6.3). He kept his word as far as the Common Market Treaty was concerned,[105] as he even sided with Monnet and the Action Committee[106] against British attempts to derail the transformation of the Common Market into a real customs union.[107] But as far as the Euratom Treaty was concerned, de Gaulle applied the same tactic used by the AEC, which consisted of abiding by the strict public presentation of the treaty while refusing to apply Euratom's rules (especially regarding controls) as they were privately interpreted by the negotiators of the Euratom Treaty.

The opaque interpretation of the jurisdictional boundaries of the Euratom Treaty thus allowed de Gaulle to bypass a complicated reform of the treaty, which his prime minister, Michel Debré (who held office from 1958 to 1962), had initially requested.[108] In this case, the classification struggle over the correct interpretation of Euratom's jurisdictional boundaries (and where the separation between peaceful and military nuclear technologies lay) had indeed a strong effect on how the rules, especially Euratom controls, were implemented: by limiting the scope of their application, a member state (first France, but then others) could exclude what it considered "military" activities from the control of the Euratom Commission while claiming to respect the treaty.

For instance, the Euratom Treaty expressly said that the commission should control the use of all the source and special fissionable materials circulating in Euratom's territory (with the exception of the special fissionable material in operational nuclear warheads),[109] including, for instance, the plutonium processed in France (at Marcoule) that was destined for military uses.[110] The Euratom Treaty negotiators had indeed agreed in October 1956 that the only materials that the Euratom Commission would deem "military" (hence falling outside its jurisdiction and controls) were those placed in nuclear warheads.[111] As the commission noted, "When HEU [highly enriched uranium] is used for direct military applications, the French government owns it, but when it is corrupted, reprocessed and potentially used for other purposes, then it falls under the jurisdiction [and control] of Euratom."[112] The French government disagreed, and said so privately to the president of the Euratom Commission. According to de Gaulle, France would not send any information on the amount and location of the fissile materials "destined to" be weaponized—that is to say, those that were not yet placed in nuclear warheads but that might be in production.[113] The French government claimed, for instance, that the plutonium that was being reprocessed in Marcoule was already military in nature, and therefore no longer under the ownership and control of the Euratom Community, whose jurisdiction was limited to purely peaceful activities (see fig. 6.3).[114]

France and the Euratom Commission were also opposed due to interpretive conflicts regarding the extension of Euratom's control to the special fissionable materials bought by member states from outside Euratom (and not only those materials produced in Marcoule or Pierrelatte). These disputes started when France and the United States signed a bilateral defense agreement in May 1959, under the terms of which France bought a prototype submarine reactor (to be based on land) and the highly enriched uranium used to fuel it. The Euratom Commission claimed that it should be informed of and consulted on the amount of highly enriched uranium necessary to fuel the prototype reactor sold to the French (see fig. 6.3). The legal services of the Euratom Commission claimed that, if "the Community does not need be informed of treaties concerning [solely] defense (like planning the sharing of nuclear bombs on one territory)," which were contracted in a bilateral manner by the United States and importing NATO member states, it shall nonetheless "be informed of treaties of mutual security, if the activities planned by the treaty can have peaceful as well as military impact: for instance, the treaty between France and U.S. which plans that France will get some HEU for prototypes of nuclear submarines,"[115] and that could include the exchange of "knowledge necessary to build a nuclear submarine that will be useful for instance to build a cargo [ship] or a tanker [propelled by nuclear reaction]."[116] Furthermore, the Euratom Treaty stated that "where an agreement . . . for the exchange of scientific or industrial information in the nuclear field between a member state . . . on the one hand, and a third state . . . or a national of a third state on the other, requires, on either part, the signature of a state *acting in its sovereign capacity*,[117] it shall be concluded by the Commission" (art. 29). Thus, Etienne Hirsh, the president of the commission, claimed that the commission had to comment on bilateral contracts "within a month" of being informed of them, and if the commission did not agree with the contract, "the state shall not conclude the proposed agreement or contract until it has satisfied the objections of the Commission or complied with a ruling by the Court of Justice" (art. 103, 106).[118] Hirsh's argument was strengthened by the interpretation of the US Congress, which had explicitly indicated that the prototype of the submarine nuclear reactor sold to France was "peaceful," because France had not made "sufficient progress" to qualify for nuclear military cooperation as outlined by the 1958 McMahon Act. Therefore, argued the president of the commission, France could not unilaterally declare its cooperation with the United States to be military in nature.

Here again, the French government disagreed with the Euratom Commission and refused to submit the requested information.[119] De Gaulle restricted the jurisdiction of the Euratom Treaty to the activities that the US Congress considered exclusively peaceful, such as the import of power plants, and he benefited from the silence of the US Congress, which gave no indication that it intended these fuels to be controlled by Euratom. As far as "source materials" (and not just "special fissionable materials") were concerned, France also insisted on keeping the Euratom Commission at arm's length in terms of the amounts and prices of nuclear fuels imported to France. As Gabrielle Hecht shows,[120] after de Gaulle's return, France privileged its relationships with its former colonies[121] as far as access to raw nuclear materials (such as natural uranium, which was used as fuel in French power plants) was concerned. As Bertrand Goldschmidt wrote, "By 1960, the world market of uranium was in surplus, and the CEA discovered large [supplies of] uranium in Niger, which ensured French autonomy in uranium procurement."[122] France did not intend to report the amounts of "source materials" that it extracted from Niger for its nuclear program to the Euratom Supply Agency, whose authority was limited, according to the French interpretation, to the "sale" of uranium (natural or enriched) to a Euratom member state—whereas the French nuclear mining business directly "extracted" (rather than "bought") natural uranium from the Niger soil.[123] As a result, the Euratom Commission noted in 1960, "Efforts by the Commission to transfer all bilateral fuel procurement agreements from member states to the Commission, in conformity with article 106 of the treaty, have not succeeded in producing any concrete result."[124] The role of facilitator that Euratom was supposed to play in helping its member states access nuclear fuels on a phantom "market"[125] of nuclear fuels (either source or special fissionable materials) was put in jeopardy.

As these examples illustrate, the domestic changes in the United States and France left intact the visible tip of the legal iceberg—the public treaties organizing transatlantic nuclear trade—but cut off from the hidden base formed by the cluster of secret agreements. In so doing, they led to restrictions in the jurisdiction of the public treaties and to changes in the interpretation of opaque rules.

These interpretive disputes were not solved publicly: the opacity of the control rules allowed each side in the controversy to deny that such reinterpretation was taking place. In this case, the reinterpretation was finally imposed upon the commission when the commission was purged of its Euro-federalist members—in particular, its president, Etienne Hirsh. Indeed, de Gaulle fired him at the end of 1961, after a clash between de Gaulle and Hirsh on the question of voting rights in the European Council of Ministers.[126] Hirsh introduced a proposal (opposed by France) to use Euratom to create a pool of prototypes of breeder reactors (reactors using highly sensitive fissile materials, such as highly enriched uranium and plutonium) owned and operated by Euratom—a proposal that his brother-in-law, Jules Guéron, had prepared.[127] In order to bypass French opposition, Hirsh decided to use the procedure of qualified majority voting (QMV) to pass the proposal in the Council of Ministers, invoking article 215 of the Euratom Treaty. As a result, the proposal "was adopted by the qualified majority, with only France voting against it."[128] But when Hirsh's tenure was up for renewal at the end of 1961, de Gaulle unilaterally announced the replacement of Hirsh with Pierre Chatenêt (1917–97), who was then minister of the interior in Michel Debré's government.

The choice of a new president for the commission who defended views radically different from Monnet's former associates sent a clear signal to other Euratom member states: Chatenêt, a member of the French Conseil d'Etat and a former coauthor of the Constitution of the Fifth Republic,[129] was clearly in favor of the protection of national sovereignty in nuclear matters. About the Euratom Treaty he was called to protect, Chatenêt said that "if I had been a deputy at the time of the Euratom Treaty negotiations, I would have voted against it."[130] As the French delegate to NATO in Pierre Mendès France's government, he had opposed the EDC Treaty in 1954. It was therefore no surprise if Chatenêt's first fait accompli "was to renounce the use of the procedure of qualified majority to vote on the second five-year plan," a renunciation that "was pronounced during one of the Council's sessions, as a spontaneous decision made by the Commission."[131] In effect, with Chatenêt's tenure, de Gaulle abrogated the supranational rules in the Euratom Treaty (qualified majority voting and the commission's monopoly on the introduction of policy proposals in the council).[132] The decision to purge the commission of the presence of Monnet's former associates revealed how little regard de Gaulle truly had for the opinion of the Euratom Commission and/or other member states in nuclear matters.[133]

The Effect of Opacity for Declining Elites (1960–65)

Rising elites can use the multiplicity of meanings (and the hierarchy between public and private ones) to impose their new policy agenda without appearing to challenge existing legal bonds. Eurofederalists' adversaries in the United States and France used the discrepancy between public and secret interpretations of the Euratom Treaty to empty it of its original purpose. They broke the linkage between the Eurofederalists' secret goal—to create a European nuclear force—and secret interpretations of the treaty. However, the question remained as to whether the US government had also abandoned Eurofederalists' secret objective, or whether it sought to achieve this goal through instruments other than the Euratom Treaty—for instance, a treaty of nuclear military cooperation with a united Europe.

Continued Opacity, Deception, and Self-Deception (1960–62)

As Arendt writes, those who know a secret truth often believe that it possesses "an ineradicable primacy"[134] over all public charades enacted to hide it. This applies to those who know the true (secret) interpretation of a treaty or agreement: for them, the agreement possesses a reality that shapes their future expectations. Even if, for conjectural reasons—for instance, domestic changes among the signatory states of that treaty—the implementation of an opaque treaty suffers some delay or drawback, the secret ambition of its promoters gains an undeniable reality that cannot be erased with one stroke of the pen by newcomers. Those who have shaped an opaque contract will deny that their creation is born dead. They tend to believe that, in the end, their truth will dominate, despite the contingent obstacles that the realization of their objective might experience in the present.

In the face of policy reversals, such as those experienced by the Eurofederalists in the late 1950s, holders of private truths are unlikely to view temporary defeats as more than temporary. Because the Eurofederalists' strategic objective of creating a European nuclear force had been translated into legal instruments once—with the signing of the Euratom Treaty, and the tripartite treaty of nuclear military cooperation between France, West Germany, and Italy—they clung to the belief that overall Western support for their strategic goal had not evaporated with the contingent abandonment of some of their secret interpretations of Euratom Treaty rules by the United States and France. After de Gaulle and Kennedy started to unravel the European legal edifice, some Eurofederalists even thought that they were in a position to achieve their larger strategic goal by asking both the United States and the member states of Euratom to publicly support the broad objective of forming a United Europe with jurisdiction over nuclear-weapons acquisition and use.

The first public campaign in favor of a European nuclear force came from Etienne Hirsh, while he was still the president of the Euratom Commission: in June 1960, Hirsh convinced the presidents of the Common Market and the Coal and Steel Communities as well as Jean Monnet's Action Committee to endorse a proposal to merge the three communities into one European Community and to clearly extend its powers to matters of common defense and military nuclear policy. Hirsh's proposal for a "merger treaty" was even introduced in the European Parliament by the Netherlands in October 1960 (despite opposition from France). With this new campaign, Eurofederalists finally made it public and clear that the ultimate goal of the Euratom Treaty, when merged with the other communities to form a new federation, would be to develop a fully fledged European Federation with jurisdiction over the military affairs of its member states.[135]

As they engaged in this new campaign, Monnet and other Eurofederalists misperceived the extent to which the French and American governments had moved away from this larger objective. Part of this miscalculation was the result of an intentional tactic of deception followed by the Eurofederalists' adversaries. Indeed, faced with Eurofederalists' mobilization, President de Gaulle and his advisor on European matters, Alain Peyrefitte (1925–99), a gifted intellectual and diplomat, decided to avoid a direct confrontation with the Eurofederalists, which could have antagonized Chancellor Adenauer. Each side (Eurofederalists and Gaullists) had shifted position on the question of whether opacity was an acceptable tool that could be used in diplomatic negotiations: the Eurofederalists now argued in favor of transparency, whereas the Gaullists, now in power, argued in favor of opacity. Indeed, in the summer of 1960, Peyrefitte wrote to de Gaulle that he should not reject Hirsh's proposals but that he should instead "let our [European] partners believe, or appear to believe, that the President of the Republic has converted himself to their federalist theses, so that scholastic quarrels between 'Europeans' and 'anti-Europeans,' promoters of the 'little Europe' vs. 'Great Europe,' 'Federation' vs. 'Confederation' shall be overcome and the Union shall be made, as it will allow the federalists to rally our French projects without losing face."[136] De Gaulle was convinced that he should not ask for a direct reform of the Euratom Treaty,[137] but that he should instead seize the opportunity offered by the negotiation of a merger treaty to subvert the European project from within, and to eliminate the Eurofederalists from the future single European Commission. As Peyrefitte wrote, de Gaulle should wait to "strangle Euratom when we shall win the upper hand."[138] In case the communities did merge, "by placing the same men to head the Communities, we could take the opportunity to create a unique new 'college' which would chloroform Euratom; we could get rid of such and such French member of the executive [such as Hirsh], and we could reduce the supranational powers of the High Authority by aligning the powers of the latter on the [less supranational] ones of the Common Market."[139]

The tactic of deception, which for de Gaulle consisted in publicly maintaining his support for European association, even extended to military questions, worked well to divide the Eurofederalist camp. Eventually, the older generation agreed to play de Gaulle's charade, and rejected Hirsh's confrontational stance toward de Gaulle. Even if they suspected that de Gaulle was not acting in good faith when he proposed a "confederation treaty,"[140] they believed that it was worth trying to find a language acceptable to de Gaulle, which, if interpreted in a certain way, would allow them to move forward with the creation of a strong Europe with jurisdiction over military affairs. Monnet remarked that "for a confederation to become a reality," it was necessary to "delegate some power to common institutions."[141] In November 1960, Monnet thus convinced Chancellor Adenauer to open new negotiations that would clarify how France and the other five Euratom members could cooperate in military (including nuclear) activities in this new community placed under a broader confederation.[142] Thus, in February 1961 in Paris, pressed by Monnet and Adenauer, the six European heads of state agreed to establish a commission chaired by the French diplomat Christian Fouchet to write a draft of the projected political union (hereafter the Fouchet Commission). The Fouchet Commission met for the first time in March 1961 to delineate the sharing of responsibilities between its permanent secretariat in Paris and the existing communities in Brussels and Strasbourg.[143] The creation of the Fouchet Commission, which quickly presented a draft treaty accepted by five out of the Six in April 1961 (with the exception of the Netherlands), gave de Gaulle an unexpected diplomatic success at a time when he scored few points on the diplomatic scene. At that time, only Monnet's former right-hand man, Etienne Hirsh, continued to criticize de Gaulle's "confederation treaty,"[144] even (and especially) after de Gaulle briefed Hirsh on the importance of supporting French views on Euratom "in the secrecy of a cabinet,"[145] as advised by Peyrefitte.[146]

In fact, by agreeing to negotiate with de Gaulle, the old Eurofederal-ists only duped themselves: de Gaulle was not interested in finding a compromise; he only wanted to buy time so that he could address European issues after the end of the Algerian war. Indeed, at the time the Fouchet Commission started its work, European discussions were far from his priorities. In April 1961, the situation in Algeria required all of de Gaulle's attention. As a result of the steps he had taken toward giving considerable "autonomy" to Algeria, some retired generals in Algeria attempted a new putsch (similar to that which had brought de Gaulle back to power) to ask for de Gaulle's resignation. Although the attempted coup aborted after a few days, de Gaulle seized emergency powers in Algeria, which he retained until the end of the conflict.[147] The situation on the ground reflected a real uneasiness, as de Gaulle increasingly moved toward granting independence to the Algerians, against the wishes of French colonists and some of his ministers (including his prime minister) who wanted France at least to retain some sovereignty over a partitioned Algeria.[148] De Gaulle's real intentions became apparent[149] when, in December 1961, he fired Hirsh, and on December 15, 1961 (the same day that the Europeans agreed to condition British membership on the British ratification of all three existing treaties as well as the "merger" treaty), he asked his foreign minister to send a new version of the Political Union Treaty (as the merger treaty was now called) to France's European partners in which no mention was made of the role of NATO in the defense of the West,[150] or of the European Communities.[151] The new draft clearly showed that de Gaulle intended to use the negotiation of the merger treaty to impose a new European regime that would suppress the jurisdiction of Euratom over all nuclear matters and that would isolate the United States from Europe. Still, at the time, the Algerian issues were not settled, and de Gaulle could not yet afford to open a new front in European affairs. So he agreed to restore the draft of the Fouchet treaty to its original form after the complaints of other Europeans.[152] The writing process dragged on from January to April 1962. De Gaulle finally dissolved the Fouchet Commission as soon as France obtained an agreement with Algerian independence fighters (the Evian Agreement, signed in March 1962 and approved by referendum in the French metropolis by a majority of over 90 percent on April 8, 1962). With his hands freed of the Algerian burden,[153] de Gaulle then pronounced the death of the merger treaty and formed a new government, led by a new prime minister, George Pompidou, replacing Michel Debré after the latter resigned in opposition to de Gaulle's policy on Algerian independence.[154] Even though de Gaulle lost the support of the pro-French-Algeria and pro-European ministers of his government,[155] the support that the French population gave at the end of the war in Algeria left him free to express more clearly his vision of Europe, and to realize it—especially since the referendum on the Evian Agreement gave the president (rather than the prime minister) full powers to implement France's new foreign policy.[156]

The collapse of the Fouchet plan should have revealed to Eurofederalists that they had clearly miscalculated their chances of obtaining de Gaulle's approval of a new treaty that would help them realize their nuclear ambitions. And some of them did understand that lesson—in particular, George Ball, Jean Monnet's preferred legal advisor in the late 1940s. At that time, Ball became involved in the discussions between Gaullists and Eurofederalists because the failure of the Fouchet plan opened the new cycle of negotiations of British adhesion to the three European Communities, which had been postponed until the signature of the "confederation treaty,"[157] which the United Kingdom would have signed at the same time as the other treaties in order to become an integral part of the European Communities. In April 1962, Hirsh's isolated voice was no longer heard since his departure from the Euratom Commission, but Undersecretary of State George Ball now understood the necessity to extract clearly and publicly expressed commitments from de Gaulle. Ball believed that the prospect of British entry into Euratom should be used to oppose de Gaulle's European design, this time clearly. In June 1962, Ball warned Kennedy that, in the context of British negotiations to enter Euratom, the British prime minister might ask him to authorize sharing with the French the technology they had acquired either indigenously or with US help (i.e., before and/or after the 1958 McMahon Act)—for instance, on nuclear propulsion technology for submarines and nuclear warhead designs. Ball wrote to Kennedy, "We should make crystal clear to the British that we would be strongly opposed to any sharing of U.S. or U.K. information with France,"[158] especially outside the Euratom Treaty framework. When dealing with an ally that consistently tried to play with the interpretation of treaty rules, Kennedy found he had to propose contracts that were as complete and transparent as possible,[159] to protect himself against future criticisms from the US Congress or Eurofederalists on the Continent.[160] As Ball stated, "Even if the sharing were thus limited to U.K. information [obtained prior to the 1958 McMahon Act], there would be a presumption in Europe that the U.S. had connived in it, at least tacitly," and "public U.S. statements to the contrary would be taken with a grain of salt, in view of the close Anglo-American relation."[161] Furthermore, Ball expected that "the French would be constantly pressing for further British elucidation, discussion and cooperation," and the "British would have a hard time, in the face of this pressure, deciding where pre-1958 information ended, and post-1959 information began." Furthermore, "if the British interpreted this line constructively, there would be continuing U.S.-U.K. friction," and "if the British interpreted the dividing line strictly, the French would claim that they were being fouled." Then "a situation would be quickly created in which the British would be pressing us to allow the U.K. to share U.S. information as well," and "U.S.-French tensions would be even greater than at present as a result."[162] Furthermore—for Ball, in particular—the objective of forming a European federation with nuclear weapons should no longer be an opaque goal privately discussed by a handful of statesmen (Eisenhower, Dulles, Monnet, Adenauer, etc.) behind closed doors, but a legitimate objective that the State Department should publicly ask its allies to pursue.

Ball's turn toward transparency reinforced the common misperception among Eurofederalists on the European Continent that the United States and the United Kingdom wished to pursue the objective of creating a European nuclear force, and that they might soon realize their dream. In the context of British negotiations with Euratom member states, Ball urged Kennedy to back up the proposal that Edward Heath, the British foreign secretary, put on the negotiating table when he told the Euratom partners in July 1962 that in exchange for British entry into the European Communities, "Euratom would take over the Capenhurst plant in isotopic separation," whose "products and personnel would be made available for the French if they wanted so,"[163] and that the British government seriously considered "the possibility of using the British isotopic separation plant of Capenhurst for the purpose of building a European nuclear force."[164] With this British proposal on the table, Eurofederalists were hopeful that their temporary defeat with the extension of Euratom to dual-use nuclear activities would be reversed, and that the American and British governments would convince de Gaulle to accept their conditions. The US commitment to the Eurofederalist goal, which Kennedy repeated in a speech prepared by George Ball and his former boss Jean Monnet,[165] delivered in Philadelphia in July 1962,[166] was given a concrete existence with the British decision to place their dual-use industries under Euratom's jurisdiction. The British decision was a step toward the realization of the US-declared objective of establishing a European federation with jurisdiction over all nuclear matters, into which the French and British nuclear activities would be subsumed.[167] The French Ministry of Foreign Affairs noticed that "many Eur-

Table 6.2 Conditions placed by the United States and France upon British entry into Euratom

Negotiation points	Nuclear cooperation along intergovernmental lines de Gaulle / Nitze / Bohlen	Nuclear cooperation along Eurofederalist lines Monnet/Hirsh/Ball/Heath
Concerning British (and French) nuclear weapons technology	Franco-British bilateral cooperation would take place outside the Euratom Treaty	The US president must prevent a secret Franco-British deal
	France will refuse to place its nuclear weapons under the jurisdiction of NATO, unless NATO is reformed according to de Gaulle's plan	Eventually, the French and the British must place their nuclear deterrents under the authority of the SACEUR, who will represent the Atlantic Federation and speak on behalf of the Atlantic Council
Concerning British (and French) dual-use nuclear technologies	French and British dual-use facilities shall not be placed under Euratom controls	The United Kingdom will place all of its dual-use facilities under Euratom control
	The Euratom Commission shall not be informed of the nature of the secret patents deposited by the French and British concerning dual-use technology	The British enrichment plant will become the property of Euratom
	The French and British will use, or not, the Euratom Supply Agency to buy fissile materials abroad and to serve as a "façade" to hide British sales of highly sensitive fissile materials for French military uses	

atom member-states [in particular, the West Germans and Italians] were not pained to see France's primacy in nuclear matters stolen by the UK" when Heath proposed to "Euratomize Capenhurst."[168]

In fact, the British position was a divine surprise to the Eurofederalists on the Continent, and a bad surprise to the French government. Indeed, de Gaulle had initially hoped that the British entry into Euratom would give France the opportunity to clearly reject once and for all the goal of placing Europe's dual-use nuclear industries under the jurisdiction of Euratom.[169] The French Ministry of Foreign Affairs noted that before 1962, the declarations of the British "clearly show that the British are less prone to apply the Rome Treaty than we are," and that "the British entry would give us a strong support in our bargaining position with the other five members."[170]

The French government immediately saw the threat that such conditions to the British adhesion to the communities represented: de Gaulle was aware that Eurofederalists could use the British bid for membership to give legitimacy to an extension of Euratom's jurisdiction to France's military nuclear affairs.[171] The French government thus consistently refused the British proposal from the beginning to the end of negotiations in 1962. It made it equally clear to the Europeans that it conditioned British membership in Euratom on their decision to share nuclear military technology and materials, which France did not have at that time, on a bilateral basis and outside the Euratom Treaty framework (see table 6.2).[172] Indeed, the French government was convinced that its nuclear-weapons program could be quickly developed "if the U.S. accepts that British knowledge be made available for France"[173]—in particular, that "France could make considerable economies" if it was granted "availability of [some weapons-grade] HEU for military studies (H-bombs and warheads) five years before the end of Pierrelatte,"[174] the future French uranium-enrichment plant. To match the British proposal to "Euratomize" their enrichment plant, the French were forced to massively increase the appropriation of funds for the construction of the uranium-enrichment plant in Pierrelatte,[175] in order to send a signal to the French military forces that the end of the Algerian war would enable the French government to spend more on its nuclear program.[176] It also signaled to France's Euratom partners that the French were committed to mastering the enrichment technology quickly and independently of British aid, and outside the Euratom Treaty framework.[177] As the French made clear, they did not "ask the British to Euratomize a British research center in exchange for their adhesion,"[178] but rather, they wanted the British "to provide us with some fuel (Pu) [plutonium] for fast reactors as well as some patented information"[179] on military designs. The discussion advanced no further until the fall of 1962: the controversy over whether the British bid for adhesion to Euratom would help Euratom extend its jurisdiction remained open, or rather, closed without any prospect of compromise.

When Opacity Failed the Eurofederalists—Again (Fall 1962–Fall 1964)

In the summer of 1962, even if Eurofederalists realized that the United States had severely limited the extent to which Euratom member states could use the Euratom Treaty to move closer to the acquisition of a European nuclear deterrent, their hopes that the adhesion of the United Kingdom to Euratom would help them realize that goal were paradoxically at their highest. Now that President Kennedy openly advocated for the realization of their secret goal, they saw the reversals of the past two years as temporary obstacles on the road toward the creation of a European nuclear force—which would be free if only de Gaulle could be forced out of power. Thus, they completely missed the fact that the US government had radically altered its strategic objectives—and abandoned such a goal—as a result of the Cuban missile crisis.

The Cuban missile crisis had (on the face of it) a paradoxical result on Eurofederalist plans: in October 1962, the Soviets sent a clear message that they wanted the United States to abrogate some of the existing bilateral NATO nuclear-sharing agreements signed by Eisenhower in 1958; Kennedy responded by proposing to NATO allies an even more ambitious multilateral nuclear-sharing plan of Eurofederalist inspiration. This was all the more surprising that the international liberals in his administration (McNamara in particular)[180] had made it clear that this very same multilateral agreement was no longer on the table in July 1962. In fact, by abrogating existing bilateral agreements, and replacing them with the (unrealistic) promise of a multilateral plan, Kennedy followed a face-saving strategy, which allowed him to respond positively to the exchange requested by the Soviets. Indeed, when the Soviet medium-range missiles carrying nuclear warheads were discovered in Cuba in the fall of 1962, the Soviets told President Kennedy that the United States would have to take back the land-based "Jupiter" missiles that were still in joint custody with Turkey in exchange for the removal of the Soviet missiles in Cuba.[181] This was not a controversial proposal for Kennedy and some of his advisors. When he learned of the Soviet proposal to trade missiles for missiles, the president said, "Most people will regard this as not an unreasonable proposal."[182] Even Kennedy's trusted advisors, such as Averell Harriman, believed that "the placing of our missiles in Turkey and Italy was counter-productive," not only because "the missiles can be destroyed so easily, but beyond, because they have been humiliating to Soviet pride that they had to permit such a threat to exist so near."[183] Yet, much of the problem that President Kennedy faced was that the public nature of the Soviet request made it difficult for the US government to act without first asking for the agreement of the Turks,[184] as the missiles were owned by the Turks, and even the nuclear warheads inside the missiles were in the joint custody of the United States and Turkey on behalf of NATO.[185] To get out of the crisis without publicly admitting before NATO allies that the United States had accepted the deal proposed by the Soviets, George Ball and his assistants in the State Department suggested in October 1962 that Kennedy should say nothing to NATO allies, not consult with them, and say directly to the Russians, "Well, sure, we'll accept your offer. If this is a matter of grave concern to you, and you equate these things [missiles in Cuba and Turkey], which we don't but if you do, ok, we can work it out, and we're going to put Polaris [submarines] in the Mediterranean because you've got the whole seas to range in, and we can't keep you out of the ocean."[186] Ball's tactic convinced Kennedy. On the evening of October 27, the president sent his brother, Robert Kennedy, to the Soviet ambassador, Dobrynin, to say that the United States accepted the secret deal, but "that any attempt to treat the President's unilateral assurance as part of a deal would simply make that assurance inoperative."[187]

The US acceptance of a secret deal with the Soviets was a risky tactic, as for some older strategists such as Norstad, Acheson, and Nitze (who all advised against it),[188] removing the Turkish missiles was "absolutely anathema as a matter of prestige and politics": for them, an arrangement with the Soviets would expose the United States to accusations of "a Munich-like sell-out."[189] Indeed, if the terms of the deal were revealed, the credibility of the American commitment to NATO would crumble. But, as Ball concluded, "I don't think NATO is going to be wrecked, and if NATO isn't any better than that, it isn't that good to us."[190]

The Kennedy administration needed to leave unacknowledged the secret agreement. For that, it counted on British support to craft a public charade about why it would ask the Turks to remove their land-based missiles, and other governments had to agree to support that charade. Indeed, Ball and others convinced Kennedy that the United Kingdom, instead of the United States, should revive the defunct plan proposed for NATO in 1960 by older Eurofederalists (such as Eisenhower, Bowie, and Norstad), which consisted in creating, within NATO, a multilateral submarine force equipped with nuclear warheads manned by European as well as American officers, and publicly inviting the Turks to join it in exchange for the removal of their land-based missiles.[191] Then, British pressure, not Soviet pressure, would be seen as explaining why the United States would press the Turks to remove the Jupiter land-based missiles in Turkey, the United Kingdom, and Italy, in exchange for those countries' participation in a multilateral force (MLF) made of NATO submarines with Polaris missiles carrying nuclear warheads. The US ambassador to Ankara wrote to Ball during the Cuban missile crisis, "[The] British abandoning of [land-based] Thors and possible Italian agreement to dismantle [land-based] Jupiters could be helpful in approaching [the] Turks."[192] As Robert McNamara (the secretary of defense) observed, it would seem quite credible that the United States had made no deal with the Soviets if the United States could say to the Turks that "the Jupiter missile is obsolete" and that "the British have recognized the obsolescence of the Thor and have decided to take it out and replace it with other systems of which Polaris is an effective one." Thus, as McNamara continued, the United States just "proposed the same thing to be done for Turkey," and "Italy too."[193]

Until the Cuban missile crisis, the Eurofederalists around Jean Monnet believed that they had a fairly good perception of the balance of power between Eurofederalists, international liberals, and nationalists in the US government. But after the crisis, they failed to realize that George Ball, their main ally in the US government, no longer espoused their cherished objective—even against the Soviets' will—and that he, Bundy, and McNamara, had moved closer to the international liberals' view on transatlantic nuclear cooperation. The public charade that Ball, Bundy, and McNamara advised the president to play was staged in early December 1962 at Nassau by the same young, civilian nuclear strategists who had been privy to the deal made with the Soviets during the Cuban missile crisis.[194] There, the United Kingdom agreed to the proposal to give up its NATO land-based missiles, only insisting that they would keep the new Polaris missiles in their own nuclear submarines (staffed exclusively by British naval officers and not manned by crews of various NATO nationalities), until the future command structure controlling a multilateral force of NATO members was created. In fact, Kennedy's advisors and Kennedy himself understood very well that the generous Anglo-American agreement signed at Nassau was not only, as Marc Trachtenberg writes, "a charade being acted out for the benefit of the British public,"[195] but also, and even more important, a charade being played out for the Turks. Indeed, the United States and the United Kingdom had to show the Turks that it was due to an extraordinary diplomatic act by the British prime minister and a mistake on the part of Kennedy that the British obtained conditions (national control of missiles until the creation of the MLF) that the Turks (and the Italians or the West Germans) should not expect to receive. Kennedy's advisors proposed that the deal would be made to appear a mistake on Kennedy's part. Kennedy would then correct it by extending the original multilateral proposal to the Turks or other European allies.[196]

One of the key questions in this debate was whether Kennedy's turn to suddenly support a defunct plan of Eurofederalist inspiration (the MLF Treaty) would be credible to the Europeans. Another related question at that point was whether France (and West Germany, to a lesser extent) would be included in the circle of trust, and whether de Gaulle should be asked to support this public charade, in exchange for benefiting from the same terms as those proposed to the British—and whether he would be willing to accept that bargain. Indeed, if the United States resumed its nuclear military cooperation with the United Kingdom, France would expect to be treated in a similar way. After all, de Gaulle had supported the United States without question when told by the US ambassador in Paris, Charles Bohlen, that the United States was considering attacking Cuba and that the situation might escalate quickly. The arrangement reached at Nassau meant that the United States would trust the United Kingdom to manage the world's nuclear affairs, but that it would not trust the other allies in Europe at the same level: in fact, the United States agreed to lie to the others. To that extent, by creating two truths, the US government created two classes of states—that is, "insiders" and "outsiders"—among allies, which was indeed a risky strategy. By including the United Kingdom in the private circle of insiders with access to the secret knowledge of US-Soviet relations, Kennedy took the risk of infuriating all the other Europeans—France in particular—who would be excluded from that inner circle.[197]

Betting that de Gaulle would support the public charade played out by the Anglo-American powers was an issue that divided the Kennedy administration. For Bohlen, who had already proposed that France benefit from the 1958 McMahon Act as early as June 1962 (a proposal that Ball himself had killed at the time), Kennedy had to extend the same offer to France as to the United Kingdom, and he had to include de Gaulle in their circle of insiders who would support the charade. At that point, Kennedy was almost convinced that it was undesirable to continue excluding France from the Western leadership: when preparing the Nassau conference, Kennedy, McNamara, and Bundy insisted that "it might be necessary to abandon the multilateral concept [of the MLF] and for the U.S. and the U.K. to make an approach to President de Gaulle to see if France would be prepared to join with their two Governments as joint defenders of Europe."[198] As Marc Trachtenberg writes, "It was a very important remark," since it meant that "Kennedy was now ready in principle to draw the line after France," and in this "new concept, Britain, France and the U.S. would be acting as a bloc,"[199] along the lines requested by de Gaulle in his September 1958 letter to Eisenhower. In fact, aligning actions with words, Bohlen privately conveyed the new US proposal to the highest French authorities a few weeks after the Nassau conference, on January 4, 1963. In a private meeting, the US ambassador to France told de Gaulle and his foreign minister, Couve de Murville, that the United States would sell to France Polaris missiles to be placed in submarines in exchange for the vague "paper commitment" to a multilateral framework, but that in times of emergency, France would be free to use these missiles unilaterally.[200] Bohlen's offer was so radically different from any proposal previously expressed by the United States that it surprised even Couve de Murville: it came close to acceptance of the terms that de Gaulle had previously set for his agreement to British accession to the European Communities.[201]

Not all top officials in the State Department agreed that the United States should openly tell the other allies that the Kennedy administration had converted to de Gaulle's theses: some of them believed that Kennedy should not reveal to anyone (with the limited exception of the British top policy makers) its new thinking on nuclear issues, even to de Gaulle himself. Although the crisis finally aligned the strategic conceptions of the US and French leaderships, top Kennedy aides, such as Ball, opted for the second approach: they were not yet ready to clearly tell West Germans and Turks that the United States now believed that the three Western nuclear powers should act as the leaders of the free world. Ball wanted to keep the Eurofederalists' charade alive, as he was not convinced that the announcement of such a drastic change in policy was timely. If the US president publicly confirmed Bohlen's private offer, he would have had difficulty convincing his other NATO allies that he had made yet another mistake when dealing with the French, a month after the first "mistake" at Nassau.[202] Then, it would mean that Kennedy no longer supported Monnet's goal of integrating both the British and French nuclear deterrents into a European framework. As the United Kingdom was negotiating its accession to the European Communities, such a revelation could have infuriated the West Germans and the Eurofederalists on the Continent. In January 1963, in Paris, a week after Bohlen met with de Gaulle, Ball explained to Couve de Murville that the American offer to let the United Kingdom claim absolute sovereignty over the use of the Polaris missiles in "times of national emergency" had been Kennedy's mistake, but that the proposal he was going to present publicly before the NATO allies was the one formulated in 1960 by Acheson.[203] To the "surprise" of Couve de Murville, and the embarrassment of Bohlen, who also attended the meeting, Ball said that the United States planned to create the MLF—that is, a fleet of "mixed-manned submarines" (manned by possibly Greeks, Italians, Turks, British, French, etc.) equipped with Polaris missiles, and placed "under the supranational control of NATO's Supreme Commander (or another NATO General having authority over that specific fleet)," during normal times *and* in times of emergency. The French authorities, who had expected to be granted conditions similar to those granted to the United Kingdom in the Nassau agreement, immediately told Ball that among West European nations, only the Turks would be interested in the new proposal.[204]

Eventually, the Cuban missile crisis revealed a new problem associated with the context of détente: as the United States and Soviets made secret deals regarding their nuclear affairs, it was no longer clear who were the insiders with private knowledge of certain deals, and who were the outsiders denied access to the private truth behind the public charades. The uncertainty that resulted from these overlapping circles of negotiations destroyed the trust that Europeans placed in Kennedy's leadership,[205] even though the Eurofederalists were still in a state of denial. The American decision to treat both West Germany and France differently from the United Kingdom actually provoked the effect that Ball had wanted to avoid: the change of plan convinced President de Gaulle to reject the whole proposal and to dramatize the French move by also rejecting British membership in the European Communities the very same day that Ball publicly announced his plan to America's NATO allies.[206] During a press conference, de Gaulle denounced what he considered an Anglo-American "betrayal,"[207] all the more difficult to stomach given that France had completely supported the United States during the Cuban missile crisis.[208] In the age of détente, West Germany also wanted the United States to be more transparent—even at the cost of angering the Turks, whom neither the French nor the West Germans considered as equals. Although the German chancellor believed that Ball "had not tried to deceive him," he told de Gaulle that he regretted the "extraordinary strategic uncertainty" that characterized US nuclear strategic thinking, and left the West Germans and Europeans "without any knowledge of their targeting plans,"[209] or future plans for reform of the alliance. One week after de Gaulle's veto, de Gaulle and Chancellor Adenauer met and signed the Paris Treaty, which planned for binational cooperation in military activities,[210] leaving unclear whether this cooperation extended to "nuclear" military activities. The Paris Treaty gave de Gaulle the public victory he needed to restore France's grandeur after the end of the Algerian war.[211] It proved to the Americans that, following the Cuban missile crisis, the West Germans no longer entirely trusted the United States or NATO.[212] In the words of Helmut Schmidt, the future chancellor, to Max Kohnstamm, the Franco-German rapprochement of January 1963 was a result of "the fear of a settlement between the two giants at the costs of the other nations, . . . and the lack of trust in automatic military assistance of the U.S. in case of war."[213]

After this crisis in European affairs, most of the observers considered the drafting of the MLF Treaty a joke. Nevertheless, the Eurofederalists around Jean Monnet agreed to the diplomatic-legal work of treaty drafting, engaging in a hopeful self-deception. Most US allies no longer believed the US government when it publicly displayed an attachment to (defunct) Eurofederalist ideas (such as the MLF) while negotiating privately with nuclear powers such as the Soviet and British governments. Only Monnet willfully agreed to continue the conversation about "the American offer to equip the forces of European countries with Polaris"[214] missiles. He gathered a group to draft the MLF Treaty in a way that would frame the British offer to use their nuclear submarines as the basis for an integrated European force.[215] Eurofederalists who agreed to play this role were ready to deceive themselves in exchange for a seat at the official negotiating table, at a time when they no longer had access to the highest echelons of power (neither in France, nor in West Germany, nor in the United States). Despite the fact that they were hardly naïve observers of international politics, their involvement proved that they were in what Stanley Cohen calls "a state of denial"[216]—a common reaction for people whose world has been shattered by a terrible turn of events. Indeed, despite their suspicions that they were no longer intimate with the US decision-making process, they agreed to open a new negotiation with the United States on the creation of a fourth European Community, devoted to the nuclear affairs of the alliance that could be characterized as "military."[217] Jean Monnet, Max Kohnstamm, and other members of the Action Committee such as Jacques Van Helmont (formerly the director of Euratom's controls and Monnet's new assistant) then started to write the draft of the MLF Treaty.

For the US leadership, the clause (hereafter the "European clause") that the Action Committee members inserted had the advantage that its direct inspiration came from defunct European treaties (such as the EDC Treaty). Thus, the initiative could appear to come from the Europeans, and the legacy of the integration movement, rather than from the United States, and its management of the fallout from the Cuban missile crisis. Indeed, the MLF Treaty "included a clear reference to Euratom, which show[ed] that in the spirit of the Action Committee, the MLF [wa]s not only a military and diplomatic political organization, but that it designate[d] a new sector to add to the European commissions (ECSC and Euratom) already in place: the sector of nuclear military activities, from research to development to industrial production." As Monnet made clear, "In the future, the MLF would basically place all activities of the European nuclear industrial complex within the sovereign realm of two commissions: Euratom on the civilian side, and MLF on the military side, which would merge in the future with the other commissions."[218] Monnet's European clause in the MLF Treaty asked the American and British governments to engage in two successive rounds of negotiation: first, an initial "negotiation with the United Europe and the United States, the goal of which will be . . . committing to a future European common force"; second, during a future "negotiation, all aspects of the nuclear question had to be envisioned, including research and development," as "Europeans must not have the feeling that they are destined to become second class citizens from the technological point of view."[219] According to Monnet's interpretation of the European clause, if "in the first phase, the multilateral force was not supposed to pool R&D in military nuclear activities, submarine technologies and missile technologies,"[220] in the second phase, "all the aspects of nuclear activities should be included in the negotiations of the planned secession charter, when the future European Union would re-negotiate with the U.S. the extent of its collaboration to the multilateral force."[221] Furthermore, Van Helmont, Kohnstamm, and Monnet hoped to obtain an American commitment to cooperate in the development of nuclear weapons with a European Community in the event that the United Kingdom was not a member state of that community, but France was (see table 6.3).[222]

It is clear what advantage the United States gained from Monnet's new campaign, as it buried the secret deal that the United States had made with the Soviets deep in Europe's historical consciousness, by distancing the new cycle of negotiation from the Cuban missile crisis. President Kennedy and then President Johnson made some considerable efforts to hide both how much they disagreed with Monnet on the terms of the MLF Treaty and the fact that neither of them had ever supported the treaty in the first place. At home, Kennedy silenced the advisors who argued in favor of honesty and transparency in the US government's dealings with Europeans. In particular, Livingston Merchant, Dulles's former assistant secretary for European affairs, whom Kennedy had nominated as special ambassador in charge of negotiating the creation of a multilateral force (MLF) two days after the signing of the Paris Treaty,[223] repeatedly warned the Europeans (including Monnet) that Monnet's ideas were unrealistic. Merchant recommended that Kennedy adopt a transparent approach to the Turks and West Germans, which consisted of drafting only proposals that conformed to what the US Congress would realistically authorize in terms of nuclear military cooperation with Europeans: thus, as the US Congress would refuse to sell submarine nuclear propulsion technologies under the terms planned by

Table 6.3 Transatlantic disputes over the "European clause" in the MLF Treaty

Contentious issues concerning the interpretation of the "European Clause"	Anglo-American liberal interpretation Ball / State Department and the British government	Eurofederalist interpretation Monnet and the Action Committee
Creating a new "center of decision" vested with the authority to start nuclear war with NATO weapons	No: The future European Community will include the British, and possibly the French, who will keep their right of veto	No: During the first phase, NATO's supreme allied commander is responsible for firing nuclear weapons Yes: During the second phase, the future president of the European Community formed with jurisdiction in the defense field will make the decision in consultation with the council; furthermore, the French and/or British will lose their right of veto because decisions will be taken by qualified majority voting in the council
Spreading military nuclear technology to more nations	No: Until the 1958 McMahon Act is revised, the United States cannot help a new European Community acquire nuclear weapons even if some of its member states have made "sufficient progress"	Yes: During the second phase, the European Community, once formed, can inherit the right to be helped by the United States that the United Kingdom has enjoyed since the 1958 McMahon Act
Entry into force	The United States maintains the right of veto on the entry into force of the European Clause	The European Clause automatically enters into force after the European Community with jurisdiction in military affairs is formed (either led with the United Kingdom, or with France, or both)

Monnet, Merchant rejected Monnet's proposal for a joint control of mixed-manned submarines by the United States and West European NATO allies, and he proposed in its stead a fleet of mixed-manned surface vessels (in simpler terms, boats with multinational crews)[224] armed with Polaris missiles.[225] In parallel, Merchant reported to Ball and Kennedy that he had "increasing doubts as to the wisdom in being too forthcoming in holding out the promise, or the likelihood, of the willingness to have the United

States abandon its veto or shift over responsibility and control of the fleet to the other allies at some time in the future."[226] Merchant believed "that to extend such a hope, regardless of the merits of the matter, would not really be to act in good faith with our allies because this would be an undertaking which in the crunch could not be delivered."[227] Not long after the beginning of Merchant's mission,[228] Kennedy and Ball terminated Merchant's assignment and encouraged Monnet to believe that they accepted the latter's proposals.[229]

In parallel, Kennedy publicly declared himself in favor of Monnet's proposed European clause, and he asked his advisors who knew better to remain silent on the issue. For instance, Kennedy told Averell Harriman (Roosevelt's former ambassador to Russia), Carl Kaysen, and the team of negotiators that he had sent to Moscow to negotiate what became the Limited Test Ban Treaty (LTBT) to keep secret the promise that in exchange for the Soviet approval of the LTBT, the United States would agree never to sign any MLF Treaty.[230] After Kennedy's assassination, Bundy convinced Lyndon Johnson to stay the course.[231] The tactic of opacity did bear its fruits for the US government: it allowed the speedy signing (and ratification) of the Limited Test Ban Treaty and the Soviet recognition in June 1963 of the legitimacy of the control of the International Atomic Energy Agency (IAEA) over the international trade of nuclear technologies and fissile materials. Secret and direct talks among Russo-Anglo-American diplomats (the French declined to attend) instead of through multilateral and public venues, such as the NATO Council or the Eighteen Nations Disarmament Committee (ENDC) in Geneva, allowed the Soviets and Americans to arrive at a consensus, which was based on the continued ignorance of the American-Soviet "deals" by NATO allies other than the United Kingdom.[232] Johnson and Ball thus considered as insiders only those powers already in possession of nuclear weapons (the United Kingdom, France, and the Soviets), but they needed the public charade produced by transnational networks with no access to the real diplomatic negotiations in order to keep the smaller NATO powers quiet.

In hindsight, it is not clear what advantage Monnet's network derived from their participation in the MLF Treaty negotiation. Short of assuming that they were delusional, it is likely that Monnet's associates knew they would have a terribly hard time convincing even the United States (which was one of the only powers to publicly support their proposal) to agree with the terms of the transatlantic military nuclear cooperation they offered. Monnet knew that Eurofederalists' ideas seemed highly unlikely to be accepted by the United States. Consenting to the European clause meant that the United States was prepared to agree that if "a group of European states establish among themselves a [European] Union having authority in the field of defense,"[233] then such a European Union would be able to inherit not only the rights held by its member states regarding the control of that multilateral force, but also the rights to use those nuclear weapons brought by the United States to the common pot. Ball had not always tried to deceive his old mentors. Early in the MLF Treaty negotiation, he told the Europeans that the United Kingdom should never lose its veto over the use of that multilateral force; that it would be their decision whether to abandon their national nuclear deterrent in phase two of the MLF, but that there would be no pressure from the State Department for the United Kingdom to accept Monnet's interpretation (see table 6.3).[234] Then, even though Kennedy publicly gave Monnet his full support, in a famous speech delivered in Frankfurt,[235] Monnet knew that most knowledgeable observers believed that the US government would never agree to most of the terms of his plan, but he still continued to animate the negotiation. Old Eurofederalists did not want to hear George Ball, when the latter told them that, eventually, the United States would insist on signing a treaty whose meaning was transparent to all parties (whose meaning was both clear and public). As State Department officials said, for instance, "The commitments taken by the U.S. Congress should be precisely enumerated"[236] in order for Congress to consider the European clause as binding; and it was unlikely that senators would accept Monnet's interpretation of the European clause if it clearly expressed Monnet's wish that the United States would cooperate with a fourth European Community in all aspects of the Western nuclear armament, "including the research and production of it."[237] In no case, said Ball to Kohnstamm,[238] would the US Congress agree to a vague binding rule to negotiate on all aspects of nuclear military assistance in the future (including the production of nuclear weapons components by Europeans) with an undetermined new European Community. At the time, even the British found this prospect to be an unacceptable form of nuclear proliferation,[239] and the only concession that Monnet's assistant obtained from them was that the British "accepted to not publicize their opinion" that the European clause would constitute a case of nuclear proliferation "in their discussions with the East."[240]

Part of the explanation for why the Eurofederalists agreed to participate in this diplomatic charade was psychological. It was all the more difficult for the Eurofederalists to let go of their dream of helping a united Europe acquire nuclear weapons since they had believed that the Euratom Treaty would achieve just that goal when it was ratified at the end of 1957. The opacity of a legally binding agreement gives a more concrete reality to a secret objective than the ambiguity and complete indeterminacy of a treaty. Ambiguity, by being open to all future interpretations, does not give precedence to any specific one. But for the promoters of a secret policy, who commit to a treaty on the basis of private promises, it is quite difficult and psychologically demanding to abandon their secret goal. As many cognitive psychologists have shown after Amos Tversky and Daniel Kahneman, the comparison between people's aversion to a real loss and their aversion to not winning an uncertain gain (the latter being much smaller than the former) reveals the existence of an "endowment effect,"[241] which explains why people do not update their strategy as quickly as rational choice theory would lead us to believe. This psychological resistance to change is illustrated by the difficulty with which Monnet and his associates came to acknowledge their failure.

Another reason for the self-deception observed among the participants in the diplomatic negotiation was sociopolitical: the old Eurofederalists preferred to keep their unrealistic hopes alive rather than see their role in transatlantic negotiations diminish. In this case, it was not only the "future-oriented"[242] character of diplomatic negotiations, as Martin Jay writes, that allowed such self-deception to persist (as it is hard to contradict a future-oriented proposal with a fact), but also the centrality that Eurofederalists sought to keep in the US decision-making process by engaging in public negotiations with the State Department. The public recognition that negotiations took place, and the central role that Monnet and others (such as McCloy) had in these negotiations, gave them back a role they had lost in the immediate aftermath of the Cuban missile crisis. Monnet and Kohnstamm were only too happy when they could report to State Department officials such as Schaetzel that they had convinced Spaak, or the Italian government,[243] or the old guard of NATO generals (including Eisenhower), for instance,[244] to support the "draft of the MLF treaty presented at a meeting with John McCloy."[245]

The Eurofederalists' persistent refusal to acknowledge the abandonment of the secret objective of the Euratom Treaty by France and the United States, the deceptive tactics sometimes adopted by the United States, combined with the absence of alternate plans proposed by Europeans, explain why it took two years for the Eurofederalists to open their eyes to the new realities of the global nuclear discussions between the East and West. Monnet's friendship with Republicans such as Dwight Eisenhower and John McCloy made it politically risky for Johnson to openly repudiate Monnet's MLF Treaty before the presidential elections in the fall of 1964—as the Republicans could have used the argument to unmask Kennedy and Johnson's betrayal of their European allies during the Cuban missile crisis.[246] Even though Johnson knew that the US Senate would refuse to ratify an MLF Treaty with Monnet's European clause,[247] only after Johnson was elected president in November 1964 did the Democrats in power publicly reveal their disagreement with the Europeans and Jean Monnet. Just after the election, in December 1964, Lyndon Johnson met with the British prime minister in Washington to announce that the nuclear submarine forces publicly offered by the British and Americans should not be mixed-manned (with other crews of Europeans), but merely placed under NATO's authority with the United States' and the United Kingdom's veto, as agreed in Nassau in December 1962; and that Europeans would not be invited to participate in the development of NATO nuclear weapons at all stages of their development (as Monnet had wished in the proposed MLF Treaty).[248] As noted by Max Kohnstamm, the British prime minister "made no concession because the President asked him none."[249] The *Times* declared the diplomatic conference "the year's most spectacular rug-pulling operation."[250] Kohnstamm concluded in January 1965, "The MLF is dead, . . . and there is nothing more Germany can do."[251]

The two years that the MLF Treaty negotiations lasted bought enough time for the United States so that the beginning of the NPT negotiations was then associated with another event—the recent Chinese nuclear test—and no longer with the outcome of the Cuban missile crisis. Even though it was the Cuban crisis that had led the United States to realize that it could not indiscriminately place nuclear warheads and missiles in Europe and jointly manufacture nuclear-weapons components with Europeans without Soviet retaliation, Johnson's government now justified the need for the NPT with the specter of nuclear proliferation in the non-European world.[252] By then, the position of strength that Johnson had gained after his election allowed him to move swiftly with a new proposal that his secretary of defense extended to the United States' NATO allies, to the dismay of the old generation of Eurofederalists. In the fall of 1964, Ball told the cabinet that the United States should replace Monnet's MLF Treaty with a NPT and pair its NPT proposal with a satisfying mechanism of consultation with its NATO allies; otherwise, the NPT would "probably be no more effective than the Kellogg-Briand Pact."[253] In August 1964, Walt Rostow's brother Eugene (1913–2002), then dean of the Yale Law School, who, like George Ball, had worked in the lend-lease administration during the war before becoming an expert on the regulation of the energy sector, crafted a "proposal for a NATO Directorate, a body smaller than the existing NATO

Council," which would become "a kind of Atlantic 'Security Council' with five (or seven) permanent and non-permanent members," and "in which Britain, France and the U.S. would be permanent members, and the others changing."[254] Such a consultative NATO Committee could be enough to satisfy West Germany: after all, when the West German chancellor signed the 1963 Paris Treaty, he only obtained the right to be consulted on France's strategic nuclear doctrine.[255]

Eventually, the sustained MLF Treaty negotiations allowed the new generation of US nuclear strategists to solve the problem of asynchrony in legal change (i.e., when intergenerational renewal among foreign policy elites occurs at different dates in different domestic fields of power). By refusing to acknowledge private disagreements for two years, they gained the time necessary for them to impose their views in a more advantageous context, both at home and abroad.[256] The clarification introduced by the new generation to the US nuclear nonproliferation designs brought an end to Monnet's efforts, and to the legitimacy that the old guard of Eurofederalists gave to opacity as a tactic to manage the affairs of the alliance. After Johnson's election, Ball immediately told Chancellor Erhard that the West Germans should request the right to participate in strategic talks concerning NATO's doctrine on the use of nuclear weapons,[257] in what became NATO's Nuclear Planning Group (or NPG), modeled after Eugene Rostow's ideas. The NPG that McNamara officially proposed to NATO allies in May 1965 thus comprised "a select committee of four or five Ministers of Defense" who would "improve and extend allied participation in planning for use of nuclear forces, including use of our strategic nuclear forces."[258] To Monnet's dismay, except for France, all the Western European nations[259] agreed that the NPG proposal rather than the MLF was the best way to fill the gap in NATO's consultation process. The proposal was so popular that the NPG was eventually extended to Canada and then Turkey,[260] in response to those countries' requests. Two months later, the United States presented its first NPT draft at the UN Disarmament Committee, spelling the death of the MLF.

The lines of conflict revealed by the withdrawal of the MLF Treaty and its replacement by the NPT showed that groups divided themselves along generational rather than ideological lines: the NPT and NPG proposals equally infuriated the old generation of Gaullists and Eurofederalists,[261] who shared Robert Bowie's opinion that there was "a danger that McNamara's proposed committee would not be conceived as a transitory measure but as a long-term solution to the German problem, which would suit the interest of those who want to find an agreement with the Soviets on the

Non-Proliferation Treaty," but at the price of reproducing "the situation created at [the 1945] Potsdam [Conference]: a status of inferiority given to the West Germans."[262] In fact, the French reaction to McNamara's NPG proposal was the most dramatic. As de Gaulle knew that Franco-German strategic consultations organized within the framework of the 1963 Treaty of Paris would become less interesting to the West Germans if the United States started to consult with them on questions of NATO nuclear strategy, he sought to block the completion of McNamara's plan as much as he could by announcing a series of unilateral moves: in June 1965, de Gaulle announced that France refused to participate in the NPG,[263] and that he would withdraw all French forces from NATO's integrated command as soon as January 1966, as France was determined to recover the full exercise of its absolute sovereignty over its armed forces.[264] But de Gaulle's gesture did not produce the desired effects: against the advice of Acheson,[265] Ball and McNamara convinced Johnson "that the French withdrawal created an opportunity to solve many alliance-related issues, from adopting the flexible response doctrine[266] to nuclear sharing to the need to revitalize the alliance and move it toward Détente with the Soviet Union"[267] by signing the NPT. By then, Monnet's associates and supporters realized that their support for the charade that the United States played for two years had failed their cause, and that they had lost their battle against the new generation.

Conclusion

The opacity of the transatlantic nuclear trade regime crafted in 1958 allowed new policy elites to privately subvert its secret purpose in a new geopolitical context. The adoption of new interpretations of past legal instruments was a result of intergenerational changes in the United States and France (see fig. 6.4). The new forms of knowledge deemed legitimate, especially in the US field of nuclear foreign policy, had changed since the mid-1950s, when Eurofederalists were mainly fighting with legal tools to impose their strategic views on international liberals. Opacity made the European and North Atlantic treaties more vulnerable to reinterpretation through extralegal means (through the imposition of unplanned interpretation) than clear treaties, whose interpretation would have needed to be changed according to the amendment procedure planned in the treaty.

Eurofederalists paid the price of opacity twice. First, by refusing to acknowledge that they sought to give nuclear-weapons capabilities to a united Europe thanks to Euratom, they could not mobilize the legal and rhetorical resources offered by the treaty in order to fight back the revi-

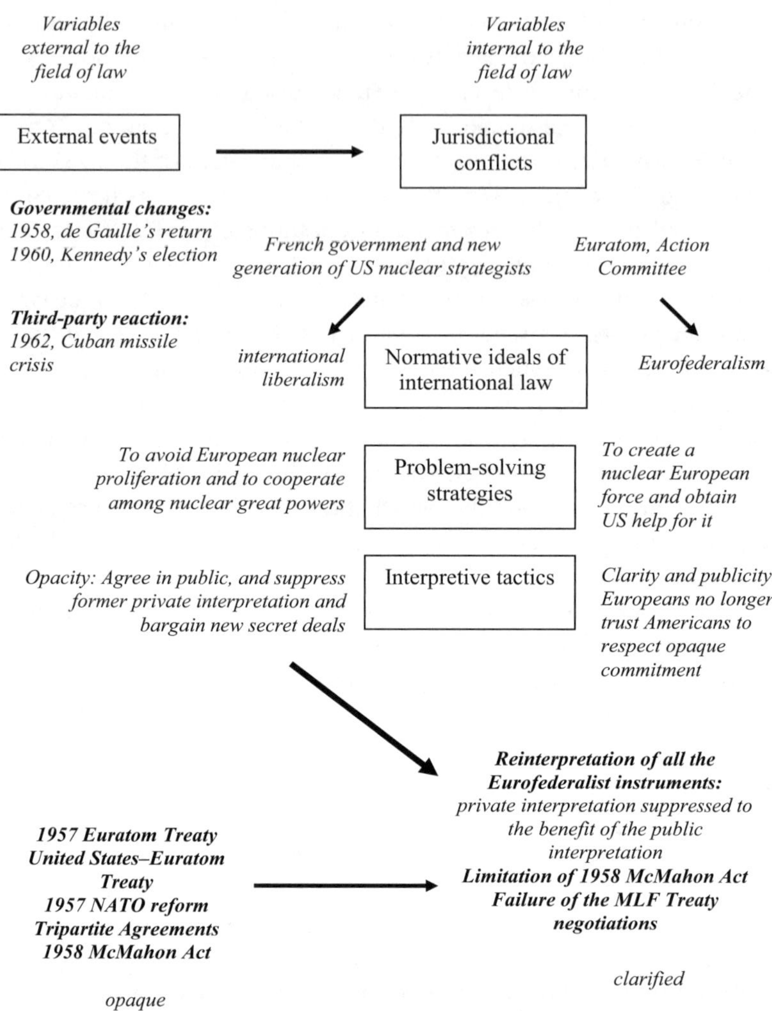

Figure 6.4. The dynamics of Eurofederalism in the early 1960s

sionist attempts of the newcomers who broke the linkage between the Euratom Treaty and its secret military objective. Here, it is important to note that because of the opacity that characterized these negotiations and reinterpretation of the jurisdictional boundaries of the Euratom Treaty and United States–Euratom Treaty, treaty interpretation occurred in diplomatic circles rather than through "judicialization"[268] of international law—that is, an incremental, nonpolitical, and professional process of clarification of a treaty's objectives led by judges. The opaque character of the Eurofederalist promises regarding future nuclear military cooperation between the United States and Europe meant that the reinterpretation of the jurisdictional boundaries of Euratom was performed outside the judicial arena: inside the Euratom Commission, or in the relationships that the commission entertained with member states and the United States. In any case, the European Court of Justice (ECJ) had no say in this process, and did not affect the outcome, which explains why domestic changes among the key signatory states of the United States–Euratom Treaty led to the victory of intergovernmental interpretations of the European Community.[269]

Second, by participating in a culture in which the truth of international legal commitments was to be found in secret rather than public interpretations of the Euratom Treaty, the Eurofederalists came to associate their own secret objectives with the concrete legal existence of the Euratom Treaty. For them, the secret interpretations had taken on an undeniable reality. As a result, when the Eurofederalists suffered an important interpretive defeat at the hands of nationalists in the US and French governments, the psychological costs of revising their expectations about the future prospects of success of their strategic dreams were still extremely high—quite unrealistically so. The open-endedness of an ambiguous treaty would not have created the impression of (secret) concreteness that the private interpretation of Euratom possessed in the minds of its promoters. To that extent, ambiguity would have been less harmful to the Eurofederalists' cause than opacity. But because they were unwilling to acknowledge that the US government might mislead them in the MLF Treaty negotiations, old Eurofederalists exchanged the ability to air criticism publicly for the illusion of being consulted on the establishment of new rules for the transatlantic nuclear trade. In hindsight, Monnet and the Eurofederalists around him certainly seemed delusional for believing that the Kennedy and then Johnson administrations could have accepted their plans, but their wide acceptance of secrecy was, to a large extent, central to their habitus: men such as Monnet, McCloy, or Bowie, who were used to walking in the hushed corridors of power in Wall Street, Paris, and Washington, but who never ran public campaigns, preferred to keep their disagreements private rather than risk losing their access to power. This tactical choice proved fateful for their cause: they gave their competitors in domestic fields of power the opportunity to choose the best moment to reveal publicly their rejection of Eurofederalist plans.

SEVEN

The Resilience of Opacity in a Changing International Legal Environment: How Europe Weighted East-West Negotiations of the NPT

Changes in the international legal environment of Europe occurred well before the NPT was signed in 1968. Indeed, the global nonproliferation regime was gradually set up in the 1960s, when the IAEA expanded its own system of rules regarding the safeguarding of nuclear materials and technologies traded between nations. These regulations, produced by the IAEA as well as other forums, formed what legal scholars call "soft law," in the sense understood by Kenneth Abbott and Duncan Snidal—that is, rules that are weak in one of the following three dimensions: their binding nature, their clarity, or the fact that contracting parties have delegated their interpretative authority to a third neutral party (in general, an international court).[1] At the time, it was not clear whether these global soft-law regulations would trump the rules of preexisting treaties, such as the United States–Euratom Treaty, which had already set regulations on issues that overlapped with the IAEA rules. To understand how such preexisting rules survive the production of soft law, we thus need a "doctrine of desuetude,"[2] which does not exist in international law. This chapter fills this vacuum by addressing the question of how hard law and soft law were articulated not only within one regime (centered around one treaty, the NPT) but also across regimes (European and global), and how they evolved together.

Two contrasting views exist on the evolution of regime complexes made of multiple soft and hard legal rules. The dominant view of the articulation between hard and soft law portrays them as *complements*, in at least two senses: first, legal scholars claim that ex ante soft law would render some points of convergence visible before treaties crystallize their rules into binding and clear hard law; second, that ex post soft law would clarify the interpretation of rules and obligations contained in hard treaty law.[3] In contrast, other authors believe that hard and soft law can be seen as *antagonists*: as Gregory Shaffer and Mark Pollack write, "Soft law can lead to the softening of hard law—that is, it can become less clear and precise in its meaning, thus reducing legal certainty and predictability."[4] In other words, soft law might not only fill the gaps left by prior hard law or prepare and ease the adoption of new hard law, but "can also be used strategically to undermine"[5] hard-law regulations in competing regimes.

Still, so far, the literature on hard and soft law has ignored the possibility that legal rules (especially hard ones, such as Euratom's rules)[6] could be opaque: for all authors, the law is "hard" when the rules are clear (and binding and interpreted by an independent court), and the law is "soft" when its rules are vague.[7] This chapter thus extends previous analyses of the conflicts of legal rules by applying the analysis to understand the articulation between systems of rules in which the rules are partly opaque. Taking the case of Euratom's control rules, this chapter argues that their opacity (and the fact that their public interpretation differed from their private one) actually facilitated harmonization between the two regimes of control—that is, the regime set up by Euratom for Europe's nuclear activities, and that set up by the IAEA for the rest of the world—in a context in which the production of soft law by the IAEA *undermined* rather than *complemented* the existing rules in Europe.

This chapter demonstrates this thesis in two sections. The first shows that the production of soft-law regulations prior to the NPT sometimes paved the way toward a general agreement on the desirability of the NPT between East and West, but that at other times, it raised strong obstacles on the road toward the NPT. In particular, the production of soft-law regulations by the IAEA threatened the hard law formed in Europe by Euratom and the United States–Euratom Treaty, as the IAEA developed an intrusive control of traded nuclear materials and technologies that differed greatly from Euratom's control rules.[8] This antagonism explains that, as Astrid Forland writes, "the European context set the framework for the [NPT] negotiations."[9]

The second section of this chapter shows how the opacity of Euratom's control rules facilitated the completion of the negotiations between Euratom and the IAEA over the future control of nuclear activities of the NPT signatory states that did not possess nuclear weapons. This section shows that the *public* interpretation of Euratom's control rules, based on a Euro-federalist reading of the Euratom Treaty as instituting a supranational organization claiming ownership and control, helped Euratom member states obtain from the IAEA some specific exceptions for Euratom. Nuclear opacity, in that case, led to a paradoxical result: the IAEA, a global agency charged with the responsibility to ensure the peaceful character of nuclear programs, adopted the control rules of an organization, Euratom, whose initial purpose had been the creation of a supranational nuclear-weapons program in Europe.

The Role of Soft-Law Regulations in the Progress of the NPT Negotiations

To some extent, the progressive production of nonbinding regulations in transatlantic and global forums (NATO and IAEA) paved the way toward the agreement reached by the Soviet and Western blocs on the NPT.

The NPT and Its Significance for NATO's Nonbinding Rules (1965–66)

The NPT regime created a system of binding and clearly expressed rules that prevented nuclear-weapon states (such as the United States) from developing nuclear-weapons technologies jointly with non-nuclear-weapon states anywhere in the world, including in Europe. To that extent, it created a regime of hard law, whose objective diverged from the prior transatlantic regime constituted by the Euratom and United States–Euratom Treaties.

The NPT was negotiated at the Conference of the Eighteen Nation Disarmament Committee (ENDC) in Geneva from 1965 to 1968, as well as in parallel private venues, especially in bilateral discussions between the United States and the Soviets.[10] After years of negotiations, the NPT was finally accepted by the UN General Assembly on June 12, 1968, after which it was opened to signature. The NPT rested on three pillars: nonproliferation, enhanced peaceful nuclear cooperation, and nuclear disarmament. These three norms had been official US policy objectives since the Baruch Plan was first proposed in 1946, and the first two norms had shaped concrete US nuclear policy proposals since the beginning of Kennedy's tenure.

In the NPT, the rights and duties of all states on these three issues were distinguished between two classes of states: the nuclear-weapon states (NWS), which were the five states that had officially manufactured and exploded a nuclear weapon prior to January 1, 1967 (art. 9.2); and the non-nuclear-weapon states (NNWS), which were all those other signatory states of the NPT—while nonsignatory states of the NPT constituted a third implicit category of states. In the NPT, the NWS committed not to help other states acquire nuclear-weapons technology, and NNWS swore not to seek that help from the NWS (art. 1 and 2). In exchange, the NWS recognized that NNWS had an "inalienable right" to peaceful nuclear development (art. 4), and they pledged to offer them privileged access to international trade in civilian nuclear technologies (over NPT nonsignatory states). This was the main part of the grand bargain between NWS and NNWS. In addition, the NWS pledged to "pursue negotiations in good faith" on nuclear disarmament (art. 6), so that the difference between NWS and NNWS would be lessened. Furthermore, NNWS could exit the NPT on three months' notice (art. 10.1) if "extraordinary events" required them to do so—for instance, if faced with the prospect of a nuclear attack.[11] This grand bargain between NWS and NNWS attained the force of law in March 1970, when the NPT entered into effect for an initial period of twenty-five years, after which the parties would decide whether they wished to extend their obligations indefinitely—which they did during the 1995 NPT Review Conference.

Until recently, most analysts presented the NPT signed in 1968 as constituting a tightly integrated regime, which placed the many preexisting agreements on nuclear trade (such as those contracted with the IAEA) and nuclear strategy (such as those organized within NATO) into a coherent framework.[12] This historical reading is largely true as far as the discussion of nuclear nonproliferation norms among NATO nations was concerned. Indeed, the NPT clearly prohibited nuclear military cooperation between a NWS and a NNWS,[13] but it did not prevent the NWS from engaging in nonbinding discussions with NNWS over how to best use their weapons in the event of a nuclear war. This policy corresponded to the NATO policy adopted by Kennedy and then Johnson with respect to NATO allies since 1962. As I have showed in the previous chapter, by the time NPT negotiations started at the ENDC, and especially after Johnson's reelection, the US government had rejected the Eurofederalist proposal that the United States would help a European Community acquire nuclear weapons of its own. The United States proposed in its stead the creation of the Nuclear Planning Group (NPG) inside NATO to enhance consultation over nuclear strategic doctrines.

The NPT thus crystallized the evolution of NATO policies into hard law. As Monnet's associates recognized from the start,[14] the NPT drafts of 1965 and 1966 did not contain any "clause which would have made possible that Europe in a state of formation (that is not yet a full-fledged federation but an association of states on the road towards federation) could absorb [the] existing nuclear capacity of Member States."[15] Indeed, the first June 1965 version of the NPT presented by the British to NATO allies, which was introduced (with slight changes) by the US representative William Foster at the Geneva Disarmament Committee in August 1965, only allowed nuclear military cooperation between two legitimate NWS, such as the United States and the United Kingdom.[16] This meant that the American and British governments now conditioned future US nuclear military help to Europeans on the formation of a real European federal state that would be the successor state of the United Kingdom,[17] and not on the formation of a looser type of European Union, as Monnet wished.[18] This policy decision was confirmed in December 1966, when "Dean Rusk delivered to the German representative of the NATO Council the text of articles 1 and 2 of the NPT, . . . which made any kind of nuclear-sharing impossible, unless (according to the American interpretation) a federated European state would become the successor of the present European nuclear powers, i.e. France and Great Britain."[19]

All NATO parties agreed to respect this consensus when the NPT deliberations started at the Geneva Conference. If the United States insisted on turning clear prohibitions into binding obligations (hard law), Monnet and Kohnstamm insisted on getting the written approval of the Americans and Soviets that they accepted the "so-called 'successor state' theory, i.e., that the emergence of the new political entity of a United States of Europe would naturally assume this responsibility"[20] to manufacture nuclear weapons for the European federation and to receive outside help from the United States—to the extent that the European federation would inherit the British rights protected by the 1958 McMahon Act. In December 1966, Monnet and the Europeans had not received this written approval from the two superpowers, whose commitment to the "successor state theory" remained only an implicit promise.[21] Seeing the obstacles they faced, Max Kohnstamm reported that in January 1967 the West German foreign minister, Willy Brandt, told Monnet and him that "he believed we should not try to obtain a European formula from the Americans," but that "Germany, Italy, etc. should sign the NPT and reserve the possibility to negotiate the European clause after the formation of a political Europe,"[22] which meant that West European nations would include in the instruments of ratification of the NPT a statement "that the text does not exclude a European force encompassing the French and/or British nuclear forces once a political Europe exists."[23] Monnet accepted Brandt's proposition after "the American government explained that a united Europe will have the possibility of becoming a nuclear power on condition that it becomes a federation with, within it, a full delegation of sovereignty on external political and defense matters."[24] By the time the Disarmament Committee in Geneva reconvened in February 1967, the compromise proposed by Brandt, and accepted by the United States and the Soviets, allowed the NPT negotiations not to stumble over the European requests.[25]

When West Germans and Italians ratified the NPT in 1975, they refer-
enced this compromise by adding to their instruments of ratification of
the NPT a statement that a future European federal state that included the
United Kingdom or France would be recognized as a NWS.[26] Even though
the West Germans and Italians kept open their Eurofederalist dream, all
agreed that such a European Federal State would never be created in the
short or midterm, after the British entry into the European Community
in January 1973.[27] As a German parliamentarian wrote to George Ball in
October 1973, "The coming together of the European partners in a federation is highly unlikely, and Europe will depend for an indefinite period upon the nuclear strategic deterrent of the U.S."[28] The Eurofederalist dream of a European nuclear force thus survived only on paper, in the
instruments of ratification of the NPT.[29] At last, the legal division inside
the NPT between NWS and NNWS crystallized the nuclear status quo in
Europe, with the United Kingdom and France being the sole two European
legitimate NWS.[30]

In that way, the relationship between the NPT and NATO's nonbinding
rules (as illustrated in the proposed consultation mechanisms) illustrates
the relationship between hard and soft law as reinforcing *complements*,
which is characteristic of situations in which an integrated regime emerges
in which soft- and hard-law agreements distribute rights and duties to contracting parties in a coherent fashion (see table 7.1). As Gregory Shaffer
and Mark Pollack write about this kind of situation, "Non-binding soft-law
instruments help pave the way into binding hard-law instruments, just as
discrete state practices can aggregate and give rise over time to a consensus
regarding general binding customary international law."[31] The long negotiation of NATO consultation rules, which I have described in its domestic dimensions in the previous chapter, and which pitted Eurofederalists
on one side against international liberals on the other side, paved the way
to the hard-law agreement between East and West. That hard and soft law
worked as complements might explain why the compromise has been re-
markably stable since the signing of the NPT: the division of the European
continent between NWS and NNWS was left unchallenged even when a
new chapter of European integration in conventional military operations
opened after the Saint Malo meetings of 1998.[32]

The NPT and the Incremental Development of IAEA Rules (1961–67)

The relationship that Europe's hard law (in the Euratom Treaty) entertained with a growing body of soft-law regulations incrementally produced

Table 7.1   The interaction of hard and soft law in integrated regimes and regime complexes

	Intensity of the distributive conflicts between hard and soft law	
Type of regime	Low	High
Single integrated regime	Hard and soft law as reinforcing *complements*: For example, soft law further clarifies how binding rules apply to unplanned cases, or soft law paves the way to hard-law agreements that crystallize a consensus (*NATO's consultation rules and NPT from 1965 to 1968*)	Hard and soft law as *weak antagonists*
Regime complex	Hard and soft law as *substitutes*: For example, parties to overlapping but distinct regimes can engage in forum shopping (or rules shopping), as the advantages they derive from either soft law or hard law differ only slightly (*Harmonization between IAEA and Euratom safeguarding rules after the NPT from 1970 to 1975 lead to greater integration*)	Hard and soft law as *strong antagonists*: For example, parties to overlapping but distinct regimes perceive the production of soft law in parallel regimes as undermining their own hard law (*IAEA safeguards document from 1965 to 1968 seen as undermining the Euratom and United States–Euratom Treaties by Euratom member states*)

by the IAEA Secretariat and approved by the IAEA Board during the decade leading up to 1968 is less clearly one of complementarity. In 1968, the NPT signatories agreed that, in order to guarantee compliance with the first two pillars (nonproliferation and enhanced nuclear peaceful cooperation), the NNWS granted the IAEA the "exclusive purpose of verification of [their] obligation with a view to preventing diversion of nuclear energy from peaceful uses to nuclear weapons" (art. 3.1).[33] The global nonproliferation regime thus formed by the NPT and by a dense web of Safeguards Agreements that NNWS would sign with the IAEA, either "individually or *together with other states*"[34] (art. 3.4), gave the IAEA a right of "*verification*" that proper controls were in place. Although this language seems straightforward, in the sense that it gives primacy of place to the IAEA as a monitoring organization, it would be wrong to believe that the increased legitimacy that the IAEA gained in the 1960s by producing a range of safeguards regulations actually eased the NPT negotiations among the United States, Europe, and the Soviets.

In fact, article 3 was probably the most disputed article of the NPT, partly because there existed various systems of controls of nuclear trades depending on the region of the world, and because each system of controls distributed rights and duties differently to nuclear importing and exporting countries (see the bottom half of table 7.1). In these cases, as Gregory Shaffer and Mark Pollack explain, "Hard and soft law interact as antagonists and not complements [nor alternatives] because of the conflicting distributive implication of law and legal change for states"[35]—in the sense that new rules distribute rights and prerogatives differently as compared to old rules.

As Astrid Forland, the main historian of the IAEA, has shown, at least three years elapsed from the moment the Statute of the IAEA was defined in 1956 to the moment when negotiations about its safeguards document started. This time lapse was mainly the result of the pressure mounted by Eurofederalists in the State Department, and more particularly Robert Schaetzel, who wanted to first complete negotiations of the United States–Euratom Treaty, before they would deal with global IAEA rules from which the Euratom zone would be exempted.[36] As I said in chapter 5, the prior hard-law agreement signed between Euratom and the United States in August 1958 represented a victory for Eurofederalists, for three reasons: it did not prohibit military use of imported (or locally produced) source and special fissionable materials by Euratom member states as long as such use was declared to Euratom; it did not grant to nuclear importers (such as the United States) a "right of pursuit" over degraded fissile materials (for instance, plutonium extracted from the waste of nuclear fuels imported by Euratom); and it did not authorize foreign inspections on its soil—instead, the United States was granted a right to "verify" (or rather, to read) the accountancy books of nuclear materials circulating in Euratom territory.

Thus, immediately after the United States–Euratom Treaty was signed in 1958, the US negotiator of the deal on Euratom controls noticed that "a degree of conflict unavoidably implicit between American objectives regarding Euratom and those regarding the IAEA"[37] was likely to make the development of IAEA safeguards the object of difficult negotiations. The United States developed not only double but also triple standards on issues of control. For instance, in February and March 1959, important discussions were held by the "Ottawa powers"—that is to say, the former signatory states of the Quebec Agreement (the United States, the United Kingdom, and Canada)—and two of Britain's main exporters of source materials (Australia and South Africa): these Anglophone countries insisted that not only among themselves, but also between themselves and Euratom countries, they would not require the imposition of IAEA safeguards on their nuclear trade.[38] Furthermore, during these meetings, Schaetzel accepted Canada's incremental approach to IAEA safeguards—that is, that the IAEA Board would first define safeguards to be imposed on research reactors (the technologies most likely to be sold to non-European countries) before it would study safeguards for other kinds of facilities. This focus on research reactors meant that the IAEA would concentrate mostly on controlling sales to the developing world. In contrast, the "comprehensive" approach that the AEC initially defended (i.e., that IAEA safeguards be defined at once for all kinds of nuclear facilities) would have meant that the IAEA would have focused on Europe, where the uranium-enrichment and plutonium-reprocessing plants were being built (those facilities in which diversion from peaceful to military uses of nuclear energy was the most likely to occur).[39]

The difference between Euratom controls and the envisioned IAEA controls became the focus of criticism not only by the Eastern bloc but also (and even more important) by the nonaligned countries, with India at their forefront.[40] The criticism grew as the double (triple) standard regarding the US approach to controls became more apparent. Commenting upon the US policy regarding controls at the IAEA Board in September 1959, India (and other nonaligned nations such as Egypt) denounced the exceptions that were granted by the Anglo-American nuclear exporters: they saw in it a neocolonial mind-set at work, which divided the world between the white-dominated Western nations (whose nuclear trade would be excluded from safeguards by the IAEA) and the rest (whose nuclear trade, especially concerning research reactors, would be strictly controlled by the IAEA).[41]

Despite these criticisms, which targeted the plurality of rules for different regions of the globe—or rather, the conflicts between the distribution of rights and duties for the participants of each distinct regime of control—the production of soft-law regulations on safeguards by the IAEA progressed along the lines decided by the Ottawa powers, with only some small measure of accommodation to the demands expressed by India.[42] The first safeguards document adopted by the board in 1961 only concerned research reactors.[43] The United States adroitly argued that although the limits placed on the safeguarded reactors specifically targeted the non-Western world, at the same time, the limits allowed the United States to accept similar safeguards on its soil (principle of reciprocity). Indeed, in order to deflect the criticism expressed by India that the IAEA controls represented an infringement on national sovereignty that was all the more impossible for decolonizing nations to suffer since only their facilities would become subject to such safeguards, the United States opened the four US research reactors "of the type to which the proposed [IAEA safeguards] would apply"[44] to IAEA controls. The United Kingdom followed suit, as these unilateral gestures did not cost it much: the British dual-use activities were not conducted in small reactors but in larger facilities such as uranium-enrichment plants.

Although limited to research reactors, the first IAEA safeguards document instituted tougher controls than those of Euratom, as Euratom controls adopted a materials-based approach to controls (focused on nuclear fuels), which aimed at ensuring the conformity between declared and real use (with no control of the finality of the use), whereas IAEA controls included reactor design reviews by the IAEA, so that the IAEA could verify ex ante both that the design allowed for the application of safeguards, and that the design would not allow an easy and quick diversion from peaceful to military purposes.[45] Furthermore, the IAEA safeguards allowed exporters to require that such safeguards be applied to reactors built indigenously but in which imported nuclear fuels would be loaded.[46] This provision represented an infringement of sovereignty that the West Germans would never have accepted from the IAEA, although it was actually in line with the IAEA Statute of 1956. To this extent, we can say that the production of the first IAEA safeguards document participated in creating a facilities-based and finality-oriented approach to control that was tougher than that adopted by Euratom.

However, the first safeguards documents also incorporated the criticisms made by India that the IAEA and Euratom would institute discrimination against the non-Western world in other aspects. Indeed, the IAEA safeguards did not require the permanent presence of foreigners in the research reactors (as the US AEC had originally proposed), but instead mostly established audits with occasional spot inspections (as the Canadians had proposed).[47] In fact, the IAEA adapted its system to the political realities of the time in order to be able to detect possible diversion with a 90 percent measure of confidence. Furthermore, the French obtained the concession that the trade of some source materials (such as thorium) and that of sensitive nonnuclear materials (hence falling outside the purview of Euratom controls, which only applied to source and special fissionable materials) such as heavy water would be excluded from IAEA safeguards on reactors.[48] At last, in order to deflect the criticisms expressed not only by

India but also by Latin American countries such as Brazil, the United States accepted a safeguards document in which no clear "right of pursuit" was imposed on fissile materials in all subsequent forms after they were first traded. Although the United States insisted that its bilateral treaties would include a right of pursuit for bigger reactors than those targeted by this first IAEA safeguards documents, it agreed that such a right of pursuit would be negotiated at a later date.[49] This was a victory for India, whose prime minister, Nehru, had rejected the possibility that nuclear powers could have a right of pursuit on materials sold to developing nations if the great powers did not subject themselves or Euratom to the same rules[50]—and later, India used that loophole to extract plutonium from nuclear waste in order to build its first explosive devices.[51]

Thus, the first concrete document that the IAEA produced regarding safeguards clearly represented an example of soft law, in the sense that it contained nonbinding[52] and sometimes vague obligations, which some of the IAEA member states (such as the United States) wanted to toughen in future bilateral treaties, and that others (such as India) wanted to dilute even further. Still, as is often the case with soft-law regulations, each regulation had to be judged not only for itself, but for the process it allowed to start. By crystallizing a consensus in a difficult diplomatic situation involving many actors, this first document served as a confidence-building measure that buttressed the legitimacy of the concerned international organization: in this case, the IAEA.[53]

Progress in negotiation was facilitated further after the Soviets recognized the legitimacy of IAEA controls in June 1963, ten days after Kennedy announced the visit of his emissaries to negotiate the LTBT in Moscow. Then, through an incremental process, the first IAEA safeguards document was strengthened, and some of its loopholes closed, thus paving the way for negotiations of the NPT to include discussions about IAEA safeguards. Indeed, in January 1965, shortly before the NPT negotiations publicly started in June 1965 at the Disarmament Conference, the first safeguards document adopted in 1961 was revised and extended to cover larger reactors, and the resulting document (INFCIRC/66) was adopted.[54] The new document strengthened the controls by reintroducing the "right of pursuit" in the IAEA soft-law regulations;[55] by including a right for the IAEA to access the facilities "at all times";[56] and by establishing a list of nonnuclear items (such as heavy water) whose sale would "trigger" IAEA controls on the facilities in which they were used. Furthermore, the United States and the United Kingdom held yearly talks in London with other nuclear exporters (including the "Ottawa powers" but also France) in the hope that a consensus would be found to establish a "trigger list" of nonnuclear equipment (used exclusively in nuclear reactors) whose sale would trigger IAEA safeguards. Even though France and South Africa (from which France started buying natural uranium in the early 1960s)[57] rejected any such "trigger list," and insisted on a case-by-case policy for controls of nonnuclear materials,[58] both nuclear exporters and importers gradually came to expect that nuclear nonproliferation policy needed to apply to nonnuclear materials as well.

However, the continued exclusion benefiting Euratom still represented a looming threat to the possibility that East and West would arrive at an agreement on controls in the hard law of the NPT. The Soviets and some nonaligned nations, especially "the representatives of India and Pakistan" at the IAEA, routinely "declared that the truly international system of surveillance is much better than the multinational system of Euratom,"[59] and that the existence of Euratom's controls illustrated the discriminatory and neocolonial nature of the world nuclear trade that the United States and its allies wanted to impose on the decolonizing world. In 1965, when the first drafts of the NPT were introduced by the United Kingdom and the United States, the plurality of regimes of control was acknowledged, but no work of commensuration was attempted to harmonize the rules of the two regimes (IAEA and Euratom).

Instead, the West made it clear that the Euratom Treaty would trump any new soft or hard law as far as the application of safeguards was concerned in Europe. Under the leadership of George Ball and Robert Schaetzel at the State Department, the US government took great care to show that its new global agenda did not renege on the US commitments contracted in prior European and transatlantic treaties—in particular, the 1958 United States–Euratom Treaty. For instance, the first article on safeguards that appeared in the US draft of the NPT in August 1965 left open the possibility that Euratom controls could still apply on Euratom territory, as it prescribed cooperation between future state parties to the NPT (both the NWS and the NNWS) and the IAEA or an "equivalent international safeguards" agency, such as Euratom. As William Foster, the director of the Arms Control and Disarmament Agency (ACDA) in charge of NPT negotiations in Geneva, acknowledged in August 1965, "We have drafted the safeguards provision to take account of the view of countries who do not seem prepared at this time to accept IAEA safeguards in all applicable circumstances."[60] Even after the 1965 NPT draft was rewritten in January 1966 by Senator John Pastore, chairman of the JCAE, and fifty-four other senators, in order to take into account Soviet demands that the application of safeguards on peaceful activities would concern the NNWS only, the new 1966 NPT draft still reflected Europe's continued preference for the Euratom Treaty framework—in particular, regarding the issue of controls. Indeed, Senator Pastore's 1966 version still left open the possibility for nuclear trade to be safeguarded by IAEA safeguards or "equivalent safeguards," meaning Euratom safeguards.

Even if the United States appeared to respect the continued plurality of safeguards regimes, the Europeans who were already part of hard-law agreements (the Euratom and United States–Euratom Treaties) felt that the production of IAEA soft law *undermined* the hard-law rules of their own regime: the legitimacy of Euratom controls at least was threatened, as progress in the production of IAEA regulations enhanced the legitimacy of this institution to the detriment of that of Euratom. Eurofederalists feared that the production of IAEA soft law would sooner or later force the United States to adapt the Euratom controls to fit with the IAEA controls, if only to respond to criticisms of double standards. This situation, which corresponds to the lower-right cell of table 7.1,[61] explains why France voted against the IAEA 1965 Safeguards Agreement at the IAEA Board and why it accepted Euratom controls (although with some restrictions, as described in the previous chapter), which had the advantage for France that Euratom did not require France to limit its use of imported materials to peaceful goals. The possibility that progress in the definition of IAEA controls would undermine the legitimacy of Euratom controls also explains why the West Germans were against the idea that Euratom should "establish official relations with the IAEA,"[62] and why West Germans consistently resisted the attempts by the AEC chairman Glenn Seaborg to convince Euratom member states to sign an agreement of cooperation with the IAEA that would give the IAEA a role in the control of Europe's nuclear activities.[63]

Fears that the IAEA soft law would undermine the legitimacy of the Euratom controls were not groundless, as segments of the US administration, especially the AEC and its chairman, Seaborg, redoubled their pressure to universalize IAEA controls on NNWS, and substitute IAEA safeguards for alternative forms of controls such as Euratom's.[64] After Johnson's election in 1964, the AEC chairman tried to impose "a far more restrictive approach of providing atomic assistance that has prevailed in the last ten years," which was "to permit the export of reactors on case-by-case basis,"[65] taking into consideration the stability of the country and the importer's willingness to accept the IAEA's safeguards on reactors.[66] The Euratom Commission then noted with distress that the AEC's diplomatic drive was meant to establish "an international agreement that all future foreign sales of atomic power plants will provide for inspection by the IAEA," and the "acceptance by the nuclear powers of IAEA safeguards over the atomic power plants built in their own countries."[67] It was only due to Ball's effort that Seaborg was blocked from interfering with the opening negotiation of the NPT in the summer of 1965.[68]

The possibility that the soft law produced in the IAEA regime would substitute itself for the hard law adopted in Europe was serious, as the United States still had to get the Soviets to accept that Euratom member states would keep their own system of control in order to obtain their agreement on the NPT. This task proved unlikely as, when the Soviets recognized the legitimacy of the IAEA safeguards on nuclear reactors in June 1963, their criticisms turned exclusively against Euratom, which they routinely accused of being "a military operation," which could not be trusted for the control of European nuclear activities.[69] After the US senators made public their draft of the NPT in January 1966, the Soviets did not express their opinion of Senator Pastore's resolution in matters of controls, but instead let Poland and Czechoslovakia, followed by the German Democratic Republic, lead the offensive against Euratom controls. Indeed, in the fall of 1966, the Soviet satellites offered to place their nuclear facilities under IAEA safeguards provided that West Germany reciprocated by also accepting IAEA safeguards on its nuclear imports and nuclear facilities. Faced with the Eastern European proposal, the French government urged the West German government to reject the proposal, arguing that "legally, France could veto a German decision to accept controls by the IAEA as well as by Euratom."[70] France consistently refused IAEA safeguards on its imports, and when it finally accepted IAEA safeguards on its nuclear exports in August 1966, it still exempted all exports to Euratom member states from IAEA controls.[71] The West Germans had no intention of accepting the proposal either,[72] even if AEC chairman Glenn Seaborg was "enthusiastic about the Polish and Czech offers."[73] Eurofederalists in the State Department agreed with West Europeans: if Walt Rostow, who replaced McGeorge Bundy as national security advisor in the winter of 1996, remained "noncommittal,"[74] his brother Eugene Rostow, who replaced George Ball after the latter resigned from his post as undersecretary of state in September 1966, interpreted the "East Germans' proposal as an attempt to gain national recognition by the agency—something that would be completely unacceptable to the Bonn Government."[75] Furthermore, Eugene Rostow, who oversaw the negotiations with the Europeans at the State Department, refused to "single out West Germany among the Western European nations as the one that must accept international agency safeguards," as such a move would depart "from their twenty-year old policy of solving the German problem within the broader West European context."[76] Still, as the facility-based approach to controls adopted by the IAEA was gradually extended from one type of nuclear facility to the next,[77] the proposal by Eastern European states made it harder for Euratom member states to claim that the IAEA system of safeguards was not advanced enough to substitute for that of Euratom,[78] whose controls were initially placed upon a much larger number of facilities than those of the IAEA, including large-scale facilities such as power plants and reprocessing plants. Progress in the IAEA control rules meant increased danger for Euratom controls.

In a traditionally envisioned legal world, one would deduce that hard law would eventually impose itself on soft-law regulation, but as many analysts have emphasized, the conflicts between soft and hard law in a fragmented legal world are characteristic of a mode of networked governance, in which legal rules no longer fall into relatively clear categories and hierarchies, with international law binding states.[79] Rather, "in networked governance, normative systems overlap and inter-penetrate each other, and the determination of the legitimacy of an activity under any one system of norms is rarely definitive, since powerful actors are usually able to mount a challenge by reference to another system."[80] In this case, the mounting fears that the Euratom Treaty might be endangered by the production of IAEA soft law and the need to harmonize both systems in order to complete negotiations between East and West materialized at the end of January 1967, when Eugene Rostow informed Max Kohnstamm and Jean Monnet that the US government was about to introduce changes to article 3 that would make IAEA controls mandatory even for Euratom member states. In response, Kohnstamm immediately told Rostow that Europeans would reject the altered language of the new article 3 because it "accepts the Soviet position that the European Communities do not exist and that Euratom safeguards are not effective."[81] But the draft of article 3 that the United States circulated among Euratom countries in February 1967 reflected the ascendancy of the AEC in the US decision-making process and the willingness showed by Johnson to reach an agreement on the NPT with the Soviets before the end of his tenure.[82] Indeed, the new American proposal suppressed the legal possibility that Euratom controls could be maintained after the entry into force of the NPT with the specific wording "equivalent international safeguards were not to be acceptable"[83] in the new version.

At that point, the European reaction to the new draft of article 3 showed that two extreme possible resolutions to the problem of legal fragmentation would both bring a dead end in East-West negotiations of the NPT: if Europe's hard law trumped global soft law in Europe, or if IAEA's global soft law trumped Europe's hard law in Europe. Indeed, faced with the latter possibility, the Europeans immediately denounced the new American draft NPT as a violation of prior treaty commitments. Shortly before he died, Konrad Adenauer qualified the new article 3 proposed by the United States in February 1967 as being a "Morgenthau plan squared."[84] The West German Euratom commissioner was particularly adamant that "article 3 is incompatible with the Euratom Treaty, and proceeds from a will to discriminate between nations."[85] Not only Euratom non-nuclear-weapon states, but also France rejected the new article 3 of the NPT, which reintroduced the specific "right of pursuit" that Euratom member states, and France in particular, disliked. Therefore, France threatened to blockade all controls if IAEA controls were superimposed on existing Euratom controls.

The crisis revealed the necessity to open negotiations not only between the Americans and Soviets, but with the Europeans as well, in order to find a way to harmonize the two existing international safeguards regimes. Otherwise, the road toward the creation of hard law in the form of the NPT would be blocked. As Daniel Halberstam writes, given the two extreme alternatives represented by "hierarchy" (between hard and soft law) and "anarchy" (when the latest system of rules imposed by the great powers prevails over previous ones), the only option to advance on the road toward new law is to adopt a form of "global legal pluralism," which is based on "mutual autonomy and lack of hierarchy [between normative orders], but also on mutually embedded openness of the various participants to the authority of the other or to some form of collective governance."[86] In the case of the NPT, European jurists emphasized that harmonization between two autonomous but open systems of controls was the only possible option in a context in which "the NPT raise[d] an exemplar case of a new kind of problem, which [wa]s to harmonize the numerous engagements that States take, for themselves and their citizens, toward other states or international organizations," as "the obligations subscribed can become contradictory simply because of the inadvertence of the negotiators who do not know of engagements taken elsewhere and in another conjecture."[87]

The United States and European nation-states realized they were not unbound Ulysses, free to tie their hands to a mast. If they wanted to tie new knots to draw a new picture on the world's legal tapestry, they would have to untie a few knots, like Penelope, but the new picture they wanted to draw would inescapably be influenced by the many preexisting treaties and agreements signed between the United States and Europe.

Global Legal Pluralism in Practice:
How Control Regimes Were Harmonized

Even though the Americans, Europeans, and Soviets realized that Europe's regime of nuclear trade controls needed harmonization (rather than suppression) before the NPT could be signed, such harmonization was not easily achieved, as this little-known story shows.[88]

Double Delegation of Interpretative Authority (1967–73)

Immediately after talks about harmonization started, most diplomats and foreign policy makers realized that the prior creation of either soft or hard law by Euratom and the IAEA meant that states were no longer free to do as they wished, but that some authority had been transferred to the organizations in charge of ensuring proper controls in each region. In this regard, whether the rules about safeguards were clear or not, binding on all member states of the organization or not, their very recognition by some member states of each organization meant that the harmonization between the two systems of rules would have to be performed by the international organizations themselves, and not just by the state parties negotiating behind closed doors. Thus, a double delegation of authority was a precondition for any attempt to make the two systems of rules commensurate with each other: the Soviets would have to implicitly recognize the authority of Euratom to negotiate with the IAEA (as they did in 1968 when they signed the NPT); and vice versa, the Euratom member states would have to recognize the authority of the IAEA to negotiate with Euratom (see fig. 7.1).

The idea that the negotiation of article 3 of the NPT regarding safeguards should no longer be conducted in the context of negotiations among the United States, the Soviets, and European states was first defended by Euro-federalists after the US government asked Euratom to abandon its controls in January 1967. In February 1967, Jean Monnet told Willy Brandt, the West German secretary of foreign relations in Chancellor Kurt Kiesinger's Grand Coalition government, that "the U.S. and Russia are on the way to conclude gradually agreements on various problems,"[89] so that "the negotiations should not be between you and the U.S. but between as many members of Euratom as possible and the U.S."[90] To Monnet, the West Germans, whose nuclear activities would fall under IAEA controls if the latter were substituted for Euratom controls, should not act as if they were free to change the Euratom Treaty without following the proper procedure.

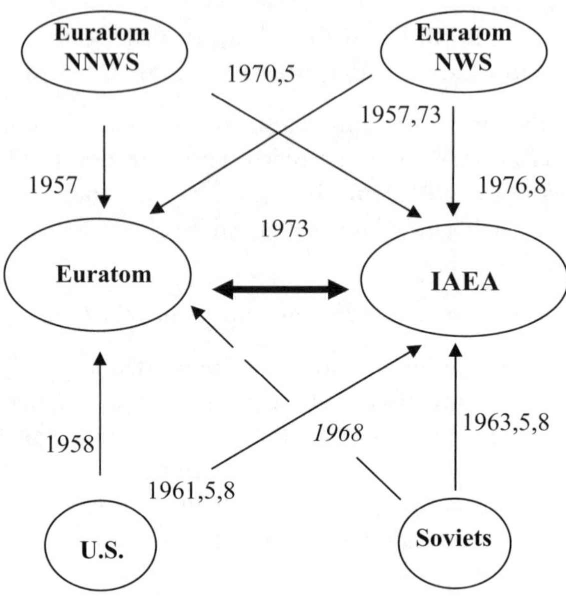

Figure 7.1. The double delegation that made possible
the harmonization of control regimes

As Monnet told Brandt, "The question of Euratom control over peaceful
nuclear activities is not a matter of interpreting the Treaty, but of changing
the present text,"[91] which could only be done by following the proper procedure defined in the Euratom Treaty.[92] To Monnet and the legal services of
the Euratom Commission,[93] "Even if the [Euratom] non-nuclear-weapon
members were to accept to submit to the IAEA, it is difficult to see how the
existing situation could be changed without the consent of all members"
(including France), since "this situation results from the Euratom treaty
and from the Euratom-U.S. agreement which both proceed of a common
decision of the Six."[94] Monnet thus believed that the only chance for the
NPT negotiation to move forward was for a United Europe to "be accepted
practically as an equal by the U.S. and Russia," and for "Europeans to speak
with one voice,"[95] through the Euratom representative.[96]

As all the Western European governments opposed the extension of
IAEA controls to Europe, they followed Monnet's advice, trying to convince both the United States and the United Kingdom that the negotiation should not take place between them and Euratom member states but
with the Euratom representatives. As Monnet reminded Eugene Rostow,
the United States had recognized explicitly some limitation of their right

to change controls in Europe, in "paragraph 11E of the memorandum of understanding which had preceded the agreement itself between the two negotiators (letter Kohnstamm/Butterworth July 18, 1958), which said: 'I want to confirm the interpretation of the Commission . . . that in case an international system of safeguards and control would be instituted by the IAEA, the U.S. and Euratom will concert one another about the IAEA exercising controls and safeguards of the fissile materials used or produced within our programs.'"[97] As the West German Euratom commissioner also remarked, the fact that "Euratom has passed an agreement with the U.S. to import fissile materials which will only end in 1995 . . . [wa]s a major card in our game"[98] because it forced Americans to mold their NPT proposal within the overall framework of the United States–Euratom Treaty. As a result of the binding nature and clarity of these past commitments, the US government itself was forced to first take into consideration the legal obstacles to the worldwide extension of IAEA controls posed by the preexisting transatlantic (non)proliferation treaty regime before it could debate the political desirability of its universalization.

The European pressure on the United States worked. Recognizing that "the intervention of the Commission on the discussions of the NPT results from conventional obligations,"[99] the American negotiator of the NPT, William Foster, came to Brussels in March 1967 to hear the opinion of the Euratom Commission on the new draft of article 3. On that matter, there was little ambiguity: as the legal services of the Euratom Commission noted, "The new [NPT] article [3] would lead to substituting for the principle of equality of rights between member states, the principle of discrimination between nuclear and non-nuclear powers."[100] As Monnet wrote to Eugene Rostow, the undersecretary of state for political affairs, the new draft article 3 ran counter to Euratom legal commitments, "as the IAEA intervention would recreate an administrative border line splitting the nuclear common market and shrinking industrial integration in a vital technological sector."[101] Indeed, the new article 3 "would thus create and institutionalize discrimination [between France and the other Euratom member states] where it does not exist up to now,"[102] since the Euratom Treaty clearly mentioned that in the "application of safeguards, no discrimination shall be made" (art. 84) between member states based on their final use of the materials.[103] The West German Euratom commissioner agreed. After seeing the new draft article 3 in February 1967, he said that "it would be impossible to sign this actual draft of the Treaty" because, "while it is a clear demonstration of a will for peace, article 3 is incompatible with the Euratom Treaty, and proceeds from a will to discriminate between nations."[104]

The arguments heard in Europe forced the US government to back-pedal: in March 1967, Senator John Pastore gave support to Monnet's interpretation of the US responsibility to include the Euratom Commission in the discussion when he declared that if "there appears to be developing in the minds of some the idea that a choice must be made of one of these organizations [Euratom or IAEA] to the exclusion of the other," then "this is wrong."[105] As Pastore added, "We need Euratom safeguards, we need the IAEA safeguards, and we need any additional regional safeguard systems that may hereafter be set up," and even "an organization of Warsaw Pact nations that might be formed to further the civilian uses of atomic energy."[106]

Eurofederalists also turned to the *"bons offices"* of the United Kingdom to defend the cause of Euratom controls in the private discussions that the United States and Soviets held in parallel to the public Disarmament Committee in Geneva. When Monnet and the Action Committee passed a declaration calling for British entry into the European Community in March 1967, they explicitly stated that their call should help "the organization of the European Community's technological development," and "the further uniting of Europe, not only in the economic and social field, but in that of foreign policy and defense."[107] The power that Monnet's group had over the British adhesion to the European Communities was clearly understood by the British government, which immediately promised to defend the community's rights regarding nuclear safeguards. The British foreign secretary, Lord Chalfont, also met the Euratom commissioners in Brussels in March 1967 and reassured them that even though "the Soviet Union has already let us know that the only form of control that it accepted would be the one of IAEA" and "a regional safeguards system like the one of Euratom would not be considered as equivalent," he added, "The British Government does not have rigid exigencies on control," and it "has in mind to act as a European power" and "will do whatever is necessary to avoid dissociating itself from Euratom."[108] The Dutch and German Euratom commissioners expected a strong support for Euratom controls from the United Kingdom, as "the Community d[id] not see how Euratom could accept a regime of control leading to potential sanctions, including the confiscation of fissile material after a[n] IAEA decision."[109] Max Kohnstamm as well warned Eugene Rostow that if the United States and the United Kingdom insisted on substituting IAEA controls for Euratom controls on their nuclear exports to Europe, they would put the United Kingdom in an awkward position, as the resulting situation "will be resented by the Germans, harm the British negotiations for membership in the Common Market, and give the French a major excuse for arguing that the UK does not share the same interests as Continent[al] Western Europe," and that "this issue could in fact play the same role that the Nassau agreement played in 1962, the catalyst of the breakdown."[110]

If at this point the United States accepted the principle that the negotiations needed to involve Euratom acting in some legal capacity, it remained to be seen whether the French government was ready to accept that such interpretive authority be delegated to Euratom. Indeed, to give such a role to Euratom meant that European governments would recognize the Euratom Commission as a legitimate actor in European foreign nuclear policy. Originally appointed by the French government to suppress the supranational features of the Euratom Commission in its day-to-day operation (as seen in the previous chapter), the president of the Euratom Commission, Pierre Chatenêt, had many reservations. In March 1967, the day after William Foster discussed the new article 3 with the commission, Chatenêt took a stand on its illegality when he told members of the European Parliament that the IAEA controls would raise "economic and industrial problems"—in particular, concerning the access to fissile material provided by the United States within the framework of the United States–Euratom Treaty. But he did not propose to take the lead to defend the "non-discriminatory principle underlying the Euratom treaty"[111] against the Americans and the Soviets. During the same session of the European Parliament, Walter Hallstein, who presided over the Common Market Commission until its merger with Euratom in the EEC, made the political case against the draft article 3 on safeguards much more clearly than Chatenêt, as he "confirmed the logical link between economic integration–political integration–common defense–common nuclear policy."[112] It was the responsibility of the president of the Euratom Commission—not the president of the Common Market Commission—to defend the European interpretation of the United States' commitments under the United States–Euratom Treaty, but de Gaulle did not encourage Chatenêt to step into transatlantic negotiations as the legitimate representative of the Six.[113] Rather, de Gaulle wished to use the NPT negotiations as leverage to further disentangle the French CEA from Euratom Treaty commitments and to blockade any Euratom controls (especially if these were redefined along the lines followed by the IAEA controls) on France's military activities (conceived broadly).[114]

Here, the opacity of the interpretation of Euratom's controls actually helped the cause of Eurofederalists. Indeed, despite the fact that France had radically undermined the supranational aspects of the Euratom Treaty in private, as far as the "property" rights that Euratom claimed to have with respect to nuclear fuels were concerned (and the kind of industrial joint venture that Euratom could decide to conduct), Euratom officials impressed the Americans with the view that Euratom "owned" all the nuclear materials in the community, and that the decision to let the IAEA control their use was therefore Euratom's and not its member states'. The American chief nuclear diplomat, William Foster, echoed the Europeans' legal arguments when he told the Soviets that "based on the NPT draft of February 1967," the United States would not have any legal grounding to sue the Euratom Commission if it refused to submit its imports of nuclear fuels to the IAEA controls, especially if "the materials are sent to *the Community*, a lawful actor with a legal personality distinct from one of the member states."[115] Before the Soviets, Foster argued that, as "all special fissionable material for peaceful purpose within Euratom territory was the property of Euratom" (art. 86),[116] "the Soviet draft contained a very large loophole, as under the Soviet article 3, all fissionable material owned by Euratom would be excluded from safeguards, not to mention the four facilities owned by Euratom over which even national governments have no independent inspection rights."[117] As the West emphasized in its negotiation with the Soviets, the crux of the problem derived from the fact that the Euratom Treaty system had created a supranational system of property, accountability, and control of fissile materials, whereas the proposed language of the NPT and the IAEA Statute were traditional Westphalian legal instruments open to signature by nation-states only: indeed, the NPT only created obligations for states, which meant that "the Community could not be attacked on behalf of the NPT" if it refused to let the IAEA control nuclear installations in Euratom territory.[118] France did not object to the public charade according to which Euratom had supranational "property rights," as long as, de facto, Euratom rather than IAEA controls persisted in Europe after the NPT.

Eventually, the opacity of the legal rules contained in the Euratom Treaty helped the United States convince the Soviets to implicitly recognize the authority of the Euratom Commission to interpret how the NPT would change its control rules, and whether the existence of IAEA soft law would impact its new regulations. Indeed, in July 1967, the US negotiator finally obtained assurance from the Soviets that the new article 3 of the NPT would leave the matter of establishing commensurability between the two types of controls in the hands of the two international organizations concerned: the Euratom Commission and the IAEA. The two organizations were given the responsibility to prove clearly the equivalence of their safeguard system within 180 days of the entry into force of the NPT (art. 3.4 of the NPT).[119]

In the fall of 1967, the legal point of view defended by the Euratom Commission thus prevailed: the Soviet negotiator accepted the idea, even though in July 1967, he still stressed the nonequivalence of Euratom and IAEA safeguards, as the first was based on a nonintrusive materials approach and the latter on an "intrusive facility-based approach."[120] As Foster told the Euratom Commission in August 1967, the deadlock was broken when the Soviets suggested "in a private conversation that article 3 be based upon the IAEA statute and the IAEA safeguards document," which both refer to "bilateral or multilateral" arrangements with the IAEA—the term *multilateral* being interpreted to include international organizations as well as groups of states. Thus, "the Soviets did not exclude the possibility that Euratom and IAEA might come to some agreement covering verification by the IAEA of compliance with the terms of the NPT."[121] As Robert Schaetzel, who had monitored the United States–Euratom negotiations in 1958, and who still worked at the State Department on European affairs, confirmed to the commission in October 1967, "In private conversations, the U.S. made it quite clear that this language ["multilateral arrangements"] would have to permit members to negotiate and conclude an agreement with the IAEA through Euratom to carry out their safeguards obligation and that a Euratom-IAEA agreement could result from these negotiations," and "the Soviets have indicated that they agreed."[122]

The legal discussion on the equivalence of Euratom and IAEA safeguards was thus postponed until the discussion of a future Euratom-IAEA treaty of cooperation, which, the Euratom Commission insisted, "in no case would organize the legal subordination of Euratom to the IAEA."[123] This compromise represented a great victory for European legal experts, as the new article 3 "d[id] not create any real legal obligation," but "just mention[ed] the need to plan a negotiation."[124] With this stratagem, the Soviets could compromise without losing face, as they maintained that as far as they were concerned, Euratom controls were not equivalent to IAEA controls.[125]

The last version of article 3 of the NPT acknowledged that the two sets of hard- and soft-law regulations negotiated in two very different political, strategic, and military contexts had yet to be harmonized, but it changed the institutional players in charge of that harmonization. The negotiation of Euratom and IAEA controls no longer confronted strong states (the United States and the USSR) with a weaker international organization (the Euratom Commission), but an international organization (the Euratom Commission) with a weaker one (the IAEA), whose rules had yet to be put into operation on a wide scale. Furthermore, the Europeans refused to allow any ambiguity regarding controls to persist in the future NPT regime when they ratified the NPT. To escape the deadline of 180 days on negotiation between the IAEA and NPT signatory states in the "guillotine clause" (art. 3.4 of the NPT),[126] all Euratom NNWS signed the NPT in 1968 and 1969 but agreed to wait to ratify the NPT until the end of negotiations between Euratom and the IAEA, so the outcome of those negotiations on controls would be clear to them at the time of ratification. As the US AEC chairman noted, "The fact that all Euratom members delayed their ratifications of the NPT until after the date [when they signed the IAEA-Euratom Agreement] gave Euratom increased bargaining power in its negotiation."[127]

Negotiations between Euratom and the IAEA began in November 1971 and ended in September 1972, when a Euratom-IAEA Safeguards Agreement was approved between the five NNWS of the Euratom Community—whose extension also covered the territory of the British and Irish isles and Denmark after they completed their adhesion to the European Community and entered as full members on January 1, 1973.[128] The negotiation between Euratom and the IAEA was a major victory for Euratom NNWS. Indeed, as a result of the negotiation with Euratom, the "NPT safeguards system has been greatly influenced by and adapted to the Euratom system in several respects,"[129] as Mohamed Shaker writes. For instance, in anticipation of the coming negotiations with Euratom, the IAEA Safeguards Committee decided in March 1971 to ease possible tensions between the two systems of control by adopting a materials-based approach similar to that of Euratom for the NPT signatory states. Indeed, the new safeguards concept was largely inspired by the "Karlsruhe Doktrin,"[130] developed by West German scientists in Karlsruhe. Consistent with Euratom's controls, West Germans insisted on a materials-based approach; a discontinuous approach that focused on "strategic" points where diversion was most likely; and on nonhuman inspection, in order to prevent industrial espionage (by Communists). The materials-based approach (focusing on source and special fissionable materials) meant that transfer of nonnuclear equipment (listed by art. 3.2b of the NPT) would be excluded from the Euratom-IAEA Safeguards Agreement. The nonhuman inspection techniques privileged good record-keeping practices aimed at ensuring material balance accountancy in "all the civilian" nuclear programs of each country (the "full-scope" approach to safeguards), which could be complemented by the presence of sensors and monitors in facilities, to watch for any suspect interruption in the normal operation of plants. As West Germans and Italians emphasized, the NPT aimed at control of materials and not of plants as such, and IN-FCIRC/153 (the new document produced by the IAEA) made no mention of "continuous inspection and access at all times,"[131] which meant that the old IAEA safeguards model of INFCIRC/26 and INFCIRC/66 no longer provided an adequate template for the control of nuclear trade among signatory states of the NPT.[132]

The negotiation between Euratom and the IAEA thus created a major discontinuity in the production of regulations by the IAEA. As Astrid Forland writes, even though the United States had insisted on including a right of review for the IAEA over the design of future nuclear facilities in both its 1961 and 1965 documents on safeguards for reactors, INFCIRC/153 "no longer permitted [taking] a closer look at facilities before or during their construction."[133] Instead, the new document merely signaled that information about new facilities should be provided to the agency "as soon as possible" before the introduction of nuclear materials into the plant.[134] This discontinuity explains, for instance, why the Islamic Republic of Iran, which signed a "full-scope" Safeguards Agreement with the IAEA in 1974 based on the new model (INFCIRC/153), claimed in 2003 that it did not have to inform the IAEA of the construction of new plants designed to enrich uranium before the introduction of source or special fissionable materials into the centrifuges.[135] Whereas the old IAEA system of safeguards addressed "some individual nuclear installation to IAEA safeguards in connection with assistance received from some third party,"[136] the new IAEA safeguards were applied "for the purpose of verifying the fulfillment of the obligation which they had entered by signing the NPT"[137]—that is, the effectiveness of the regional or national system of control to detect possible diversion of nuclear materials from peaceful to military use, whether the country (or group of countries) received outside assistance or not.

The soft law produced by the IAEA clearly moved closer to Euratom's approach to controls. Euratom made only slight changes to its control procedures before and after the signing of the NPT by its non-nuclear-weapon member states. Indeed, the agreement that Euratom signed with the IAEA in September 1972 not only adopted many of the provisions of the IAEA's new control procedure (INFCIRC/153), which was founded on Euratom's materials-based approach, but it even included special provisions for Euratom NNWS that recognized the specific rights granted to Euratom by its member states, such as the exclusive right that Euratom retained to invite (or not) IAEA inspectors.[138] Furthermore, this agreement was the first and only time that a regional organization, Euratom, was recognized as a party to the application of article 3 of the NPT. As a result, the Safeguards Agreement regarded the territories of NNWS that were part of Euratom as a single unit. This provision meant that there would be no IAEA safeguards on nuclear materials traded among them, and no need to send advance notification of bilateral trade in nuclear materials or equipment to the IAEA, as was required between all other states.[139] In that sense, the Euratom-IAEA Agreement recognized that the "property" rights (ownership) of fissile materials in Europe belonged to Euratom, according to the public charade found in the Euratom Treaty (despite the fact that the rights were in practice kept by the individual owners and users of these fuels), and that this "property" was essential to the maintenance of a common market of nuclear fuels in Europe. Finally, Euratom obtained the assurance that in compliance with the United States–Euratom Treaty of November 1958, no nuclear material exported from the United States to Euratom was to be safeguarded by the IAEA.[140] The only concession that the IAEA obtained was that Euratom controls would no longer apply to the safeguarding of nuclear materials only (as planned by the Euratom Treaty of March 1957), but that Euratom inspectors could also visit the facilities where these fuels were used, processed, and produced, and that Euratom inspectors could decide to invite IAEA inspectors to visit facilities,[141] in order to prove *on the ground* the compatibility of its controls with those of the IAEA. But still, IAEA inspectors could not visit European facilities without first informing Euratom inspectors, a particularity that survived the inclusion of Eastern European countries (which were more used to IAEA than to Euratom inspections) in Euratom after the collapse of the Soviet Union and their accession to the EU.[142]

The clear recognition of the specificity of the transatlantic treaty regime within the global NPT regime cleared the road for ratification of the NPT by five founding Euratom NNWS: they all ratified the NPT the same day: May 2, 1975. The process of harmonizing the rules of the IAEA and Euratom not only contributed to the integration of Europe into the NPT regime, by allowing the Euratom controls to substitute themselves for IAEA controls in Europe (see the lower-left cell in table 7.1), but it also contributed to the rapid rate at which non-European nations signed Safeguards Agreements with the IAEA. Indeed, most of these nations were not unhappy that the IAEA had modeled its system of safeguards on the nonintrusive "full-scope" approach of Euratom rather than on the intrusive facility-based approach of the IAEA soft law produced before the NPT was signed. Nations were prompted to set up safeguards systems similar to Euratom on a national basis, leaving to the IAEA the responsibility to "verify" that the national system in place worked effectively: for instance, Japan waited until the end of the ratification process by Euratom NNWS to conclude the negotiations of its Safeguards Agreement with the IAEA (modeled after Euratom's agreement) and to ratify the NPT, which it did in 1976.[143] In many ways, the "full-scope" approach provided an incentive for nations to sign the NPT, and thus escape the more intrusive INFCIRC/66 safeguards document.

As the new IAEA soft law adopted the nuclear materials–based approach, the IAEA admitted that it was not in charge of establishing the export control lists of nonnuclear materials used to build nuclear reactors (heavy water, for instance) that would "trigger" IAEA controls. Thus, an informal committee chaired by a Swiss professor of international law, Claude Zangger, was named to constitute such a list (in compliance with article 3.2). Until the Indian test of an explosive nuclear device in 1974, France boycotted any attempt to create a global trigger list of nonnuclear materials, either by the Zangger Committee or by the Nuclear Suppliers Group (NSG), which continued to meet in London. Still, the IAEA endorsed the consensus reached in this external committee, and it eventually published Zangger's "trigger" list in September 1974 as one of its documents. The same list was also incorporated into the work of the NSG, which resumed its cooperation with France in September 1974 after the Indian test.[144] In so doing, the global nonproliferation regime was reinforced, rather than undermined, by the multiplicity of interpretative authorities charged with coordinating the control of nuclear and nonnuclear materials that triggered IAEA safeguards.

Nuclear Opacity Clarified: Two Rules in Two Contexts (1967–73)

The negotiation between the IAEA and Euratom also gave an opportunity to all Euratom member states (NWS and NNWS) to settle their disagreement privately: the new interpretations made clearer the context in which Euratom's control rules were to be privately interpreted according to a Eurofederalist lens (in the territory of the NNWS) and the context in which a minimalist interpretation of these rules would be privately accepted (in the territory of the NWS). If, when dealing with the IAEA, Euratom publicly claimed that all activities and all nuclear materials circulating within Euratom territory fell under a nondiscriminatory supranational system of property and control, France continued to privately argue (within the council) that all nuclear activities that could have a military as well as peaceful use fell outside of Euratom's controls, including its activities in the field of uranium enrichment and plutonium reprocessing. In private, Euratom controls had thus been interpreted in a discriminatory fashion, since they were applied differently in France and in the Euratom NNWS.

Through the negotiation between Euratom member states and the IAEA,

Euratom members had an opportunity to clarify this previous opacity. A first attempt to align the private and public interpretations of the nondiscriminatory nature of the Euratom Treaty along Eurofederalist lines had been attempted (in vain) in 1967, during the NPT negotiations. In the context of the 1967 negotiations of British entry into the European Community, Euratom NNWS argued that the United Kingdom should help them enforce nondiscriminatory Euratom "supranational" controls in the future NPT regime, and that the United Kingdom should also help them convince France that Euratom's "supranational" system of controls and property applied to all dual-use activities (in particular, uranium-enrichment and plutonium-reprocessing activities) in all the territories of Euratom member states (whether NWS or NNWS).[145] Responding to the Euratom commissioners' concerns about the permanence of Euratom controls after the entry into force of the NPT, Lord Chalfont responded that "the British government w[ould] not sign the NPT if it grant[ed] the IAEA the right to prohibit persons and enterprises the right to pursue peaceful scientific and technological activities which could eventually lead to military applications."[146] At this point, however, the Dutch and German commissioners wanted a clear and public recognition by all powers of their right to access dual-use nuclear technologies within the Euratom Treaty regime without preapproval by the IAEA (or by Euratom), and that all dual-use activities in Euratom territory should be equally controlled by Euratom (rather than by the IAEA), whether they were located in the territory of a NWS or a NNWS. To align promises with deeds, as a price for British membership, the Dutch and German commissioners asked the British government to "plan the extension of the Capenhurst [uranium-enrichment] facility and the possibility to transform it into the heart of the European industry in isotopic separation," as well as the "Europeanization of the [plutonium-]reprocessing center of Windscale,"[147] to be placed under Euratom controls.

A positive response to such a proposal by all parties involved would have clearly moved the private interpretation of Euratom's controls closer to their public interpretation as a nondiscriminatory system of control encompassing all dual-use nuclear activities (except for the design of nuclear warheads) in Euratom's territory. But although the United Kingdom accepted the "Euratomization" of its enrichment and reprocessing plants, as requested by the West Germans,[148] France blocked the proposal in December 1967 by vetoing British admission to the European Communities for the second time. Instead, General de Gaulle proposed to open participation to the West Germans in a new French-led "European gaseous diffusion plant," which would "straddle the Rhine with the actual separation unit on the French side (secrecy being maintained on the more specialized components) and the necessary electric power station on the German side of the river."[149] The French proposal would give the Germans, "if not all the 'know-how,' at least one key to the plant's operation,"[150] and it would keep Euratom far from the secret operations. The West Germans, though, found it humiliating that de Gaulle would refuse to accept them as full partners in the French program of isotopic separation, and that de Gaulle had once again blocked British membership in the European Community without consulting with them.[151] Thus, Bonn rejected the French proposal. The Germans did not accept being treated as a second-rate nuclear power, especially at a time when they insisted in East-West negotiations that Euratom was based upon the principle of nondiscrimination: they wanted to create a de facto precedent showing that they could enrich uranium under Euratom (rather than IAEA) controls before the NPT was signed and the negotiation between Euratom and the IAEA started.[152]

The West Germans and the Dutch insisted on securing de jure and de facto access to the joint development of dual-use technologies with a NWS (and under Euratom supervision) prior to the entry into force of the NPT. Disappointed with France's Eurodif proposal, they encouraged the British to pursue their proposal of joint collaboration in the field of uranium enrichment along new lines. France had refused to allow the "Euratomization" of British plants for strategic and normative reasons,[153] but France could not prevent the West Germans from conducting joint cooperation on a trilateral basis with the British and the Dutch. Thus, the West Germans turned to the Dutch and British with a proposal for joint production of a uranium-enrichment plant using the centrifuge technique for isotopic separation, an alternative to the gaseous diffusion separation technique used by the British in Capenhurst and the French in Pierrelatte.[154] The choice of technology was partly the result of legal considerations: the British government could not share with third parties the information on gaseous diffusion technologies, some of which it had obtained from the United States through the 1958 McMahon Act, but it could share information on technologies for which it had not received any help from the United States, such as centrifuge techniques.[155] The West Germans and the Dutch got their wish, obtaining equality with the United Kingdom when they signed the treaty establishing a new multinational firm—the Uranium Enrichment Company (Urenco), whose facilities in the Netherlands were placed under Euratom controls—in March 1970, on the very day that the NPT became effective.

In fact, this tripartite treaty constituted what I have called in chapter 4 a "preemptive interpretation" of the ambiguous rules of the NPT, rather than a strategic statement on the parties' willingness to develop nuclear weapons: with the tripartite Urenco Treaty, the West Germans made it clear that, as the NPT entered into force, they recognized no limit placed on their development of dual-use nuclear technologies; that except for the making of nuclear warheads, they would engage in nuclear cooperation of all sorts with NWS as well as NNWS; and that, unlike the French, they agreed to impose "full-scope" Euratom controls on their (new) enrichment facilities. The director of foreign affairs of the French CEA, Bertrand Goldschmidt, concluded in a quite melodramatic fashion, "It was as [if] Germany had wanted to show that it had freed itself from Konrad Andenauer's pledge renouncing the manufacture on home territory of nuclear weapons or their vital components."[156] But such a claim was exaggerated, as the West Germans did not want to make bombs but wanted to ensure that their participation in uranium-enrichment cooperation would not be challenged under the provisions of articles 1 and 2 of the NPT, and that their project would not be subject to preapproval by the IAEA.[157]

The entry into force of the NPT precipitated a series of preemptive interpretations of Euratom's control rules from NNWS, but also from the only NWS that was party to Euratom at the time: France—a confirmation that an ambiguous treaty creates incentives for all of the parties concerned with its implementation to unilaterally clarify the meaning of its rules between the moment of its signature and its ratification. As Bertrand Goldschmidt writes, after the Euratom NNWS signed the NPT in 1969, "The French government did not see why it should be subjected to the consequences of a treaty [the NPT] it had not signed."[158] In particular, the French government wanted to continue to benefit from the nuclear materials imported through the Euratom Supply Agency (ESA) without being subjected to IAEA controls, especially after the "signature of the AEC Omnibus Bill [in] 1967 by President Johnson, which authorized the increase of ceilings for plutonium and uranium for Euratom."[159] Therefore, after de Gaulle vetoed the British entry into Euratom, the administrator general of the French CEA told AEC officials that the French were happy "to continue Euratom inspections but were opposed to IAEA controls," and that, "in the case the U.S. would insist on IAEA controls in the Community, which might affect the Euratom control program, France would rather abandon its plans [to buy US] light water reactors than make such concessions toward international controls other than Euratom's."[160] France feared that if Euratom failed to maintain its system of control in its future negotiation with the IAEA, the United States would apply the same IAEA safeguards to fissile materials imported by the French as it did with the British.[161] The French government wanted to avoid this situation, an objective that it could only achieve by maintaining Euratom controls in place in the future NPT regime.

With the entry into force of the NPT, France succeeded in shaping the new control rules that would ensue from the negotiations between the IAEA and Euratom by limiting to the greatest extent the jurisdiction of Euratom controls over the French nuclear activities. With de Gaulle replaced by Georges Pompidou in 1968, the French government agreed to recognize the right of the European Commission to negotiate with the IAEA on behalf of the five Euratom NNWS after Pompidou obtained from the commission "an understanding that the future Euratom control [redesigned to fit with the IAEA standards] should not apply to nonrestricted materials in France"[162] (that is to say, to materials produced or processed for military uses, but not yet placed in French nuclear warheads, such as the uranium being enriched at Pierrelatte). Thus, France agreed to let the commission "sign an agreement between the IAEA and Euratom" as long as Euratom restricted its control "to fissile materials in France which are for peaceful purposes *and* which are subjected to an international agreement, or if France unilaterally decides to subject them to international safeguards."[163] This discriminatory stance was part of an ongoing French effort to break free from the Euratom Treaty obligations. In 1971, France even refused to submit its exports and imports of fissile materials (enriched uranium exported to Italy, and natural uranium imported from South Africa since 1969) to the preapproval of the ESA.[164]

This time, the European Commission and the European Court of Justice recognized France's right to exclude the enriched uranium it produced for its military nuclear program from Euratom controls, but they asked France to respect the rules of the Common Market for the civilian nuclear fuels it imported and exported (and the "right of option" that member states could use after being informed of future sales of ores by the ESA). The private interpretive arrangement reached by France and the member states in the European Council solved a decadelong struggle between the commission and the CEA, which since 1958 had rejected the right of the Euratom Commission to control all nuclear materials in the community until they were placed in nuclear warheads (as seen in the previous chapter).[165] This arrangement also paved the way for the tripartite Safeguards Agreement that France signed jointly with the IAEA and Euratom in 1978, by which France authorized Euratom to report to the IAEA on the "peaceful" nuclear activities that France declared to Euratom. With this last agreement (along with the prior United Kingdom–Euratom–IAEA Agreement of 1976), the

IAEA could close its yearly reviews of Euratom NNWS, as France would account for the "peaceful" source and special fissionable materials that, for instance, it reprocessed in France on behalf of the Germans in the French reprocessing plant at the Hague.[166] In this case, France carefully avoided sending to Euratom (and thus to the IAEA) any information regarding its dual-use program.

In fact, the harmonization between the European and global nonproliferation regimes was completed with the end of these negotiations between Euratom member states, Euratom, and the IAEA. The opacity of Euratom's control rules facilitated the process of harmonization. Indeed, the interpretation that Euratom member states gave to the Euratom controls differed between the NNWS and the NWS (such as France and the United Kingdom). In the first case, direct IAEA controls were rejected by Euratom because Euratom had an all-encompassing (or "comprehensive") system of property (ownership) and control of all the nuclear fuels in the territory of NNWS; in the latter case, IAEA controls were rejected by Euratom because NWS had no obligation to apply IAEA safeguards on their nuclear activities (as art. 3.1 of the NPT only created obligations for NNWS) and because France claimed that Euratom had no jurisdiction over the control of nuclear fuels used in dual-use facilities. Interestingly, this political compromise was actually turned into European jurisprudence when the European Court of Justice ruled in two important decisions in 2005 and 2006 (contrary to the original interpretation of the Euratom Treaty negotiators in 1957) that Euratom controls did not apply to the decommissioning of a British military nuclear reactor and that the safety risks arising from a damaged British nuclear-powered submarine did not require the British government to advise the Euratom authorities of the "military" information regarding special fissionable materials.[167]

Conclusion

After the ratification of the NPT by Euratom member states, the Eurofederalist dream of a European nuclear force had lived out its life. In many ways, Eurofederalists had achieved their purpose: they successfully preserved a certain amount of autonomy for the European nuclear trade regime so that Germany could feel that it was treated in international treaty negotiations as an equal to France or the United Kingdom, even though Germany was eventually denied the right to unilaterally own and produce nuclear weapons. Without the Eurofederalists' thirty-year crusade for Europe to have a right to build, own, and target its own nuclear weapons, the problem of

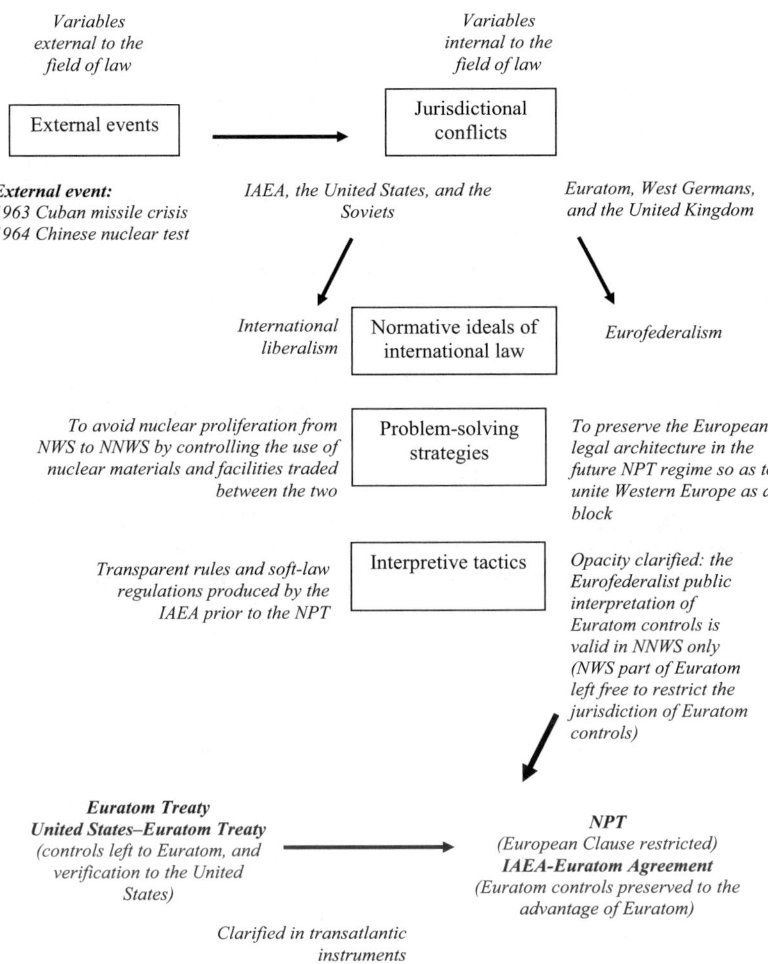

Figure 7.2. Opacity clarified: European federalism in the late 1960s and early 1970s

nuclear proliferation in Europe might never have been solved, and the European nuclear order would not have been clearly recognized in global legal instruments such as article 3 of the NPT and the ensuing Euratom-IAEA Agreement (see fig. 7.2).

Quite paradoxically, the opacity of Euratom's control rules helped Euratom member states bargain a better position when negotiating with the IAEA on the extent to which the IAEA regulations would be applied to Euratom. The existence of the prior European treaty regime, which appeared publicly to give clear rights to a nonstate actor (Euratom), meant that all the parties of the future NPT regime (the United States but also the Soviets) had to allow Euratom to keep an important role within the new global regime, or the Euratom member states would be excluded from the future interstate control regime of the IAEA.

At the same time, the very success of the Eurofederalists in preserving (through clarifying and therefore limiting) the interpretation of their exclusive rights within the broader global NPT regime triggered an angry reaction from the rest of the world—in particular, in the former colonies that aimed at great-power status. Indeed, the stories of nuclear programs in India, Iran, and Pakistan, and the challenges each of these nations mounted against the NPT framework, found their origins in the European nuclear settlement of the mid-1970s. India subsequently denounced the NPT as a farce reproducing the division between colonial and colonized powers, and in May 1974, it exploded its first nuclear device. Similarly, when France denied Iran the right to own its shares in the French-led consortium Eurodif at the end of the 1970s, in response to the ousting of the Shah, Iran started a process of state-led terrorism and nuclear proliferation the result of which we see now. And last, when a young Pakistani engineer named A. Q. Khan left the Urenco company with secret documents on centrifuge technologies that he used to develop the Pakistani nuclear program and that he later sold to Iranians,[168] the Europeans were forced to admit the limits of the global nuclear control regime that they had crafted. This sequence of events, and the reactions of the European powers, the United States, and the Soviets as they tried to protect the European and global nuclear regimes that they had constructed, is the story that I will address in the final chapter.

EIGHT

The Singular Legacies of Nuclear Opacity: The Difficult Road toward the Universalization of the NPT Regime

The evolution of the European treaty regime and its gradual harmonization with the global NPT regime has an important bearing on contemporary discussions of nuclear proliferation. In this conclusion, I will draw some lessons for the universalization of the NPT. In particular, I will discuss whether the process of harmonization between the European and global rules of the nuclear trade could be replicated in the case of the three countries that have never signed the NPT nor adhered to the rules of the NPT regime—namely, Israel, India, and Pakistan. I will argue that the inclusion of Israel, India, and Pakistan raises the question of how one might create a legal dynamic through which various nuclear trade regimes are made to converge, and how the veil of opacity over each of these countries' nuclear status could be lifted gradually, through the very same process of harmonization between treaty regimes that took place in the case of Euratom member states with respect to the global NPT regime.

Drawing some lessons from the successful harmonization of Euratom rules with the rules of the NPT regime could bring valuable insights to the debate over whether the NPT regime can survive the present challenges. The existence of de facto nuclear-weapon states outside the global NPT regime, while included in other regional nuclear trade regimes, poses one of the gravest threats to the existence and effectiveness of the NPT regime. Only three years after the NPT regime was given a formidable vote of confidence in 1995, when all the NPT signatory states agreed to extend its duration, due to expire twenty-five years after ratification (art. 10.2), two out of these three de facto nuclear-weapon states, India and Pakistan, publicly conducted a series of nuclear tests. Furthermore, less than ten years later, it was publicly revealed that Pakistan had organized a vast proliferation network that subverted the rules of the NPT regime. These events shattered the hope that the indefinite extension of the NPT regime would block nuclear proliferation forever. As the team of experts led by George Perkovich under the auspices of the Carnegie Endowment for International Peace write, the public acknowledgment that Pakistan had organized a secret regional nuclear trade regime with Iran, Libya, Iraq, and North Korea "highlight[ed] the challenge of persuading the states that have not joined the NPT—India, Pakistan, and Israel—to nevertheless accept rigorous nonproliferation obligations."[1] Indeed, as the authors note, "in varying degrees their status beyond its boundaries undermines the entire NPT-based regime."[2]

In this conclusion, I will show that the nuclear opacity that was characteristic of European countries' nuclear status during this earlier period was far from being an exception. Indeed, the US government has long kept the nuclear status of these three NPT outliers opaque in ways that were similar to how it initially kept Euratom's nuclear status opaque (as shown in chapter 5). Unsurprisingly, each language has its own word to designate such opacity: for instance, *amimut* in Hebrew "refers to the taboolike social aspects of Israel's prohibitions and restraints in connection with its nuclear weapons";[3] in Arabic, as IAEA director ElBaradei notes, the word used to refer to opacity and dissimulation is "*taqiyya* [*tagiyeh* in Persian], meaning to protect oneself or those under one's care from harm"[4] through deception. Europe is not exceptional in the fact that its nuclear status was kept opaque, in large part with US help. Rather, European exceptionalism consists in the fact that its nuclear opacity was gradually overturned, first when a new generation of state leaders and nuclear experts arrived to power in the United States and France at the same time as the Euratom Treaty was implemented (chapter 6), and second, when the rules of Europe's nuclear regime were harmonized with the global rules of the NPT regime (chapter 7).

This comparison between the fate of European and non-European opaque nuclear programs after the NPT entered into force shows that the emergence of new global norms does not necessarily lead states to clarify their nuclear status. Over the long term, the *harmonization* between treaty regimes is just one possible outcome of such processes, and not the most likely one. Israel's nuclear status, discussed first here, has consistently been an *unacknowledged exemption* to the global treaty regime before and after the NPT. In many ways, Israel is still a black hole in the NPT regime because everyone seems to have had an interest in maintaining Israel's nuclear opacity intact. In contrast, when India progressed on the road toward nuclear weapons, it rejected opacity and favored instead a tactic that Itty Abraham calls "ambivalence," by which Indian diplomats referred to an ontological inability of the NPT to characterize unambiguously which nuclear activities were prohibited by the new regime.[5] To the extent that nuclear ambivalence was more threatening than nuclear opacity, the United States and other guardians of the NPT tried to render India's nuclear status opaque in order to defend (rather than to subvert) the NPT. Thus, in the case of India, nuclear opacity was used to produce some *acknowledged exception* in the global regime. Unfortunately, in the case of Pakistan, nuclear opacity, which has largely been produced by the US government, extended to the nuclear export agreements signed by Pakistan and state buyers of forbidden nuclear weapons technologies that had signed the NPT as NNWS: North Korea, Iraq, Iran, Libya. By permitting an opaque nuclear trade regime to develop in juxtaposition with the NPT regime, the United States allowed a *silent subversion* of the global regime to take place. This subversion has become the main threat to the effectiveness and existence of the NPT regime today, which the United States and its Western partners need to tackle, although, I suggest here, on a systematic rather than ad hoc basis.

By highlighting the different effects of nuclear opacity on the global NPT regime, this conclusion shows that the modalities of inclusion of the three last NPT outliers will differ, because the existing webs of agreements to which they belong differ in goals, scope, and degree of opacity. Consistent with the central assumption made in this book (i.e., that regimes do not emerge ex nihilo, as if states moved from anarchy to order), I emphasize that Israel, India, and Pakistan are not unbound Ulysses who could be easily convinced to tie their hands to the central mast of the NPT regime through persuasion and coercion, but that they are part of singular trade regimes that preceded the NPT regime. The transition from their past adherence to parallel nuclear trade regimes to their inclusion in the NPT regime needs to be achieved through a process of harmonization between their past legal commitments and the new legal commitments they will be asked to respect. But again, the extent to which their past and possible future commitments diverge is different for each of these three countries. Such a process of inclusion cannot, and should not, be similar in each case, as these NPT outliers are not all in a similar position with respect to the NPT regime.[6] To detail some of the challenges ahead, I will present how nuclear opacity was constructed in each of these three cases, and what effects it had on the global nuclear trade regime, starting with Israel, then moving to India, and finally Pakistan.

Israel: The Worst-Kept Secret . . . but the Least Embarrassing for the West

How Israel, France, and the United States Produced Israel's Nuclear Opacity

The predicament that the international community faces with regard to Israel's nuclear status comes closest to the situation in which the world found itself when Europe had to normalize its relations with the global nonproliferation regime in the mid-1970s. The origins of Israel's nuclear opacity are rooted in the same events—in particular, the Suez crisis. Thus, to understand how Israel's position with regard to the global nonproliferation regime has been constructed over the years, it is important to recall how the opacity of Israel's nuclear program was originally coproduced by the United States, France, and Israel—a process described by the foremost expert on the issue, Avner Cohen.

Israel's nuclear story, like that of many other countries, started with the launch of the Atoms for Peace program by Eisenhower and AEC chairman Lewis Strauss in 1953. Still, Israel soon realized that the AEC would not provide Israel with reactors that could produce "the slightest quantity of plutonium,"[7] which forced Israel's prime minister, David Ben-Gurion, to search for other forms of cooperation that left the nuclear weapons option open. The opportunity came in the summer of 1956, when Israel's top nuclear administrator, Shimon Peres, exchanged the promise of intelligence cooperation regarding President Nasser's involvement in Algerian politics for a vague promise of nuclear cooperation extended by the French defense minister. As Avner Cohen has shown, the Suez crisis gave Israel the opportunity to forge strong nuclear ties with France: the nationalization of the Suez Canal, followed by the failed invasion by Israeli, French, and British troops, and the adverse reaction from the two superpowers, convinced France not only to extend nuclear cooperation with Germany (and Italy) to military activities (as seen in chapter 5), but also to jump-start the creation of a secret Israeli plutonium-reprocessing plant and a small uranium-separation plant at Dimona.[8] On November 8, 1956, Golda Meir and Shimon Peres negotiated with the French defense minister in Paris the sale of a nuclear reactor capable of producing fifteen kilograms of plutonium a year (enough to produce two bombs per year), and a hidden reprocessing plant that would allow Israel to extract plutonium from the spent fuel.[9] On October 3, 1957, a month before the tripartite agreement between France, West Germany, and Italy was signed, a secret Franco-Israeli agreement was signed between the two governments to start construction of the nuclear facilities at Dimona. They hired a French private contractor (with strong ties to the state sector), Saint Gobain, to construct a replica of the power plant that France had built at Marcoule, alongside a reprocessing plant.[10] Thus, this secret Franco-Israeli nuclear-weapons program was another hidden side of Europe's legal iceberg of nuclear agreements signed in the wake of the Suez crisis.

At the start of the Franco-Israeli cooperation, secrecy reigned. But as Avner Cohen shows, secrecy was soon replaced by opacity when, in the first and only public reference to Israel's nuclear activities in Dimona made by Israel's state officials, Prime Minister Ben-Gurion publicly declared to the Israeli parliament in December 1960 that Israel had started a purely civilian program, without mentioning French cooperation to build the hidden plutonium-reprocessing facility and a small uranium-separation plant.[11] This announcement was made immediately after the signs of the plutonium production site were picked up by the CIA and leaked to the *New York Times*.[12] In this context, Ben-Gurion's "revelation" was both an acknowledgment of the presence of a nuclear program and a lie. By concealing French involvement, Ben-Gurion allowed France to escape pressure from either the United States or the Soviets to reveal what technology it had delivered to the Israelis; and by welcoming "scientific visits"[13] from US scientists and carefully rejecting international "inspections" by the IAEA or other inspectors, Ben-Gurion shifted the burden of spelling out the truth about Israel's nuclear program to the shoulders of the US government.

In contrast to some earlier interpretations,[14] even expressed by Cohen himself, according to which French president Charles de Gaulle had given orders to cut all ties with Israel when he returned to power,[15] it seems that, as long as the United States agreed to turn a blind eye to the nature of Franco-Israeli cooperation, de Gaulle agreed to let it live, provided Israel's nuclear status remained opaque.[16] In fact, as Mathew Kroenig writes, when the United States started its visits to Israeli sites, "de Gaulle made a calculated decision [upon his return to power] to cut off official cooperation, to provide the French government plausible deniability [opacity] while simultaneously utilizing private French firms to honor the nuclear cooperation agreement with Israel."[17] For instance, after the US inspectors started their visits, de Gaulle not only left the nuclear agreement untouched, he also let the French firm Dassault cooperate on the production of the (nuclear-capable) Jericho missiles after 1961.

Since then, the United States (not the French) has thus become the guardian of the opacity of the Franco-Israeli program in Dimona: first Kennedy, then Johnson, and then Nixon all ensured that the US government assuaged the fears expressed by other countries (especially Arab countries) that Israel would soon become the sixth nuclear-weapon state. Despite the fact that the US engineers sent to visit Dimona were not allowed to take measuring instruments, nor to take papers back to the United States for translation (all papers shown to them were in Hebrew), and that they were even shown "a mock-up control room provided by France that displayed data consistent with a small reactor,"[18] successive US presidents positively asserted in public that the Israeli program was purely civilian.[19] Furthermore, none of the top US civilians officially asked French leaders "why the French-Israeli nuclear deal was kept secret," and whether "a promise that Israel would not develop a nuclear weapons capability in the future" could be extracted from Israel.[20] In fact, Kennedy's role was more than passive: he not only let the AEC inspectors be deceived by the Israelis during their visits; he also actively compartmentalized information so that the information extracted by the CIA in early 1963 on Dimona's true military nature would not reach the AEC.[21] As Cohen writes, "Kennedy did not ask about Israel's future plans to separate plutonium; . . . Kennedy . . . limited himself to making the U.S. position on nonproliferation clear, pointing out the need to assure others of Israel's intentions."[22]

Throughout the negotiations of the NPT among the United States, the Soviet Union, and Europe, the United States maintained the opacity of Israel's nuclear program, as Israel's nuclear opacity and its public acceptance of the principles of nonproliferation "prevented a head-on collision with U.S. nuclear nonproliferation and legislation."[23] The US tactic of opacity ensured that Israel's nuclear status would not harm the president's global nonproliferation agenda. Indeed, Kennedy consistently favored a three-pronged approach to the Middle East: nuclear opacity on the part of Israel, conventional deterrence (with arms procurement contracts signed between the United States and Israel as well as Arab states),[24] and Arab-Israeli public support for the US global nonproliferation efforts (starting with the LTBT, which Israel signed in 1963). During that decade, all that the United States asked from Israel was therefore a pledge of "nonintroduction" of nuclear weapons in the Middle East. The term was first used by Prime Minister Ben-Gurion and by his deputy minister of defense Shimon Peres when dealing with the US government in 1962. Then, in 1965, *nonintroduction* was used in a written statement in which Israel pledged that it would "not to be the first to introduce nuclear weapons into the Arab-Israel area," in exchange for US acknowledgment that Dimona was not to be placed under IAEA safeguards.[25] This pledge meant that Israel acknowledged that it would not be granted the same legal status and rights as the other NWS,[26] although it had started producing nuclear weapons before the deadline set in the NPT of January 1, 1967 (art. 9.3).[27] Since Israel's nuclear opacity did not derail American global nonproliferation efforts in favor of the NPT, President Johnson continued to support it, and he focused his negotiating efforts instead on Euratom member states, which had expressed strong concerns about the role that the IAEA would have in the future NPT regime.[28]

Israel's nuclear opacity was further strengthened after the election of President Nixon, whose views on the NPT were shaped by Henry Kissinger, his national security advisor. As far as Israel's nuclear status was concerned, both Nixon and Kissinger differentiated the "secret" possession of nuclear weapons, which they acknowledged as a fait accompli, from their "public" possession, which they discouraged as a condition for Israel to receive more US aid toward its conventional deterrent.[29] For Kissinger, this distinction meant that the United States would privately tell Israel that it could keep its existing nuclear weapons and continue assembling some others, but that, in public, the United States would insist that Israel should not have any assembled devices and that Israel would not be allowed to sign the NPT as a NWS. During a meeting between President Nixon and Prime Minister Golda Meir in September 1969, the United States agreed with top Israeli authorities that "nonintroduction" of nuclear weapons meant no public revelation of secretly readied nuclear weapons (rather than no readying of nuclear weapons at all). After this meeting, the US president dropped the pressure on Israel to sign the NPT and let the IAEA take over the occasional bilateral visits that the AEC had recently concluded in Dimona, in exchange for Golda Meir's agreement never to publicize the secret nuclear weapons already in existence. This compromise allowed Washington "to be on record that it had Israel's assurances that it would remain a non-nuclear-weapons state as defined in the NPT."[30] As Avner Cohen concludes, "This did not mean that America had dropped the issue of NPT universality as a policy objective but that for all practical purposes, Israel had received an exemption,"[31] an unacknowledged exemption of a different kind than that offered to the Germans and other European members of Euratom.

Overall, Israel complied with its pledge: not only did it not use nuclear weapons, even when its military was crushed in the early days of the 1973 war, nor refer to the possibility that it would use them on the battleground, but it also refrained from criticizing the legitimacy of the NPT. In fact, since the beginning of NPT negotiations, Israel has maintained that it did not sign the NPT on pragmatic grounds rather than on philosophical grounds (such as those expressed by India or Pakistan). Shai Feldman writes, "In contrast to India, Israel did not dispute the rationale of the NPT, . . . it only viewed the application of the treaty as flawed,"[32] illustrated by the fact that the IAEA could not prevent clandestine nuclear proliferation as in the case of Pakistani sales of centrifuges to Iraq, Libya, and Iran in the 1980s and 1990s. For instance, Israel criticized the fact that although the IAEA had the legal power to conduct "short-notice" and "challenge" inspections, it had never used that right and "has given much prior notice before launching inspections, leaving governments ample opportunity to conceal prohibited activities,"[33] in order to maintain good relationships with member states, despite the duplicitous behavior that some of them have adopted with regard to the IAEA. To that extent, the real reasons why Israel decided not to sign the NPT (its possession of nuclear weapons) might be the world's "worst kept secret," to paraphrase Avner Cohen, but it was also the least embarrassing for the West's global nonproliferation agenda.

Toward Israel's Inclusion in the Global Nonproliferation Regime

In many ways, the process through which Israel could be included in the global NPT regime needs to take into account these past public commitments if it is to have any chance to move forward. The best opportunity that Israel has had to normalize its relationship with members of the global NPT regime,[34] in concert with its regional neighbors, occurred in the mid-1990s during the Arab-Israeli peace process (known as the "Madrid peace process"), which started after the revelations about Iraq's secret nuclear weapons program and which was interrupted by the start of the Second Intifada. Key lessons can be drawn from this experience. Indeed, in that context, the Arab and Israeli parties to the Madrid peace process agreed to engage in conversations regarding the steps that could lead toward a weapons of mass destruction (WMD)–free zone in the Middle East.[35] The Arab-Israeli dialogue on nuclear issues was facilitated when the Israeli foreign minister, Shimon Peres, the architect of Israel's nuclear program and defense posture since the mid-1950s, signed the Chemical Weapons Convention in January 1993 and approved the "Mubarak initiative" of 1990, which conceived of the Middle East as a WMD-free zone.[36] As a result of the Israeli goodwill and the US insistence on engaging Israel and its neighbors in strategic talks, after the Madrid conference of 1991, the United States and Russia organized a series of conferences in Moscow (January 1992) and in Washington (May and September 1992), which institutionalized the working group under the name "Arms Control and Regional Security" (ACRS), comprising experts from Israel as well as the thirteen Arab states that had taken part in the Madrid peace process (without Syria and Iran).

This process proved that progress could be made as long as Israel kept three commitments: to keep its nuclear-weapons program unacknowledged; to affirm the legitimacy of the NPT regime; and to work toward achieving the goals of the NPT,[37] by calling for more intrusive inspections than those performed by the IAEA in the future WMD-free zone envisioned for the Middle East.[38] In exchange, the official statements coming from Arab participants to ACRS did not single out Israel's nuclear past as the only one outside the nuclear nonproliferation regime. Israel and most of the Arab participants to ACRS (except for Egypt) agreed that solving the problem of Israel's legal standing before the NPT could be postponed until the end of a process of harmonization between Israel's nuclear status and the global rules of the nuclear trade regime as interpreted by the IAEA and other bodies such as the Nuclear Suppliers Group (NSG). In fact, the progressive sequence that diplomats envisioned in ACRS would have been very much the same as the one followed by Euratom member states in the early 1970s, when the five Euratom member states considered as NNWS under the NPT category waited until they had collectively signed a Safeguards Agreement with the IAEA in 1972 before they agreed to finally ratify the NPT as NNWS three years later. Through the ACRS talks, all Arab states (eventually, with the exception of Egypt) agreed that the question of Israel's accession to the NPT as a NNWS should be postponed to a later stage, in order not to force Israel to reveal transparently its nuclear past.[39] Even when Egypt eventually insisted that Israel should immediately commit to sign the NPT as a NNWS (as is reflected in the Egyptian version of the Final Statement)[40] before the creation of any new regional organization in charge of mutual verification, it did not state that Israel's signature should come with a full disclosure of its nuclear past or an opening of military bases in which Israeli nuclear weapons might be stored. As the NPT's main objective is nuclear nonproliferation from NWS to NNWS (art. 1 and 2) rather than nuclear disarmament (only mentioned in art. 6), it leaves obscure how the IAEA could be involved in verifying that special fissionable materials are removed from warheads.

The example set by Euratom member states when they normalized their relationship with the IAEA is all the more important to remember now that criticisms of Israel's opacity have started to appear,[41] and the guardians of Israel's opacity, such as Israel's president Shimon Peres, are reaching the end of their careers and will soon be replaced by new generations of nuclear strategists who might not share their "ethos of secrecy and invisibility."[42] As seen in chapter 6, opacity is particularly vulnerable to domestic governmental changes brought by intergenerational dynamics, and critics of opacity, such as Avner Cohen himself, claim that opacity, or *amimut*, which offered great payoffs in the first forty years of Israel's life with the bomb,[43] is now hampering Israel's harmonious development: in particular, Israel's policy of *amimut* is blamed for serving as a powerful model for other countries of the region—such as Iran—to follow, and for reproducing a military structure of censorship and habits of secrecy among political elites that Israelis have inherited from their wartime experience (and actually from the rules of the British mandate).[44] But until now, Israel's tactic of nuclear opacity (and Arab states' cooperation in that opacity) has allowed all states in the region to continue in a process of constituting the "Middle East" they envisioned as a WMD-free zone.[45]

Through the ACRS talks, it was clear that Arab states did not want to see Israel "come clean," in the words of those who advocate for Israel to declare its nuclear-weapons arsenal, even as a precursor to nuclear disarmament and regional peace.[46] The public charade has a force of its own, which would be destroyed if the unacknowledged exemption from which Israel benefited were turned into an acknowledged exemption—as is now the case with India. While some see a "missed opportunity"[47] for Israel, such as members of the Israeli AEC Arms Control Division, who believe that Israel could have benefited economically from a deal with the IAEA similar to that recently obtained by India (as explained in the next section), it is also important for Israel to take into consideration the kind of "Middle East" in which it wants to project itself before it decides to raise the veil that renders its nuclear program opaque. Indeed, the general consensus is that if Israel went public with its nuclear-weapons program in the context of negotiations with its neighbors (or worse, unilaterally, as India did first in 1974 and later in 1998), it would convince some Arab states to leave the NPT (which is permissible with three months' notice, per art. 10.1), as Arab statesmen would view such a disclosure as a major threat to their security. If Israel were given the same status as India (should it become an acknowledged de facto nuclear-weapon state), the agreed-upon constitution of the "Middle East" would have to change: no longer would Arab states be able to conceive of the "Middle East" as a WMD-free zone; instead, they would conceive of a regional order characterized by the proliferation of nuclear-weapon states deterring one another—that is, the kind of regional order in which India, Pakistan, China, and North Korea live.[48]

Already the "revelations" made during the "Va'anunu affair"[49] in 1986 (which Israel did not officially endorse) showed that increased transparency over Israel's nuclear status could destroy trust rather than increase it. Many Arab countries were shocked by Va'anunu's disclosure that Israel's nuclear arsenal could amount to about two hundred operational nuclear warheads, as the large size of that stock contradicted Israel's justification that its nuclear weapons were weapons of last resort (in which case, ten to twenty nuclear weapons would be enough to deter Arab countries from using WMDs on Israel's soil).[50]

Negotiations over the creation of a WMD-free zone are bound to continue in the future, as the creation of such a zone has been one of the pillars of the agreement reached during the 1995 Review and Extension Conference of the NPT—and as a result, the 2010 NPT Review Conference (vainly) called on all parties to facilitate a multilateral conference in 2012. Furthermore, after the P5+1 (the permanent members of the UN Security Council and Germany) reached a deal with Iran in Geneva in November 2013, which defines a phased approach toward a mutually agreed comprehensive solution that would ensure that Iran's nuclear enrichment program would serve exclusively peaceful objectives,[51] the state parties of the NPT can seize the momentum to turn their promises of 1995 into concrete negotiations. As these discussions proceed, the lessons of the ACRS process should not be lost: Israel can advance on the road toward full inclusion in the global nuclear trade regime if its nuclear opacity is preserved to some extent during the process of disarmament and peacemaking; and if, in turn, its neighbors avoid employing the "labeling and shaming"[52] tactics that are so often used in international politics, especially in the Middle East, when talking about Israel's nuclear status. Indeed, when, in early 1995, as the NPT Review and Extension Conference was approaching, President Mubarak said that Egypt would not agree to extend the NPT for an unlimited period if Israel did not also sign the NPT as a NNWS in 1995,[53] Egypt singled out Israel as the only obstacle to the creation of a WMD-free zone, and in so doing, he imperiled the continued Arab-Israeli discussions on the topic. Egypt's campaign to label and shame Israel in the NPT Review Conference proved that such tactics cannot be successful, as they failed in two important respects: first, no Arab block coalesced around Egypt's strategy in the 1995 NPT Conference, as all Arab states agreed to sign the NPT for an unlimited period;[54] second, the Egyptian move was sanctioned by the United States, which canceled other ACRS sessions, under pressure from Israel, whose government "rejected the imposition of linkages that might have made the process hostage to the preferences of the least cooperative party."[55]

In fact, the reference to the past harmonization between Euratom and the IAEA and the future normalization between Israel and the IAEA should be more than an analogy made for academic purposes; this analogy and its present validity for the Middle East could actually become itself the object of deliberation between Israel and former ACRS participants in any future forum of discussion of the WMD-free zone in the Middle East. Indeed, the analogy between Europe's past and the Middle East's future has become a central trope in the rhetoric of arms control talks between Israelis and Arabs since ACRS.[56] From 1990 to 1992, President George Bush and his secretary of state, James Baker, repeatedly drew parallels between the two contexts.[57] When ACRS discussions started, their call to "learn from Europe" was joined by Shimon Peres, as the latter publicly entertained "the hope that the Middle East's future w[ould] duplicate Europe's past—where modest experiments in cooperation snowballed into greater interdependence and nation-building."[58] As the Jordanian head of delegation, Abdullah Toukan, writes, initially the ACRS talks were "basically a seminar for mutual familiarization of terms in the field of arms control based on the European example,"[59] which led from the Conference on Security and Cooperation in Europe (CSCE) held in 1973 in Helsinki to the adoption of arms reduction and peace treaties in Europe in 1990 (at the end of the Cold War). This analogy thus helped "constitute" the reality of the "Middle East," in a context in which its ontological status as an object of deliberation and intervention was especially problematic.[60]

During ACRS talks, the parallel with Europe was not just a historian's fancy: it was actually a condition of possibility for these Arab-Israeli talks. The "learning process" based on the European case gave a fictional quality to the discussion that helped lessen the tensions of mutual recognition (or lack thereof). In fact, the analogy between Europe and the Middle East institutionalized a dramaturgy of deliberation, which allowed participants to discuss their preferred nuclear futures and to deny at the same time that they had participated in any "official" negotiations with warring states on each side of the Arab-Israeli conflict. This measure of deniability was important at the time and is still key today, as "the Israeli government seems to believe that once discussions are initiated, it is difficult to ensure that they do not 'slip' into negotiations."[61] As each party's conception of the "Middle East" did not include the other with whom they needed to compromise to reach a peaceful settlement,[62] it was also particularly important that Arabs could deny that they had engaged in "official" discussions with Israel.[63]

At the time, the point of reference in the ACRS discussions was not Euratom and its relationship with the global regime,[64] but the Euratom precedent could actually become the focal point of future talks on the WMD-free zone in the Middle East. As the director for arms control in the Israeli Foreign Ministry told US diplomats in 2009, Israel was not against instituting "a forum to share experiences on previously created nuclear weapon–free zones" or other regional security arrangements, if the "discussion [was] used as 'a means for learning,' and not as an opportunity to negotiate with the Egyptians and other" Arab states.[65] Since reference to the Helsinki process proved successful through the ACRS process,[66] reference to the Euratom process of nuclear integration could become the focus of renewed negotiations at this time when nuclear opacity is at risk in Israel, due to internal and external factors.

India: The Worst-Told Truth, and the Easiest to Criticize

India's Tactic of Nuclear Ambivalence

As Gabrielle Hecht argues, each country's relationship with its colonial past was central to determining how it situated itself with regard to the NPT and other nuclear trade regimes.[67] In particular, since the beginning of the nuclear age, India has criticized most nonproliferation initiatives coming from either the United States or Europe as hiding neocolonial designs: for instance, at the United Nations in 1946, India backed the Soviet claim that the Baruch plan was only meant to prolong the Western monopoly over nuclear weapons for another century.[68] India has maintained this position over time, advocating that disarmament efforts should be made before or in conjunction with nonproliferation efforts rather than postponed to a later date (as in the Baruch plan and then the NPT), and that nuclear disarmament and nuclear nonproliferation efforts should be universal: if exceptions were tolerated, particularly in the West (or in Israel), the nonproliferation plans would be worse than the maintenance of anarchy, as they would reinstitute in the nuclear age the colonial division of the world.

These core principles were articulated by Indians to justify why they refused to sign the NPT. India rejected what it called the "nuclear apartheid"[69] that the NPT organized, despite the late addition of the nuclear-weapon states' commitment to move toward nuclear disarmament (art. 6) and their general security guarantee not to threaten any nation with nuclear weapons, which was added by the United States, the United Kingdom, and the Soviet Union through a UN Security Council resolution one week after the passage of the NPT at the General Assembly (in June 1968). As George Perkovich summarizes the reasons for India's opposition to the NPT, "The

U.S. and the Soviet Union were designing a treaty to stop the spread of nuclear weapons to other countries, while India was seeking a treaty that would, as part of the bargain, freeze and ultimately roll back the production of nuclear weapons that had already occurred."[70]

Extremely protective of its new national sovereignty, India adamantly opposed any attempt to transfer the ownership of these materials to an international organization, especially one created by the great powers—and especially by Western great powers, which Indians consistently criticized for their hypocrisy. In doing so, India achieved some important successes. For instance, in the mid-1950s, it was in large part due to India's rhetoric that Eisenhower's proposal that the IAEA would serve as a fuel bank owning dangerous "special fissionable materials" was watered down.[71] In the early 1960s, as Astrid Forland shows, India led the campaign against the IAEA's "right of pursuit"—that is, the right of the IAEA to safeguard fissile materials sold as fuel to power plant importers wherever those fuels went, in whatever form they took.[72] As Prime Minister Nehru sought to buy India's first large-scale power reactors, he argued that any safeguards system needed to be based on reciprocity of duties and universality, thus rejecting the possibility that nuclear powers could have a "right of pursuit" with regard to materials sold to India (for instance, plutonium extracted from nuclear waste) as long as European states, such as Euratom states, did not subject themselves to the same rules.[73] It was in large part to assuage India's demands that the IAEA's right of pursuit was abandoned in the first IAEA safeguards document of 1961.

At last, India championed the postcolonial rhetoric of "ambivalence"[74] to defend the new nations' "inalienable rights"[75] to produce any kind of source materials and "special fissionable materials"[76] (such as weapons-grade enriched uranium), as long as that nation's intent was peaceful. In the context of the NPT negotiations, India consistently argued that intent rather than "possession" should serve as the only criterion to establish the "peaceful" or "military" character of a nuclear program, as George Perkovich observes.[77] During the NPT negotiations, India reiterated its claim that the evaluation of intent itself should be based on a country's declaration about its own nuclear future rather than determined from outside by the international community. Thus, Indians resisted President Lyndon Johnson's attempt in 1967 to declare developmental nuclear explosions illegal (rather than "peaceful" and thus permissible under the NPT). Of course, the main effect of this postcolonial rhetoric was to maintain that any limitation placed by international law on India's national sovereignty could be subverted. In contrast to Israel, which never officially revealed the truth about its nuclear-weapons capability in technoscientific terms, India made a point of officially revealing to the world the kind of explosive nuclear technologies it was acquiring and developing. At the same time, India denied that anyone (especially the West) could say that the NPT rules were breached by India's progress.

Four years after the NPT entered into force, India applied these normative principles with regard to international law when it finally exploded a nuclear device underground—a space not covered by the LTBT signed by India in 1963, which prohibited nuclear explosions only in seas, oceans, and aboveground spaces. Then, Indians claimed that their first "peaceful" explosive nuclear device thus conformed to the Indian interpretation of their legal obligation, as their test was purely peaceful, and could not be evaluated in any different way by other nations or international organizations. In effect, India played on the legal loopholes it had introduced in the agreements it had signed with the West. For instance, when the United States signed an agreement with India in 1963 to supply the fuel for India's first power reactor (in Tarapur), the United States agreed to allow India less stringent safeguards conditions than usual.[78] Indeed, whereas the US AEC initially insisted on India accepting IAEA safeguards on the Tarapur plant, India limited the IAEA safeguards agreement to only the US-supplied fuel rather than allowing it to be applied to the whole plant.[79] Thus, the agreement adopted a fuel-based approach rather than the plant-based approach of the IAEA; in so doing, the United States–India Agreement indirectly helped India produce its first nuclear weapon, as restricting the IAEA safeguards to the US-sourced fuel allowed India to use non-US-supplied fuel (Canadian fuel) not subject to IAEA safeguards (as India did not recognize any right of pursuit on the IAEA's part), to make a nuclear explosive device from the spent fuel in Tarapur.[80] As George Perkovich sums it up, Indian scientists had understood that they "could use international [US] aid under safeguards to augment an unsafeguarded parallel explosives program."[81] Some could (and did) argue that India violated the letter of its 1961 fuel supply agreement with Canada, as India had agreed that the spent fuel (plutonium extracted from the reactor) would only be used for "peaceful purposes," but since India did not regard a "peaceful" nuclear explosion as constituting a violation of that agreement, India's diplomats claimed that the 1974 nuclear test did not violate any agreement (with Canada or with the United States).[82]

The United States' Tactic of Nuclear Opacity with India

Truthfulness, however, can be costly when no one besides oneself shares the same conception of the proclaimed truth. The policy adopted by the United States with regard to India's nuclear development differed in important respects from that followed with regard to Israel's nuclear development, not only because of each country's different role in the United States' Cold War strategy,[83] but also because of the direct challenge that India's tactic of ambivalence posed to the existence and effectiveness of the NPT regime. Of course, India resented what it perceived as a US bias in favor of Pakistani interests to the detriment of India, especially after Sino-American relationships warmed as a result of Nixon's policy of rapprochement with China, and as Pakistan's strategic value increased when Pakistan became a base from which to strike the Soviets in nearby Afghanistan. Still, Indo-American nuclear relations cannot be subsumed under larger Cold War logics, and the outcome of many years of negotiation between the United States and India also had to do with how India (in contrast to Israel, for instance) justified its nuclear decisions—in particular, its decision to proceed with the 1974 "peaceful" nuclear test. Indeed, from the 1970s onward, Indo-American relationships were fraught with distrust and acrimony, sometimes verging on direct insult, especially when the discussion concerned the United States' nonproliferation agenda, which was reduced by India to the establishment of a "nuclear apartheid,"[84] characteristic of a neocolonial and racist mind-set that entrusted humanity's future to the White Man.

To confront the challenge that India's tactic of ambivalence posed to the NPT regime, the United States turned to a tactic of opacity, because it found hypocrisy (opacity) less threatening than confusion (ambivalence). At least, opacity did not challenge the general conceptual categories upon which the NPT was based; rather, opacity challenged the application of those general categories to a particular nuclear behavior—here, that of India. Thus, when India conducted its first nuclear test, the United States did not publicly dispute India's claim that its nuclear program only served "peaceful" purposes, even though it knew that Indira Gandhi's decision had been based on strategic concerns as well: in particular, to emulate the Chinese in their assertion of nuclear power.[85] Although privately, the US government disagreed with the Indian interpretation, officially the Nixon administration stated that "the Indian test did not violate any agreement with the U.S.,"[86] just as India claimed. Finally, the United States applied no direct sanction against India; Nixon's national security advisor, Henry Kissinger, effectively silenced any talk of sanctions in the administrative ranks of the State Department, and allowed the US AEC to continue fueling the Tarapur plant even after the Indian test.[87]

But for Perkovich, "Indira Gandhi and her advisors . . . did underestimate the punitive costs of the [1974] blast."[88] Rather than bringing India closer to the NPT regime by bending its general categories to the point that India could fit in, India's peaceful nuclear explosion brought most of the NPT signatory states closer to one another at the expense of India. India's tactic of ambivalence did not help it gain recognition as a NWS of equal standing with China, nor did it help India obtain a certificate of good nuclear conduct from the world powers in charge of safeguarding the nonproliferation architecture instituted by the NPT. As George Perkovich aptly summarizes in his authoritative book on India's nuclear development and its relationship with the global nonproliferation regime, from the 1960s onward, "India had neither the power nor the resources with which to hurt the United States, but it was willing to hurt itself in the process of defying Washington over principle."[89]

Although the United States did not target India with "labeling and shaming" tactics by adopting sanctions precisely aimed at India, the United States did adopt an indirect approach to sanctions, amending the legal rules so as to clearly prohibit nuclear actions similar to those taken by India, and then sanctioning India if it did not comply with the new rules. First, the US Congress amended its domestic laws. After the Indian test, Congress amended the International Development Assistance Act to direct the United States to vote against any allocation of aid by the World Bank to any state that developed nuclear devices without being a member of the NPT (as India was).[90] A few years later, in 1976, Congress enacted the Symington Amendment to the Foreign Assistance Act, which denied US economic and military assistance to any country engaged in enrichment and reprocessing activities unless that country accepted "full-scope" IAEA safeguards (those safeguards modeled after the safeguards that Euratom applied on all its source materials and special fissionable materials).[91] This nonproliferation policy was toughened further under Jimmy Carter's presidency: in March 1978, Congress passed the Nuclear Non-proliferation Act, which expanded this prohibition of US exports to cover all "source materials" and "special fissionable materials" sold to a country without full-scope IAEA safeguards.[92]

Second, the US government sought to reinforce the global NPT regime by amending international law, or rather, by complementing the NPT with a series of soft-law regulations that clarified the West's interpretation that a test such as that conducted by India was not permissible and that future replications would trigger sanctions.[93] In August 1974, twenty nuclear exporting nations that were part of the Nuclear Exporters Committee chaired by Claude Zangger met to determine tighter export controls on a "trigger list" of materials and equipment crucial for making a nuclear weapon. Henry Kissinger, by then the secretary of state under President Ford, revived the Nuclear Suppliers Group (NSG), and convinced it to adopt the "trigger lists" established by Zangger's committee and act as a "relatively effective nonproliferation cartel,"[94] as George Perkovich writes, so that the group's members would join the United States (and Canada) in adopting tougher safeguards when exporting materials to India. The NSG member states agreed in 1976 to make export of sensitive nuclear and nonnuclear materials conditional upon acceptance of full-scope IAEA safeguards by the importing nation.[95] Finally, in 1992, the NSG, in consultation with the IAEA, adopted a policy on "full-scope safeguards," similar to the Symington Amendment, stating that "transfer of nuclear facilities, equipment, components, material and technology as referred to in the export trigger list" of the NSG "should not be authorized to a non-nuclear-weapon State unless that State has brought into force an agreement with the IAEA requiring the application of safeguards on all source and special fissionable material in its current and future peaceful nuclear activities."[96] This NSG decision was included in the NPT regime by the declaration of the 1995 NPT Review and Extension Conference (paragraph 12).[97]

This tactic allowed the United States to appear not to directly sanction India for its test, when it fact, it did. Indeed, after this new wave of national and international legislation was passed, the United States effectively revised its relationship with India, not as a result of India's violation of its international commitments, so it claimed, but as a result of the necessity to adapt all American nuclear trade agreements to the changing domestic and international legal environment. For instance, the new 1978 Nonproliferation Act forced the US chief executive to renegotiate the United States' 1963 fuel supply agreement with India regarding the Tarapur reactor. The United States then threatened to discontinue fueling the Tarapur reactor unless India accepted full-scope IAEA safeguards (rather than IAEA safeguards limited to the US-supplied fuels).[98] Negotiations between the two countries reached an impasse,[99] as India considered this revision a breach of international law, and did not recognize the principle that new soft law (or new domestic law) can trump past hard-law agreements. In effect, India was forced to find a third party to provide the necessary fuel, and Russia replaced the United States as a supplier of fuel for Tarapur.[100]

The difference between the West's reaction to the Indian tests of 1998 and its reaction to the 1974 test illustrates the power of public charades in international relations. India decided to conduct new tests in 1998, after some progress was made toward the negotiation of the Comprehensive Test Ban Treaty (CTBT) as a result of the unlimited extension of the NPT: China, France, and then India, followed by Pakistan, conducted a series of underground tests before the CTBT (which has yet to enter into force) would make those tests unlawful. As no claim was made on the part of India (or Pakistan) that the tests were peaceful, India's and Pakistan's series of tests brought universal condemnation in the West.[101] India and Pakistan were the object of a specific UN Security Council resolution (1172), which "encouraged States to prevent the export of equipment, materials or technology that could in any way assist programmes in India or Pakistan for nuclear weapons or for ballistic missiles capable of delivering such weapons" (point 8),[102] and enumerated a series of conditions for the resumption of civil nuclear cooperation with these two outliers to the NPT. These conditions included: helping the United States pass a Fissile Material Cutoff Treaty (FMCT), designed to freeze nuclear arsenals at their existing levels (before India could produce other nuclear weapons); signing and ratifying the Comprehensive Test Ban Treaty (CTBT) then in negotiation,[103] so that India would commit not to test any other nuclear device (point 14); adhering to the Missile Technology Control Regime (MTCR) already in place since 1987; adopting stringent nonproliferation measures, with the effect that India would behave as if it were a signatory of the NPT. In addition, the NSG helped the United States enforce the UN Security Council resolution by asking Russia, which continued fueling the Tarapur reactor despite the 1998 test, to stop transfers of fuels and materials to India until the conditions were met.

As Surabhi Ranganathan writes, when "the US again initiated dialogue with India in 1998, it was to find a way of absorbing India within the nuclear non-proliferation regime,"[104] not by having India become a party to the main treaty of that regime (i.e., the NPT), but by having India adhere to all the other rules derived from the NPT. After less than ten years of negotiation, India finally agreed with the terms of the grand bargain proposed by the United States: although the initial declaration by President George W. Bush and Prime Minister Singh in 2005 was criticized at first by the nonproliferation community (as there was little clarification of the guarantees obtained by the United States), the "123 Agreement" signed in 2006, which was ratified by the US Congress in 2008, was welcomed by the guardians of the NPT regime, including the IAEA director general.[105] During the three years of negotiation that led to the signing of an IAEA Safeguards Agreement with India, the international community verified that India would gradually transfer all international obligations from the NSG and MTCR regimes into its national legislation, in very much the same way as an "EU aspirant country internaliz[es] the Acquis Communautaire,"[106] as the US assistant secretary for arms control Stephen Rademaker told the Indian foreign secretary Shyam Saran in bilateral meetings. For instance, one of the main pieces of legislation that India passed before the United States signed the agreement in 2006 was the "Weapons of Mass Destruction and Their Delivery Systems (Prohibition of Unlawful Activities) Bill, 2005 (Bill No. 70)," which subjected the nuclear and nonnuclear materials identified by the NSG "trigger lists" to stringent export controls, and which criminalized the behavior of individuals trading such technologies.[107] The State Department declared the bill a major success of the new US strategy, and "a clear indicator of India's commitment to nonproliferation and the U.S.-India relationship."[108] As India's top diplomats recognized, India succeeded in convincing its "nuclear and high-tech communities" to support the bill, but it was not an easy task,[109] since all Indian nuclear scientists had the (right) perception "that the NSG control lists were adopted after the [Indian] nuclear tests, which fed the almost universal perception in India that they [we]re targeting us."[110] As the Indian foreign secretary stated before the US delegation that came to verify India's commitment to the global nonproliferation regime in late 2005, "Although India is not a member of the NPT, our behavior is such that we [now] are."[111]

By taking these actions, the United States and other nuclear exporters forced India to abandon its postcolonial rhetoric of ambivalence, which challenged the conceptual categories on which the NPT and its subsequent rules (such as the lists made by the NSG) were based. The United States forced India to abandon the idea long expressed by India that it was impossible to find a technoscientific criterion by which one could separate peaceful from military nuclear activities. As a result, India stopped criticizing the general conceptual architecture behind the "trigger lists" and export control rules adopted by the Zangger Committee and the NSG; it adopted comprehensive IAEA safeguards on all its peaceful activities; and it stopped publicly criticizing the NPT as constituting a nuclear apartheid, and adopted a line much closer to that of Israel on that matter. As the Indian foreign secretary said, since 2003, India "has been pursuing a careful policy, declining to make statements about the inequitable nature of the NPT, for example," although India "recognized that the NPT contained serious inadequacies, particularly [regarding] non-state actors, which presented new challenges."[112] In addition, India agreed to adhere to the MTCR and abide by NSG rules concerning export controls;[113] and it declared a unilateral moratorium on nuclear testing (although it failed to mention the CTBT on the grounds that it had not yet entered into force).

Such a clarification of India's nuclear status helped the international community accept that India's inclusion would bend some NPT categories (such as the distinction between NWS and NNWS), but would not break its conceptual boundaries. In a sense, India's nuclear status became an acknowledged exception (in contrast to Israel, still an unacknowledged exception) in the global nonproliferation regime. The IAEA agreed to apply some measure of "positive discrimination"[114] with regard to India, as Indian officials asked IAEA director general Mohamed ElBaradei when the latter visited India. Indeed, the IAEA carefully avoided granting the same rights to India as those held by NWS under the NPT definition.[115] But the IAEA still implicitly recognized that India (although not a NWS) would keep a nuclear black hole within its territory (its military program). The Safeguards Agreement that India signed with the IAEA did not conform to any model enacted before: it was the result of a concerted effort to have India and the international community come to an agreement over where the boundary between military and peaceful activities in India (and in the rest of the world) would be drawn. When the administration of George W. Bush presented its agreement of civil nuclear cooperation with India through the NSG, in order to gain its acceptance in the form of a waiver (to the United States' own 1992 policy targeting India), the United States declared that although India did not have "full-scope" IAEA safeguards (since some of the special fissionable materials in its military activities were excluded from IAEA safeguards), the IAEA still safeguarded all of its special fissionable materials in the peaceful sector. The NSG thus decided that the IAEA-India Agreement represented a compromise that was acceptable enough to authorize NSG member states to initiate nuclear trade with India. When the forty-five member states of the NSG accepted the model agreement between the United States, India, and the IAEA as being in harmony with the goals of the NPT regime (or at least, not in contradiction to those goals), they accepted India's position outside of the NPT categories (as either a NWS or a NNWS).[116]

The West did not object to this plurality of rules (or rather, this plurality of nuclear ontologies), although it refused to go as far as publicly recognizing India as a NWS.[117] In the process of negotiation with the NSG and the IAEA, India's nuclear ontology was turned opaque: all the members of the IAEA Board (even Pakistan), strongly pressured by the United States,[118] agreed to silence their public criticism of the United States–India deal inside the IAEA Board, in spite of the fact that some of them (like Pakistan) privately objected that the Safeguards Agreement "did not fit with the two accepted models: a nuclear weapon states agreement and model INFCIRC/66 agreements,"[119] the latter based on the 1965 Safeguards Agreement, which was generally applied to NPT nonsignatory states. It remains to be seen if such opacity placed on India's nuclear ontology, which did not lead to a complete harmonization between the rules of nuclear trade with India and those adopted by the rest of the world, can be sustained in the long term without tensions.

Pakistan: The Best-Kept Secret . . . and the Most Subversive

How the United States, China, and Pakistan Coproduced the Nuclear Opacity of a Black Market in Nuclear-Weapons Technologies

The story of Pakistan's development of nuclear weapons provides a perfect example of how the construction of opacity can also lead to a gradual subversion of the objectives of the global nonproliferation regime. Pakistan's relationship with the United States dates back to the early days of the Cold War, and India's perceived position as being closer to the Soviets than to the West. The US-Pakistani tie was strengthened in August 1971, when Nixon's national security advisor, Henry Kissinger, announced a breakthrough in the Sino-American relationship, which convinced the Indians to sign a peace treaty with the Soviet Union that same month.[120]

Still, in the aftermath of the May 1974 Indian test, Pakistan was also subject to restrictions imposed by the US government, especially after the Carter administration got the 1978 Non-proliferation Act passed by Congress. Thus, when Pakistan signed an agreement with a French firm to construct a plutonium-reprocessing plant in response to the Indian nuclear test,[121] the United States immediately pressured the French into limiting the extent of its envisioned nuclear cooperation with Pakistan.[122] As France now insisted on placing its future plant under IAEA safeguards (in contrast to France's prior policy),[123] and as the United States insisted that future US nuclear fuel supply agreements would be conditional upon the importer's acceptance of full-scope IAEA safeguards on all its source and special fissionable materials (not just US-imported fuels),[124] the Pakistanis lost interest in the French plutonium-reprocessing technology, and Prime Minister Zulfikar Ali Bhutto dropped the plan to purchase that plant in 1978. But Pakistan's decision came with little cost, since it abandoned the plutonium road toward nuclear-weapons acquisition only to concentrate its efforts on the uranium path.[125]

As a result of the strengthening of the global rules of the nuclear trade in the aftermath of the Indian test, the Pakistani nuclear-weapons program began in great secrecy, or rather, with a breach of secrecy of centrifuge plans being developed in the Urenco facilities of Capenhurst (United Kingdom), Alemo (Netherlands), and Gronau (West Germany) by a young Pakistani engineer named A. Q. Khan. Khan worked at Urenco as a technical translator in the early 1970s. After various unsuccessful attempts at connecting with the Pakistani military, Khan seized the double opportunity offered by India's nuclear test in May 1974 and his theft of the most recent Urenco centrifuge designs to convince Prime Minister Bhutto to fund a secret program of uranium-enrichment technology that he would lead to completion in Kahuta (Pakistan).[126] Although Bhutto did not survive the military coup of General Zia that ousted him in 1977, Khan did, and the military clique of generals who seized power decided to internationalize Khan's secret program of uranium enrichment from the start. As Adrian Levy and Catherine Scott-Clark write in their authoritative study of Pakistan's nuclear program, General Zia immediately instructed the military in charge to "make certain that the enrichment program was successful not just for Pakistan but for the Muslim *ummah* [people]: Khan's bomb, if he ever got that far, was to be shared with the entire Islamic world."[127]

From the start, Khan's project aimed not just at strengthening Pakistan as an isolated nation-state facing the threat of a nuclear India, but also at placing Pakistan at the center of a hidden regional nuclear trade regime whose objectives—to share the benefits of nuclear energy used for military purposes among Islamic states—subverted the very same goal that most Islamic states claimed to pursue when they signed the NPT and Safeguards Agreements with the IAEA.[128] In parallel, with the benevolent support of one NWS (i.e., China), North Korea became the hub of secret exports of missile technologies. As Pakistan defied the NPT limitations on unsafeguarded international sales of dual-use nuclear technologies (particularly uranium enrichment), North Korea defied the Missile Technology Control Regime (MTCR), which complemented the NPT regime, as it sold Pakistan the prohibited components of the delivery systems for nuclear weapons.[129]

Still, secrecy was not very well maintained with regard to the covert Pakistani program. Almost from the beginning, signs of the Pakistani-led international nuclear black market were picked up by British and American intelligence agencies.[130] In 1978, although Khan initially worked "in the margins of the IAEA [and NSG] trigger list"[131] of prohibited technologies, the British started noticing the alarming purchase of dual-use materials that could be employed as centrifuge parts (or as mechanisms of oil extraction, as the Pakistanis claimed) by Pakistani military officials from European firms.[132] In April 1979, two days after Zia's new regime condemned Zulfikar Bhutto to be hanged, the US Congress invoked the 1976 Symington Amendment to block US economic and military aid to Pakistan on proliferation grounds.[133] In retaliation, a Pakistani mob burned the US embassy in Islamabad, worsening the US-Pakistani relationship. The US government went even further at the end of 1979, when the Carter administration was on the verge of revealing the secret nuclear-weapons program whose enrichment side was built in Kahuta. Indeed, President Carter dispatched Gerard Smith, Dulles's former nuclear advisor under Eisenhower and the former head of the Arms Control and Disarmament Agency (ACDA) under Nixon, to brief the IAEA director, Sigvard Eklund, on the US findings about the secret enrichment plant being built in Kahuta. Still, Smith asked the IAEA director to keep the information confidential until Carter made a further decision, as he was trying to convince Carter to launch a preemptive strike against Kahuta—similar to the strike that Israel would conduct against the Osiraq reactor in Iraq in 1981—and such action required secrecy.[134]

If the Pakistani program began in secrecy from 1974 to 1978, it was soon turned into an opaque program at the end of 1979: a program whose technoscientific content was privately known to Western spy agencies and heads of states, but not publicly acknowledged as such by Western politicians. Indeed, Cold War politics dictated against the public revelation of the secret Pakistani operations, either by way of public condemnation in the IAEA forum,[135] or by preemptive military action, because of events that suddenly turned Pakistan into the new front line of the West's war with the Soviets (in Afghanistan) and with Islamist extremists (in Iran): in November 1979, Iranian revolutionaries sent the Shah into exile and stormed the US embassy in Teheran; at the same time, the Soviets mounted an invasion of Afghanistan. Pakistan was the only US ally left in the region, and to buy its support, the United States rendered Pakistan's nuclear-weapons program opaque.

Since that time, US administrations have not only turned a blind eye to intelligence showing that Pakistan was developing a nuclear-weapons program, but even actively concealed the existence of that intelligence from the US Congress for more than a decade. Indeed, in order to prevent Congress from stopping the flow of US aid to Pakistan—a flow of hundreds of millions of dollars with few strings attached—which the Pakistani military elite used not only to aid the Muslim fighters against Soviet forces in nearby Afghanistan, but also to fund their own nuclear-weapons program, the US president had to certify that Pakistan's nuclear program was peaceful: this was required by the 1976 Symington Amendment to the Foreign Assistance Act, which the United States had passed to sanction India for its nuclear test. If Carter's administration reluctantly abandoned its plan to condemn Pakistan's nuclear-weapons program, the Reagan administration very actively turned that program opaque. After Reagan's election, in May 1981, the new Republican administration granted a six-year waiver on the aid restrictions imposed on Pakistan under the terms of the 1977 Glenn Amendment,[136] which mandated a certification of nuclear good conduct by the US president before Congress was allowed to sign off on US aid. The certification that Reagan gave to Congress authorized more than $3 billion of US aid to Pakistan,[137] and it gave the US government permission to sell the most advanced US airplanes (F-16 fighters), capable of carrying nuclear weapons after reengineering—which Pakistan did, when the F-16s were finally released, after having been blocked by Congress for more than ten years.[138]

Privately, Republican insiders knew that Pakistan did not merit such a certificate of good conduct, but they believed that Pakistan's nuclear-weapons program would ensure a regional balance of power between India and Pakistan.[139] For instance, former president Nixon made clear that it was a good thing that Pakistan caught up with India, and Reagan's secretary of state, Alexander Haig, believed that if the United States turned a blind eye to Pakistan's nuclear activities, it would bolster the US rapprochement with China, which provided Pakistan with highly enriched uranium and warhead designs.[140] So when the time came again in 1986 for the US president to give a formal certification to the US Congress that Pakistan had neither developed nor acquired nuclear weapons so that US aid could flow, Reagan did so, to the dismay of the ACDA director,[141] who privately asserted that "the President lied" to Congress.[142] As a result, Reagan's policy vis-à-vis Pakistan resulted in a paradoxical situation in which, as Levy and Scott-Clark write, "U.S. taxpayers unwittingly funded Pakistan's nuclear weapons program."[143]

The insiders in the Reagan administration who were in favor of turning Pakistan's secret nuclear trade (mostly with European firms and China) opaque not only chose to conceal some information from the public, but they also became proactive in asking America's European allies to remove the evidence that Pakistan was building a secret nuclear trade regime. The

Reagan administration launched an effective public campaign aimed at assuring all foreign skeptics (including Israel) that Pakistan was years from obtaining nuclear-weapons technology.[144] To do so, the Reagan administration not only quashed the legal actions taken in the United States by the Department of Justice against US firms suspected of selling materials to the Pakistani nuclear-weapons program, it also lobbied European governments, particularly the Urenco member states, where Khan had developed his network of suppliers, to drop any charges against them.[145] As Levy and Scott-Clark write, "The nuclear bazaar that Khan claimed to have orchestrated certainly existed, but where the public and private stories diverged was that the covert trade in doomsday technology was not the work of one man, but the foreign policy of a nation, plotted and supervised by Pakistan's ruling military clique, supposedly a key ally in America's wars. The true scandal was," they add, "how the trade and the Pakistan military's role in it had been discovered by high-ranking U.S. and European officials many years before, but rather than interdict it, they had worked hard to cover it up."[146]

Throughout his two presidencies, Reagan publicly claimed that he strengthened the global NPT regime as he successfully convinced China to enter the IAEA in 1983, the first step before Reagan's successors convinced China to sign the NPT as a NWS in 1992 (like France), to refuse any nuclear assistance if foreign nuclear facilities were not under IAEA safeguards in 1996, and then to enter the NSG and to pledge adherence to its nuclear export restrictions in 2004.[147] But the cost of getting China into the NPT regime by lying about its nuclear ties with Pakistan greatly subverted the NPT regime. As Levy and Scott-Clark write, at the time when Reagan completed the rapprochement between the United States and China, as manifested by the economic cooperation agreement signed in April 1984 (which included the sales contracts for the US nuclear industry), the US president and the CIA "had known for almost a year that Pakistan had twice successfully cold-tested a nuclear device, that A. Q. Khan had gone way beyond the red line, having achieved 95 percent enrichment, and that China was likely to have hot-tested a complete device on Pakistan's behalf."[148] Then, Reagan not only lied to the US Congress, but at the global level, he also lied to the IAEA, the international watchdog that was supposed to monitor the implementation of the NPT, as he refused to share with the IAEA the information that China had provided help in weapons design and highly enriched uranium to Pakistan.[149] As IAEA director Mohamed ElBaradei writes, this decision was in direct violation of the United States' obligation, since the United States had to inform the IAEA of such underground dealings, especially when they also involved nuclear trade with NPT signatory states such as the Muslim nations with which Pakistan traded technologies, and the European firms with which Khan contracted to procure centrifuge components for his global trade.[150]

When signs of the global trade deals made by Pakistan were picked up by foreign intelligence agencies, such as the Israeli Mossad, the United States once again backed up the Pakistani military, and adopted new rhetoric to turn Pakistan's nuclear-weapons program opaque. Indeed, the "success" of Pakistan's uranium-enrichment program made it harder to hide: as Khan turned from an importer to an exporter of nuclear centrifuge technologies, he acquired a base in Dubai, from which he exported to Iran all the first-generation centrifuges that he had initially assembled for Pakistan but that he no longer used, having developed better technologies.[151] Moreover, the Pakistani military started selling abroad the products and services that Khan's network of entrepreneurs could provide to Muslim countries interested in acquiring a centrifuge program to make nuclear-weapons technology: not only Iraq and then Iran, but also Syria and Libya.[152] India also started picking up signs of these trades: as Indian diplomats later reported to the United States, "The program was not the work of an individual motivated by greed or ambition but had explicit state support," and India could cite many "examples of equipment delivered via Pakistani military aircraft."[153]

To counter these arguments, as Levy and Scott-Clark write, the US government consistently "created as much space as possible between the smuggler [A. Q. Khan] and the Islamabad regime"[154] in order not to threaten the $4 billion aid package that Congress had approved in 1986 to help the Pakistanis fight the Soviets in Afghanistan. The US rhetorical tactic was to publicly present Pakistan's secret nuclear trade regime as the one-man work of a brilliant but immoral entrepreneur seeking financial gain,[155] rather than the foreign policy of a country that sought resources and alliances to contain the Soviet threat (by allying with Iran, which also had a border with Soviet-occupied Afghanistan) and the Indian threat (by allying with China).[156] Even though the US policy toward Pakistan slightly changed after the end of the Cold War, particularly when, in October 1990, US president George H. W. Bush announced that he no longer could certify to Congress that Pakistan had not developed a nuclear weapon,[157] the main tenet of the US policy remained unchanged: even though "Pakistan's sensitive nuclear exports qualify as state-sponsored"[158] nuclear proliferation, if Pakistan was caught with its hand in the bag, the United States would support the claim that the international proliferation network was not the foreign policy of Pakistan but the "private" action of adventurous individuals who tarnished Pakistan's image in the world.

As I showed in chapter 6, nuclear opacity is likely to be abandoned, gradually or suddenly, only to the extent that newcomers enter en masse one of the governments producing opacity with the goal of abrogating private agreements. That was clearly not the case in the United States during the Clinton and George W. Bush presidencies. The Clinton administration continued past administrations' double-truth and lobbied to resume military cooperation with Pakistan, with Clinton keen on providing Pakistan the F-16s that the Congress had blocked previously. In 1996, the US Congress passed the Brown Amendment, which authorized the resumption of military cooperation with Pakistan in 1998.[159] Even after Pakistan revealed its possession of nuclear weapons by following the 1998 Indian nuclear tests with its own tests, the CIA advised the State Department, and in particular Robert Einhorn, the assistant secretary for nonproliferation from 1991 to 2001, not to interfere with the Pakistani proliferation ring, organized by Pakistan's new strongman Pervez Musharaff,[160] with A. Q. Khan acting as a salesman.[161]

The "war on terror" that started after September 2001 provided a new framework for America and its British ally to exonerate Pakistan for its proliferation activities and resume military cooperation with Pakistan.[162] The movement toward greater cooperation was accelerated during the George W. Bush administration when the so-called Vulcans, the group of hawks working around Vice President Dick Cheney and Secretary of Defense Donald Rumsfeld, decided to confront "Pakistan's clients (Iran, Iraq, Libya, and North Korea)"[163] rather than attack head-on the main supplier of secret centrifuge technology: Pakistan. The policy that Reagan had adopted with regard to Pakistan was resumed, as "many of those in the new inner circle [of Bush, Cheney, and Rumsfeld] had actively participated in . . . the rewriting of intelligence that had thrown U.S. nonproliferation policy off-kilter for a decade" during the Reagan administration, "something that [Paul] Wolfowitz would come close to admitting at his nomination hearing for the job of deputy defense secretary."[164] During the presidency of George W. Bush, Albert Wohlstetter's protégés Wolfowitz,[165] Richard Perle, and Zalmay Khalilzad came back to occupy central posts in the administration of the younger Bush, and they continued to deny that the United States knew that it had been Pakistan's foreign policy to create a nuclear-weapons program whose centrifuge component was being shopped around in Muslim states and Chinese satellites.

The Problems of Double Standards and "Labeling and Shaming" Tactics

The proliferation regime built by Pakistan, Iran, Libya, and North Korea, and the US response to the challenge it represented, raise important concerns. Indeed, if the behavior of Pakistan's clients is clearly condemnable, both legally and politically, it also seems clear that the US strategy has failed to convince the violators of the global nonproliferation regime to respect its rules. A particularly distressing aspect of this case is that, until the November 2013 Joint Plan of Action between Iran and the P5+1, the United States has consistently undermined the legitimacy of the IAEA when dealing with Pakistan's client states: Iraq, Libya, and Iran. Successive US administrations decided to protect Pakistan from international inquiries into its secret trade agreements with importing states, such as Iran or North Korea. But Pakistan's clients instead became the object of US sanctions, one after the other, especially following the election of George W. Bush to the US presidency. As George Perkovich and his coauthors write about the United States' particular treatment of Iran, "The Bush administration has spurned treaties that demand painstaking verification, and instead has shifted the focus from eliminating weapons to eliminating regimes."[166]

Reluctant to undertake the legal and diplomatic effort of working with international organizations such as the IAEA, the Bush administration moved to engage each buyer of Pakistani centrifuge technologies in bilateral action in inconsistent fashion: in some cases, the United States agreed to make deals; in other cases, it instead used labeling and shaming tactics by singling out countries as being part of George W. Bush's infamous "axis of evil" (from which Pakistan was absent). Bush's strategy was particularly hurtful to the global nonproliferation regime, as he applied double (or triple) standards to deal with each case and he consistently sidelined the IAEA, to which the United States was supposed to have delegated interpretative authority regarding NPT and IAEA safeguards violations when it signed the NPT.[167]

First came Iraq, against which the United States and the United Kingdom waged war in March 2003 on the basis of faulty (and rewritten) intelligence about its nuclear behavior.[168] Despite the advice of former IAEA director Hans Blix, who led the UN Monitoring, Verification and Inspection Commission prior to the 2003 war, and who declared that his team found no proof of a renewed nuclear-weapons program, war ensued. It was only after the postwar inspections by the US-led team (called the "Iraq Survey Group")[169] that the United States acknowledged that Iraq had stopped its nuclear-weapons program as a result of the UN sanctions of the 1990s. In this case, faulty intelligence that was rewritten by the same men (among others, Paul Wolfowitz) who had exonerated Pakistan and helped it cover up its nuclear-weapons sales during the Reagan years[170] trumped compliance with international law in the nuclear nonproliferation field. The United States preferred to sideline both the IAEA and Blix's inspection team to wage an illegal preventive (rather than preemptive) war against a country that the United States' top civilian leadership had decided to invade.

Next came Libya. A new branch in the Pakistani proliferation regime was revealed to the public when Libya's ruler, Qaddafi, bargained his way out of the Pakistani network in exchange for a promise of absolution and inclusion in the Western regime of nuclear trade. Qaddafi made his decision after an American-British intelligence team intercepted a shipment of centrifuge components traveling from A. Q. Khan's post in Malaysia to Libya in October 2003.[171] The example set by Iraq helped convince Qaddafi that participation in the nuclear trade regime led by Pakistan could be more costly than he originally believed. In December 2003, Qaddafi renounced the materials intended for Libya's future nuclear-weapons program, which were then shipped to the United States. Here again, the IAEA was sidelined: it was only informed of Libya's violation of its NPT and safeguards obligations after a secret deal was made between the United States, the United Kingdom, and Libya, which showed not only that the United States would adopt different standards for its treatment of proliferation cases, but also that the United States refused to commit to informing the IAEA of violations of the rules of the NPT regime. Furthermore, after the IAEA was allowed to inspect Libya's nuclear-weapons sites, the United States sent all confiscated materials to the United States, as President Bush asserted that only NWS should have possession of nuclear-weapons designs.[172] This decision sidestepped open questions about the source of these designs.

In the case of Libya, an important part of the deal struck by Bush and UK prime minister Tony Blair was to make no mention of the role that the Pakistani military clique played as an exporter and middleman in the delivery of nuclear-weapons components to Libya: that part of the deal was brokered by Richard Armitage, the assistant secretary of state for South Asia, in order to protect Pakistan's president Pervez Musharraf (and the United States, for that matter, since the United States had for twenty years sat on critical information without acting upon it).[173] In Pakistan, a public acknowledgment and an apology were extracted from A. Q. Khan, who was immediately pardoned by Musharraf (and kept away from questioning by Western intelligence and media), and fewer than ten top Pakistani engineers were charged with the crime of forming a "private" black market.[174] The ten engineers were spirited away by the Pakistani secret services, with the indirect result that Western intelligence agencies were not able to investigate their side of the story.[175] The United States exerted silent pressure on Pakistan to enact national legislation criminalizing dealings such as those engaged in by A. Q. Khan. Since then, the State Department has noted, "the Government of Pakistan recognized it had serious deficiencies in its nuclear control practices; and . . . in large part due to assistance from the U.S., the U.K., and the IAEA . . . Pakistan has passed a weapons of mass destruction law, improved physical protection of weapons-related materials, established an interagency export control authority, and expanded the mandate of its nuclear regulator to enforce security and safety standards, among other actions."[176]

After Iraq and Libya, Iran was third on the list of US targets, and the treatment was, again, quite different from the other two cases. To deal with Iran, the United States turned neither to war (reserved for Iraq), nor to a secret deal (Libya), nor to silent pressure (Pakistan), but instead adopted comprehensive economic sanctions as well as shaming tactics. The news that Iran had bought uranium-enrichment technologies from Pakistan was not a revelation for insiders in the Bush administration. Since "the CIA was well aware that Pakistan had forged a nuclear pact with Tehran as far back as 1987,"[177] every US administration had known about it but failed to act upon the information. Tired of talking to an unresponsive United States, in August 2002, the Mossad leaked the information to a group of Iranians in exile,[178] revealing that Iran had planned and constructed a secret centrifuge program with the help of Pakistan. This time, the public revelation that Iran constructed secret uranium-enrichment facilities forced the United States to let the IAEA investigate the claims, as was its duty to do so since Iran had signed a full-scope Safeguards Agreement with the IAEA in 1974, and the introduction of some source or special fissionable materials inside the centrifuges would have been considered a violation of this agreement.

The involvement of the IAEA in the negotiation with Iran proved at first effective. Initially, Iran claimed it had not informed the IAEA yet because it had no legal obligation to do so before the introduction of uranium into the centrifuges (a consequence of the changes in the IAEA Safeguards Agreements before and after the NPT, as seen in chapter 7). But when Iranians let the IAEA director Mohamed ElBaradei and a team of former Urenco engineers visit the site in Natanz (as well as a second site where small tests had been conducted on the centrifuge), the IAEA inspectors found traces of enriched uranium in their samples, which proved that the centrifuges had been operated somewhere, either in Iran or in Pakistan.[179] The IAEA now had legitimate concerns and legal arguments from which to press Iran to open its sites for closer investigation: as ElBaradei writes, "Iran was caught, dead to rights."[180] Furthermore, the former Urenco engineers brought by the IAEA immediately recognized their design: it became clear that A. Q. Khan and Pakistan were behind the Iranian program—despite claims that Iran had worked indigenously.[181]

The place that Pakistan occupies outside the NPT regime allowed it to escape inquiries by the IAEA when its clients, such as Iran, were found in violation of their Safeguards Agreement with the IAEA.[182] Not being able to trace the extent of Pakistan's tentacles by investigating directly within Pakistan itself, the IAEA pressured Iran into disclosing its imports of nuclear technologies well in advance, and into signing the "Additional Protocol," adopted in 1997 by the IAEA Board of Governors after the inspections in Iraq following the 1991 war had proved that "conducting international safeguards by 'honor code' was no longer adequate."[183] The Additional Protocol allowed the IAEA (tipped off by national intelligence services)[184] to verify the "completeness" of the nuclear activities that each NPT signatory state reported to the IAEA. Furthermore, it allowed the IAEA to inspect any suspicious building and plant, even if the state that signed the Additional Protocol had not declared the building to be hosting nuclear activities. In October 2003, after having demonstrated a pattern of Iranian deception in its enrichment program, ElBaradei obtained from the Iranian leadership the concession that Iran would sign the Additional Protocol (in the Teheran Declaration),[185] which it did in December 2003, in exchange for suspending his written judgment in the IAEA report that Iran had been found building a nuclear-weapons program. In other words, Iran was given the benefit of the doubt, in exchange for its acceptance of a strong program of intrusive inspections. But ElBaradei "retained the possibility [of referring Iran to the UN Security Council] as a bargaining chip."[186]

However, despite these early successes when dealing with Iran, the IAEA was again sidelined by the Bush administration, in which the "hawks" overruled the initial decision made by the IAEA director general to give Iran the benefit of the doubt. Although Secretary of State Colin Powell and Richard Armitage advocated dialogue with Iran on a number of issues (such as nuclear proliferation and the stabilization of Iraq), the opinion of the undersecretary of state for arms control and international security, John Bolton, who rejected the strategy of the IAEA director general, prevailed. Bolton was furious when he saw that the IAEA report on Iranian centrifuge activities did not conclude that those activities proved the existence of a vast nuclear-weapons program in Iran.[187] Thus, Bolton and the so-called Vulcans led a successful campaign to move the Iran issue to the Security Council after a split vote in the Board of IAEA Governors in 2005. Rather than appease the Iranians, this country-specific decision led to a confrontation between the United States and Iran, which discontinued the six-month voluntary suspension of its enrichment program, as well as its application of the Additional Protocol, in the fall 2005.[188] The conflict escalated, leading to more discrepancies between the treatment of Libya and that of Iran. The UN Security Council adopted Resolution 1747, which banned Iran's arms imports and exports, froze assets, and imposed travel restrictions. In retaliation, Iran announced the indigenous production of more modern centrifuges based on Pakistani designs of the P-2 centrifuges.

The discrepancies in the treatment that each party in the Pakistani-led network received from the United States only added fuel to the escalating crisis with Iran. Opportunities to reach a solution were missed as long as Iran was singled out as the crux of the problem, when both the heads of the Pakistani-led nuclear proliferation regime and Libya's leaders still escaped any sanction. Besides, more deception was employed on each side, with the United States hiding intelligence from the IAEA for two years that Iran had started construction of a secret facility north of Qom.[189] In many ways, the dramaturgy of negotiation through "labeling and shaming" gave the impression that the main parties were not interested in using the IAEA and diplomacy to arrive at a workable solution before Iran moved closer to getting the bomb. The multilateral efforts of George W. Bush in response to "revelations" about Pakistan's proliferation ring systematically sidelined the IAEA, and served to reinforce the myth that "private" individuals were behind the Pakistani-led nuclear trade regime. For instance, the United States and its allies took the opportunity offered by the revelation of Iran's violation of its Safeguards Agreement to blame the inner logic of the NPT, as they claimed that they had identified a "loophole" in the NPT, which they sought to close by passing UN Security Council Resolution 1540 in April 2004. Indeed, Resolution 1540 asked all states to pass national legislation that criminalized the proliferation practices of private actors;[190] to strengthen their commercial export controls; and to authorize the seizure of illegal material transfers by making them subject to chapter 7 of the UN Charter.[191] But here no mention was made of the IAEA as a guardian of the global nonproliferation regime, and the diagnostic was based on the myth that the secret Pakistani-based trade in enrichment technologies was headed by a private individual who acted within a legal vacuum, outside the purview of his government. Of course, this diagnosis was wrong, as the main problems with Pakistan and Iran were related to the fact that the IAEA was not given all the monitoring power it required to detect Libya's or Iran's violations of their Safeguards Agreements (a problem that the Additional Protocol aimed to solve); that the guardians of the NPT, such as the United States, did not inform the IAEA of these violations when they knew about them; and that an NPT outlier could remain outside the main regime with the support of the United States and China.

The escalation stopped only after President Barack Obama's reelection in 2012 (and the replacement of Hilary Clinton by John Kerry in the post of secretary of state) and the election of President Hassan Rouhani in June 2013 in Iran. A decade was lost. But the Joint Plan of Action signed by the P5+1 and Iran in November 2013 takes up many of the conditions that IAEA director general ElBaradei had expressed with regard to Iran's nuclear program in 2003, although this time, Iran seems to have secured its right to enrich uranium at low levels and for exclusively peaceful purposes.[192] Bringing the IAEA back to the center of the nuclear debate (according to the model of double delegation that I have illustrated in the case of the harmonization between IAEA and Euratom rules) seems to be the new position adopted by the second Obama administration, in order to convince former violators to respect their (strengthened) IAEA Safeguards Agreements, and to harmonize their conceptions of the nuclear trade with the rules of the global nonproliferation regime.

Still, in the case of the Pakistani-centered proliferation regime, which silently subverted the NPT regime, no discussion has brought to the table all the not-so-secret buyers of dual-use nuclear technology (Libya, North Korea, Iraq, Iran, etc.) and their supplier—in this case, Pakistan (and to some extent, China).[193] In contrast, discussions between the United States and Euratom member states engaged a collective dialogue about how rights in one prior regime would be transferred into the next regime as these states agreed to abide by the NPT rules. This collective consultation about rights enabled a process of harmonization between regimes that put the IAEA at the center of the diplomatic discussion. To ensure that Pakistan (or Iran) does not create a new secret nuclear trade regime tomorrow, the United States needs to engage both those countries in concert with the IAEA, which means that both the United States and Pakistan need to agree to delegate the interpretative authority regarding rules and violations in the global nonproliferation regime to the IAEA.[194] The precedent set by the discussion between the IAEA and Europe in the mid-1970s, and between the IAEA and India in the 2000s, should clearly show a way forward for the hard discussions that are bound to occur if Pakistan is to be included in the nonproliferation regime in the near future.[195] These precedents show that opaque nuclear programs can be gradually included in the global regime if the legitimacy of the IAEA is strengthened rather than undermined.

Conclusion

The construction of opacity is never completely stabilized: opacity requires vast amounts of resources to be sustained over time. In fact, whether the opacity of rules will endure depends on different factors—in particular, whether governmental insiders among state parties to a regime of opaque rules stay in power, and whether strong outside pressures are put on these governments so that they work to harmonize their system of rules with other systems in place. This chapter has examined how these factors operated to clarify opaque nuclear regimes and harmonize them with the global nonproliferation regime—or not. Each case (harmonization, unacknowledged exception, acknowledged exception, and silent subversion) differed depending on how each of these factors operated. The harmonization of Euratom's rules with those of the IAEA, which resulted from strong foreign pressures that were exerted upon Europe by outside powers (the United States and the Soviet Union) during the NPT negotiation, and from domestic changes in the signatory states of two of the various regimes, might be the exception rather than the norm.

The story of Europe's harmonization of its nuclear trade rules with global nonproliferation rules thus provides a unique example, which the international community should study to find insight into how to include the remaining NPT outliers within the global NPT regime. As far as Europe was concerned, the process was successful because it placed the IAEA at the center of discussions with Euratom, and because most parties avoided the "labeling and shaming" tactics that were so often used in international politics at the time. Labeling and shaming tactics can work as preventive and reparative measures in fields in which the responsibility for treaty (and conventions) violations can be clearly assigned to a government (for instance, in the field of human rights, as human rights violations are usually conducted by one government against its own citizens).[196] But as far as the violations of the IAEA Safeguards Agreements observed in the last two decades were concerned, the Western nuclear exporters, especially the United States, collectively shared with proliferators the responsibility for letting parallel trade regimes exist. Thus, it was not a surprise if, as Mohamed El-Baradei observes, the shaming strategy adopted by the United States to denounce Iranian violations of its Safeguards Agreements radicalized Iran's response.[197] Such tactics did not attack the main roots of the problems of nonproliferation: the existence of NPT outliers willing to sell forbidden technologies to would-be proliferators. As Perkovich and others recognize, "The threat [of nuclear proliferation] cannot be eliminated by removing whichever foreign governments the United States finds most threatening at any given time."[198]

Recognizing the collective responsibility that the United States (and China, among others) shared in the silent subversion of the global NPT regime led by Pakistan requires debunking the myth that nuclear trade could grow outside a legal framework (in particular, without having trading partners abide by secret interstate pledges and agreements). This realization will hopefully convince the international community to again employ the tools of diplomacy, by engaging each NPT outlier and the countries that have violated their Safeguards Agreements in a process of gradual harmonization of their rules of nuclear conduct with those of the global nonproliferation regime. Diplomats should examine the example of Euratom, to learn how Europe's nuclear opacity was gradually but successfully reduced. In this endeavor, global legal pluralism, which acknowledges the plurality of rules and openness of regimes, could provide a more fruitful and pragmatic road to solve the problem of nuclear proliferation than country-specific sanctions. To attain the universalization of the NPT regime, the modalities of state adhesion to the NPT need not be similar for everyone, as long as the process of harmonization strengthens the central international organizations in the global nonproliferation regime—here, the IAEA. The diplomatic challenges lying ahead are great, but as this book shows, diplomacy can achieve great things—provided it is not conducted in a blunt and one-sided manner.

NOTES

CHAPTER ONE

1. Jay 2010, 141.
2. Michel 2013.
3. Krasner 1999.
4. Jay 2010, 90.
5. Woodrow Wilson 1918.
6. Hecht 2010.
7. Alterman 2004.
8. Ellsberg 2010.
9. With the relative exception of Mearsheimer 2011.
10. Waltz 2008.
11. Keohane 1983.
12. Meyer, Boli, Thomas, and Ramirez 1997.
13. For notable exceptions, see Alter 2001; Koskenniemi 2002; Halberstam 2010; and Klabbers 2011.
14. With the exception of the advisory opinion on the legality of the use of nuclear weapons given by the International Court of Justice in 1995. Boisson de Chazournes and Sands 1999; and Shaffer and Pollack 2011.
15. Foucault 1995, 2003, 2007.
16. Latour 1987.
17. Knorr Cetina 1999; and Hecht 2012.
18. Camic, Lamont, and Gross 2011.
19. Nye 1980.
20. Block-Lieb and Halliday 2011, 4.
21. Treaty on the Non-proliferation of Nuclear Weapons 1968.
22. Nye 1980; Tate 1990, 402, 403.
23. Scheinman 1967, 1987; and Tate 1990, 410.
24. Forland 1997, 235.
25. Cannizzaro, Palchetti, and Wessel 2011.
26. Mazower 2010.
27. International Law Commission 2006; and Koskenniemi 2002.
28. Perkovich 1999, 138.
29. Halberstam 2010.

30. This methodology departs from the study of the Cold War policies, which focus on US-Soviet relations and ignore European sources. See Gaddis 2005. In addition to the cables published in the *Foreign Relations of the United States*, I consulted the archives of the French Foreign Ministry (Ministère des Affaires Etrangères Français) and the archives of the Euratom Commission.
31. Frankfurter 1941.
32. To select the individuals involved in the making of both the European and global nonproliferation regimes, I thus used a technique that sociologists call "snowballing." I also consulted the papers of other individuals (such as J. Robert Oppenheimer or Vannevar Bush) unrelated to that key individual.
33. In the book, I use the term *Eurofederalist* rather than *European federalist* in order to avoid confusion: not all Eurofederalists are European citizens.
34. Bits and pieces can be found in Shaker 1976; Scheinman 1967, 1987; and Skogmar 2004.
35. Political scientists and sociologists interested in the European Union (EU) tell the history of the EU exclusively from the economic perspective of the Common Market and pay no attention to Europe's nuclear obligations. Moravcsik 1993; Milward 1992, 2002; Fligstein and Stone Sweet 2002; and Parsons 2002.
36. Milward 1992, 281–304.
37. Fontaine 1974; Brinkley and Hackett 1991; and Duchêne 1994.
38. Halliday and Carruthers 2009.
39. Alter and Meunier 2009, 16.
40. Krige 2008, 10.
41. Arendt 1971, 2.
42. Dezalay and Garth 2008.
43. Avner Cohen 2010.
44. Abraham 1998.
45. ElBaradei 2011, 258.

CHAPTER TWO

1. A tactic is closer to the realm of practice than a strategy; unlike a strategy, a tactic is an immediate response that practitioners face on the spot instead of after a rational calculation *ex ante*. De Certeau 1984.
2. Hall 1989; and Krasner 1983, 1.
3. Mérand and Pouliot 2008.
4. Dezalay and Garth 2002, 2008.
5. Steinmetz 2007.
6. Antonin Cohen and Vauchez 2007; Hagan 2003; and Madsen 2010.
7. Bourdieu 1987.
8. Halliday and Carruthers 2007, 2009.
9. Ewick and Silbey 1998, 20; Silbey and Sarat 1987; and Latour 2009.
10. Halliday and Carruthers 2009; and Karpik 2007, 29.
11. Riles 1999.
12. Bourdieu 2002, 9.
13. Fish 1982.
14. Bourdieu 1987, 812.
15. Meyer, Boli, Thomas, and Ramirez 1997.
16. Jay 2010, 8; see also 56–58.
17. Jay 2010, 9.

18. Elster 1998, 111.
19. Morgenthau 1960, 277; and Tallberg 2002.
20. Halliday and Carruthers 2007, 1149.
21. Morgenthau 1960, 281.
22. Although the Statute of Rome, which established the International Criminal Court, designates "crimes of aggression" as one of the four crimes under its jurisdiction (along with crimes against humanity, war crimes, and genocide), it is the only crime with no clear definition in the statute.
23. Hecht 2006, 26.
24. Hecht 2006, 26.
25. Katzenstein 1996.
26. Bourdieu's insistence on the flexibility of international law leads to the proposal that law is always subject to the latest interpretation imposed by the dominant power, a theory not unlike that proposed by realists such as Hans Morgenthau. Morgenthau 1960, 278.
27. Abbot and Snidal 2001, 444, 445.
28. Shaffer and Pollack 2011, 1157.
29. Risse and Sikkink 1999; and Finnemore 1993.
30. Finnemore and Sikkink 1998.
31. Abraham 1998.
32. As Itty Abraham writes, "The 'strategy' of ambivalence is not a strategy used to deceive or confuse, but rather [is] seen as an effect of the inability of discourse to fix itself unambiguously on one or another nuclear meaning." Abraham 2006, 56.
33. Mearsheimer 2011, 63.
34. Jay 2010, 8.
35. Avner Cohen 2010.
36. Jay 2010, 8.
37. Mearsheimer 2011, 26–27.
38. Until now, historians and anthropologists of science have focused on the epistemic effects of secrecy rather than opacity. Galison 2004; and Gusterson 1996, 2004.
39. Avner Cohen 1998, 5.
40. Avner Cohen 2010, 45.
41. Arendt 1971, 3.
42. Arendt added, "The presence of what Ellsberg has called the process of 'internal self-deception' is beyond doubt, but it is as though the normal process of self-deceiving was reversed; it was not as though deception ended with self-deception." Arendt 1971, 3.
43. Adler 1992; Adler and Haas 1992; Kratochwil 1989; and Slaughter 2004.
44. Dezalay and Garth 2002.
45. Dezalay and Garth 2002.
46. Bourdieu 1987, 812.
47. Dezalay and Garth 2011, 145.
48. Alter and Meunier 2009, 16; Benvenisti and Downs 2007, 597; and Drezner 2009, 66.
49. Antonin Cohen 2009, 139.
50. Dezalay and Garth 2002.
51. Antonin Cohen 2009, 145, 154.
52. Dezalay and Garth 2008, 165.
53. Dezalay and Garth 2008, 145.

54. Dezalay and Garth 2002, 19.
55. Murphy 1985, 155.
56. The exact same formulation is first used in the LTBT (art. 4.1)—which, like the NPT, adds that three months' notice is necessary for a state to exit its treaty commitment (art. 4.2)—and then it made its way into the NPT (art. 10.1, 10.2).
57. In general, Germany's constitutional court in Karlsruhe has consistently insisted on getting clear definitions of the amount (and type) of decision-making power that the German parliament would share with other European nations.
58. Hooghe and Marks 2001, 3; Ernest Haas 1968; Scharpf 1999; and Fligstein and Stone Sweet 2002, 1216.
59. Sagan 1994, 1996, 65; Scheinman 1966, 1967; and Perkovich 1999.
60. A point emphasized in Moravcsik 1993.
61. Isaacson and Thomas 1986.
62. Antonin Cohen 2009, 145.
63. This is true of the US public as far as decisions to launch aggressive wars are concerned. Mearsheimer 2011, 58.
64. Halliday and Carruthers 2007, 1148.
65. Morgenthau 1960, 277.
66. The role of Eleanor Roosevelt and Harry Truman in blocking the attempt by African Americans to create such a global judiciary has recently been highlighted. See Anderson 2003.
67. Scheppele 2006.
68. Alter and Meunier 2009, 13.
69. Benvenisti and Downs 2007.
70. Halberstam 2010.
71. Abbott and Snidal 2001.
72. Halliday and Carruthers 2007, 1149.
73. Levy and Scott-Clark 2008.
74. Avner Cohen 1998, 5.
75. Perkovich 1999.
76. Ranganathan 2011.
77. Mian and Ramana 2006.
78. Morgenthau 1960, 40; and Posen 1984.
79. Strange 1983, 345; but also Yergin 1977; Stein 1983; Jervis 1983; Waltz 1981; Walt 1988; and Mearsheimer 1990.
80. Keohane, Macedo, and Moravcsik 2009, 19.
81. Koskenniemi 2001; and Guilhot 2008.
82. Elster 1984. For approaches that draw on this metaphor, see Young 1983; Donnelly 1986; Hemmer and Katzenstein 2002; and Moravcsik 2000.
83. Nye 1980.
84. As it is reflected in the fact that during the second half of the century, 4,065 new multilateral treaties were signed—an average of almost 90 new treaties per year. Shirley V. Scott 2004, 5.

CHAPTER THREE

1. Elster 1998, 98.
2. Weiss 1968, 226.
3. Krige 2006a, 161. This chapter builds upon Mallard 2008b.

4. On the origins of this declaration and the decision to drop the bomb, see Bernstein 1974.

5. Philpott 2001, 157, 172; Koskenniemi 2001, 148–53; and Mazower 2010.

6. Byrnes infamously justified lynching and other forms of southern justice on the floor of Congress; Byrnes did everything to circumvent the power of the soon-to-be-created Commission on Human Rights and to protect the legislative sovereignty of southern states. See Anderson 2003, 69–71.

7. After Oppenheimer told Truman that he had "blood on his hands," Truman concluded by saying to Dean Acheson, "I don't want to see that son-of-a-bitch ever again." Bird and Sherwin 2006, 325.

8. Nitze 1987.

9. Gordin 2007, 41.

10. Conant 1945c.

11. Gordin 2007.

12. Isaacson and Thomas 1986, 308; and Maddock 1997, 85.

13. Krasner 1999, 4. At the same time, treaties signed by the United States with like-minded democracies of the New World gave the United States certain rights to interfere in their domestic affairs. Nys 1909, 145, 146; and Schmitt 1950, 252.

14. Rhodes 1986.

15. Bernstein 1974.

16. Maddock 1997, 89.

17. Cited in Bird and Sherwin 2006, 342.

18. Bird and Sherwin 2006, 325.

19. Gordin 2007, 29.

20. McCloy addressed problems ranging from the nuclear issues to the internment of Japanese Americans and the production targets for America's arsenals.

21. Dulles and Oxnam 1945; and Dulles 1946a.

22. We call this conception of law "Westphalian" in reference to the Peace of Westphalia, signed in the seventeenth century, which saw the replacement of canonical law by civil law and the new understanding of a treaty as a legal contract signed by two independent monarchs. Schmitt 1950, 252; and Corbett 1959, 7.

23. Cited in Isaacson and Thomas 1986, 311.

24. Stimson 1945.

25. Cited in Bird and Sherwin 2006, 318.

26. Cited in Bird and Sherwin 2006, 323.

27. Cited in Bird and Sherwin 2006, 323.

28. Bush 1945b.

29. Conant 1945c.

30. Conant 1945a.

31. Conant 1945a, 1945b; see also Bush 1945c.

32. Conant 1945c.

33. Shotwell was of the same generation as John Foster Dulles, whom he had met at the 1919 Peace Conference in Paris.

34. Shotwell 1925.

35. The resolution was titled "Outlawry of Aggressive War." In 1928, the resolution led the French president Aristide Briand and the secretary of state Frank Kellogg to promote the interstate declaration banning any type of aggressive war. See Schmitt 1950, 306.

36. Shotwell 1946b.

37. Viner 1946; and Brodie 1945.

38. Shotwell 1946a, 1946b.

39. Considering the production of atomic weapons as an "act of aggression," the UN Security Council would be empowered to use massive retaliation acting under the right to individual or collective self-defense (art. 51 of the UN Charter). Carnegie Endowment for International Peace 1946.

40. Frankfurter 1945.

41. Bohr 1944a.

42. Bohr 1944b; and Bird and Sherwin 2006, 269.

43. The Polish physicist Joseph Rotblat, who later created the "Pugwash Conferences" in the 1950s with British philosopher Bertrand Russell, was the only scientist who quit Los Alamos after the capitulation of Germany. Wittner 1993, 1997.

44. Franck et al. 1945.

45. Price 1995, 224.

46. Ward Wilson 2008.

47. Cited in Bird and Sherwin 2006, 296.

48. Kramish 1983.

49. Bird and Sherwin 2006, 296.

50. Bird and Sherwin 2006, 289. Oppenheimer later wrote that, at that time, scientists in Los Alamos "proposed that in the field of atomic energy, there be set up a world government; that in this field, there be a renunciation of sovereignty." Oppenheimer 1953b.

51. In November 1945, it became the Federation of American Scientists.

52. Furthermore, even though the 1946 McMahon Act created a civilian AEC, it also created the Military Liaison Committee, chaired by General Groves himself, which was responsible for reviewing the military implications of atomic energy development in the AEC. Bush 1945f.

53. Gordin 2007, 43.

54. Rhodes 1986.

55. Guéron was the first person to inform de Gaulle, during a visit to Montreal, where Guéron worked on the Allied nuclear weapons project, that the Americans had developed a weapon of such strength that "one bomb equaled one city." Goldschmidt 1991, 11–12.

56. The first two points of the Anglo-American Quebec Agreement included a pledge not to use the bomb against each other's territory (art. 1), and to seek each other's consent prior to the use of atomic bombs outside Anglo-American territory (art. 2).

57. Quebec Agreement 1943.

58. Maddock 1997, 104; and Hershberg 1993.

59. The Quebec Agreement prolonged the Anglo-American tradition of ex ante consultation and ex post arbitration of disputes between governments, which had started with the Jay Treaty of 1796 (their peace treaty). Corbett 1959, 141.

60. The British scientists found article 4 unfair, as the United Kingdom had provided most of the scientific research needed for the construction of nuclear reactors in America. So, the British reasoned, it was fair that they should receive "industrial" and "commercial" information that could be useful in producing electricity on a mass scale. Bernstein 1974, 1008. But Bush, who was considerably annoyed at "the British tendency to call us robbers," believed otherwise. Bush 1952b; and Conant 1952b.

61. Bush 1952a.

62. In 1940, the French scientists Hans von Halban and Lew Kowarsky smuggled most of France's heavy water to the United Kingdom on the basis of a British promise that the French contribution gave them the right to be consulted by Anglo-American allies to organize the postwar nuclear order. The same promise was reiterated in 1940 by the British officials to Jules Guéron, a French chemist, and his brother-in-law, Etienne Hirsh, that the United Kingdom would fairly represent France's interests in their dealings with the United States. Oliphant 1941; and Goldschmidt 1991, 11–12.

63. Isaacson and Thomas 1986, 283.

64. Bird and Sherwin 2006, 295.

65. Galison 2004; see also Hogan 1998.

66. Truman 1945.

67. A public version exposing the philosophy was published in Oppenheimer 1953b.

68. Cited in Sokolski 2001, 26–27; see also Oppenheimer 1953a, 27, 19.

69. Bird and Sherwin 2006, 444–45.

70. Saito 2006, 366.

71. A few days after the Hiroshima bombing, General Groves authorized the publication of the report (known as the *Smyth Report*) commissioned to Princeton professor Henry Smyth by Bush and Conant, on the knowledge that the United States could safely share with the rest of the world. Norris 2003.

72. Lilienthal 1963a, 216, 203.

73. Bush 1945f.

74. Bush 1945f. This does not mean that, if informed, the senators would have voted differently, since the Republican majority distrusted Clement Atlee and his Labour government, which in 1945 replaced the Conservative government of Winston Churchill. A year later, when the congressional Joint Committee on Atomic Energy (JCAE), which oversaw the work of the AEC, was informed of the content of the Quebec Agreement during the congressional debates on the "Marshall Plan," they requested its explicit abrogation. Maddock 1997, 146; and Bush 1947.

75. It was only after Winston Churchill returned to power in 1954 that Churchill (with the agreement of Eisenhower) revealed the content of the Quebec Agreement, in order to respond to the heavy opposition of members of Parliament, who accused him of having sold out to the Americans during the war. Bush 1954; Eisenhower 1954b; and Hewlett and Anderson 1962, 113–14.

76. Polanyi 1949.

77. Hollinger 1998, 168.

78. Wang 2002.

79. Still, Conant, then the president of Harvard University, passed the policy of not "knowingly" employing communists as teachers. Bird 1998, 122.

80. Bird and Sherwin 2006, 401.

81. McCarthy's aide Roy Cohn used Fuchs's statements to implicate Julius and Ethel Rosenberg and Rosenberg's brother-in-law David Greenglass in passing secret information to the USSR. They were convicted in 1951 and executed two years later. Robert Williams 1987. As a result, British scientists and world federalists, such as Polanyi, were denied visas to the United States. See Shils 1952; and Polanyi 1952.

82. Cited in Isaacson and Thomas 1986, 490–95.

83. Cited in Maddock 1997, 146.

84. Lilienthal 1963a.

85. Before the November conference, even Byrnes had warned Truman against this idea by saying that "the Russians will simply not agree to have the Urals and Siberia roamed over by international surveyors of raw materials." Maddock 1997, 92.
86. Maddock 1997, 90.
87. As Bush acknowledged, their plan "became the administration plan." Bush 1945d, 1945e.
88. Conant 1945d.
89. Maddock 1997, 92.
90. Hurd 2007.
91. Oppenheimer 1946a.
92. Hollinger 1998. On the anti-Semitic attacks that Lilienthal had to face during his chairmanships at the TVA and AEC, see Mallard 2008b, 106–7.
93. The TVA's chairman did not report to the state of Tennessee, but directly to the federal authorities, despite the fact that its mandate was to foster industrial production in the Tennessee Valley. The most probable international legal precedent was the Congo Act of 1885, which recognized the sovereignty of an international society (the "Congo Society") over the development of an African territory. Schmitt 1950, 228.
94. For traditional legal scholars such as Carl Schmitt, this cosmopolitan ideal "means nothing else than the utopian idea of total depoliticalization," which is only true if one defines the political as the struggle to kill an enemy. See Schmitt 1932, 54, 72.
95. Lilienthal 1963b, 4.
96. State Department, Board of Consultants 1946.
97. Lilienthal 1963a.
98. Kennan 1951.
99. Kennan 1946.
100. Oppenheimer 1946c.
101. Lilienthal 1963a, 130.
102. Lilienthal 1963a, 130.
103. Analysis of Bernard Baruch's memorandum of September 24, 1946, to Truman, 1949.
104. Oppenheimer 1946a.
105. Oppenheimer 1946a. For Oppenheimer, the classical interstate approach that McCloy and Shotwell defended "will provide no security and indeed will be some source of insecurity." Oppenheimer 1946c, 1947.
106. Lilienthal 1963a, 134.
107. Urey 1946; Shils 1946; Cousin and Finletter 1946; Teller 1946; and Bohr 1946. Bohr had an ethical position (Moore 2008): he fought the sole cause of international scientific cooperation, and he refused to sign the pamphlets prepared by the French nuclear scientist Joliot Curie, who sought to label the use of nuclear weapons as "war crimes" and crimes against humanity. Bohr 1950.
108. Cited in Bird 1998, 91.
109. Stimson wrote to Frankfurter that "the full enumeration of the steps in the tragedy will excite horror among friends." Cited in Bird 1998, 102.
110. The article, to Conant's delight, claimed, wrongly, that there had been no alternative but to bomb Hiroshima and that the *Franck Report* had been discussed by Truman. Bird 1998, 102.
111. Tannenwald 2007, 88.
112. Ward Wilson 2008.

113. Maddock 1997, 122.
114. Monnet 1976, 93.
115. Lilienthal 1963a, 43.
116. Knoll 1946.
117. Baruch 1946a.
118. Knoll 1946.
119. To Hancock's mind, equalizing the bargaining positions was impossible, as it could only mean that the United States must "give up all the information, destroy all our plants, kill all the scientists, destroy the know-how of production and the plants in which such know-how could be applied." Hancock 1946.
120. Hancock 1946.
121. Baruch 1948.
122. A related source of concern, especially to Oppenheimer, was Baruch's desire to add "a call for total disarmament," which, as Lilienthal remarked, "would hopelessly confuse and mix issues, and obscure the hope of working out something on the atom bomb." See Lilienthal 1963a, 43. Though Baruch did not mention this call when he presented the US position at the United Nations, he did not completely abandon the idea. Baruch 1948; see also Dulles 1948.
123. Baruch 1948.
124. Groves 1946.
125. Lilienthal 1963a, 43.
126. Baruch 1946a.
127. Cited in Maddock 1997, 128. Dulles did so even though he had been opposed to giving a "permanent" veto to the five permanent members of the Security Council in the first place (he considered a "temporary" one to be better). Dulles 1945.
128. Dulles 1946b.
129. Baruch 1947b.
130. On other aspects, Baruch realigned the official US position presented at the United Nations closer to the Anglo-American "trusteeship" announced by Truman in August 1945. Baruch 1946a.
131. Lilienthal 1963a, 106.
132. Bird and Sherwin 2006, 346.
133. Bush 1946b.
134. Finletter 1946.
135. This was not a surprise to members of the Carnegie Endowment who had told James Conant, at his presentation of the Acheson-Lilienthal plan, that "the proposal for complete internationalization provides the ideal technical solution, but not the ideal political solution." Shotwell 1946c.
136. Lilienthal 1963a, 65.
137. Knoll 1946.
138. Baruch 1946b.
139. Oppenheimer 1946b.
140. "Russia Says Bikini Test Banished Faith in US" 1946.
141. Lilienthal 1963a, 56.
142. Lilienthal 1963a, 56.
143. For instance, Baruch's aides insisted that "the Russian plan, which proposes the destruction of the U.S. stockpile within three months," was unacceptable, and that the demilitarization of the US nuclear project should "be left in the hands of the body which would have the duty of imposing sanctions." See Knoll 1946. Baruch read in

"[the] Soviet Plan, which defends the great power veto [in the UN Security Council] . . . [the] ambition to expand the Russian system." Hancock 1946, 2.

144. Lilienthal 1963a, 106.

145. Lilienthal 1963a, 106.

146. Wallace 1946; and Baruch 1946b.

147. Baruch 1946c.

148. Baruch 1948.

149. Baruch 1947a.

CHAPTER FOUR

1. Most specialists of the EDC Treaty do not take into account ambiguity. They focus instead on coalition strategies to explain the outcome. Aron and Lerner 1956; Milward 2002; and Kaiser 2005.

2. The US government was the most powerful Western occupying power in Western Germany, and therefore the most likely to impose its point of view on the creation of the postwar legal order in Europe. For a focus on France, see Antonin Cohen 2009; on the United Kingdom, see Milward 2002.

3. Scholars who use principal-agent models to study the "delegation" of sovereignty to supranational institutions use this metaphor. See Garrett and Weingast 1993; and Majone 1993.

4. Some of the scientific managers of the Manhattan Project (Vannevar Bush) tried to relax this protectionism for basic nuclear science in the context of the Marshall Plan, but failed. Krige 2006b, 31.

5. When the armistice with Germany was signed, the joint chiefs of staff ordered the immediate destruction of all the nuclear weapons and missiles research laboratories in Western Germany. See Krige 2006b, 46. At the end of the war, it was also John McCloy, then assistant secretary of war, as well as Secretary of War Henry Stimson, who decided to prevent the capture of "German nuclear physicists and technicians by the advancing Soviet armies," and rounded up German physicists to avoid that prospect. See Maddock 1997, 49; and Schrafstetter and Twigge 2004, 21.

6. Marshall 1947.

7. Monnet believed that basic science was not, in 1947, key to the economic recovery of France, whose economic infrastructure was in ruins. See Krige 2006b, 38.

8. Brinkley 1989.

9. The European states had first created the Western European Union (WEU) in March 1948.

10. Like the OEEC in Europe, NATO was also organized along classical intergovernmental lines.

11. Acheson 1969, 437.

12. Acheson 1969, 437.

13. This also meant that the Saar war industries (administered as an international territory by the three Western powers) would fall under the authority of the West German chancellor, since Acheson intended to authorize the organization of a referendum (as the West Germans wanted) on the issue.

14. According to the "London recommendations" of June 1948.

15. Trachtenberg 1999, 78.

16. Acheson 1969, 440.

17. Cited in Monnet 1976, 400.

18. After Algerian independence in 1962, Bidault was exiled because he supported the

pro-French Algeria militias. But during the 1940s and 1950s, he often occupied the post of foreign minister.

19. When he was appointed secretary-general of the newly formed League of Nations in the early 1920s, Monnet had tried (unsuccessfully) to place the Saar under the management of the League of Nations. In 1945, Monnet and Bidault believed that the Saar and the Ruhr could actually be merged to form a separate Rhineland Republic in the middle of Europe. Monnet 1976, 107, 356.

20. From 1945 to 1950, the International Authority limited levels of German coal production to 50–60 percent of its prewar production, and steel production to 25 percent. Judt 2006, 110.

21. Monnet 1976, 263.

22. Monnet 1976, 347; and Mayer 1956.

23. Monnet remained opposed to a referendum on the attachment of the Saar region to West Germany.

24. Debré 1988, 170.

25. Monnet 1976, 357.

26. Monnet 1976, 401, 403; and Antonin Cohen 2009.

27. European Defense Community Treaty 1952.

28. Monnet 1976, 357.

29. A customs union, which was what Monnet proposed, was not the same as a free-trade zone, which was what the Anglo-American international liberals were willing to accept. Monnet 1976, 357.

30. Monnet 1976, 357.

31. Trachtenberg 1999, 104–10.

32. Milward 2002, 49.

33. Dulles 1950.

34. Acheson 1969, 440.

35. Trachtenberg 1999, 110.

36. Antonin Cohen 2009. Bourdieu and his followers say that these individuals are generally positioned at the intersection of various positions in the field: those practitioners who have moved across positions in a field because of their "split habitus" are legal innovators. See Dezalay and Garth 2008, 155.

37. Monnet 1976, 322, 324; and Bissel 1971.

38. Antonin Cohen 2009, 145.

39. In 1947, John Foster Dulles, Monnet's good friend, was also thinking of "a federal formula" (like the TVA and IADA) for the regulation of coal and steel industries in the Rhine valley. Dulles 1947.

40. McCloy 1981.

41. Monnet 1976, 364; and Stone 1982.

42. Monnet 1976, 250. A shock therapy is a mixture of public spending cuts and public borrowing on international financial markets.

43. Monnet met Roosevelt as early as October 1938 to warn him of the necessity for the United States to produce weapons for the French and British governments. Monnet 1976, 139, 158.

44. Monnet 1976, 249.

45. In 1946, Ball joined the executive council of the United World Federalists, presided over by Cord Meyer Jr. United World Federalists 1947. Ball became the deputy chairman of the ad hoc European committee of the OEEC in Paris, and he helped Monnet draft his proposals. Bill 1997.

46. Monnet 1976, 420.
47. Cited in Monnet 1976, 421.
48. Galambos 1989, 369.
49. Trachtenberg 1999, 122.
50. Cited in Stirk and Weigall 1999, 68.
51. Still, Konrad Adenauer did not accept the French imposing the separation of the Saar from the rest of West Germany. Monnet 1976, 356.
52. McCloy even said of Adenauer, "[Adenauer] did have an idea of a united Western Europe and he was something of a Holy Roman Emperor: the Holy Roman Empire had occurred only the day before yesterday so far as he was concerned." McCloy 1981, 8.
53. Moravcsik 2000.
54. Bird 1992.
55. Milward 2002, 51. The British diplomats also resented the fact that Monnet had informed Acheson and McCloy of the ECSC before informing them. Acheson 1969, 437.
56. Debré 1988, 163.
57. Monnet 1976, 376.
58. A process found in other European defense treaties. See Mallard and Foucault 2011.
59. For instance, the disagreements between the Dutch, who wanted to maintain their national control of the High Authority through the European Council, and the French, who did not want to let small powers veto decisions of the High Authority, were partly solved thanks to the introduction of vague provisions: in the final ECSC Treaty, the High Authority could submit its proposals for adoption by the council to majority ruling (art. 13) on simple decisions, and to a unanimous vote on "important decisions" (the difference between "simple" and "important" not being defined in clear terms).
60. Article 38 stated that the parliament of the EDC and ECSC should constitute an "assembly" charged with the responsibility to write the "constitution of an Assembly of the EDC elected on a democratic basis" (art. 38.a); that the future "permanent organization . . . of federal or confederal character that will substitute itself to the provisionary organization" will respect the "principles of separation of powers and bicameral representation" (art. 38.c); and that the constituent assembly will have a "six month timeline" to present its constitution to the council of the EDC (art. 38.c).
61. Judt 2006, 126.
62. European Defense Community Treaty 1952.
63. For instance, the EDC Treaty charged the European Commission to fight against national cartels in armament industries (naval, aircraft, and nuclear missile industries, among others) by opening defense industrial markets to fair competition among the defense industries of Europe.
64. Monnet 1976, 409.
65. Abbott and Snidal 2001.
66. The promotion of Eurofederalist ideals addressed the two ideological factions of the Republican Party, which sought in Eisenhower its new champion: the nationalists, such as Senator Vandenberg; and the internationalists, such as Senator John Foster Dulles (see table 4.1). Friedberg 2000.
67. For Eisenhower, the indifferent reaction (verging on hostile) to the EDC Treaty of Acheson, Bevin, and Truman was not neutral: it had a negative effect on Monnet's project. Eisenhower 1951.

68. Milward 2002, 93.
69. Monnet 1976, 421.
70. For the Dutch and Belgians, the defense of their territory fell as much to the French and West Germans who controlled the land as it did to the Anglo-American powers who controlled the sea.
71. Milward 2002, 51. The Labour government feared that Monnet's proposal would lead to stronger competition for British mines. Monnet 1976, 357.
72. Ball 1976.
73. Council on Foreign Relations 1951, 3.
74. The design reflected the French legal tradition of administrative independence, as illustrated by the statutes of the French Planning Commission created by Monnet in 1945. Lindseth 2010.
75. Milward 2002, 49.
76. The British government also objected that with the EDC, the cost of maintaining British troops in West Germany would no longer fall on West German shoulders in the form of reparations.
77. Monnet agreed that its members would be selected from members of the parliament of the Council of Europe, created in 1949, to which the United Kingdom belonged.
78. Debré 1988, 177.
79. Debré 1988, 180.
80. Even if the EDC Treaty gave the military power to a European commander, the treaty said that as soon as European forces were mobilized by the European Defense Commission, those forces would be placed under the jurisdiction of NATO's supreme commander (art. 2 and 5).
81. Krige 2006b, 65.
82. MAEF 1955a.
83. Krige 2006b, 46.
84. Furthermore, the European Defense Community Treaty created strong mechanisms of compliance, as the European Commissariat was responsible for the licensing of new plants and for "inspection and verification" (art. 76).
85. The European Defense Community Treaty "contains no discrimination between member-states" (art. 6, European Defense Community Treaty 1952).
86. The pile produced up to fifteen hundred megawatts. MAEF 1955a.
87. "Nuclear weapons" in the EDC Treaty were defined broadly: not only as "any weapon containing or meant to contain nuclear fuels or radioactive isotopes, which by explosion or any other uncontrolled transformation, can bring massive destruction," but also as "any constitutive part conceived for the fabrication of nuclear weapons" (annex 2 of art. 107, European Defense Community Treaty) such as nuclear fuels enriched at low levels, uranium-enrichment plants, and plutonium-reprocessing plants.
88. Guéron 1970, 116.
89. Debré 1988, 176, 177, 197.
90. Stromseth 1988.
91. Trachtenberg 1999, 90.
92. Even though US experts publicly rebuked the conclusions reached by the British and French, most of them, including Conant himself, privately agreed with them. See Conant 1952a.
93. Rosenberg 1983.
94. Since 1947, Eisenhower faulted the US AEC for letting the British down: Eisenhower

had backed the British demand to test their nuclear weapon in the US test site, but General Groves (who sat on the AEC Military Liaison Committee) refused. Lilienthal 1963a, 219.

95. The three Allies "promised to regard a West German defection from the EDC as a threat to their own security" and to take preemptive action. Trachtenberg 1999, 121, 126.

96. Scheinman 1966, 74.

97. Gaillard 1951.

98. Hecht 1998; and Scheinman 1966, 28.

99. Vaïsse 1994, 47.

100. Debré 1988, 183.

101. Milward 2002, 111.

102. Debré 1988, 184.

103. Although they welcomed observers from the member states of the Council of Europe, such as the United Kingdom, Monnet and Spaak refused to grant their observers the right to speak or vote in the ad hoc assembly (composed of three Frenchmen, three Germans, and three Italians). Milward 2002, 111.

104. He was elected by the French socialists, as the latter wanted a critical observer inside the committee. Debré 1988, 184.

105. Spaak 1953; and Mayer 1956.

106. Others such as Fernand Dehousse, the Belgian legal advisor of the Assembly of the ECSC and a staunch Eurofederalist, were called on to give their opinion.

107. Radoux 1952; and Bowie and Friedrich 1954.

108. Milward 2002, 113.

109. Spaak 1953.

110. Draft Treaty Embodying the Statute of the European Community 1953.

111. In January 1953, when Debré proposed a counterproject, a "confederate" treaty that claimed to establish the future Europe on a politically realistic basis.

112. Debré 1988, 186.

113. Debré 1988, 185.

114. Loewenstein 1955, 806.

115. West German sociodemocrats believed that the EDC Treaty would delay the possible signing of a peace treaty between a unified Germany and the four occupying powers. Loewenstein 1955, 812.

116. The opposition claimed that this article was "equivalent to an assignment of military emergency powers to the Federal Government." Loewenstein 1955, 826.

117. The Federal Council found that the diplomatic immunities granted to EDC officials did affect the rights of the Landers. Loewenstein 1955, 827.

118. The West German constitutional disputes were not an isolated case in Europe, but their repercussions on the ratification process were much greater than elsewhere, because the West German Basic Law contained a process of ex ante constitutional review. In France, similar disputes erupted in June 1953 when Michel Debré asked the French Parliament to postpone ratification until after a constitutional reform, but without a constitutional court in France, the criticism was defeated by proponents of the EDC Treaty. Thus, when he drafted the Constitution of the Fifth Republic in 1958, Debré included an ex ante constitutional review of laws by a Constitutional Council. Debré 1988, 199.

119. The adoption of constitutional amendments required two-thirds of the votes, as

opposed to the ratification of a treaty, which could be accomplished by a simple majority.

120. Loewenstein 1955, 811.

121. The highest French military authorities, such as Marshall Juin and the French Defense Ministry, were adamant that these protocols be added in the instruments of ratification.

122. Skogmar 2004, 38.

123. Skogmar 2004, 41.

124. Skogmar 2004, 55. Not only West Germany but all of France's European partners rejected the French interpretation presented in February 1953.

125. Bird 1992. Instead, McCloy came back to New York to take the chairmanships of the Ford Foundation, Chase Manhattan Bank, and the Council of Foreign Relations. The epitome of the insider-outsider, he could influence the making of US foreign policy from outside the administration.

126. With these picks, Eisenhower gained the approval of the Republican senators in Congress, who strongly supported the EDC Treaty. Skogmar 2004, 48.

127. Cited in Charlton 1987.

128. Bruce 1953.

129. Merchant 1964a.

130. Milward 2002, 118.

131. Skogmar 2004, 44.

132. This demand contradicted article 107, which did not specify any geographic exception to the jurisdiction of the European Defense Commissariat.

133. Milward 2002, 118.

134. Dulles also refused to recognize the right of the French government to unilaterally decide the number of conventional troops it would transfer from French European soil to non-European soil to fight its colonial wars. Milward 2002, 123.

135. Although the French would be required to send their proposal to construct power plants to the European Commissariat for review, the acceptance would be almost automatic. Skogmar 2004, 56.

136. Skogmar 2004, 48.

137. Trachtenberg 1999, 53. In reality, American and NATO forces had been "preparing and training for nearly a decade for massive preemption." Rosenberg 1983, 66.

138. Trachtenberg 1999, 195–99.

139. That same day, the US Congress passed an amendment to the US Military Security Act, which conditioned the American aid to Europe on the ratification of the EDC Treaty. Skogmar 2004, 60.

140. Soutou 1994, 87.

141. In November of 1954, Eisenhower again told his allies that he would soon issue an executive order to "delegate to local commanders the power to decide to launch a military preventive attack" in the event of an emergency. Cited in Trachtenberg 1999, 166.

142. In contrast to Mayer and Bidault, Mendès France did not want to maintain the French Empire unchanged: he not only concluded the negotiations with the Viet Cong in the summer of 1954, but also undertook negotiations toward the transition with the protectorates in Tunisia and Morocco.

143. Aron and Lerner 1956; and Soutou 1994, 90.

144. Soutou 1994.

145. Skogmar 2004, 49.

146. Debré 1988, 240.

147. Merchant 1964a.

148. Furthermore, there was no guarantee that France would later agree to Germans participating in the construction of their enrichment plant, and West German nuclear development would then be completely dependent on the will of France. Skogmar 2004, 55.

149. The people of the Saarland voted for the return of the Saar to West Germany in January 1957.

150. Dulles did not consult with the French government of Pierre Mendès France, who, he believed, "had forfeited the right to intimate discussions and negotiations." Merchant 1964a.

151. Dulles 1955.

152. West European Union Paris Agreement 1954.

153. The French planned to produce four to five raw nuclear weapons by 1960 and to accelerate the construction of their uranium-enrichment plant in order to produce H-bombs. Scheinman 1966.

154. Skogmar 2004, 99. The Paris Agreements increased the asymmetry between the US and European powers, which is why French Gaullists even talked of rejecting their ratification. But Debré convinced them that Eurofederalists would then impose the EDC and EPC Treaties. Debré 1988, 229–35.

155. This was the solution that the West German chancellor discussed with James Conant, the US ambassador to West Germany, after the rejection of the EDC Treaty. Skogmar 2004, 66.

156. West European Union Paris Agreement 1954.

157. Skogmar 2004, 84.

158. Skogmar 2004, 83.

159. To raise the prohibition, West Germany needed a majority of two-thirds of the Council of the WEU and the approval of NATO's supreme commander (protocol III). This rule applied to all armaments except for nuclear weapons, which West Germany could produce only if it received the unanimous approval of all members of the Council of the WEU.

160. A member of the French Ministry of Foreign Affairs reported "that the 3 kg and a half of fissile materials that the Germans have agreed not to exceed are not a limit but a simple program," and "the Agency of WEU cannot do verifications on this matter." Cantu 1973.

161. Cantu 1973, 18.

162. MAEF 1955b, 1955c.

163. Skogmar 2004, 89.

164. Cited in Duchêne n.d.

165. Cited in Skogmar 2004, 108.

166. Soutou 1994, 86.

167. Skogmar 2004, 76.

168. Soutou 1996.

169. General de Gaulle, cited in Monnet 1976, 415.

170. For other examples of European influence over the United States, see Risse-Kappen 1995.

CHAPTER FIVE

1. Weiss 1968, 226.
2. Machiavelli 1532, 61.
3. Avner Cohen 2010, 45.
4. Bourdieu 1984.
5. In the case of Israel, the definition of the nuclear activities that Israel would privately deem of a "military" nature (contradicting its public characterization as "peaceful") is pushed to the limit: the assembly of nuclear warheads is even deemed "peaceful" if not revealed. Avner Cohen 2010.
6. Mallard 2009; on Euratom negotiations, see also Mallard and Lakoff 2011.
7. In the sense that Americans hoped to use Euratom to tie Western Europe to the United States. Krige 2008, 10.
8. The EDC Treaty limited the size of piles to those that produced fifteen hundred megawatts, whereas Brookhaven's pile could produce sixty thousand megawatts. See MAEF 1955a.
9. Only the power plants imported from the United States would be safeguarded by American inspectors. Indeed, the Paris Agreements only planned loose West German inspections of future indigenous West German atomic industries through the Western European Union (WEU). Cantu 1973.
10. Eisenhower 1954a.
11. Sokolski 2001.
12. MAEF 1955a.
13. Originally, the IAEA was meant to become an inspection agency and a "fund," having the ownership of all traded fuels; the latter proposal was abandoned in February 1956. Forland 1997, 57.
14. India, which used the waste (plutonium) from a reactor bought in Canada to produce a nuclear explosive device, shows that Strauss's fears were not unjustified. Perkovich 1999.
15. The United States, United Kingdom, and Canada decided that IAEA safeguards would first be implemented on research reactors, which were mostly sold to non-European states (i.e., the least likely candidates for diversion of fuels). This decision revealed their discriminatory approach to controls. Forland 1997, 57.
16. MAEF 1955a.
17. Skogmar 2004, 149.
18. Shaw 1979, 20.
19. Winand 1996, 95.
20. Even though Monnet and Spaak favored the "sectorial approach" to European integration in limited but dual-use strategic fields (such as the nuclear sector), they agreed to open the negotiations for a Common Market Treaty in Messina in June 1955 to please the Dutch.
21. Cited in Shaw 1979, 29; see also Kohnstamm 1957f.
22. Mallard 2009.
23. Sokolski 2001.
24. The AEC power plant program met with financial difficulty in the mid-1950s. Sokolski 2001.
25. Cited in Duchêne n.d.
26. As John Krige observes, the AEC even insisted that in sales contracts with Europe, the nuclear fuels that Europe would buy from the United States should only be

leased to the Europeans, with the United States keeping the ownership of (and control over) these fuels. Krige 2008, 36.

27. Duchêne n.d.

28. Dulles 1956c.

29. Dulles 1956c.

30. Dulles 1956a.

31. Comité Inter-Gouvernemental crée par la conférence de Messine 1955b.

32. Comité Inter-Gouvernemental crée par la conférence de Messine 1955a, 1955b.

33. Dulles 1956a.

34. Krige 2008, 10.

35. Dulles's deputy for atomic policy, Gerard Smith, disagreed with Livingston Merchant on that matter, but Robert Schaetzel's and Livingston Merchant's ideas prevailed. Skogmar 2004, 124, 137.

36. Duchêne n.d.

37. Dulles 1956b.

38. Dulles 1956b.

39. As well as his assistant at the High Authority, Max Kohnstamm, who became the vice president of the Action Committee.

40. Monnet only let the British join the Action Committee in 1968.

41. Stone 1982, 10. Shepard Stone, McCloy's former press representative in West Germany and his new deputy at the Ford Foundation, added, "Anything we could do within the charter of the Ford Foundation to help German-French understanding . . . fitted right into our concept of history."

42. As a result, two months after the signing of the Euratom Treaty, only half of the French, Germans, and Italians, and no less than 10 percent of Britons, had heard of Euratom, and among these knowledgeable populations, those who were in favor of it were no more than 15 percent in France, and only half in Germany. See Merritt and Puchala 1968, 295.

43. Action Committee 1955.

44. State Department 1955a.

45. Cited in Monnet 1976, 492.

46. The administrator general of the CEA, Pierre Guillaumat, said in 1955 that any proposal in favor of a "European Directorate of nuclear activities would be . . . dangerous," as "the integration of the nuclear private sector is very hard because the atomic industry is so dependent on the state." MAEF 1955b, 2.

47. Comité Inter-Gouvernemental crée par la conférence de Messine 1955b.

48. Comité Inter-Gouvernemental crée par la conférence de Messine 1955a.

49. MAEF 1956a.

50. MAEF 1956a.

51. MAEF 1955c.

52. State Department 1955a.

53. MAEF 1956b, 1956c.

54. The pressures exerted by the State Department were private, not public: in February 1956, the US ambassador in Paris told the secretary of state that Monnet "stresses overt support by the U.S. for Euratom as counter-productive." Duchêne n.d. But as a Dutch diplomat on the Spaak Committee acknowledged, US pressures to accept Monnet's plan intensified. Charlton 1987, 18.

55. Dulles 1957b.

56. Duchêne n.d.
57. Duchêne n.d.
58. The French experts knew that it was necessary for France "to avoid giving Germany the impression that France wants to reintroduce controls and verification on behalf of cooperation." MAEF 1956b.
59. Guéron 1963a.
60. Dulles's assistant, Robert Schaetzel, was particularly instrumental in delaying the opening of negotiations over the IAEA's system of control until after the Euratom Treaty was signed. Forland 1997.
61. It is now relatively well known that during the preparation of the Franco-British response to the Suez crisis, in September 1956, Guy Mollet also proposed to Antony Eden a Franco-British Union, merging the French and British Empires, to maintain control over their African and Asian colonies.
62. Indeed, the Franco-British intervention was all the more untimely in that it occurred at the same time as the Soviets entered Budapest to crush the Hungarian revolt.
63. Avner Cohen 1998.
64. Chancellor Adenauer also realized that the United States might come to an agreement with the Russians on the European issue: during the Suez crisis, the Soviets proposed to the United States that they should deal with the crisis between the two of them, a proposal that Eisenhower did not reject. Skogmar 2004, 217.
65. Since the "reparation agreements" that Chancellor Adenauer signed in 1951 and 1952 with Israel, West Germany was funding the Israeli government up to 80 percent of its budget, and most of Israel's defense capacity had been built after West Germany turned military material over to the Israelis. The two nuclear agreements that France signed with West Germany and with Israel (separately) closed the triangle.
66. Skogmar 2004, 200.
67. MAEF 1956c.
68. The Italian minister proposed to create the legal notion of a "Community military secret." MAEF 1956c.
69. MAEF 1956c.
70. MAEF 1956c.
71. France was promised the chairmanship of the Euratom Commission and West Germany that of the Common Market Commission.
72. The German foreign minister rejected these solutions, arguing that the notion of a "military Euratom" would risk engendering too broad an extension of the military domain. MAEF 1956c.
73. MAEF 1956c, 1956d.
74. Maurice Bourgès-Maunoury was in charge of overseeing all military affairs in Algeria, including most of the justice matters (as military tribunals judged terrorist suspects). Malye and Stora 2012, 196–97.
75. MAEF 1957c.
76. Kohnstamm 1957a.
77. Euratom Treaty 1957.
78. MAEF 1957a.
79. The notion of property in the Euratom Treaty resembled the notion of sovereignty granted to the League of Nations (the French and British states had in fact all the sovereign rights over the administration of the mandates). Philpott 2001, 157.

80. To that extent, Goldschmidt was wrong when he said that Euratom "was inspired by the Acheson-Lilienthal plan of 1946, which planned the establishment of a world research community" with the "property" (ownership) of all "'dangerous' materials." See Goldschmidt 1982, 294. For a critique, see Guéron 1984.
81. Cited in Skogmar 2004, 232.
82. Skogmar 2004, 200.
83. Kohnstamm 1957a.
84. Kohnstamm 1957a.
85. Euratom Commission 1960a.
86. MAEF 1956d.
87. MAEF 1957a.
88. Forland 1997, 79.
89. Forland 1997, 163.
90. MAEF 1955d.
91. Goldschmidt 1982, 295. Spaak, as a proof of goodwill from the Belgian government, offered to let the future ESA manage the exports of natural uranium from the Belgian Congo that were not already under the supervision of the Combined Development Trust created by the Anglo-American Quebec Agreements.
92. MAEF 1955e.
93. MAEF 1956c.
94. American observers saw in this compromise the influence of the Suez crisis. State Department 1956b.
95. Soutou 1996, 153.
96. Euratom Commission 1958c, 1958d.
97. MAEF 1958a.
98. MAEF 1958b.
99. Perrin 1956; and Armand 1956.
100. Guéron 1983.
101. Hecht 1998, 44.
102. Armand 1956.
103. Armand 1955.
104. Dulles 1956a.
105. Skogmar 2004, 148.
106. Gerard Smith 1955.
107. Krige 2008, 18.
108. Eisenhower 1956.
109. Knorr 1956.
110. Farley 1956.
111. The other two Wise Men were Frantz Etzel, a fifty-five-year-old West German parliamentarian, who served as vice president of the first European Community, the ECSC, under the presidency of Jean Monnet; and Francesco Giordani, a fifty-nine-year-old chemist, who had authored the first postwar bill organizing Italian nuclear research and then presided over the Italian Nuclear Research Council.
112. Kohnstamm 1957c.
113. Armand 1957.
114. Dulles 1956d.
115. Krige 2008, 35.
116. Kohnstamm 1957b.

117. Surprisingly, these briefings contain no mention of the assumptions under which the Europeans would consider their long-term economic forecasts reasonable. All the briefings concerned the control of the sensitive nuclear materials exported from the United States to Euratom. Kohnstamm 1957a, 1957b, 1957c.
118. Armand 1957.
119. Kohnstamm 1957b, 1957d.
120. Kohnstamm 1957a.
121. Kohnstamm 1957b.
122. Kohnstamm 1957d.
123. As Kohnstamm told a distinguished audience of the Council on Foreign Relations, the Euratom Treaty "covers all fissile material, imported or produced locally," whereas the "bilateral agreements signed by the U.S. refer only to nuclear material received from the United States," so that "a country receiving atomic fuel from the United States could divert uranium obtained elsewhere to any other country or any use excluded in the agreement with the United States," whereas "Euratom ownership would bar any unauthorized diversion" (without adding that no military use was unauthorized under European law). Kohnstamm 1957f. As a result of these lies, Kohnstamm's "visit was a miraculous success," according to Schaetzel 1957b.
124. Latour 1987.
125. Guéron 1957.
126. Action Committee 1955, 1958.
127. They monitored the opposition of these other groups, especially those "experts from the Euratom countries," who "worked out a new research program for the Community," rather "than the one aimed at nuclear power decided by the Three Wise Men." Schaetzel 1957b.
128. Kramish 1957; and Guéron 1983.
129. Kohnstamm 1957e.
130. Schaetzel 1957b, 1957c.
131. Then, "the U.S. would not seek or be given rights to verify or inspect to assure whether the guarantee was being observed." Schaetzel 1958b.
132. Schaetzel 1958a. In particular, the head of Westinghouse was convinced by the Three Wise Men's economic arguments. See Knox 1958.
133. Schaetzel 1958a.
134. Kohnstamm 1958a.
135. Kohnstamm 1958a.
136. Avner Cohen 2010, 45.
137. "Euratom Resists Inspection by US of Future Plants" 1958.
138. "Prospects of Euratom" 1958.
139. Herter 1958b.
140. Baruch 1958. Eisenhower responded to Baruch that "the news report which you saw was incorrect. Euratom did ask for self-inspection but Lewis [Strauss] objected, and our right to inspect is clearly established in the document initialed last night." Eisenhower 1958, 1.
141. Herter 1958a.
142. Kohnstamm 1958b.
143. Kohnstamm 1958b.
144. Kohnstamm 1958b.
145. Securing the legal validity of the instruments created by the Euratom Treaty for the

fifty years during which the bilateral treaty was in force. When the United States–Euratom Treaty was renegotiated fifty years later, the Europeans successfully lobbied the United States to keep the provisions on controls intact.

146. Ball 1958.

147. Schaetzel 1958c.

148. Breithut 1958.

149. Greene 2007.

150. Shaw 1979, 26.

151. Eurofederalists faced the problem of "asynchrony" between the differential speeds with which Anglo-American and European legal instruments evolved. On asynchrony, see Delmas-Marty 2006, 28, 204.

152. Gilpin 1962, 173.

153. The tripartite agreements were signed in France by Félix Gaillard, the former author of the CEA's second plan; Christian Pineau; Maurice Faure, who had signed the Euratom Treaty; and the defense minister, Chaban-Delmas. See MAEF 1957c; and Barbier 1994a.

154. MAEF 1956d.

155. France and West Germany would share 45 percent of the cost of Pierrelatte, and Italy 10 percent. These percentages determined voting rights on the use of nuclear weapons. See Soutou 1996, 113; and Soutou 1996, 157.

156. Not all historians agree. For instance, Soutou writes that "we are stunned by the secrets and lies that these European countries proffered before the Anglo-Saxons." Soutou 1996, 124.

157. Skogmar 2004, 205.

158. From the beginning, the French government kept the British government informed of the "French views on Euratom," which "emphasized military use of atomic energy as most important," as "the projected Community will have ultimate authority to manufacture atomic weapons." State Department 1956a.

159. Hans-Peter Schwartz 1992, 43.

160. MAEF 1957e.

161. MAEF 1957c, 1957d. The tripartite agreements' preamble stated that "the signatories of the tripartite agreements will keep the authorities in NATO and in the WEU informed of the specific cooperation agreements which become conclusive."

162. Trachtenberg 1999, 206.

163. Schaetzel 1958a. Thus, the number of US nuclear weapons in Europe continued to rise steadily: in 1954, the United States had no nuclear weapons in Europe; in 1956, it had about four hundred nuclear weapons; in 1958, about one thousand. Christensen 2005.

164. Dulles 1957f.

165. Dulles 1957f.

166. For Dulles, the atomic Atlantic Federation was in conformity with "the Federalist Papers." Dulles 1957e.

167. Gerard Smith 1965.

168. So Eisenhower instead relied on the secret executive orders he had issued. Trachtenberg 1999, 149.

169. Dulles 1957d.

170. In November 1957, Eisenhower extended to European Continental nations (except West Germany) the terms of the offer he had made to the British at the Bermuda conference in March 1957, in which he proposed to sell them medium-range bal-

listic missiles (MRBMs), on the condition that the British would own, man, and operate the missiles, while the nuclear warheads inside the missiles remained under a two-key system, with one key in British hands and the other remaining in US hands. Dulles 1957e.
171. Owen 1966.
172. MAEF 1957d.
173. Moravcsik 1998, 157.

CHAPTER SIX
1. Avner Cohen 2010.
2. Robert Schaetzel had been warned by Euratom officials that "when we send Euratom's views to the AEC, we do not hear anything for weeks, and then we receive their communications back and they are almost like 'Ukases,' with ridiculously short deadlines," adding, "This way of acting destroys the meaning of joint-cooperation, and creates a deleterious atmosphere within Euratom." Euratom Commission 1959b.
3. The United States–Euratom Treaty planned a research and development program worth $100 million.
4. Euratom Commission 1959e.
5. Maddock 1997, 267.
6. Robert Bowie's panel included Livingston Merchant, Klaus Knorr, and Henry Owen, a Harvard graduate who entered the State Department. Trachtenberg 1999, 212.
7. Report to Honorable John F. Kennedy 1960, 6.
8. Seaborg 1987, 88. Other advisors thus preferred the European nuclear force based on land proposed by NATO supreme commander Norstad. Owen 1966.
9. Ball 1978.
10. Report to Honorable John F. Kennedy 1960. Although the authors were not named, I attribute the authorship of this report to Stevenson and Ball, based on the names of people who are cited in the report as having "seen" it, and the ideas developed.
11. Report to Honorable John F. Kennedy 1960.
12. Walt Rostow later became known for his advocacy of the escalation of US military operations in Vietnam, which set a stigma on the "modernization theory" that he had pioneered at MIT. See Gilman 2003.
13. The Eisenhower administration particularly disliked Nitze and did not mobilize his expertise during Dulles's tenure. See Kuklick 2006, 44, 50; and Nitze 1986. Nitze was famous for having written the NSC-68 document, which urged Truman to accelerate the thermonuclear program. Isaacson and Thomas 1986, 504; and Galison and Bernstein 1989, 347.
14. Herter 1963.
15. Maddock 1997, 270.
16. France protested that the tripartite consultations remained at the subsecretary level, although the US government regarded the claim as unfounded. MAEF 1959g, 1961b; Eisenhower 1960; and State Department 1961.
17. Acheson was alerted by RAND analyst Henry Rowen that the deployment of MRBMs in Europe would amount to "placing these strategic missiles in European hands," a consequence that RANDites deeply disagreed with. Trachtenberg 1999, 311.
18. Trachtenberg 1999, 305.
19. When Dean Rusk became the president of the Rockefeller Foundation in 1953, he funded the new foreign policy center that Paul Nitze created at Johns Hopkins University. Kaplan 1983, 315–17, 355, 390.

20. MAEF 1961b.
21. Greene 2007, 78.
22. Rowan Gaither was ill at the time and died shortly after the committee's formation. Snead 1999.
23. Andrew May 1998, 41–65; and Kaplan 1983, 91.
24. Kahn 1961. On Kahn's intellectual trajectory, see Gharmari-Tabrizi 2005.
25. Wohlstetter 1959.
26. In a paper written in 1953, Wohlstetter argued that 80 percent of SAC's B-47 bombers on the ground in Western Europe would be destroyed if the Soviets launched as few as a hundred missiles. Andrew May 1998, 150.
27. Wohlstetter 1959; and Nitze 1959.
28. For them, it was an unrealistic assumption that NATO's commander would have advance warning of an attack in the age of intercontinental missiles. Kuklick 2006, 105.
29. Brodie 1945, 1946; and J. D. Williams 1946.
30. When Eisenhower received a copy of Bernard Brodie's essay "The Absolute Weapon" in 1948, "he considered it so important that he made it available to his staff and senior members of the War Department." Greene 2007, 14.
31. Cited in Lilienthal 1963c.
32. Gaither and Nitze had ties with RAND experts that went back a long way: with Ford Foundation money, Rowan Gaither, a Republican and director of the Ford Foundation until 1953, had ensured the RAND Corporation's financial autonomy from the air force in the late 1940s. Amadae 2003, 38; and Nitze 1987.
33. Wohlstetter's theses were then popularized by RAND analyst Herman Kahn. Kahn 1961.
34. Knorr 1956.
35. Cited in Kuklick 2006, 66.
36. MAEF 1959h.
37. Still, Nitze and McNamara deeply rejected Eisenhower's philosophy of fiscal conservatism: as Nitze said, the quality that he liked most in McNamara was that he operated under the assumption "that the country could afford whatever was necessary for its defense." Nitze 1978.
38. Bird 1998, 136; see also Mallard 2014.
39. Quite characteristically, when Nitze offered Thomas Schelling, the Harvard professor who imported the tools developed by RAND into the Department of Governmental Studies at Harvard, a job as his arms-control deputy, Schelling declined but convinced his friend and Harvard colleague John McNaughton to take the job, assuring McNaughton that he did not need any knowledge of international law to assess arms-control agreements, but only a mastery of statistics and game theory. Kaplan 1983, 330–35.
40. Henry Rowen, an economist who worked with Wohlstetter in 1951 at RAND, also joined McNamara to rationalize the decision-making process along the lines recommended by the Gaither report. Andrew May 1998, 150.
41. Bundy 1972.
42. McGeorge started his career by defending his father's policies to quell the postwar controversy over the bombing of Hiroshima. See Acheson and Bundy 1952; and Bird 1998, 102, 104.
43. John F. Kennedy 1961.
44. Herken 1985, 163–64; and Trachtenberg 1999, 316.

45. Seaborg 1971, 41–48.
46. Thanks to the report written in 1954 by Eisenhower's scientific advisor. Killian 1955, 1977. On Killian's role, see York 1988, 2.
47. The doctrine of flexible response in the sense understood by RAND analysts had the advantage for Nitze and McNamara that it further distanced Norstad's finger from the button that would fire NATO's nuclear retaliation. To join words with acts, in the spring of 1961 Bundy commissioned Kaysen and Rowen to review and change the operational plans of the Joint Chiefs of Staff. Joxe 1990.
48. Trachtenberg 1999, 298.
49. Trachtenberg 1999, 300.
50. MAEF 1961b.
51. *Flexible response* had been the official term for NATO's doctrine since the 1956 NATO meetings, but the new strategy meant that the US president, rather than NATO's supreme commander, would be the judge of how, when, and where the US nuclear strategic force and NATO's tactical nuclear force would be used in the event of a Soviet attack in Europe. Maddock 1997, 316. Few nuclear strategists sided with President Eisenhower on the issue of leaving the right to start nuclear warfare to NATO's supreme commander. For an exception, see Kissinger 1959.
52. Trachtenberg 1999, 289, 299. The European negative reaction made Kennedy pause: in May 1961, Kennedy presented both Norstad's and Acheson's NATO policies as acceptable, thus giving "new life to a proposal that seemed already dead and buried." MAEF 1961b.
53. Maddock 1997, 370.
54. Brodie observed the irony that Kennedy had dismissed Norstad because of "his unreadiness to accept some of those McNamara doctrines which the Europeans themselves did not like." Brodie 1967, 14.
55. Eugene Rostow 1962a, 1962b.
56. Cited in Maddock 1997, 367.
57. Brodie 1967, 20.
58. Maddock 1997, 270.
59. MAEF 1961a.
60. Peyrefitte 1994, 167.
61. MAEF 1958c; and Soutou 1996, 254.
62. West Germany canceled its contract to purchase French bombers capable of carrying nuclear weapons (Mirage III and Mirage IV). The contract had been signed during the Rome conference of April 1958, at which the Europeanization of Pierrelatte had been decided. Soutou 1996, 255.
63. Jervis 1976.
64. MAEF 1959e.
65. MAEF 1959h. The issue of France's veto power over the use of American nuclear weapons was first discussed by de Gaulle and Norstad in June 1958. State Department 1961.
66. De Gaulle argued that West German participation also ran counter to Chancellor Adenauer's 1954 pledge not to produce nuclear weapons and their components. de Gaulle 1959b.
67. De Gaulle thought that NATO's limitation to the European continent was too narrow to permit the allies to really defend their interests in the face of Soviet military support of decolonization movements.
68. Except in the event of a direct Soviet attack on their soil, in which case France, the

United Kingdom, and the United States reserved an absolute right to retaliate without consultation. De Gaulle 1958.

69. MAEF 1959a.

70. MAEF 1959e.

71. De Gaulle believed that the growing "missile gap" controversy might convince "the White House and the Pentagon that the U.S. . . . had only a small window of opportunity" to strike first. MAEF 1959b, 1959d.

72. Gallois 1960; and Tertrais 2004.

73. Behind the extension of the jurisdiction of de Gaulle's tripartite directorate from Europe to the whole world, the State Department saw a neocolonial mind-set. State Department 1961.

74. De Gaulle 1959a, 1959b. De Gaulle reiterated his plan to divide the jurisdiction of Western global strategy into three zones: French, British, and American. MAEF 1959i.

75. MAEF 1959b.

76. State Department 1961.

77. Vaïsse 1994, 119.

78. De Gaulle 1959b.

79. Soutou 1996, 134.

80. Soutou 1996, 162, 170.

81. Euratom Commission 1959d.

82. Goldschmidt 1982, 308, 309.

83. Goldschmidt 1982, 308; and Jasper 1990.

84. Yondorf 1965.

85. Guéron 1965, 1984.

86. Goldschmidt 1982, 372.

87. Guéron 1973b.

88. Euratom Commission 1960c; and Finney 1959.

89. Euratom Commission 1959b.

90. Guéron 1963b.

91. Euratom Commission 1959b.

92. Euratom Commission 1960b.

93. Euratom Commission 1960e.

94. Euratom Commission 1960e.

95. Goldschmidt 1982, 310.

96. Euratom Commission 1961.

97. Hirsh 1960. Indeed, the Euratom Treaty "confers to the Community the right to transfer to Euratom the rights and duties convened within the framework of bilaterals signed by member states before the Rome Treaties were signed" (art. 101, 106).

98. Euratom Commission 1960c; Goldschmidt 1982, 308; and Hirsh 1960.

99. Guéron 1984.

100. Hirsh 1961.

101. Guéron related the anecdote that when de Gaulle read the treaty, de Gaulle said with indignation, "Pfft! It's only *that!*" Guéron 1965. In particular, de Gaulle was aware that the commission could not force member states to start joint research projects in dual-use activities with other Euratom member states.

102. Guéron 1984.

103. Guéron 1984.

104. Milward 2002, 289.

105. Moravcsik 1998, 183–85.
106. Action Committee 1958, 1959a, 1959b.
107. Camps 1965, 111, 147, 165.
108. Peyrefitte 1960. The procedure was cumbersome and the results highly uncertain, as the "amendments shall enter into force after being ratified by all the member-states" (art. 204).
109. The legal advisor to the Euratom Commission warned Hirsh in February 1959 that the French were trying to set this dangerous precedent: "If the control stopped because of the communication by the military forces that fuel would have military uses, then, member states could just apply the label 'military' on all their installations, which would allow them to prevent the Commission from conducting its activities in an important domain." Euratom Commission 1959c.
110. Hirsh proposed a regime of secrecy managed by the commission "in domains where the Community's activities meet the military activity of one of its member states." But the French refused. Euratom Commission 1959b.
111. MAEF 1956c.
112. Euratom Commission 1959d.
113. Hirsh confronted Guillaumat, when he was minister of the armed forces from 1958 to 1960, and again when Guillaumat was the minister of atomic energy from 1960 to 1962, but "Guillaumat noted that some data concerning the French production of plutonium fell under the realm of military secrecy." Hirsh 1960.
114. Euratom Commission 1959c, 1959d.
115. Euratom Commission 1959d.
116. Euratom Commission 1959c.
117. Emphasis mine.
118. Euratom Treaty 1957.
119. Euratom Commission 1959c.
120. Hecht 2012.
121. Goldschmidt 1982, 295.
122. Goldschmidt 1982, 295.
123. Interview with a French nuclear executive in fuel procurement, October 2011.
124. Euratom Commission 1960c.
125. The notion of a "market" for nuclear fuels is problematic: prices are not fixed by the laws of supply and demand, as prices and quantities have long been negotiated in the secrecy of governmental cabinets where neocolonial relationships of patronage are reproduced (such as France in Niger). See Hecht 2012.
126. Krief 1964; and "How International?" 1961.
127. It was the Euratom Commission's right to do so, as it had a monopoly on the decision to introduce proposals in the council.
128. As Guéron added, "This vote confirmed, or even triggered, the decision in Paris to replace Hirsh by a man who could obey orders." Guéron 1984.
129. Soustelle 1965.
130. Chatenêt 1966.
131. Guéron 1984. Chatenêt also attacked the monopoly of the commission on the introduction of proposals to be discussed by the Council of Ministers in his first speech before the European Assembly. He limited the role of Euratom to serve "as a link which coordinates national programs." European Parliament 1962.
132. The same reform that he would then impose on the Common Market Commission three years later.

133. It was during Chatenêt's tenure that the controversy over the meaning of article 29, which stated that member states should submit bilateral agreements with third parties to the review of the commission, was finally settled, when France signed a bilateral treaty with Pakistan, without consulting the commission or even informing the commission of the content. Euratom Commission 1963a, 1963d. Then, Chatenêt argued that article 29 of the treaty did not apply "because of the vagueness of the provisions planned in the exchange of information with Pakistan" (Euratom Commission 1964), an opinion accepted by the West German government, which declared that when a government has "limited knowledge of the content of a deal, then, the action would not be considered an *act of sovereignty*." Euratom Commission 1964.

134. Arendt 1971, 3.

135. Hirsh planned that the future community would be given more democratic legitimacy by instituting universal suffrage to elect its parliamentarians. Camps 1965, 291.

136. Peyrefitte 1960.

137. For Peyrefitte, when Debré "asks to revise the Treaties," he "takes great risks . . . as the Germans, Belgians, and Dutch could get rid of the dispositions that prevent Great Britain from entering the Community." Peyrefitte 1960.

138. Peyrefitte 1960.

139. Peyrefitte 1960.

140. Kohnstamm 1961.

141. Kohnstamm 1961. Monnet remarked "that a confederation cannot exist without a kind of 'confederate government' which is something else than the simple aggregation of national governments." Monnet 1961.

142. Soutou 1996, 178.

143. Cattani 1967.

144. Hirsh worried that the new permanent secretariat of the confederation "w[ould] turn itself against the [three] Commissions." European Parliament 1960, 1589. He urged federalists to "dispel the myths entertained by the adversaries of Euratom who wear the European mask." Hirsh 1962b.

145. The day after the Fouchet Commission met, de Gaulle summoned Hirsh into his office, as advised by Peyrefitte (1960).

146. Hirsh's fears were aggravated by his interview with de Gaulle, who told him that France was "not predisposed to give any information on questions relative to national defense, to whomever, and particularly not to Euratom." Hirsh 1961.

147. Shepard 2008.

148. Peyrefitte 1994, 89.

149. Historians have trouble explaining why de Gaulle almost killed the Fouchet Plan in such a way. George Henri Soutou, whose father actively participated in writing the draft of the Fouchet treaties, believes that the French president wanted to assuage the moral loss for the French people after the decision to retreat from Algeria. Soutou 1996, 190. For Moravcsik, de Gaulle's decision was a sign not of weakness, but of strength. He writes, "The second revision was drafted . . . just four hours after the decisive agriculture compromise of January 1962, which assured that the CAP [Common Agricultural Policy] would move forward: with agriculture secure, de Gaulle set forth a more intransigent position." Moravcsik 1998, 226.

150. Soutou 1996, 188.

151. Soutou 1996, 190.

152. Cattani 1967.

153. Peyrefitte 1994, 88.

154. Christian Fouchet then organized the "return" of the Algerian white population from Algeria, and the correlate filtering of the Algerian "Muslims," most of whom were denied French nationality. Shepard 2008.

155. Three days after the Fouchet Commission was disbanded in April 1962, Prime Minister Michel Debré resigned as a consequence of de Gaulle's policy on Algeria, which, according to Soustelle, violated the constitution of the Fifth Republic (on the "integrity of the territory") and process (on the amendment procedure). Soustelle 1965, 84, 163; and Shepard 2008.

156. Shepard 2008.

157. Macmillan accepted this in January 1961, to the surprise of Gaullists who, like Peyrefitte, had bet that the merger treaty "was likely to be ignored by the British." Peyrefitte 1960.

158. Ball 1962b.

159. In general, "when opportunism threatens the interest of the contracting parties, then, the latter ask for more complete contracts." Karpik 2007, 30.

160. Ball predicted that the "Congress would probably react critically to anything which appeared to be a U.K.-French 'deal' whereby the British sought to obtain better terms for their admission to the Common Market, in exchange for nuclear help to France." Ball 1962b.

161. Ball 1962b.

162. Ball 1962b.

163. MAEF 1962a.

164. MAEF 1962c.

165. Monnet 1976.

166. Ball's calling on the French and British governments to place their existing warheads in mixed-manned NATO submarines that could form the basis of a European nuclear force converged with McNamara's NATO strategy, toward a policy of nuclear rollback in Europe.

167. In 1960, Ball supported Bowie's proposal to establish a joint American-European Atomic Authority, through which the United States would develop "alternatives regarding isotopic separation," and all the "production and research on missiles." Report to Honorable John F. Kennedy 1960.

168. MAEF 1962a.

169. In December 1962, French diplomats insisted that discussions with the British "concerning Euratom controls necessitated a legal revision of the Euratom treaty before the U.K. entered Euratom." MAEF 1962c, 1.

170. As far as the Euratom Treaty provisions "concerning controls, secrets and fuel procurement," French diplomats had noted that "our interests are similar to the British, who will soon meet the same problems we faced, with even greater difficulties because they share such intimate relations with the U.S." MAEF 1962a.

171. British membership was seen as a risk by the French government not only for the interests of French farmers but also for the French nuclear industry. Moravcsik 1998, 183; and MAEF 1961a.

172. MAEF 1962c.

173. MAEF 1962c.

174. MAEF 1962c, 1962b.

175. Kohl 1971, 214, 118.

176. Peyrefitte 1994, 166.
177. For de Gaulle, France had to show that "Euratom, it's over!" Cited in Peyrefitte 1994, 168.
178. The French suspected the British were passing off a decaying facility, since "the British know that enriched uranium in Capenhurst is not competitive with American enriched uranium." MAEF 1962c.
179. MAEF 1962a.
180. In March 1962, Paul Nitze and Carl Kaysen (by then McGeorge Bundy's deputy at the National Security Council) were contradicted by the US Congress, when they offered to trade information on nuclear weapons for the French acceptance of the original Fouchet plan and British membership in the European Communities. Maddock 1997, 341.
181. Most of the analyses have reinforced the official perception of the Cuban missile crisis as a case study of successful "crisis management"—Allison 1971, 42; Janis 1972; Neustadt and Ernest May 1986; Len Scott and Steve Smith 1994, 662; and Ernest May and Zelikow 1997—which confirmed the validity of past policies of "flexible" nuclear deterrence (Schelling 1960), illustrated by Kennedy's decision not to destroy the missile launchers in Cuba but to blockade the island first and then ask Khrushchev to remove the missiles before he would escalate the conflict. As a corollary, the literature on the "crisis" has tried to explain how—irrationality aside, an explanation defended by Lebow (1983, 451)—the Soviet premier could have made such a bad calculation: some argued that Khrushchev could not read the signals sent by Kennedy because of national cultural differences (Wohlstetter and Wohlstetter 1965, 21), or that the signals were reinterpreted as they moved within the Soviet command and control posts (Allison 1971; and Ernest May and Zelikow 1997), or that Khrushchev's move was rational from the domestic bureaucratic side of things (Allison 1971, 240). Only recently have new analyses taken into account the fact that the Cuban missile crisis was solved diplomatically. Bernstein 1980, 116; Kuklick 2006; and Gibson 2011a, 2011b.
182. Bundy 1987, 3; and Center of Science and International Affairs 1987, 25, 28.
183. Harriman 1962. The new generation of American nuclear strategists participating in the meetings of the Executive Committee of the National Security Council (Ex-Comm), specially called to resolve the crisis, understood that destroying the Soviet missiles in Cuba with a preemptive military attack would have destroyed the island, leading the conflict to escalate much more rapidly than theorists of flexible and gradual response had believed. Center of Science and International Affairs 1987, 31.
184. Bundy 1987, 5.
185. Bundy 1987, 9.
186. Bundy 1987, 52.
187. Rusk et al. 1982; and Schlesinger 1978.
188. Kennedy reported that General Lauris Norstad "thinks that we ought to have a meeting of the NATO Council to present this to them." Ball advised against it because "if you have a NATO Council meeting, I think you're going to get a flat rejection of this [deal], which then ties your hands." Bundy 1987, 18.
189. Bundy 1987, 10. Bundy initially sided with Nitze. Trachtenberg 1999, 354.
190. Bundy 1987, 52.
191. As Ball's assistant wrote, "Such a step, as a precursor to the establishment of a larger multilateral sea-based force would reaffirm our nuclear commitment to Europe's

defense, make clear that we would not make deals at Allied expense, and also perhaps pave the way for Turkish and Italian statements that they would phase out IRBMs in view of this substitute." Walt Rostow 1962.

192. State Department 1962.

193. Bundy 1987, 9.

194. Owen 1966.

195. Trachtenberg 1999, 362; see also Kohnstamm 1963d.

196. The myth was created by Kennedy's advisors, in particular Neustadt (1970); see also "Weary Titan" 1963.

197. Even though specialists of European integration never discuss the effect that the Cuban missile crisis had on the process of British admission to Euratom, the consequences of the US turn to a tactic of opacity when dealing with Europeans were quite dramatic. Some, such as Moravcsik, disagree that there is even a relationship between Nassau and the French veto: for him, de Gaulle's opposition to the British entry into the European Community was strictly grounded in "trade policy, not military policy," and more particularly, in agricultural policy. Moravcsik 1998, 183.

198. Trachtenberg 1999, 364.

199. Trachtenberg 1999, 365.

200. Furthermore, when de Gaulle told Bohlen that, unlike the United Kingdom, France could not place these missiles in nationally owned submarines, because, unlike the United Kingdom, France did not have nuclear-powered submarines, Bohlen told the president that the two countries could soon talk about submarines. MAEF 1963a.

201. MAEF 1963d.

202. Ball 1962b.

203. MAEF 1963b.

204. MAEF 1963b.

205. Schlesinger 1963.

206. MAEF 1963c.

207. De Gaulle 1963.

208. The timing of de Gaulle's veto can be explained by Ball's visit to Europe, as the Anglo-American conference in Nassau had occurred a month before, without provoking any reaction on the part of de Gaulle. Camps 1965, 489. My interpretation differs from the "uniquely British variant," which states that de Gaulle's veto was also "a revenge on Britain which put an end to all hopes of Anglo-French nuclear cooperation." Milward 2002, 464.

209. MAEF 1963d.

210. Kohl 1971, 134.

211. Then, Kennedy withdrew his support for Adenauer, who was replaced six months later by the international liberal Ludwig Erhard, even though "the Germans have taken great pains to emphasize . . . that the provisions of the [Paris] Treaty calling for joint efforts in 'drawing up [an] appropriate armament plan' have absolutely no application to the field of nuclear weapons." Rusk 1963.

212. MAEF 1963d. Besides, as the West German defense minister wrote to Kohnstamm, "On the military plan, West Germany is the battlefield and France is the backcountry. This situation calls for a particularly tight form of cooperation." Von Hassel 1963, 1.

213. Schmidt 1963.

214. Duchêne 1963.

215. Monnet, Stikker, and Spaak were favorable to the MLF idea only if it would help

them start anew the negotiations toward British membership in the European Communities. Merchant 1963c.

216. Stanley Cohen 2001, 15.

217. His European clause planned the possibility that dual-use (uranium-enrichment) and military (warhead design) nuclear activities would fall under the jurisdiction of the new European "Community of research, production and control of nuclear armament." Duchêne 1963; Van Helmont 1964a; and Kohnstamm 1964g, 1964h, 1964i, 1964j.

218. Monnet 1965b. Gerard Smith noted that Monnet's European clause "is following the classic pattern of European integration." Van Helmont 1964a, 1964c; and Kohnstamm 1964m, 1964n.

219. Ball 1963c.

220. Kohnstamm 1964j; and Van Helmont 1964o.

221. Van Helmont 1964k.

222. But Ball refused the latter possibility. Van Helmont 1964l, 1964m, 1964n.

223. A job that "came out of the blue," as Merchant had retired in 1961. Merchant 1965, 137.

224. Merchant 1963c.

225. Ball 1963a.

226. Merchant 1965, 175.

227. As he added, "If the time came when the Europeans asked the U.S. [to opt] out of the multilateral force, the circumstances, by definition, would be such that the Congress and anyone else in this country looking at it open-mindedly would not be willing to step aside and leave our missiles and warheads in the hands of Europeans who were splitting from us." Merchant 1965, 175.

228. Monnet 1963b.

229. Merchant 1965, 146. In fact, when Merchant visited London in March 1963, the British foreign secretary told Merchant that he did not accept that plan. Merchant 1963a. Robert Bowie also warned Merchant in February 1963 that for German politicians the multilateral force of boats would only be "second choice" (Bowie 1963), a fact confirmed in Livingston Merchant 1963b; 1965, 146. Only the Turks were still very supportive of his plan for NATO surface vessels, which they saw as "compensation for the withdrawal of our missiles a few months earlier." Merchant 1963d, 1963e. In general, the Dutch were not interested in the MLF Treaty. See Vondeling 1964.

230. Maddock 1997, 417; and Seaborg 1971, 177.

231. Seaborg 1987, 96.

232. Not only did Kennedy make that promise to the Soviets, but Ball also convinced Kennedy that the United States should try "to persuade de Gaulle to sign the test ban if we give him the technology he would otherwise derive from testing" (Ball 1963f, 2) and to ask de Gaulle, "as a *quid pro quo*, to assign the [French] *force de frappe* to NATO" under the same "terms of assignment as were employed with respect to the British Polaris" in the Nassau agreements. Ball 1963g.

233. Van Helmont 1964a.

234. On these issues of who would have the authority to fire Europe's nuclear weapons, see Van Helmont 1964c, 1964f, 1964o; and Kohnstamm 1963c, 1964j, 1964m, 1964q.

235. Ball 1963f. This speech was the result of the direct influence of Ball and Monnet. Ball 1963e.

236. Van Helmont 1964g.

237. Van Helmont 1964c.

238. Van Helmont tried to argue that the notion of "sufficient progress" in the 1958 McMahon Act was not more precise than the proposed European clause, but Ball remained firm. Van Helmont 1964e. Even Robert Bowie claimed that the US Congress would oppose any commitment if the terms of that future treaty were not expressed in writing. Stabler 1964, 18; and Merchant 1965, 157. Monnet, Kohnstamm, and Van Helmont hoped to privately arrive at a consensus with Ball and Schaetzel. See Kohnstamm 1964a, 1964b, 1964c, 1964d, 1964e, 1964f, 1964k, 1964p, 1964r; and Ball 1963f.

239. Van Helmont 1964c.

240. Van Helmont 1964b.

241. Kahneman and Tversky 1984, 349.

242. Jay 2010, 8.

243. Tuthill 1964.

244. Schaetzel 1964.

245. Kohnstamm 1963d.

246. When, in the fall of 1964, after the explosion of the first Chinese nuclear weapon, the president appointed a Special Task Force on Nuclear Proliferation to assess the alternatives to the MLF Treaty (the "Gilpatric Committee," named after Roswell Gilpatric, the former deputy of Paul Nitze and Robert McNamara at the DoD), McCloy, who sat on it, "went on at such length about the need to preserve the Atlantic Alliance system [and the MLF Treaty], despite U.S. interest in nonproliferation," that Ball concluded that rejection of the MLF Treaty would be too risky before the elections. Seaborg 1987, 143.

247. In December 1964, McGeorge Bundy informed the president that "at most twenty-five Senators are in favor of the MLF, with Humphrey and Fulbright clearly opposed." Seaborg 1987, 125; and Merchant 1964b.

248. Van Helmont 1964r.

249. Kohnstamm 1964q.

250. "The New Alliance" 1964.

251. Kohnstamm 1965a. See also Kohnstamm 1965b, 1965c. In fact, the Germans were happy that the MLF Treaty was off the table. Soutou 1996, 268; and Barbier 1994b, 176.

252. The Chinese test also increased the pressure from US scientists to drop the MLF Treaty and replace it with a NPT to be negotiated with the Soviets. Silard 1964; and Newhouse 1964. At the NSC, McGeorge Bundy used a group of nuclear scientists and political scientists, gathered around Paul Doty and Henry Kissinger at Harvard, to diffuse the idea that the Western Europeans themselves liked the MLF Treaty prepared by Jean Monnet. See Van Helmont 1964h, 1964i, 1964j; Kissinger 1961; Kissinger 1963, 32, 33; and Kubbig 1996.

253. Maddock 1997, 460.

254. Eugene Rostow 1964b.

255. In November 1964, after some informal consultations, Eugene Rostow confirmed to Ball that the West Germans would be satisfied with a simple procedure of consultation on the use of nuclear weapons. Eugene Rostow 1964a, 1964c.

256. Van Helmont noted, however, that, among other RAND experts, "Herman Kahn now favors the creation of a European nuclear force independent from a U.S. veto." Van Helmont 1964s. The West German parliamentarian Helmut Schmidt agreed with Van Helmont. Schmidt 1963.

257. McCloy 1965a.

258. McNamara 1965.

259. Kohnstamm 1965d. Chancellor Ludwig Erhard applauded the American conversion to a more limited objective, which was in line with his liberal philosophy. Maddock 1997, 483.

260. Turkey saw its inclusion as a form of closure to the Cuban missile crisis. Van Helmont 1965.

261. Monnet told Kohnstamm that McNamara's NPG "could only confuse European nations" (Monnet 1965a), a point with which Kohnstamm (1965d) agreed.

262. Van Helmont 1965.

263. McCloy 1965a.

264. By leaving the integrated command, but remaining a party to the North Atlantic Treaty, de Gaulle made a legal point regarding the sharing of legal authority, without removing French forces in West Germany. Thomas Alan Schwartz 2003, 102–3; and McCloy 1965a.

265. Thomas Schwartz claims that "as with the MLF, Johnson's decision brought him into conflict as much, if not more, with the traditional U.S. foreign policy establishment as with other Atlantic leaders," without noticing that the conflict pitted two generations against each other. Thomas Alan Schwartz 2003, 110. For instance, whereas McCloy and Acheson pushed the president to retaliate against de Gaulle's bold move, Ball and Bator easily convinced Johnson "to continue to have the wisdom to ignore de Gaulle." McCloy 1965b.

266. In exchange for the NPG, they obtained the recognition by all NATO allies (with the exception of France) of the validity of RAND's concept of flexible deterrence, which has, to this day, been at the center of NATO's strategic concept—although Nixon and Kissinger recognized in April 1974 that the French and British nuclear deterrents increased Western security.

267. Thomas Alan Schwartz 2003, 110.

268. Alter 2001.

269. It is therefore not surprising if most scholars who study the jurisprudence of the ECJ thus arrive at different conclusions than I do when analyzing how the European treaties were interpreted in the formative years of the Common Market and Euratom by the ECJ—in particular, when they emphasize the rise of Eurofederalist doctrines such as the supremacy of European law over national legislation, as expressed by court decisions in the ECJ. European Court of Justice 1964.

CHAPTER SEVEN

1. Abbott and Snidal 2001, 444, 445.

2. Shaffer and Pollack 2011, 1166.

3. Abbott and Snidal 2001.

4. Shaffer and Pollack 2011, 1148; see also Shaffer and Pollack 2010.

5. Shaffer and Pollack 2011, 1148.

6. Euratom's rules on controls cannot be said to have formed "soft law," as member states had all recognized the rules as binding and had delegated their interpretative authority to the European Commission and Court of Justice. Howlett 1990.

7. Abbott and Snidal 2001; Shaffer and Pollack 2010, 2011.

8. Euratom Commission 1967d.

9. Forland 1997, 235.

10. Seaborg 1971, 227. After the Cuban missile crisis, Kennedy realized that the four

nuclear great powers had to work together to better control the spread of nuclear armaments. John F. Kennedy 1963.

11. To prevent the use of the "exit clause" for this reason, the United States, the United Kingdom, and the Soviets issued a resolution in the UN Security Council in the summer of 1968 by which they pledged to provide assistance to any NNWS facing the threat of nuclear attack.

12. Nye 1980.

13. Dean Rusk and McGeorge Bundy officially made the completion of the NPT and NATO's Nuclear Planning Group the primary goals of US policy in July 1965. Maddock 1997, 487.

14. The reaction to the American draft of the NPT was first one of disappointment on the Continent. Kohnstamm 1967c. This was especially true in West Germany. The new German chancellor, Kurt Kiesinger, denounced what he called the "atomic complicity" and the "*diktats*" of Washington and Moscow. Thomas Alan Schwartz 2003, 152–67.

15. Kohnstamm 1967b, 1967c.

16. The formal recognition of that principle was only expressed officially by Soviet ambassador Gromyko at the Disarmament Conference in Geneva in December 1966. Thomas Alan Schwartz 2003, 136–38.

17. If the United Kingdom also retained its veto power in that federal state. See Kohnstamm 1966a, 1966b.

18. When Senator Pastore and fifty other senators passed a resolution in January 1966 in favor of the draft NPT, they made it clear that they were "reluctant to accept the concept of multilateral force [with its European clause]" in the NPT. Seaborg 1987, 181.

19. Birrenbach 1973.

20. Kohnstamm 1967c.

21. Birrenbach 1973.

22. Kohnstamm 1967c.

23. Kohnstamm 1967a.

24. Monnet 1967a.

25. Monnet 1967b.

26. Tertrais 2004.

27. As Eugene Rostow remarked in 1973, "The United States guaranteed the legal option that Europe could become a nuclear power under the NPT, but it was not presently feasible for Europe to contemplate that course," as "most people—Europeans and Americans alike—much prefer not to think about Europe becoming a nuclear power." Eugene Rostow 1973.

28. Birrenbach 1973.

29. The Germans definitely lost their dream of participating as equals in the creation of the European force when, in 1990, the Soviets signed the Moscow Treaty, which recognized the reunified Federal Republic of Germany as a NNWS under the NPT (art. 3.1 of the Treaty on the Final Settlement with Respect to Germany, 1990). In exchange, all the Eastern European satellites (including Ukraine) also signed the NPT as NNWS when they attained legal sovereignty and political autonomy in the 1990s.

30. Soutou 1996, 341.

31. Shaffer and Pollack 2011, 1157. As they write (p. 1158), in that sense, soft law represents a modern variant of the *lex ferenda*, or the "law to be made."

32. Mérand 2008. When France reentered the military structure of NATO in 2009, President Sarkozy refused to let France enter NATO's NPG.
33. Treaty on the Non-proliferation of Nuclear Weapons 1968.
34. Emphasis mine.
35. Shaffer and Pollack 2011, 1148.
36. Forland 1997, 87; and Howlett 1990.
37. Walton Butterworth, cited in Forland 1997, 89.
38. Forland 1997, 108.
39. Such as the Eurochemic plant developed in Belgium. Forland 1997, 141.
40. Euratom Commission 1963c; and Howlett 1990.
41. Euratom Commission 1963c.
42. British policy was torn between the Commonwealth Bureau, which did not want to lose the Indian bid for large-scale reactors, and the Ministry of Defense, which insisted that no deal with India should jeopardize the "special relation" with the United States. Forland 1997, 130–35.
43. International Atomic Energy Agency 1961.
44. Cole, cited in Forland 1997, 129.
45. Forland 1997, 146.
46. International Atomic Energy Agency 1961.
47. Forland 1997, 135.
48. At the time, Norway provided heavy water to both France and Israel for their respective nuclear weapons program. Forland 1997, 161. The French were the most vocal Western state in their opposition to being policed by the IAEA. Goldschmidt 1982, 283.
49. Forland 1997, 164.
50. Forland 1997, 116, 118. A provision in INFCIRC/26 (called the "substitution paragraph") allowed the country in which reprocessing was done to place a similar quantity of materials as that being reprocessed under IAEA controls, which allowed the United Kingdom to avoid having IAEA controls on its reprocessing plants (which were used for military ends). Forland 1997, 201.
51. Forland 1997, 166.
52. In the sense that these regulations did not apply to some IAEA member states, such as Euratom nations.
53. Abbott and Snidal 2001.
54. This document is still applied to controls of nuclear trade with nonsignatory states of the NPT.
55. The inclusion was due to the US representative to the IAEA. Forland 1997, 196. Some loopholes introduced in INFCIRC/26 (such as the "substitution paragraph") were nonetheless retained in INFCIRC/66.
56. Forland 1997, 196.
57. After Canada insisted on selling source materials to France only if IAEA safeguards were in place.
58. Goldschmidt 1982, 390, 391.
59. Euratom Commission 1963c.
60. Cited in Seaborg 1971, 277.
61. Euratom Commission 1963c.
62. Euratom Commission 1967k.
63. The proposal, which was relayed in February 1963 by the Dutch representative to

the commission, was immediately killed by the French representative to the commission. Euratom Commission 1963a, 1963b.

64. The struggle between the AEC and the State Department continued the bureaucratic battle between Lewis Strauss and John Foster Dulles begun in 1957, this time opposing Seaborg and Ball from 1963 until the moment when Ball finally quit the State Department in September 1966.

65. Finney 1965.

66. Finney 1964.

67. Finney 1966c.

68. As Seaborg acknowledged, "He received no encouragement from any quarter" to pursue the imposition of universal IAEA safeguards on all NNWS (including Euratom members). Seaborg 1971, 288.

69. Euratom Commission 1963c.

70. Finney 1966b.

71. Cowan 1966. In the summer of 1965, the AEC succeeded in convincing Canada to require IAEA safeguards on its exports of fifty thousand tons of uranium to France, which the French government denounced as treason. In retaliation, de Gaulle canceled the deal with Canada. Pryor 1966.

72. Among Euratom member states, only the Netherlands relayed the Eastern European call for universalization of IAEA safeguards. Euratom Commission 1967k.

73. Cited in Seaborg 1971, 278.

74. Cited in Seaborg 1971, 278.

75. Finney 1966a.

76. Finney 1966b.

77. By that time, the IAEA had extended its safeguards from reactors in June 1963 to the control of power plants in March 1964, and reprocessing plants in June 1966. Seaborg 1987, 269. IAEA safeguards on enrichment plants were eventually put in place in 1968.

78. For instance, in May 1964, Couve de Murville told Dean Rusk that "the control mechanisms of the Vienna Agency [IAEA] planned by the U.S. are insufficient to prevent states from building nuclear weapons," as they did not cover reprocessing plants. MAEF 1964.

79. Halberstam 2010.

80. Picciotto 2011, 95.

81. Kohnstamm 1967d.

82. Seaborg 1971, 288.

83. The new text of article 3 presented by the United States to NATO allies read: "Each non-nuclear-weapon state party to this treaty undertakes to accept the safeguards of the IAEA on all its peaceful nuclear activities as soon as practicable." Kramish 1967, 4.

84. In reference to the postwar plan of "pastoralization of Germany." Thomas Alan Schwartz 2003, 258.

85. Euratom Commission 1967b, 1967d.

86. Halberstam 2010, 152.

87. Giljssels 1968, 1. This interpretation was the most favorable, as it assumed that the US government had changed article 3 without knowing that it threatened the United States–Euratom Treaty.

88. Even Astrid Forland's detailed account of the NPT negotiations fails to include the role of the Euratom Commission. Forland 1997, 256, 257.

89. Monnet 1967b.

90. Monnet 1967c.

91. Monnet 1967b.

92. The would be implemented only after being "ratified by all member-states" (art. 204).

93. Euratom Commission 1967b.

94. Monnet 1967c. As the legal services of the Euratom Commission confirmed, "The U.S. had to consult with the Euratom Commission whether article 3 of the draft NPT would violate the Euratom/U.S. agreement." Euratom Commission 1967a.

95. Monnet 1967b.

96. Or, in the last instance, through the European Court of Justice (ECJ), to which Euratom member states had delegated their authority to interpret the Rome treaties.

97. Euratom Commission 1967a; Kohnstamm 1958c; and Dehousse 1968, 2.

98. Euratom Commission 1967c.

99. Giljssels 1968, 6, 7.

100. Euratom Commission 1967a.

101. Monnet 1967c.

102. Monnet 1967c.

103. And as the legal services of the commission stressed, "This discrimination could bring a delocalization of the nuclear activities (industrial and research) of certain member states toward the only territory [France] which would escape from the control of IAEA." Euratom Commission 1967a.

104. Euratom Commission 1967c, 1967d.

105. Euratom Commission 1967f.

106. Euratom Commission 1967f.

107. Action Committee 1967.

108. Euratom Commission 1967c; see also Kohnstamm 1967f.

109. Euratom Commission 1967g, 1967h.

110. Kohnstamm 1967d, 1967e, 1967f.

111. Chatenêt 1967.

112. European Press 1967.

113. Guéron 1973b.

114. Euratom Commission 1967d.

115. Giljssels 1968, 6, 7.

116. Euratom Commission 1967f.

117. Euratom Commission 1967f.

118. Giljssels 1968, 6, 7.

119. This clause, called the "guillotine clause," was initially rejected by Europeans but finally approved after Robert Schaetzel at the State Department told Europeans that "Euratom could enter into exploratory talks with the IAEA during the period before the treaty came into force." Schaetzel 1967.

120. Euratom Commission 1967f.

121. Euratom Commission 1967l.

122. Schaetzel 1967.

123. Euratom Commission 1967e.

124. European Parliament 1972.

125. Euratom Commission 1967l.

126. After that period, the IAEA controls would be automatically applied. Shaker 1976, 701; and Euratom Commission 1967m, 1967n, 1967o.

127. Seaborg 1987, 304.

128. See appendix 24 in Shaker 1976, 703.

129. Shaker 1976, 771.

130. Forland 1997, 320.

131. Forland 1997, 333.

132. Forland 1997, 327.

133. Forland 1997, 333.

134. International Atomic Energy Agency 1968.

135. ElBaradei 2011, 114.

136. In effect, the former IAEA regulations regarding safeguards (International Atomic Energy Agency 1968) would be restricted to the safeguarding of nuclear facilities built with outside help by NPT nonsignatory states.

137. Forland 1997, 326.

138. Shaker 1976, 732.

139. Shaker 1976, 733.

140. Shaker 1976, 734.

141. Shaker 1976, 706.

142. Euratom officials, private conversation with the author, October 2010.

143. Forland 1997, 328.

144. The list included heavy water (a breakthrough in regard to France).

145. Euratom Commission 1967h.

146. Euratom Commission 1967i.

147. Euratom Commission 1967j.

148. Chalfont 1968.

149. Goldschmidt 1982, 371.

150. Goldschmidt 1982, 371.

151. Euratom Commission 1967p.

152. Guéron 1984.

153. Chatenêt 1966.

154. Guéron 1984.

155. Goldschmidt 1982, 372; and Hosmer 1964.

156. Goldschmidt 1982, 373.

157. This treaty actually corresponded to the "multileveled Europe ["l'Europe à la carte"]," defended by de Gaulle. Chatenêt 1966; and Vichney 1973.

158. Euratom Commission 1971.

159. Heidenreich 1967.

160. Euratom Commission 1967p.

161. As Goldschmidt noted, even though "the British could acquire [unsafeguarded] American enriched uranium for their military program under the Anglo-U.S. Defense Agreement, . . . the JCAE whose peaceful right hand neither knew nor wished to know what its military left hand was doing, decided . . . to impose IAEA safeguards on any slightly enriched uranium supplied to the British for their civil power stations." Goldschmidt 1982, 370.

162. Goldschmidt 1982, 392.

163. Euratom Commission 1971.

164. Goldschmidt 1982, 386.

165. European Court of Justice 1971, 1010.

166. And by a very tight margin. Interview with European officials, November 2011, June 2012.

167. European Court of Justice 2005, 2006.
168. Braun and Chyba 2004.

CHAPTER EIGHT

1. Perkovich et al. 2007, 14.
2. Perkovich et al. 2007, 14.
3. Avner Cohen 2010, xxxii.
4. ElBaradei 2011, 118.
5. Abraham 2006, 56.
6. Hecht 2006, 47.
7. Avner Cohen 1998, 45.
8. Cohen does not say whether the West Germans, who funded up to 80 percent of the Israeli state budget during that same year of 1956—because of the Luxembourg Agreement on reparations signed in 1952 by Adenauer and Ben-Gurion—were informed of the content of this agreement. The expense could not have gone unnoticed for long, as Cohen estimates that the Dimona project represented 50 percent of the Israeli defense budget (paid by German reparations) in its formative years. Avner Cohen 1998, 67.
9. Kroenig 2010, 72.
10. Kroenig 2010, 77.
11. In May 1960, the French foreign minister had requested complete secrecy about France's involvement from Ben-Gurion. Avner Cohen 1998, 92.
12. In early 1960, the CIA picked up traces of Israeli visits to the French nuclear test site in Algeria, and in June 1960, the US embassy in Tel Aviv first reported French involvement in a secret facility in Dimona to Washington. Avner Cohen 1998, 85–89.
13. Avner Cohen 1998, 92.
14. Péan 1981; and Hersh 1991. Avner Cohen bases his interpretation on Péan's and Hersh's rather skewed reading of the events. Indeed, their story does not explain why de Gaulle would have been obeyed as far as his order to cut West German and Italian cooperation in France's enrichment activities was concerned (chapter 6) while French involvement in Dimona continued without his consent.
15. Cohen claims that this confusion resulted from counterorders issued by the minister of atomic energy, Jacques Soustelle, a staunch supporter of both a European nuclear-weapons program and the Israeli program (which were linked, in his mind, in the defense of Western civilization against the "Islamo-communist" threat; Soustelle 1965), but it seems hard to believe that de Gaulle ignored it. Avner Cohen 1998, 72.
16. Avner Cohen 2010, xxx.
17. Kroenig 2010, 76.
18. This mock-up control room allowed the Israelis and the French to hide the fact that the reactor produced enough plutonium for weapons purposes (after Dimona became critical in 1962) and that a secret reprocessing plant (which started operating in 1965) could extract plutonium for bombs. Kroenig 2010, 78.
19. Avner Cohen 1998, 105, 107.
20. Avner Cohen 1998, 111.
21. Avner Cohen 1998, 118. Then, President Johnson informed neither the State Department nor the NSC of CIA estimates that Israel had already produced nuclear weapons in 1967. Avner Cohen 1998, 295. On that matter, Cohen's interpreta-

tion of the role that the United States played in the construction of Israel's nuclear opacity is much more accurate than Kroenig's assertion that Kennedy's and then Johnson's administrations were duped by Israel despite their best efforts. Kroenig 2010, 78.

22. Avner Cohen 1998, 111.
23. Feldman 1997a, 17.
24. This policy overturned the 1955 declaration by the United States (along with France and the United Kingdom) that it would avoid selling conventional weapons to any of the parties to the Arab-Israeli conflict.
25. Avner Cohen 1998, 207.
26. NWS could, for instance, trade military nuclear technologies among themselves.
27. Avner Cohen 2010, 178.
28. Avner Cohen 1998, 294.
29. Avner Cohen 2010, 29.
30. Avner Cohen 2010, 29.
31. Avner Cohen 2010, 30.
32. Feldman 1997a, 17.
33. Feldman 1997b, 154. Among the severe limitations of the IAEA, Israel also often cites the chronic lack of funding for inspections, as well as the fact that "the IAEA lacks an adequate intelligence gathering and analysis capability."
34. As well as with other global regimes (such as those banning the production and use of biological and chemical weapons, and restricting the production of missiles).
35. The call for the establishment of a nuclear-weapons-free zone (NWFZ) in the Middle East was first launched by a joint Egyptian-Iranian General Assembly resolution in 1974, but it did not yet contain any reference to biological and chemical weapons.
36. Feldman 1997a, 8.
37. Especially article 7, which reaffirms the right of states that are parties to the NPT to "conclude regional treaties in order to assure the total absence of nuclear weapons in their respective territories."
38. Although the parties did not manage to agree on a consensual perspective, their joint Declaration of Principles, which was adopted during the ACRS Plenary Session in Tunis (December 1994), stated that all parties including Israel envisioned the Middle East as a WMD-free zone. The Israeli version excluded any reference to the NPT while endorsing a regional "mutual verification regime" to verify compliance with the zone requirements. Feldman 1997b, 320–25.
39. This sequence has been the object of a report commissioned by the UN General Assembly in 1990, whose conclusions made it clear that a zone should adopt more rigorous "verification procedures" than those adopted by the IAEA. Feldman 1997b, 160.
40. Feldman 1997b, 320–25.
41. Bundy, Crowe, and Drell 1993, 68–70; and Avner Cohen and Miller 2010.
42. Avner Cohen 2010, xxix.
43. Avner Cohen 2010, 45.
44. Avner Cohen 2010, 111.
45. Besides, it is not certain that the revelation of Israel's nuclear ties with other countries, such as South Africa, would put Israel in a favorable light. Polakow-Suransky 2010.
46. Bundy, Crowe, and Drell 1993, 68–70.
47. State Department 2009c.

48. Some authors argue that although the global trend is toward increased adherence to nonproliferation norms, the Middle East stands out (in contrast to "East Asia," which is supposedly more denuclearized). Solingen 2007. Still, the Middle East is less nuclearized than Europe, and even than South Asia.

49. Mordechai Va'anunu was a low-level Israeli employee working at Dimona who told the Sunday *Times* that Dimona actually produced much more plutonium than was originally thought. As a result, he was imprisoned for eighteen years (including eleven years in solitary confinement), and has been freed under strict constraints (no liberty of speech, nor movement outside Israel).

50. Feldman 1997b, 128.

51. Joint Plan of Action 2013.

52. Risse and Sikkink 1999.

53. Feldman 1997b, 217.

54. Egypt only obtained a complementary "Resolution on the Middle East," which called on all NPT signatories to facilitate the creation of the zone, with no explicit mention of Israel. Feldman 1997b, 222.

55. Feldman 1997a, 14.

56. Mallard 2012.

57. Feldman and Toukan 1997, 101.

58. Barnett 1998, 231.

59. Cited in Krause 1994, 289.

60. Barnett 1998.

61. Feldman 1997b, 26.

62. Feldman and Toukan 1997, 82.

63. The climate of trust instituted by ACRS made possible the bilateral agreement that Israel signed with the Palestinian Authority in 1993, and the peace treaty with Jordan in 1994 (which makes an explicit reference to ACRS, in art. 4.1.A and art. 4.1.B). Treaty of Peace between the Hashemite Kingdom of Jordan and the State of Israel 1994.

64. Feldman and Toukan 1997, 82.

65. State Department 2009e.

66. Mallard 2008a.

67. Hecht 2006, 47.

68. Perkovich 1999, 30.

69. Perkovich 1999, 138.

70. Perkovich 1999, 127.

71. Perkovich 1999, 28.

72. International Atomic Energy Agency 1961.

73. Forland 1997, 118.

74. Abraham 2006, 56.

75. Hecht 2012.

76. Homi J. Bhabha (the leading Indian nuclear physicist who jump-started India's nuclear program). Cited in Perkovich 1999, 28.

77. Perkovich 1999, 138. India had already affirmed that intent should be the sole criterion used to judge India's nuclear behavior in the context of prior deliberations of the IAEA Statute. Forland 1997, 116.

78. Strategic and economic reasons were the main drivers for the signing of these agreements by the United States and Canada: the United States wanted to draw India a

bit closer to the West's orbit after the invasion of India by China in November 1962. India also signed the LTBT soon after. Perkovich 1999, 55.

79. Perkovich 1999, 56.
80. In this case, Canadians rather than the IAEA were charged with the inspection of the reactor (and India was granted the right to inspect some Canadian reactor in reciprocity). See Perkovich 1999, 63.
81. Perkovich 1999, 58.
82. It is unclear if Canadians had anticipated that Indians could use this loophole, although Glenn Seaborg, the AEC chairman, was clearly aware of such a possibility in 1963. Perkovich 1999, 90.
83. Whereas Israel was strongly tied to the West, India was long perceived as a friend of the Soviet Union, despite claims made by Indian premiers that they respected a strict policy of nonalignment.
84. Perkovich 1999, 138.
85. Perkovich 1999, 178.
86. Perkovich 1999, 182.
87. Canada's reaction was less opaque than the United States', as it made further cooperation conditional on India's acceptance of IAEA safeguards on all its nuclear activities. Perkovich 1999, 186, 187.
88. Perkovich 1999, 207.
89. Perkovich 1999, 24.
90. Perkovich 1999, 182.
91. Nye 1981.
92. Nye 1981. Carter was himself a nuclear engineer with deep knowledge of the issues at stake. Nye, a student of nuclear nonproliferation and other regional security regimes (Nye 1971), was in charge of foreign nuclear policy in the Carter administration.
93. Perkovich 1999, 187.
94. Perkovich 1999, 191.
95. The IAEA included some revised version of these guidelines in International Atomic Energy Agency 2007.
96. International Atomic Energy Agency 1992.
97. NPT Review Conference 1995.
98. Perkovich 1999, 206. A deal was finally reached in 1983 when India accepted IAEA safeguards on all fuel used in the Tarapur plant (but not on all Indian nuclear facilities), while Reagan mollified the language of the Non-proliferation Act. See Perkovich 1999, 239.
99. Perkovich 1999, 207.
100. Perkovich 1999, 209.
101. Perkovich 1999, 435.
102. United Nations 1998.
103. Although President Clinton signed the CTBT in 1996, the US Senate voted in 1999 not to ratify it. Discussions in the United States over its ratification are ongoing. The FMCT is now under negotiation.
104. Ranganathan 2010, 12.
105. International Atomic Energy Agency 2006.
106. State Department 2005c.
107. State Department 2005b, 2005d.

108. State Department 2005b.
109. State Department 2005a.
110. State Department 2005c.
111. State Department 2005c.
112. State Department 2005d.
113. But India did not pledge not to transfer materials and technologies from its peaceful to its military activities. The distinction was therefore made only for the reporting goals with respect to the IAEA. See Ranganathan 2010, 14.
114. State Department 2004b.
115. Ranganathan 2010, 38. The IAEA Safeguards Agreement concluded in August 2008 with India was stronger than the type of "Voluntary Safeguards Agreement" negotiated by the five NWS and the IAEA.
116. The NSG also agreed to deliver the waiver in September 2008 after it claimed its right to terminate the waiver if India was found in violation of its nuclear freeze commitment. Ranganathan 2010, 49.
117. The deal struck between the United States and India also increased the legitimacy of the NSG and the IAEA as opposed to the review conferences of the NPT. Ranganathan 2010, 38.
118. The NSG refused to echo criticisms privately made by Pakistan that the United States–India deal "freed" some source material and special fissionable materials (as new foreign sources were added) that India could then use for its military program. State Department 2009g. The silence that Pakistan observed was the object of a deal between the US negotiator and Pakistani government officials (the "Nick Burns–F. S. Khan agreement"). State Department 2008a.
119. The State Department could obtain Pakistan's agreement because Pakistan "hopes that the India Safeguards Agreement will become a model for future civil nuclear agreements between other countries (read Pakistan)." State Department 2008b.
120. Perkovich 1999, 165.
121. Perkovich 1999, 186.
122. Perkovich 1999, 195.
123. Goldschmidt 1982, 391.
124. As required by the 1976 Symington Amendment.
125. Levy and Scott-Clark 2008, 18.
126. Levy and Scott-Clark 2008, 44.
127. Levy and Scott-Clark 2008, 52.
128. Even though Pakistan is multiplying international contracts, its political economy is still oriented toward state-based initiatives. Solingen 2007.
129. Perkovich 1999, 300.
130. Many commentators assert wrongly that secrecy over the Pakistani nuclear program was revealed only after Libya decided in December 2003 to go public with its attempt at buying uranium-enrichment technology from the Pakistanis. See Albright and Hinderstein 2005. Commentators thus absolve the United States from having missed the opportunity to crush the network in the beginning.
131. Levy and Scott-Clark 2008, 65.
132. Levy and Scott-Clark 2008, 54.
133. Perkovich 1999, 217.
134. Levy and Scott-Clark 2008, 66. Later, Gerard Smith spoke out against Reagan's Pakistani policy, which he accused in *Foreign Affairs* of being a dismal failure and a lie. Gerard Smith and Cobban 1989; see also Rydell 1991, 140.

135. The Carter administration never gave the green light to the IAEA director about the release of the information Smith had shared about the Pakistani program.
136. The 1977 Glenn Amendment introduced slight changes to the 1976 Symington Amendment.
137. Levy and Scott-Clark 2008, 85.
138. Levy and Scott-Clark 2008, 197.
139. Paul 2003.
140. Levy and Scott-Clark 2008, 76. The importance of Pakistan and Sino-Pakistani ties was not lost on the incoming US secretary of state, who had been Kissinger's aide when Kissinger secretly resumed diplomatic relations with Chinese authorities in 1971. Kissinger 1984, 382.
141. Part of the effort to cover up how US action undermined the NPT was for Reagan to decimate the ranks of the ACDA so that it lost all relevance, leaving the DoD in charge of covering Pakistan's nuclear conduct, to the dismay of CIA director Robert Gates. At the same time, Reagan's allies in Congress also passed the Pressler Amendment, which mollified the Symington Amendment. Perkovich 1999, 270.
142. Levy and Scott-Clark 2008, 148. That was not the only time the administration lied to Congress. At that time, it was also caught lying about the aid it secretly provided to Iran (in the Iran-Contra affair).
143. Levy and Scott-Clark 2008, 125.
144. Levy and Scott-Clark 2008, 88.
145. Levy and Scott-Clark 2008, 117.
146. Levy and Scott-Clark 2008, 2.
147. China publicly declared that it did not practice nuclear proliferation. Levy and Scott-Clark 2008, 100.
148. Levy and Scott-Clark 2008, 111.
149. Kroenig's assertion that "the U.S., a global superpower, intervened in an attempt to prevent Chinese-Pakistani nuclear cooperation" is largely an ex post reconstruction of the story. Kroenig 2010, 116.
150. ElBaradei 2011, 177.
151. Levy and Scott-Clark 2008, 144.
152. Levy and Scott-Clark 2008, 133.
153. State Department 2005e.
154. Levy and Scott-Clark 2008, 158.
155. An idea commonly found in the literature. Braun and Chyba, 2004; and Perkovich et al. 2007, 14.
156. Levy and Scott-Clark 2008, 266. At the same time, Pakistan sought to bolster its status in the Muslim world by challenging the NPT regime and by serving as an intermediary to sell China's weapons to Saudi Arabia and to the Gulf monarchies. Levy and Scott-Clark 2008, 173.
157. Bush's decision suited him well as it allowed him to avoid lying to Congress as well as to justify why he stopped the US aid package, which was no longer necessary since the Soviet Union had been defeated in Afghanistan. China's accession to the NPT regime in 1992 also raised the hopes that the Chinese proliferation to Pakistan would slow down. Perkovich 1999, 325.
158. Kroenig 2010, 135.
159. India was particularly resentful of this "United States–China–Pakistan" link. Perkovich 1999, 366.
160. Musharraf even chaired the "export control" committee created in 2000, which au-

thorized the sale of all nuclear dual-use technologies to foreign countries. Levy and Scott-Clark 2008, 297.

161. North Korea was turning to Pakistani centrifuge technologies as it closed down the plutonium road, because of the agreement framework it had negotiated with the United States. Levy and Scott-Clark 2008, 280.

162. Perkovich 1999, 324; and State Department 2009a.

163. Levy and Scott-Clark 2008, 304.

164. Levy and Scott-Clark 2008, 300.

165. Wolfowitz, who was undersecretary of defense during George H. W. Bush's term as president, had known from very early on that Pakistan had developed nuclear weapons. Perkovich 1999, 308.

166. Perkovich et al. 2007, 22.

167. ElBaradei 2011, 258.

168. Hecht 2010.

169. Blix 2004. The Iraq Survey Group reported directly to US secretary of state Donald Rumsfeld rather than to an international body, and absorbed the fantastic sum of $3 billion in two and a half years of inspection, "the equivalent of the IAEA's verification budget for inspections for twenty-five years." ElBaradei 2011, 80.

170. Levy and Scott-Clark 2008, 300.

171. Albright and Hinderstein 2005.

172. Levy and Scott-Clark 2008, 378–83.

173. Levy and Scott-Clark 2008, 390.

174. Levy and Scott-Clark 2008, 356, 378.

175. State Department 2009d.

176. State Department 2009b.

177. Levy and Scott-Clark 2008, 334.

178. Levy and Scott-Clark 2008, 346.

179. ElBaradei 2011, 114.

180. ElBaradei 2011, 116.

181. Levy and Scott-Clark 2008, 348; and ElBaradei 2011, 117.

182. In addition, some natural uranium imported from China was discovered, which had never been reported to the IAEA; thus, China could be asked to account for its trade. ElBaradei 2011, 117.

183. ElBaradei 2011, 28.

184. As ElBaradei recognizes, the IAEA director had to fight hard against the (Western) intelligence agencies, which "wanted as quid pro quo to have privileged access to [IAEA] inspection results" on Iraq. ElBaradei 2011, 18, 43.

185. ElBaradei 2011, 122.

186. ElBaradei 2011, 145.

187. ElBaradei 2011, 122.

188. ElBaradei 2011, 200.

189. ElBaradei 2011, 299.

190. Resolution 1540 is consistent with the new global lawmaking powers claimed by the UN Security Council since the "war on terror." States are forced, whether they participated in Security Council debates or not, to adopt in their national legislation some "model law" pioneered by the United States or other Western powers. Scheppele 2004.

191. This seems to be the true innovation of Resolution 1540, as chapter 7 of the resolution permits the Security Council to use sanctions or military force in response to

threats to international peace and security. Otherwise, Resolution 1540 asked states to pass symbolic legislation that most often already existed.

192. Joint Plan of Action 2013.

193. State Department 2009f.

194. The kind of proposals that are extended to Iran today (such as the fuel bank proposal or the multilateralization of its nuclear fuel cycle) should also concern the sections of the Pakistani nuclear-weapons program that can serve civilian purposes (and not the purely military activities, such as nuclear-weapons design, which should be treated in other disarmament negotiations with India and China).

195. State Department 2004a.

196. Moravcsik 2000.

197. ElBaradei 2011, 122.

198. Perkovich et al. 2007, 23.

BIBLIOGRAPHY

PAPERS CONSULTED

BB   Bernard Baruch, Princeton, Mudd Library
DL   David Lilienthal, Washington, DC, Library of Congress
EH   Etienne Hirsh, Florence, Archives of the European Communities
FC   Francois Chatenêt, Florence, Archives of the European Communities
FD   François Duchêne, Florence, Archives of the European Communities
FF   Felix Frankfurter, Washington, DC, Library of Congress
GB   George Ball, Princeton, Mudd Library
GK   George Kennan, Princeton, Mudd Library
GS   Glenn Seaborg, Washington, DC, Library of Congress
JFD   John Foster Dulles, Princeton, Mudd Library
JG   Jules Guéron, Florence, Archives of the European Communities
JM   Jean Monnet, Florence, Archives of the European Communities
JRO   J. Robert Oppenheimer, Washington, DC, Library of Congress
JV   Jacob Viner, Princeton, Mudd Library
JVH   Jacques Van Helmont, Florence, Archives of the European Communities
LA   Louis Armand, Florence, Archives of the European Communities
LM   Livingston Merchant, Princeton, Mudd Library
LS   Lewis Strauss, Washington, DC, Library of Congress
MK   Max Kohnstamm, Florence, Archives of the European Communities
PN   Paul Nitze, Washington, DC, Library of Congress
VB   Vannevar Bush, Washington, DC, Library of Congress

EC   Euratom Commission, Florence, Archives of the European Communities
EP   European Parliament, Florence, Archives of the European Communities
MAEF   Ministère des Affaires Etrangères Français
SD   State Department, Princeton, Mudd Library

PRIMARY SOURCES

Acheson, Dean. 1947 (June 20). Letter to Vannevar Bush. VB, box 1.
Action Committee for the United States of Europe. 1955 (October 15). Joint Declaration. JM, JMDS box 117.
———. 1958 (October 17). Joint Declaration. JM, JMDS box 117.

———. 1959a (May 11). Joint Declaration. JM, JMDS box 117.

———. 1959b (November 20). Joint Declaration. JM, JMDS box 117.

———. 1960 (July 11). Joint Declaration. JM, JMDS box 117.

———. 1964 (February 7). Draft of MLF. MK, box 26.

———. 1967 (March 16). Press communiqué. GB, box 70.

Adenauer, Konrad. 1952 (December 1). Letter to John McCloy. JFD, box 62.

Analysis of Bernard Baruch's memorandum of September 24, 1946, to Truman. 1949. JRO, box 19.

Armand, Louis. 1955 (May). "Some Aspects of the European Energy Problem." MK, box 26.

———. 1956 (July 5). "Exposé sur l'Euratom fait à la tribune de l'Assemblée nationale." EC, BAC 118/1986-1452.

———. 1957 (January 31). Letter of the Three Wise Men to John Foster Dulles. JM, JMAS box 33.

Ball, George. 1958 (July 18). Letter to Max Kohnstamm. JM, JMDS box 120.

———. 1962a (January 22). Letter to Mr. Feldman. GB, box 91.

———. 1962b (May 25). Memorandum to the president on UK nuclear cooperation with France. GB, box 91.

———. 1962c (June 17). Memorandum to the president. GB, box 46.

———. 1963a (March 26). Memorandum to the president, with Kennedy's letter to Adenauer. GB, box 49.

———. 1963b (May 6). Memorandum to the president on pros and cons of UK MLF participation. GB, box 91.

———. 1963c (May 6). Memorandum to the president, on "What Kind of an MLF Commitment Should We Seek from the UK?" GB, box 91.

———. 1963d (May 25). Memorandum of conversations with Couve de Murville. GB, box 46.

———. 1963e (June 20). Memorandum to the president, "The Mess in Europe and the Meaning of Your Trip." GB, box 46.

———. 1963f (June 21). Memorandum to the president, "Talking Points for Your Conversation with Vice Chancellor Erhard." GB, box 49.

———. 1963g (July 22). Memorandum to the president, "Proposed Nuclear Offer to de Gaulle." GB, box 46.

———. 1966 (July 22). Memorandum to the president on Harold Wilson's visit, "The Opportunity for an Act of Statesmanship." GB, box 91.

———. 1967 (May 3). "Nuclear Power and Foreign Policy." Address before the School of Advanced International Studies, Johns Hopkins University. GB, box 26.

———. 1976 (July 13). Notes for profile. GB, box 26.

———. 1978 (March 10). Notes regarding my chronology for 1947 and 1948. GB, box 26.

Baruch, Bernard. 1946a. "The American Proposal for International Control." *Bulletin of the Atomic Scientists* 4: 3–10. BB, box 52.

———. 1946b (September 17). Letter to the US president. BB, box 52.

———. 1946c (November 20). Notes on conversation at luncheon. BB, box 52.

———. 1947a (January 4). Letter of resignation from the UN Atomic Commission to the president of the US. BB, box 52.

———. 1947b (January 17). Letter to Robert Oppenheimer. JRO, box 19.

———. 1948 (October 5). Letter to John Foster Dulles. JFD, box 35.

———. 1958 (June 9). Letter to the president. JM, JMDS box 110.

Birrenbach, Kurt. 1967 (June 14). Letter to George Ball. GB, box 26.

———. 1973 (October 10). Letter to George Ball. GB, box 26.

Bissel, Richard M., Jr. 1971 (July 9). Oral history interview by Theodore A. Wilson and Richard D. McKinzie. East Hartford, CT. http://www.trumanlibrary.org/oralhist/bissellr.htm.

Bohr, Niels. 1944a (July 4). Memorandum. JRO, box 34.

———. 1944b (September 7). Letter to Franklin Roosevelt. JRO, box 34.

———. 1946 (April 17). Letter to J. Robert Oppenheimer. JRO, box 34.

———. 1950 (June 19). Letter to J. Robert Oppenheimer. JRO, box 21.

Bowie, Robert. 1963 (September 19). Letter to Kohnstamm. MK, box 24.

Breithut, Richard. 1958 (April 12). Letter to John Foster Dulles. JFD, box 125.

Brodie, Bernard. 1945 (November 27). Letter to Jacob Viner. JV, box 5.

Bruce, David. 1953. Diary entries—October 1953. JM, JMAS box 156.

Bundy, McGeorge. 1972 (November 29). Address to the Conference on External Relations of the EEC organized by Max Kohnstamm. GB, box 28.

———. 1987 (September 2). Letter to George Ball, with attached cabinet room transcripts, Cuban missile crisis. GB, box 70.

Bush, Vannevar. 1945a (July). *Science, the Endless Frontier: A Report to the President.* http://www.nsf.gov/od/lpa/nsf50/vbush1945.htm or VB, box 26.

———. 1945b (September 24). Letter to James Conant. VB, box 27.

———. 1945c (October 1). Letter to James Conant. VB, box 27.

———. 1945d (November 7). Letter to James Conant. VB, box 27.

———. 1945e (November 8). Letter to James Conant. VB, box 27.

———. 1945f (November 10). Letter to James Conant. VB, box 27.

———. 1946a (January 4). Letter to J. Robert Oppenheimer. JRO, box 23.

———. 1946b (October 21). Letter to James Conant. VB, box 27.

———. 1947 (April 10). Letter to Dean Acheson. VB, box 1.

———. 1948 (December 20). Letter to James Forrestal. JFD, box 40.

———. 1952a (September 5). Letter to James Conant. VB, box 27.

———. 1952b (October 29). Letter to James Conant. VB, box 27.

———. 1953 (March 3). Letter to J. Robert Oppenheimer. JRO, box 23.

———. 1954 (April 6). Letter to James Conant. VB, box 27.

Cantu, G. 1973. "L'agence pour l'Union de l'Europe Occidentale pour le contrôle des armements." Paris: UEO. JG, box 226.

Carnegie Endowment for International Peace, Legal Subcommittee of the Committee on Atomic Energy. 1946 (June). *Utilization and Control of Atomic Energy: A Draft Convention.* New York: CEIP. BB, box 112.

Cattani, Attilio. 1967 (April 27). "L'échec des négociations de 1961/62 pour un statut politique de l'Europe." Europe Documents. JG, box 125.

Center of Science and International Affairs (CSIA). 1987 (March 5–8). "Proceedings of the Hawk's Cay Conference on the Cuban Missile Crisis." GB, box 40.

Chalfont, Lord. 1968. "Discours prononcé par le Ministre d'Etat britannique aux affaires étrangères à Bruxelles, 9 octobre 1967." In *Union de l'Europe occidentale Assemblée-Commission des Affaires générales: L'année politique en Europe Rétrospective, 1967,* 142–45. JG, box 103.

Chatenêt, Pierre. 1966 (April 28). Interview. *Figaro.* EC, BAC 118/1986 #1453.

———. 1967 (March 16). "Discours au Parlement Européen." EC, BAC 118/1986 #1453.

Comité Inter-Gouvernemental crée par la conférence de Messine. 1955a (July 18). *Rapport de la commission de l'énergie nucléaire.* JM, JMDS box 117.

———. 1955b (November 15). *Rapport de la commission de l'énergie nucléaire.* JM, JMDS box 117.

Conant, James. 1945a (September 27). Letter to Vannevar Bush. VB, box 27.

———. 1945b (October 4). Letter to Vannevar Bush. VB, box 27.

———. 1945c (October 8). Letter to Grenville Clark. VB, box 27.

———. 1945d (December 31). Letter to Vannevar Bush. VB, box 27.

———. 1947. *On Understanding Science: A Historical Approach.* New Haven, CT: Yale University Press.

———. 1949 (May 2). Letter to James Forrestal. JFD, box 40.

———. 1952a (January 15). Letter to J. Robert Oppenheimer. JRO, box 27.

———. 1952b (July 22). Letter to Vannevar Bush. VB, box 27.

———. 1956 (February 9). Telegram from the embassy in Germany to the Department of State. In *Foreign Relations of the United States* (VI-1), p. 414.

Council on Foreign Relations. 1951 (May 9). *Discussion Meeting Report on France Today.* GB, box 37.

Cowan, Edward. 1966 (August 28). "France to Accept Controls by Euratom." *New York Times.*

de Gaulle, Charles. 1958 (September 17). Letter to President Eisenhower, with attached memorandum on NATO. GB, box 46.

———. 1959a (May 25). Lettre à Eisenhower. MAEF (Secrétariat général, entretiens et messages, 1956–66), vol. 7.

———. 1959b (June 10). Letter to President Eisenhower. MAEF (Secrétariat général, entretiens et messages, 1956–66), vol. 7.

———. 1960 (June 10). Letter to President Eisenhower. GB, box 46.

———. 1962 (January 11). Letter to President Kennedy. GB, box 46.

———. 1963 (January 14). "Conférence de presse sur l'entrée de la Grande Bretagne dans la CEE." Accessed November 10, 2013. http://fresques.ina.fr/de-gaulle/fiche-media/Gaulle00085/conference-de-presse-du-14-janvier-1963-sur-l-entree-de-la-grande-bretagne-dans-la-cee.html.

Dehousse, Fernand. 1968. *Sur la primauté du droit communautaire sur le droit des Etats membres.* Rapport de la commission juridique du Parlement Européen. EC, BAC 110/1986-18.

Draft Treaty Embodying the Statute of the European Community. 1953 (February 26). Final draft. JM, JMDS box 85.

Drouin, Pierre. 1965 (July 3). "Une hibernation de l'Europe?" *Le Monde.* MK, box 43.

Duchêne, François. 1963 (February 15). L'arrière plan aux conversations des 9, 10, 11 Février à Houjarray. JM, JMDS box 223.

———. n.d. Memo on moratorium on French nuclear tests. JM, JMDS box 235.

Dulles, John Foster. 1945 (March 17). "From Yalta to San Francisco." Paper presented before the Foreign Policy Association in New York. JFD, box 27.

———. 1946a (March 16). Memorandum of conversation with Harry Truman. JFD, box 27.

———. 1946b (July 3). Letter to Bernard Baruch. JFD, box 28.

———. 1947 (January 17). "A New Year's Resolve." Address to the National Publishers Association. JFD, box 32.

———. 1948 (October 12). Letter to Bernard Baruch. JFD, box 35.

———. 1950 (May 23). Letter to Jean Monnet. JM, JMAS box 12.

———. 1955 (January 15). Letter to the president. JM, JMDS box 102.

———. 1956a (January 9). Memorandum for the president. JM, JMAS box 33.

———. 1956b (February 9). Memorandum of conversation with Mayer. JM, JMAS box 33.

———. 1956c (May 1). Memorandum of conversation on Atoms for Peace with the president. JM, JMDS box 102.

———. 1956d (December 21). Letter to Paul Henri Spaak. JM, JMAS box 14.

———. 1957a (January 10). Memo of conversation with Monnet. JM, JMAS box 33.

———. 1957b (February). Memo on background of Euratom negotiations in Brussels. JM, box JMDS box 102.

———. 1957c (May 10). Statement before the Senate Foreign Relations Committee. JFD, box 32.

———. 1957d (November 19). News conference, *Report from the State Department N636.* JFD, box 120.

———. 1957e (December 10). News conference, *Report from the State Department N662.* JFD, box 120.

———. 1957f (December 12). Draft speech for the NATO meetings in Paris. JFD, box 120.

———. 1957g (December 15). Draft speech for the NATO meetings in Paris. JFD, box 120.

———. 1958 (April 4). Note on control from the Joint United States–Euratom working party. JM, JMDS box 120.

Dulles, John Foster, and Bishop Browley Oxnam. 1945 (August 9). "Open Letter by the Federal Council of Churches of Christ." JFD, box 26.

Eisenhower, Dwight. 1951 (July 3). "Address at the English Speaking Union Dinner." London. http://www.eisenhowermemorial.org/speeches/19510703%20English%20Speaking%20Union%20Dinner.htm.

———. 1954a. "The President's Proposal." *Bulletin of the Atomic Scientists* 10 (1): 2–5.

———. 1954b (April 1). "Letter to Winston Spencer Churchill." World Wide Web facsimile of the print edition by Dwight D. Eisenhower Memorial Commission. Baltimore: Johns Hopkins University Press, 1996. http://www.eisenhowermemorial.org/presidential-papers/first-term/documents/812.cfm.

———. 1956 (January 11). Letter sent to John Foster Dulles. JM, JMAS box 33.

———. 1958 (June 10). Letter to Bernard Baruch. JM, JMDS box 110.

———. 1960 (August 2). Letter to de Gaulle. GB, box 46.

Erler, Fritz. 1963. "L'Europe, partenaire égale des Etats-Unis: Aspects militaires et diplomatiques." MK, box 25.

Euratom Commission. 1958a (April). Memo from the joint US-Euratom working party on the nature of Western control. JM, JMDS box 120.

———. 1958b (July 8). Note about AIEA prepared by the foreign relations services, before the visit of Sterling Cole, director of the IAEA. EC, BAC 059/1980-481.

———. 1958c (September 26). Memo prepared for the second session of the General Assembly of the IAEA to oppose Eastern arguments. EC, BAC 059/1980-481.

———. 1958d. *Report of the Second General Assembly, Sept. 28 to Oct. 4, 1958.* EC, BAC 059/1980-481.

———. 1958e. *Report of the Second General Assembly, Oct. 4.* EC, BAC 059/1980-481.

———. 1959a (January 19). Memo on board of governors session in January. EC, BAC 059/1980-481.

———. 1959b (February 22). Note confidentielle de Federico Consolo à l'attention du Commissaire De Groote, Accords Euratom-US. JG, box 115.

———. 1959c (February 25). Note d'information du service juridique des Exécutifs Européens pour les membres de la Commission: Délimitation du domaine d'application du Traité Euratom—pacifique et militaire. EC, BAC 118/1986-51, JUR/10/1/59.

———. 1959d (June 19). Memo on French-US agreement, by the legal services of the Commission Euratom. EC, BAC 086/1982-72.

———. 1959e (June). Notes de Mr. Mercereau (Dir Cab Hirsh) prises au cours du voyage des Présidents aux US. EC, BAC 118/1986-1051, EUR/C/1791/59f.

———. 1959f. *Report of the Third General Assembly, from September 22 to October 3, 1959.* EC, BAC 059/1980-481.

———. 1960a (January). Memorandum from the joint US-Euratom working party of April 1958: "Nature of Western Control." JM, JMDS box 120.

———. 1960b (February 22). Criticism of Mr. Anderson of IAEA. EC, BAC 059/1980-481.

———. 1960c (March 8). Note des Services juridiques de la Commission sur Les Bilatéraux américains. EC, BAC 118/1986-51, EUR/C/3141/60f.

———. 1960d. *Report of the Fourth General Assembly, from September 20 to October 3, 1960.* EC, BAC 059/1980-481.

———. 1960e (October 9). Analyse du Rapport McKinney et Euratom, par la division des Relations Extérieures. JG, box 115; EC, EUR/C/3926/60f.

———. 1961 (June 17). The visit of President Hirsh in the US in June. EC, BAC 118/1986-1051, EUR/C/2215/61f.

———. 1962 (January 9). Mr. Le Président de la Haute Autorité, à l'attention de M. Wehrer, Président du groupe de travail des relations extérieures. EC, BAC 86/1982-69.

———. 1963a (February 4). Note to the permanent representatives by the Foreign Relations Services of the commission. EC, BAC 86/1982-69.

———. 1963b (February 12). Note to the permanent representatives by the Foreign Relations Services of the commission. EC, BAC 86/1982-69.

———. 1963c. *Report of the Seventh General Assembly, from September 20 to October 3, 1963.* EC, BAC 059/1980-481.

———. 1963d (November 17). Conclusion du Groupe des Questions Atomiques sur les Accords Bilatéraux Signés par les Etats Membres. EC, BAC 86/1982-1418.

———. 1964 (January 9). Conclusion du Groupe des Questions Atomiques sur les Accords Bilatéraux Signés par les Etats Membres. EC, BAC 86/1982-1418.

———. 1966a. *Report of the Tenth General Assembly, Sept. 1966.* EC, BAC 059/1980-481.

———. 1966b (November 9). Note of the European Commission by the Mission of Information on technico-economic aspects of nuclear energy, after a meeting with RAND Corporation economists. EC, BAC 59/1980-329.

———. 1966c (November 21). Note by Cancellario d'Alena, Foreign Relations Department of the commission, to the president of the commission. EC, BAC 59/1980-329.

———. 1967a (February 7). Notes à la Commission de Cancelario d'Alena sur les répercussions du contrôle dans le Traité et Notes de la Commission sur le projet de l'URSS d'article n.3 du Traité et sur l'aide-mémoire américain à ce sujet. JG, box 124.

———. 1967b. Extrait de *Welt am Sonntag.* EC, BAC 86/1982.

———. 1967c (February 27). Council of Permanent Representatives. EC, BAC 86/1982.

———. 1967d (February 28). Memo by Guazzuoli Marini at the meeting of the Euratom Commission. EC, BAC 86/1982.

———. 1967e (September 13). Memo to the Council of Ministers from the commission. JG, box 124.

———. 1967f (March 10). Memo to the staff on NPT remarks by Senator Pastore (JCAE). EC, BAC 86/1982.

———. 1967g (March 15). Memorandum by the commission on the visit to the commission by Mr. Foster. EC, EUR/C/1382/67f; JG, box 103.

———. 1967h (March 29). Project of response to the questions asked by the Committee of Permanent Representatives to the Council. EC, EUR/C/1581/67; JG, box 124.

———. 1967i (April 7). Project of response to the American memos of February 1, March 6, and April 3, 1967. JG, box 124.

———. 1967j (March 12). Memorandum of the meeting of the Council of Ministers of Euratom. EC, EUR/PV/R1/602/f/67; JG, box 112.

———. 1967k (June 22). Memorandum of F. Cancellario D'Alena, from the Foreign Relations Department of Euratom. EC, BAC 086/1982-29.

———. 1967l (September 10). Project of response to the questions asked by the Committee of Permanent Representatives to the Council. JG, box 124.

———. 1967m (October 6). Secret note by the Foreign Relations Service to the Secretariat. JG, box 124.

———. 1967n (October 9). Note on the American memo by the Foreign Relations Service. JG, box 124.

———. 1967o (October 10). Memo on council reaction to the commission. JG, box 124.

———. 1967p (December 17). Letter to Guéron by the Foreign Relations Service. JG, box 124.

———. 1971 (March 16). Memorandum sur les relations entre la Commission de l'Euratom et l'Agence Internationale de l'Energie Atomique (AIEA). EC, BAC 086/1982-228.

"Euratom Resists Inspection by US of Future Plants." 1958 (April 13). *New York Times.* JM, JMDS box 120.

Euratom Treaty. 1957. http://www.fissilematerials.org/ipfm/site_down/Euratom.pdf.

European Coal and Steel Community Treaty. 1951. http://mjp.univ-perp.fr/europe/1951 ceca3.htm.

European Court of Justice. 1964. Case 6/64, Flaminio Costa v. E.N.E.L. Reference for a preliminary ruling: Giudice conciliatore di Milano, Italy. http://eur-lex.europa.eu/ LexUriServ/LexUriServ.do?uri=CELEX:61964J0006:en:HTML.

———. 1971. Case 7/71, Commission v. France, ECR 1003. http://eur-lex.europa.eu/ LexUriServ/LexUriServ.do?uri=CELEX:61971J0007:EN:PDF.

———. 2005. Case C-61/03, Commission v. U.K., ECR I-2477. http://eur-lex.europa.eu/ LexUriServ/LexUriServ.do?uri=OJ:C:2005:132:0003:0004:EN:PDF.

———. 2006. Case C-65/04, Commission v. U.K. http://eur-lex.europa.eu/LexUriServ/ LexUriServ.do?uri=CELEX:62004J0065:EN:NOT.

European Defense Community Treaty. 1952. Paris. http://mjp.univ-perp.fr/europe/1952 ced.htm.

European Parliament. 1960 (November 22). Transcript of debates, p. 1589. EH, box 17.

———. 1962 (February). Discours de Pierre Chatenêt. EC, BAC 118/1986 #1453.

———. 1972 (July 7). Transcript of debates. *Journal officiel des communautés européennes*, 80–104. EC, BAC 86/1982.

European Press. 1967 (March 16). Strasbourg. JG, box 124.

Farley, Philip. 1956 (December 23). Memo to Dulles. MK, box 14.

Finletter, Thomas K. 1946 (March). "Timetable for World Government." *Atlantic Monthly.* GB, box 99.

Finney, John. 1959 (May 24). "US Hopes Revive on Euratom Plan." *New York Times.* EC, BAC 86/1982-48.

———. 1964 (December 19). "US Asks Industry to Avoid Helping France's A-Tests." *New York Times.* JG, box 24.

———. 1965 (February 12). "US Reappraising Its Policy of Atoms-for-Peace Program." *New York Times*. JG, box 204.

———. 1966a (October 25). "US Is Considering Polish-Czech Plan on Atom Controls." *New York Times*. JG, box 204.

———. 1966b (October 26). "Paris Resists Plan for European Atom Control." *New York Times*. JG, box 204.

———. 1966c (November 28). "US Seeks Curbs on Atom Plants." *New York Times*. JG, box 204.

Fischer, David. 2007 (September). "Nuclear Safeguards: The First Steps." *IAEA Bulletin* 49 (1). http://www.iaea.org/Publications/Magazines/Bulletin/Bu11491/pdfs/49103480711.pdf.

Franck, James, Donald J. Hughes, J. J. Nickson, Eugene Rabinowitch, Glenn T. Seaborg, J. C. Stearns, and Leo Szilard. 1945 (June 11). *Report of the Committee on Political and Social Problems, Manhattan Project*. University of Chicago, Metallurgical Laboratory. http://www.dannen.com/decision/franck.html.

Frankfurter, Felix. 1941 (November 14). Letter to Viscount Halifax. FF, box 85.

———. 1945 (May 6). Memorandum. JRO, box 34.

———. 1946 (May 8). Letter to Jean Monnet, with attached memorandum on judicial review of congressional action. FF, box 85.

Franklin, George. 1963 (June 27). Letter to Merchant. LM, box 10.

Gaillard, Félix. 1951 (November 13). *New York Times*. JG, box 113.

Giljssels, Jan. 1968. "Euratom et le projet de traité de non-prolifération des armes nucléaires sous l'angle du droit." *Les cahiers du droit de l'énergie atomique*. EC, JUR/CEEA/963/1/68; BAC 86/1982.

Goldschmidt, Bertrand. 1991. "Jules Guéron, l'aventure canadienne." In "Jules Guéron," edited by George Guéron and Maurice Guéron, 10–18. GS, box 292.

Gordon, Lincoln. 1958. "NATO and European Integration." Paper presented at the World Peace Conference in Paris, March 27–April 3, 1958. GB, box 99.

Groves, Leslie. 1946 (October 17). Letter to John M. Hancock. BB, box 56.

Guéron, Jules. 1957 (July). Note sur ma visite aux Etats-Unis. JG, box 130.

———. 1963a (January 24). Letter to Professor Sheinman. JG, box 130.

———. 1963b (September 4). Letter to Robert Schaetzel after their talks with the ambassador to the communities. JG, box 130.

———. 1965 (October 23). Note à Monsieur Nicolas Vichney sur L'Euratom et le Général. JG, box 104.

———. 1969 (August 21). "Euratom, un échec pour l'Europe." Interview with Francois de Closets in August. *Sciences et Avenir*. JG, box 119.

———. 1970. "Atomic Energy in Continental Western Europe." *Bulletin of the Atomic Scientists* 61 (June): 116.

———. 1973a (January 28). Letter to Henry Nau. JG, box 205.

———. 1973b (February 12). Letter to Dr. Donnelly. JG, box 205.

———. 1983 (January 3). Lettre à Renou, note sur le livre de Renou. JG, box 194.

———. 1984. Remarques sur le livre de Goldschmidt, L'aventure atomique. JG, box 194.

Hancock, John M. 1946 (November 21). Report to the staff. BB, box 56.

Harriman, Averell. 1962 (October 22). Letter to George Ball, titled "Memorandum on Kremlin Reactions." GB, box 39.

Heidenreich, Curt. 1967 (December 15). Letter to Jules Guéron. JG, box 124.

Helsinki Final Act. 1975 (August 1). "Final Declaration of the Conference on Security and Conference in Europe." http://en.wikisource.org/wiki/Helsinki_Final_Act.

Herter, Christian. 1958a (April 17). Letter to Lewis Strauss. JM, JMDS box 110.

———. 1958b (June 11). Memorandum to the president. JM, JMDS box 110.

Hindu. 1954 (April 9). http://www.hindu.com/2004/04/09/stories/2004040900010902 .htm.

Hirsh, Etienne. 1960 (May 4). Conversations confidentielles avec Mr. Guillaumat. EH, box 17.

———. 1961 (March 17). Notes prises par E. Hirsch durant son allocution avec le général de Gaulle à l'Elysée, de 3h à 3h40. EH, box 17.

———. 1962a. "Three into One Would Go." *European Atlantic Review*. EH, box 17.

———. 1962b (June 26). Notes. EH, box 46.

"How International?" 1961 (December 23). *Times* (London). MK, box 41.

International Atomic Energy Agency (IAEA). 1961. "The Agency's Safeguards." INFCIRC/26. Accessed November 14, 2013. www.iaea.org/Publications/Documents/Infcircs/ Others/infcirc26.pdf.

———. 1968. "The Agency's Safeguards System (1965, as Provisionally Extended in 1966 and 1968)." INFCIRC/26. Accessed November 14, 2013. www.iaea.org/Publications/ Documents/Infcircs/Others/inf66r2.shtml.

———. 1992. "Statement on Full-Scope Safeguards Adopted by the Adherents to the Nuclear Suppliers Guidelines." In INFCIRC405. Accessed November 14, 2013. http:// www.iaea.org/Publications/Documents/Infcircs/Others/inf405.shtml.

———. 2006. "Press Release." Accessed November 14, 2013. http://www.iaea.org/News Center/PressReleases/2006/prn200605.html.

———. 2007. "Guidelines for Nuclear Transfers." In INFCIRC/254 parts I and II. Accessed November 14, 2013. http://www.un.org/sc/committees/1737/pdf/INFCIRC_254 _Rev.9_Part1.pdf.

Joint Plan of Action. 2013 (November 24). Full text of the agreement between the Republic of Iran and the P5+1. Accessed December 2, 2013. http://mrzine.monthlyreview .org/2013/iran241113.html.

Kennan, George. 1946. "Telegram Sent to the Secretary of State." Accessed November 8, 2013. http://www2.gwu.edu/~nsarchiv/coldwar/documents/episode-1/kennan.htm.

———. 1951 (September). Summary of the differences between his views and those of the State Department. GK, box 24.

Kennedy, John F. 1961 (December 30). Letter to de Gaulle. GB, box 46.

———. 1963 (June 10). "Commencement Address at American University in Washington." http://www.ratical.org/co-globalize/JFK061063.html.

Killian, James. 1955 (February 14). "Meeting the Threat of Surprise Attack." PN, box 29.

Kissinger, Henry A. 1959 (February 17). "The Impact of Technological Progress in Armaments on Strategy and Diplomacy." Paper presented at the Bilderberg Conference. PN, box 30.

———. 1961 (February 2). "For an Atlantic Confederacy." *Reporter*. MK, box 19.

———. 1963 (March). "NATO's Nuclear Dilemma." *Reporter*, 32–33. MK, box 19.

Knoll, Denys W. 1946 (July 1). Memorandum for the secretary, Joint Chiefs of Staff, "Comparison of the US and Soviet Proposals." BB, box 52.

Knorr, Klaus. 1956 (May 16). *Euratom and American Policy: A Report*. Center of International Studies, Princeton University, Stokes Library.

Knox, W. E. 1958 (April 2). Letter to Admiral Strauss. JM, JMDS box 110.

Kohnstamm, Max. 1957a (January 20). Note sur le régime de contrôle et les pouvoirs de la Commission en matière d'exportation et de propriété des matières fissiles en préparation de la tournée des Trois Sages. EC, CEAB1–79/DOC539/57f.

———. 1957b (February). Compte-rendu des réunions du comite des sages. MK, box 7.

———. 1957c (February). Memorandum on background of Euratom negotiations in Brussels. JM, JMDS box 102.

———. 1957d (February 10). Lettre à Jean Monnet. MK, box 7.

———. 1957e (July 26). Memorandum. MK, box 46.

———. 1957f (October 23). Europe and Atoms for Power. Council on Foreign Relations, Study Group on Western European Integration. MK, box 2.

———. 1958a (April). Memo from the joint US-Euratom working party on the nature of western control. JM, JMDS box 120.

———. 1958b (May 7). Letter to Admiral Strauss. JM, JMDS box 120.

———. 1958c (June 12). Memorandum of understanding. JM, JMDS box 110.

———. 1961 (March 13). Note sur la situation après la Conférence des Six. MK, box 19.

———. 1963a (November 19). Letter to Monnet. MK, box 25.

———. 1963b (November 27). Letter to Monnet. MK, box 25.

———. 1963c (December 2). Conversation avec George Ball, et son assistant, George Springsteen, au Plaza Athénées. MK, box 41.

———. 1963d (December 18). Conversation with Robert Schaetzel. MK, box 25.

———. 1964a (January 27). Letter to Robert Schaetzel, deputy assistant secretary, European affairs, State Department. MK, box 26.

———. 1964b (February 11). Conversation with P. Farley. MK, box 26.

———. 1964c (March 24). Dinner at the Council on Foreign Relations. MK, box 27.

———. 1964d (April 27). Letter to Robert Schaetzel. MK, box 40.

———. 1964e (July 13). Conversation with Robert Bowie. MK, box 40.

———. 1964f (July 22). Conversations avec Mr. Pangenhardt. MK, box 40.

———. 1964g (September 7). La M.L.F. et les forces nucléaires nationales. MK, box 41.

———. 1964h (September 8). Dénomination de la MLF. MK, box 41.

———. 1964i (September 8). Aide mémoire relatif à la procédure de décision dans la MLF. MK, box 41.

———. 1964j (September 10). Question relatives aux aspects politiques de la MLF. MK, box 41.

———. 1964k (September 13). Talk with Robert Schaetzel in Brussels. MK, box 41.

———. 1964l (October 10). Main political provisions of the MLF. MK, box 41.

———. 1964m (October 14). Situation actuelle de la MLF et nécessité de la transformer. MK, box 41.

———. 1964n (October 29). Mémorandum sur le processus d'évolution des rapports des Etats-Unis et de l'Europe dans les question nucléaires (MLF). MK, box 41.

———. 1964o (December 12). Letter to Mr. Henry Owen. MK, box 41.

———. 1964p (December 14). Conversations with Cattani and Helmont. MK, box 25.

———. 1964q (December 18). Conversation with David Bruce in London. MK, box 41.

———. 1965a (January 6). Conversation with Barzel. MK, box 42.

———. 1965b (January 6). Conversation with McGhee. MK, box 42.

———. 1965c (June 19). Conversation with Mr. Robert Kleiman. MK, box 43.

———. 1965d (August 12). Co-ownership or no co-ownership. MK, box 43.

———. 1966a (June 10). Memo of conversations. MK, box 45.

———. 1966b (December 21). Letter to Henry Owen. MK, box 45.

———. 1967a (January 3). Memo of conversation to JM, MK, Brandt. MK, box 46.

———. 1967b (January 9). Memo of conversation JM, MK, Wehner, Brandt. MK, box 46.

———. 1967c (January 19). Memo of conversation Kramish–Kohnstamm. MK, box 46.

———. 1967d (January 30). Memo of conversation with Eugene Rostow. MK, box 46.

———. 1967e (January 30). Memo for the record, sent to Gene Rostow. MK, box 46.

———. 1967f (March 20). Letter to Jean Monnet. MK, box 46.

———. 1967g (July 25). Letter to McCloy. Art. Cit. MK, box 46.

Kramish, Arnold. 1957 (November 18). "Euratom, First Phase: Financial Evaluation of Costs." MK, box 14.

———. 1983 (April 14). Letter to Glenn Seaborg. GS, box 341.

Krief, Claude. 1964 (May 21). "L'avenir de l'Euratom." *L'express*. JG, box 104.

Lilienthal, David. 1963c (November 26). Letter to Jacob Viner, with his notes on Jacob Viner's presentation during the Chicago Conference of 1945. JV, box 13.

MAEF (Ministère des Affaires Etrangères Français). 1955a (January 15). Note de Mr. Coignard, relative aux activités allemandes en matière de réarmement. Haut Commissariat de la République Française en Allemagne. Commissaire français à l'Office militaire de sécurité. Coblence, 100/HC/OMS/COM/S Olivier Wormser 28.

———. 1955b (April 14). Note. MAEF 000611.

———. 1955c (April 25). Compte rendu des réunions du 22 et 25 avril 1955 au Ministère des Affaires étrangères sous la direction de M. Massigli. MAEF 000611.

———. 1955d (April 26). *Rapport de Bruxelles*. MAEF 000611.

———. 1955e (November 15). Télégramme, de Christian De Margerie. MAEF 000111.

———. 1956a (February 13). Lettre de Louis Joxe, à Christian Pineau, Ministre des Affaires Etrangères. MAEF 000111.

———. 1956b (April 16). *Rapport des Experts du Comité Spaak*. MAE120/56eve ou CM3/NEGOC.0091/ac-a.

———. 1956c (October 21). Proposition de la délégation française a la conférence des Six au Quai d'Orsay en Octobre sur les utilisations militaires de l'énergie atomique. MAEF 000613.

———. 1956d (November 13). Projet de procès verbal, de la conférence des affaires étrangères des Etats membres de la CECA des 20 et 21 octobre 1956. MAE460f/56mts ou CM3/NEGOC.0095/ab-a.

———. 1956e (December 13). Conférence intergouvernementale pour Euratom. "Groupe de l'Euratom: Projet de procès verbal," MAEF822f/56gd MAEF Traité de Rome 608.

———. 1957a (February 26). Note de Couve de Murville. MAEF 000019–21.

———. 1957b (November 19). Entretiens Généraux. Communiqué à Ambassade de Washington, questions militaires, de la part de Pineau. MAEF 000019–21.

———. 1957c (November 25). Protocole secret entre les Ministres Français, Allemand, Italien de la défense. MAEF 000019–21.

———. 1957d (November 19). Communiqué, à Ambassade de Washington, questions militaires de la part de Pineau. MAEF 000019–21.

———. 1957e (November 26). Communiqué, sur la rencontre avec Macmillan, pour le Président Pineau. MAEF 19–21.

———. 1958a. Entretiens Généraux. Compte-rendu de l'entretien Pineau, Dulles, Lloyd, Mars, Manille. MAEF 000019–21.

———. 1958b (March 28). Entretiens Généraux, entretien à Bonn avec Heinrich Von Brentano. MAEF 000019–21.

———. 1958c (June 30). Entretiens avec Harold Macmillan, Selwyn Lloyd, et Général de Gaulle, Couve, Joxe, Pompidou, à Paris. MAEF 000019–21.

———. 1959a (January 15). Compte-rendu sommaire de l'entretien de M. le Président de la République et de M. Gaitskell. Secrétariat général 1956–66, vol. 7.

———. 1959b (January 27). Note très confidentielle pour le secrétaire général. Secrétariat général 1956–66, vol. 7.

———. 1959c (March 27). Note très confidentielle du Secrétaire Général. Secrétariat général 1956–66, vol. 7.

———. 1959d (March 28). Note de la Présidence de la république, pour le ministre des affaires étrangères. Secrétariat général 1956–66, vol. 7.

———. 1959e (March 31). Entretien: ministre des armées—M. Gates. Secrétariat général, entretiens et messages, vol. 7.

———. 1959f (April 21). Télégramme à l'arrivée, réservé secret. Secrétariat général, entretiens et messages, 1956–66, vol. 7.

———. 1959g (April 29). Directive atomique. Secrétariat général, entretiens et messages, 1956–66, vol. 7.

———. 1959h (September 1). Notes pour l'ambassadeur. Secrétariat général, entretiens et messages, 1956–66, vol. 7.

———. 1959i (March 31). Note pour le Général Gelée. Secrétariat général, entretiens et messages, 1956–66, vol. 7.

———. 1961a (May 17). Direction politique, Service des Affaires atomiques: Secret, loi MacMahon. Olivier Wormser, vol. 102.

———. 1961b (May 23). Observations Secrètes du Service des Pactes sur les suggestions américaines. Direction Politique, Olivier Wormser, vol. 102.

———. 1962a (October 31). Lettre de Mr. Palewski concernant l'adhésion de la GB à Euratom. Direction Politique, service des affaires atomiques. Olivier Wormser, vol. 50; MAEF 120f/56.

———. 1962b (November 7). Secret Bordereau collectif N° 323 de la direction des affaires politique Europe, direction d'Europe Occidentale. Secrétariat général, entretiens et messages, 1956–66, vol. 18.

———. 1962c (December 11). Note de la direction politique, service des affaires atomiques. Olivier Wormser, vol. 50; MAEF 120f/56.

———. 1963a (January 4). Audience accordée par le général de Gaulle à monsieur Charles Bohlen. Secrétariat général, entretiens et messages, 1956–66, vol. 18.

———. 1963b (January 10). Entretien entre M. Couve de Murville et M. George Ball au Ministère des Affaires Etrangères. Secrétariat général, entretiens et messages, 1956–66, vol. 18.

———. 1963c (January 14). Compte rendu, traduction: Le Chancelier fédéral a reçu G. Ball. Secrétariat général, entretiens et messages, 1956–66, vol. 18.

———. 1963d (January 21). Tête à tête de Gaulle et Adenauer. Secrétariat général, entretiens et messages, 1956–66, vol. 18.

———. 1963e (April 23). Entretien entre M. Rusk et M. Couve de Murville le dimanche 7 avril, à 17 heures. Secrétariat général, entretiens et messages, 1956–66, vol. 18.

———. 1963f (April 23). Entretien entre M. Couve de Murville et Lord Home. Secrétariat général, entretiens et messages, 1956–66, vol. 18.

———. 1963g (June 27). Entretien entre le président des Etats-Unis et le Ministre des Affaires Etrangères, en date du 25 mai 1963, à Washington. Secrétariat général, entretiens et messages, 1956–66, vol. 18.

———. 1964 (May 12). Entretien tripartite de Couve, Butler et Dean Rusk. MAEF 019–21.

Marshall, George. 1947 (June 5). Commencement speech. Harvard University, Cambridge, MA. http://www.oecd.org/document/10/0,3343,en_2649_201185_1876938_1_1_1_1,00.html.

Mayer, René. 1956 (May). Presentation before the Council on Foreign Relations. MK, box 14.

McCloy, John. 1965a (June 11). Letter to George Ball, with attached memo on conversation Kissinger–de La Grandville. GB, box 68.

———. 1965b (December 8). Letter to George Ball, with attached memo on conversation McCloy–Erhard in Bonn, December 6, 1965. GB, box 68.

———. 1981 (July 15). Interview with Philip Crowl. JM, JMDS box 180.

McNamara, Robert. 1962 (July). "Speech at the University of Michigan." *Department of State Bulletin.*

———. 1965 (May 31). Statement relating to improvement of NATO consultation. MK, box 43.

Merchant, Livingston. 1952 (September 1). Letter to Averell Harriman. LM, box 1.

———. 1960 (January 22). "The Missile Gap." *New York Times*, 1. LM, box 9.

———. 1963a (February 14). Conversation with Robert Bowie. LM, box 10.

———. 1963b (n.d.). Ambassador Merchant's notes. LM, box 10.

———. 1963c (March 22). Notes for meeting with president. LM, box 10.

———. 1963d (April 29). Overall thoughts on the MLF en route from Ankara to Naples. LM, box 10.

———. 1963e (June 11). Excerpts from statement by Secretary Gates. LM, box 10.

———. 1963f (November 7). Notes. LM, box 10.

———. 1964a (March 13). Interview with Philip Crowl. LM, box 12.

———. 1964b (December 3). Notes. LM, box 11.

———. 1965 (Spring). Interview by Philander Claxton for the John F. Kennedy Library. LM, box 13.

Michel, Serge. 2013 (November 25). "Nucléaire Iranien: L'accord répond à toutes les attentes occidentales." *Le Monde.* Accessed November 25, 2013. http://abonnes .lemonde.fr/proche-orient/article/2013/11/25/nucleaire-iranien-l-accord-repond-a -toutes-les-attentes-occidentales_3519944_3218.html.

Ministère Belge des Affaires Etrangères. 1957 (March 30). "Coopération politique euro- péenne—Questions diverses. Adhésion de la Grande-Bretagne aux Communautés eu- ropéennes 1968." Accessed November 10, 2013. http://www.ena.lu/mce.cfm.

Monnet, Jean. 1943 (February 3). Letter to Felix Frankfurter, with attached memo on proposed course of action. FF, box 85.

———. 1952 (December 31). Letter to John McCloy. JFD, box 62.

———. 1956 (January 19). Letter to John Foster Dulles. JM, JMAS box 15.

———. 1961 (March 2). Letter to Kohnstamm. MK, box 41.

———. 1963a (January 23). Address by Monnet before the US president, for the Freedom Award ceremony. JM, JMAS box 53.

———. 1963b (July 17). Letter to Eisenhower. MK, box 24.

———. 1964a (November 9). Letter to Max Kohnstamm. MK, box 41.

———. 1964b (December 19). Jean. Conversation JM–Cattani. JM, JMDS box 223.

———. 1965a (June 4). Letter to Max Kohnstamm. MK, box 43.

———. 1965b (July). Letter to Felix Frankfurter, with joint declaration by the AC for the USofE, June 1, 1964. JM, JMAS box 53.

———. 1965c (September 9). Interview. MK, box 43.

———. 1965d (December 14). Letter to Ludwig Erhard. MK, box 43.

———. 1966a (December 25). Letter to Willy Brandt. MK, box 46.

———. 1966b (December 25). Memo of conversation to JM, MK, Brandt, January 3, 1967. MK, box 46.

———. 1967a (February 3). Letter to Willy Brandt. MK, box 46.

———. 1967b (February 14). Letter to Willy Brandt. MK, box 46.

———. 1967c (February 14). Letter to Eugene Rostow. MK, box 46.

Neustadt, Richard. 1983 (June 28). Interview with General Maxwell Taylor. GB, box 40.

"The New Alliance." 1964 (December 3). *Times* (London). MK, box 26.

Nitze, Paul. 1956 (September 24). Letter to Charles Bohlen. PN, box 18.

———. 1959 (February 12). Letter to John F. Kennedy. PN, box 29.

———. 1977 (January 20). Memorandum of conversation. PN, box 31.

———. 1978 (January 10). Letter to Thomas Morris. PN, box 34.

———. 1986 (March 10). "Interview for *War and Peace in the Nuclear Age*." http://openvault.wgbh.org/wapina/barcode49036nitze1_3/index.html.

———. 1987 (January 21). Letter to James Hershberg. PN, box 21.

NPT Review Conference. 1995. "Decision 2: Principles and Objectives for Nuclear Nonproliferation and Disarmament." Accessed November 14, 2013. http://www.un.org/disarmament/WMD/Nuclear/1995-NPT/pdf/NPT_CONF199501.pdf.

Nuclear Planning Group. 1967 (April 7). "Final Communiqué." http://www.nato.int/docu/comm/49-95/c670406a.htm.

Obussier, Félix. 1968 (January 18). "Incidences possibles du projet de Traité de Non-prolifération sur le traité d'Euratom." Presentation to the Institut de droit international, Gottingen University. EUR/C/1124/68f. JG, box 112.

Oliphant, Marc L. 1941 (September 25). Memorandum. GS, box 313.

Oppenheimer, J. Robert. 1945 (December 11). Letter to Vannevar Bush. JRO, box 23.

———. 1946a (February 2). Letter to David Lilienthal. JRO, box 46.

———. 1946b (May 3). Letter to Harry Truman. JRO, box 73.

———. 1946c (May 19). Letter to Bernard Baruch. JRO, box 19.

———. 1953a (February 17). "Atomic Weapons and American Policy." Discourse at the Council on Foreign Relations. VB, box 89.

———. 1953b. "Atomic Weapons and American Foreign Policy." *Foreign Affairs*, 529.

———. 1955 (April 12). Letter to George Kennan. JRO, box 43.

Owen, Henry. 1966 (May 26). Letter to George Ball, with attached chronology concerning MLF proposals. GB, box 74.

Perrin, Francis. 1956 (July 5). Exposé sur l'Euratom fait à la tribune de l'Assemblée nationale. EC, BAC 118/1986-1452.

Peyrefitte, Alain. 1960 (August 29). Note très secrète anonyme sur la négociation européenne et les conditions de son succès. JM, JMDS box 223.

"The Prospects of Euratom." 1958 (June 8). *New York Times*. JM, JMDS box 120.

Pryor, John. 1966 (March 9). "EEC Stressing Nuclear Safeguards." *Journal of Commerce* 2. JG, box 204.

Quebec Agreement. 1943 (August 19). "Articles of Agreement Governing Collaboration between the Authorities of the U.S.A. and the U.K. in the Matter of Tube Alloys." http://www.radiochemistry.org/history/manhattan/03_quebec.shtml.

Rabi, Isidor. 1946 (February 16). *New York Times*. BB, box 112.

Radoux, Lucien. 1952 (July). Lettre à Bob Bowie et Carl Friedrich. FD, box 89.

Report to Honorable John F. Kennedy. 1960 (November). GB, box 89.

Rostow, Eugene. 1962a (June 11). Letter to Jean Monnet. GB, box 70.

———. 1962b (June 19). Letter to George Ball. GB, box 83.

———. 1964a (May 4). Letter to George Ball. GB, box 83.

———. 1964b (August 5). Letter to George Ball, with attached memorandum. GB, box 83.

———. 1964c (November 20). Letter to George Ball, with attached address to the American Society for Friendship with Switzerland. GB, box 83.

———. 1973 (February 17). Letter to the ad hoc Steering Committee to organize American participation in the Amsterdam conference of March 26–28, 1973. GB, box 43.

Rostow, Walt. 1962 (October 26). Letter to Dean Rusk and George Ball about alliance missiles. GB, box 39.

Rusk, Dean. 1963 (February 2). Memorandum to the president on "Possible Arrangements in Nuclear Weapons Field." GB, box 46.

Rusk, Dean, Robert McNamara, George Ball, Roswell Gilpatric, Theodore Sorensen, and McGeorge Bundy. 1982 (September 7). Draft statement on the twentieth anniversary of the Cuban missile crisis. GB, box 28.

"Russia Says Bikini Test Banished Faith in US." 1946 (July 4). *New York Times*. JRO, box 19.

Schaetzel, Robert. 1957a (November 14). Letter to Max Kohnstamm. ECA. MK, box 14.

———. 1957b (November 19). Letter to Max Kohnstamm. ECA. MK, box 14.

———. 1957c (December 17). Letter to Max Kohnstamm. ECA. MK, box 14.

———. 1958a (January). Memo to Max Kohnstamm. JM, JMDS box 120.

———. 1958b (January 28). Letter to Max Kohnstamm. JM, JMDS box 120.

———. 1958c (June). Letter to Jean Monnet, with attached to memo on Macmillan talks, June 9–11, 1958. JM, JMDS box 110.

———. 1963 (October 16). Letter to Max Kohnstamm. MK, box 25.

———. 1964 (January 21). Letter to Max Kohnstamm. MK, box 260.

———. 1967 (October 6). Memorandum to Commissioner Martino. JG, box 124.

———. 1974 (April 13). Letter to George Ball, with attached memo on Western Europe to be sent to the 1974 Democratic candidates and Governor Carter. GB, box 30.

Schlesinger, Arthur. 1963 (February 12). Memorandum to George Ball. GB, box 46.

Schmidt, Helmut. 1963 (July 5). Letter to Max Kohnstamm. MK, box 24.

Seaborg, Glenn. 1962 (September 18). Letter to Mr. Chatenêt. EC, BAC 118/1986-1051, EUR/C/5356/62f.

———. 1967 (June 26). "Symposium on Safeguards Research and Development at Argonne." EC, BAC 059/1980-481.

Shaw, Edwin. 1979. *The Three Virtues: A History of the Dragon Project, 1959–1976*. JG, box 218.

Shotwell, James T. 1946a (April 13). *Report of the Meeting of the Committee on Atomic Energy*. Carnegie Endowment for International Peace. BB, box 112.

———. 1946b (May 8). Letter to Dean Acheson. BB, box 112.

———. 1946c (May 11). *Report of the Meeting of the Committee on Atomic Energy*. Carnegie Endowment for International Peace. BB, box 112.

Smith, Gerard. 1955 (December 8). "Telegram Sent to Livingston Merchant on December 8." *Foreign Relations of the United States*, 6:1.

———. 1965 (October 13). "Interview with Philip Crowl." JFD Oral History Project.

Spaak, Paul-Henri. 1953 (March 10). Discours devant le Parlement Européen. JG, 103.

Stabler, Elizabeth. 1964 (December 7). "The MLF: Background and Analysis of Pros and Cons." 75 pp. LM, box 10.

State Department. 1955a (June 8). Telegram to Brussels. JM, JMDS box 99.

———. 1955b (March 4). Telegram to embassy in Paris. JM, JMDS box 98.

———. 1955c (November 8). Telegram from Strasbourg. JM, JMDS box 99.

———. 1956a (June 20). Telegram from London. JM, JMDS box 99.

———. 1956b (November 28). Telegram from Brussels. JM, JMDS box 99.

———. 1961 (May 22). Background paper on US-UK-French consultation. GB, box 46.

———. 1962 (October 26). Telegram to Ambassador Finletter. GB, box 39.

———. 2004a (November 4). "NSSP Phase 1: Reviewing Achievements and Pending Issues." Cable from New Delhi. http://wikileaks.org/cable/2004/11/04NEWDELHI7013.html.

———. 2004b (November 11). "IAEA DG on India, Iran and Nonproliferation." Cable from New Delhi. http://wikileaks.org/cable/2004/11/04NEWDELHI7380.html.

———. 2005a (January 11). "MEA Warns of Nuclear Impasse in NSSP." Cable from New Delhi. http://wikileaks.org/cable/2005/01/05NEWDELHI551.html.

———. 2005b (May 5). "Assessing of India's Export Control Legislation." Cable from New Delhi. http://wikileaks.org/cable/2005/05/05NEWDELHI3603.html.

———. 2005c (June 16). "Get NSSP Out of the Way, the Indian Way." Cable from New Delhi. http://wikileaks.org/cable/2005/06/05NEWDELHI4690.html/cable/2005/05/05NEWDELHI3603.html.

———. 2005d (June 21). "Scenesetter for Indian Defense Minister Visit to the U.S." Cable from New Delhi. http://wikileaks.org/cable/2005/06/05NEWDELHI4721.html.

———. 2005e. "U.S.-India Nonproliferation Dialogue." Cable from New Delhi. http://wikileaks.org/cable/2005/06/05NEWDELHI4961.html.

———. 2008a (July 21). "Pakistani Reaction to the India-IAEA Safeguards Agreement." Cable from Islamabad. http://wikileaks.org/cable/2008/07/08ISLAMABAD2457.html.

———. 2008b (July 24). "Pakistan Will Not Impede the IAEA-India Safeguards Agreement." Cable from Islamabad. http://wikileaks.org/cable/2008/07/08ISLAMABAD2514.html.

———. 2009a (March 18). "Saving the F-16 Program." Cable from Islamabad. http://wikileaks.org/cable/2009/03/09ISLAMABAD586.html.

———. 2009b (April 2). "Constraints on Nonproliferation Cooperation with Pakistan." Cable from Islamabad. http://wikileaks.org/cable/2009/04/09ISLAMABAD690.html.

———. 2009c (May 27). "Nuclear Suppliers Group Outreach to Israel." Cable from Tel Aviv. http://wikileaks.org/cable/2009/05/09TELAVIV1153.html.

———. 2009d (July 17). "A. Q. Khan Defends Pakistan's Nuclear Weapons." Cable from Islamabad. http://wikileaks.org/cable/2009/07/09ISLAMABAD1607.html.

———. 2009e (September 14). "Response to Egyptian Meeting Request with Egyptians on NPT/IAEA/Middle East Issues." Cable from Tel Aviv. http://wikileaks.org/cable/2009/09/09TELAVIV2020.html.

———. 2009f (October 8). "Pakistan Welcomes Progress on Iran Issue." Cable from Islamabad. http://wikileaks.org/cable/2009/10/09ISLAMABAD2431.html.

———. 2009g (November 24). "Pakistani Views on Fissile Material Cutoff Treaty." Cable from Islamabad. http://wikileaks.org/cable/2009/11/09ISLAMABAD2840.html.

State Department, Board of Consultants. 1946 (March 16). *A Report on the International Control of Atomic Energy.* BB, box 112.

Stimson, Henry L. 1945 (September 11). Letter to Harry Truman. JRO, box 34.

Stone, Shepard. 1982 (July 23). Interview. JM, JMDS box 58.

Treaty of Peace between the Hashemite Kingdom of Jordan and the State of Israel. 1994. Accessed November 14, 2013. http://www.kinghussein.gov.jo/peacetreaty.html.

Treaty on the Final Settlement with Respect to Germany. 1990 (September 12). http://en.wikisource.org/wiki/Treaty_on_the_Final_Settlement_with_Respect_to_Germany#Article_3.

Treaty on the Non-proliferation of Nuclear Weapons (NPT). 1968. United Nations website. Accessed November 2, 2013. http://www.un.org/en/conf/npt/2010/npttext.shtml.

Truman, Harry S. 1945 (August 9). "Radio Report to the American People on the Conference in Potsdam on August 9." Accessed November 8, 2013. http://www.presidency.ucsb.edu/ws/index.php?pid=12165.

Tuthill, John. 1964 (January 21). Letter to George Ball, with memorandum of conversation between Monnet and Tuthill on January 17, 1964. GB, box 70.

United Nations. 1998. "Security Council Condemns Nuclear Tests by India and Pakistan." Accessed November 14, 2013. http://www.un.org/News/Press/docs/1998/sc6528.doc.htm.

United World Federalists. 1947 (November). "Beliefs, Purposes and Policies." GB, box 99.

"U.S. Sets Heart on Polaris Ships." 1963 (March 14). *Guardian*. MK, box 41.

Van Helmont, Jacques. 1964a (June 19). Conversation avec Phil Farley, Jacques Van Helmont. Destinataires, Monnet, Kohnstamm. MK, box 40.

———. 1964b (July 15). Note sur l'historique de l'Alliance atlantique. MK, box 40.

———. 1964c (July 17). Conversation with Mr. Finletter and Von Pagenhart. MK, box 40.

———. 1964d (July 25). Article 2 of the draft treaty, letter to Jean Monnet. MK, box 40.

———. 1964e (September 2). Letter to Monnet. MK, box 41.

———. 1964f (September 14). Memorandum, VH/dz. MK, box 41.

———. 1964g (September 15). Conversation avec M. Finletter, Schaetzel, Bowie, Farley à Londres. MK, box 41.

———. 1964h (September 18). Memorandum. MK, box 41.

———. 1964i (September 27). Memo sur le problème nucléaire. MK, box 43.

———. 1964j (October 10). Conversation JM–Phil Farley. VH/cm. MK, box 41.

———. 1964k (October 23). Conversation avec M. Finletter le 23 octobre. VH/cm, 23/10/1964. MK, box 41.

———. 1964l (October 24). Aide mémoire sur la position italienne. VH/dz. MK, box 41.

———. 1964m (October 24). Memorandum. MK, box 41.

———. 1964n (October 26). Conversations with Cattani. VH/cm. MK, box 41.

———. 1964o (November 11). Note à l'attention de M. Monnet. VH/cm. MK, box 41.

———. 1964p (December 19). Conversation JM–Cattani. JM, JMDS box 223.

———. 1964q (December 21). Entretiens JM–Dillon, le 16 dec. 1964. JM, JMDS box 223.

———. 1964r (December 21). La situation vue à Washington, le 12 déc. JM, JMDS box 223.

———. 1964s (December 21). Note à l'attention de Mr. Monnet, réflexions sur la situation au 21 décembre 1964. JM, JMDS box 223.

———. 1964t. "Existing Arrangements for the International Control of Warlike Material—Euratom." *Disarmament and Arms Control* 1 (2): 43–58. JM, JMDS box 223.

———. 1965 (September 29). Memo sur le problème nucléaire et NATO. MK, box 43.

Vichney, Nicolas. 1965 (May 7). "Les négociations sur la livraison d'uranium canadien à la France se heurtent à de sérieuses difficultés." *Le Monde*. JG, box 225.

———. 1971a (March 13). "Un Pierrelatte pacifique et européen?" *Le Monde*. JG, box 225.

———. 1971b (December 12). "Pierrelatte cherche des clients." *Le Monde*. JG, box 225.

———. 1973 (November 6). "L'aggravation de la bataille du pétrole." *Le Monde*. JG, box 225.

Vondeling, M. 1964 (January 20). Letter to Monnet. MK, box 26.

Von Hassel, Kai-Uwe. 1963 (June). Letter to Kohnstamm. MK, box 24.

"Weary Titan." 1963 (March 23). *Economist*. JG, box 122.

West European Union Paris Agreement. 1954 (October 23). http://www.weu.int/Treaty .htm.

Williams, J. D. 1946 (August 22). Letter to Jacob Viner. JV, box 9.

Wilson, Woodrow. 1918. "President Wilson's Fourteen Points." World War I Document Archive, 1918 Documents. Accessed November 2, 2013. http://wwi.lib.byu.edu/index .php/President_Wilson%27s_Fourteen_Points.

York, Herbert. 1988 (June 29). "Interview with Martin Collins." http://www.nasm.si.edu/ research/dsh/TRANSCPT/YORK1.HTM.

SECONDARY SOURCES

Abbott, Kenneth, and Duncan Snidal. 2001. "Hard and Soft Law in International Governance." *International Organization* 54 (3): 421–56.

Abraham, Itty. 1998. *The Making of the Indian Bomb: Science, Secrecy and the Post-colonial State*. New York: Zed Books.

———. 2006. "The Ambivalence of Nuclear Histories." *Osiris* 21: 49–65.

Acheson, Dean. 1969. *Present at the Creation: My Years in the State Department*. New York: Norton.

Acheson, Dean, and McGeorge Bundy. 1952. *The Pattern of Responsibility*. Boston: Houghton Mifflin.

Adler, Emanuel, ed. 1992. "The Emergence of Cooperation: National Epistemic Communities and the International Evolution of the Idea of Nuclear Arms Control." *International Organization* 46 (1): 101–45.

Adler, Emanuel, and Peter Haas. 1992. "Conclusion: Epistemic Communities, World Order, and the Creation of a Reflective Research Program." *International Organization* 46 (1): 367–90.

Albright, David, and Corey Hinderstein. 2005. "Unraveling the A. Q. Kahn Network and Future Proliferation Networks." *Washington Quarterly* 28 (Summer): 111–28.

Allison, Graham T. 1971. *Essence of Decision: Explaining the Cuban Missile Crisis*. 2nd ed. New York: Longman.

Alter, Karen. 2001. *Establishing the Supremacy of European Law: The Making of an International Rule of Law in Europe*. Oxford: Oxford University Press.

Alter, Karen, and Sophie Meunier. 2009 (March). "The Politics of Regime Complexity." *Perspectives on Politics* 7 (1): 13–24.

Alterman, Eric. 2004. *When Presidents Lie: A History of Official Deception and Its Consequences*. New York: Viking.

Amadae, S. M. 2003. *Rationalizing Capitalist Democracy: The Cold War Origins of Rational Choice Liberalism*. Chicago: University of Chicago Press.

Anderson, Carol. 2003. *Eyes Off the Prize: The United Nations and the African American Struggle for Human Rights, 1944–55*. Cambridge: Cambridge University Press.

Arendt, Hannah. 1951. *Imperialism: The Origins of Totalitarianism*, vol. 2. New York: Harcourt.

———. 1963. *On Revolution*. New York: Viking Press.

———. 1971. "Lying in Politics: Reflections on the Pentagon Papers." *New York Review of Books*. http://www.nybooks.com/articles/archives/1971/nov/18/lying-in-politics -reflections-on-the-pentagon-pape/?page=1.

Aron, Raymond, and Daniel Lerner, eds. 1956. *La querelle de la CED: Essais d'analyse sociologique*. Paris: Armand Collin.

Barbier, Colette. 1994a. "Les négociations franco-germano-italiennes en vue de l'établissement d'une coopération militaire nucléaire au cours des années 1956–58." *Revue d'histoire diplomatique*, 1–2.

———. 1994b. "La force multilatérale." In *La France et l'atome: Etudes d'histoire nucléaire*, edited by Maurice Vaïsse, 163–219. Brussels: Bruylant.

Barnett, Michael N. 1998. *Dialogues in Arab Politics: Negotiations in Regional Order*. New York: Columbia University Press.

Ben Dor, Gabriel, and David Dewitt. 1994. "Confidence Building Measures in the Middle East." In *Confidence Building Measures in the Middle East*, edited by Gabriel Ben Dor and David Dewitt, 3–32. Boulder, CO: Westview Press.

Benvenisti, Eyal, and George Downs. 2007. "The Empire's New Clothes: Political Economy and the Fragmentation of International Law." *Stanford Law Review* 60 (2): 595–632.

Bernstein, Baron J. 1974. "The Quest for Security: American Foreign Policy and International Control of Atomic Energy, 1942–1946." *Journal of American History* 60 (4): 1003–44.

———. 1980. "The Cuban Missile Crisis: Trading the Jupiters in Turkey?" *Political Science Quarterly* 95: 97–125.

Bill, James. 1997. *George Ball: Behind the Curtains*. New Haven, CT: Yale University Press.

Bird, Kai. 1992. *The Chairman: John J. McCloy, the Making of the American Establishment*. New York: Simon and Schuster.

———. 1998. *The Color of Truth: McGeorge Bundy and William Bundy, Brothers in Arms*. New York: Touchstone.

Bird, Kai, and Martin Sherwin. 2006. *American Prometheus: The Triumph and Tragedy of J. Robert Oppenheimer*. New York: Random House.

Blix, Hans. 2004. *Disarming Iraq: The Search for Weapons of Mass Destruction*. New York: Pantheon.

Block-Lieb, Susan, and Terence Halliday. 2011. "Social Ecology, Recursivity and Temporality: Toward a Sociology of Global Lawmaking." Paper presented at the American Sociological Association Meetings, Las Vegas.

Bohr, Niels. (1955) 1958. *Atoms and Human Knowledge*. New York: Wiley.

Boisson de Chazournes, Laurence, and Philippe Sands. 1999. *International Law, the International Court of Justice and Nuclear Weapons*. Cambridge: Cambridge University Press.

Bourdieu, Pierre. 1984. *Distinction: A Social Critique of Judgement*. Cambridge, MA: Harvard University Press.

———. 1987. "The Force of Law: Toward a Sociology of the Juridical Field." *Hastings Law Journal* 38: 805–53.

———. 2002. "Les conditions sociales de la circulation des idées." *Actes de la recherche en sciences sociales* 145: 8.

Bowie, Robert, and Carl Friedrich, eds. 1954. *Studies in Federalism*. Boston: Little, Brown.

Braun, Chaim, and Christopher Chyba. 2004 (Fall). "Proliferation Rings: New Challenges to the Nuclear Nonproliferation Regime." *International Security* 29 (2): 5–49.

Brinkley, Douglas. 1989. "Dean Acheson and the European Integration Movement." Paper presented at the Harry Truman Library Institute, September 21, 1989. JM, JMAS box 33.

Brinkley, Douglas, and Clifford Hackett, eds. 1991. *Jean Monnet: The Path to European Unity*. New York: Saint Martin's Press.

Brodie, Bernard, ed. 1946. *The Absolute Weapon: Atomic Power and World Order*. New York: Harcourt, Brace.

———. 1967 (March 9). "How Not to Lead an Alliance." *Reporter*.

Brzoska, Michael. 1992. "Is the Nuclear Non-proliferation System a Regime? A Comment on Trevor McMorris Tate." *Journal of Peace Research* 29 (2): 215–20.

Bundy, McGeorge, William Crowe Jr., and Sidney Drell. 1993. *Reducing Nuclear Danger: The Road away from the Brink*. New York: Council on Foreign Relations.

Butcher, Sandra Ionno. 2005 (May). "The Origins of the Russell-Einstein Manifesto." http://www.pugwash.org/publication/phs/history9.pdf.

Camic, Charles, Michèle Lamont, and Neil Gross, eds. 2011. *Social Sciences in the Making*. Chicago: University of Chicago Press.

Campbell, John. 1998. "Institutional Analysis and the Role of Ideas in Political Economy." *Theory and Society* 27: 377–409.

Camps, Miriam. 1965. *Britain and the European Community, 1955–1963*. Princeton, NJ: Princeton University Press.

Cannizzaro, Enzo, Paolo Palchetti, and Ramses Wessel, eds. 2011. *International Law as Law of the European Union*. Leiden: Nijhoff Publishers.

Charlton, Michael. 1987. "How and Why Britain Lost the Leadership of Europe." MK, box 2.

Chayes, Abram. 1972. *The Cuban Missile Crisis*. Oxford: Oxford University Press.

Christensen, Hans M. 2005. "US Nuclear Weapons in Europe: A Review of Post–Cold War Policy, Force Levels, and War Planning." Natural Resources Defense Council. http://www.nrdc.org/nuclear/euro/euro.pdf.

Cohen, Antonin. 2005. "La Constitution européenne: Ordre politique, utopie juridique et guerre froide." *Critique internationale* 26: 130.

———. 2009. "Le jour où l'Europe est née: Socio-histoire d'une décision politique." In *Pratiques et méthodes de la socio-histoire*, edited by Antonin Cohen, F. Buton, and N. Mariot, 123–65. Paris: PUF.

Cohen, Antonin, and Antoine Vauchez, eds. 2007. "Law, Lawyers, and Transnational Politics in the Production of Europe." *Law and Social Inquiry* 32 (1).

Cohen, Avner. 1998. *Israel and the Bomb*. New York: Columbia University Press.

———. 2010. *The Worst-Kept Secret: Israel's Bargain with the Bomb*. New York: Columbia University Press.

Cohen, Avner, and Marvin Miller. 2010. "Bringing Israel's Bomb out of the Basement." *Foreign Affairs*. Accessed November 14, 2013. http://www.foreignaffairs.com/articles/66569/avner-cohen-and-marvin-miller/bringing-israels-bomb-out-of-the-basement.

Cohen, Stanley. 2001. *States of Denial: Knowing about Atrocities and Suffering*. New York: Polity Press.

Corbett, Percy E. 1959. *Law in Diplomacy*. Princeton, NJ: Princeton University Press.

Cousin, Norman, and Thomas Finletter. 1946. "A Beginning for Sanity: A Review of the Acheson-Lilienthal Proposal." *Bulletin of the Atomic Scientists* 4: 3–10.

Debré, Michel. 1988. *Trois Républiques pour une France: Mémoires, 1946–58*. Paris: Albin Michel.

De Certeau, Michel. 1984. *The Practice of Everyday Life*. Translated by Steven Rendall. Berkeley: University of California Press.

Delmas-Marty, Mireille. 2006. *Les forces imaginaires du droit*. Vol. 2, *Le pluralisme ordonné*. Paris: Seuil.

Dezalay, Yves, and Bryant Garth. 2002. *The Internationalization of Palace Wars: Lawyers, Economists, and the Contest to Transform Latin American States*. Chicago: University of Chicago Press.

———. 2008. "National Usages for a 'Global' Science: The Dissemination of New Economic Paradigms as Strategy for the Reproduction of Governing Elites." In *Global Science and National Sovereignty: Studies in Historical Sociology of Science*, edited by Grégoire Mallard, Catherine Paradeise, and Ashveen Peerbaye, 143–67. New York: Routledge.

———. 2011. *Asian Legal Revivals: Lawyers in the Shadow of Empires*. Chicago: University of Chicago Press.

Donnelly, Jack. 1986. "International Human Rights: A Regime Analysis." *International Organization* 40 (3): 599–642.

Drezner, Daniel. 2009. "The Power and Peril of International Regime Complexity." *Perspectives on Politics* 7 (1): 65–70.

Duchêne, Francois. 1994. *Jean Monnet: The First Statesman of Interdependence*. New York: Norton.

ElBaradei, Mohamed. 2011. *The Age of Deception: Nuclear Diplomacy in Treacherous Times*. New York: Metropolitan Books.

Ellsberg, Daniel. 2010 (December 8). "Ex-Intelligence Officers, Others See Plusses in WikiLeaks Disclosures." Daniel Ellsberg website. Accessed November 2, 2013. http://www.ellsberg.net/archive/public-accuracy-press-release.

Elster, Jon. 1984. *Ulysses and the Sirens*. Cambridge: Cambridge University Press.

———. 1998. "Deliberation and Constitution Making." In *Deliberative Democracy*, edited by Jon Elster, 97–123. Cambridge, UK: Cambridge University Press.

Ewick, Patricia, and Susan Silbey. 1998. *The Common Place of Law: Stories from Everyday Life*. Chicago: University of Chicago Press.

Feldman, Shai. 1997a. "Israel's National Security: Perceptions and Policy." In *Bridging the Gap: A Future Security Architecture for the Middle East*, 7–33. New York: Rowman and Littlefield.

———. 1997b. *Nuclear Weapons and Arms Control in the Middle East*. Cambridge, MA: MIT Press.

Feldman, Shai, and Abdullah Toukan. 1997. *Bridging the Gap: A Future Security Architecture for the Middle East*. New York: Rowman and Littlefield.

Finnemore, Martha. 1993. "International Organizations as Teachers of Norms: The UNESCO and Science Policy." *International Organization* 47 (4): 565–97.

Finnemore, Martha, and Kathryn Sikkink. 1998. "International Norm Dynamics and Political Change." *International Organization* 52: 887–917.

Fish, Stanley. 1982. *Is There a Text in This Class? The Authority of Interpretive Communities*. Cambridge, MA: Harvard University Press.

Fligstein, Niel, and Alec Stone Sweet. 2002. "Constructing Politics and Markets: An Institutionalist Account of European Integration." *American Journal of Sociology* 5 (2): 1206–43.

Fontaine, Pascal. 1974. *Le Comité d'Action pour les Etats-Unis d'Europe de Jean Monnet*. Lausanne: Centre d'Etudes Européennes.

Forland, Astrid. 1997. "Negotiating Supranational Rules: The Genesis of the International Atomic Energy Agency Safeguards System." PhD diss., University of Bergen, Norway.

Foucault, Michel. 1995. *Discipline and Punish: The Birth of the Prison*. New York: Vintage Books.

———. 2003. *Society Must Be Defended: Lectures at the College de France, 1975–76*. New York: Picador Editions.

———. 2007. *Security, Territory, Population: Lectures at the College de France, 1977–1978*. Houndsmills, UK: Palgrave.

Friedberg, Aaron L. 2000. *In the Shadow of the Garrison State: America's Anti-statism and Its Cold War Grand Strategy*. Princeton, NJ: Princeton University Press.

Gaddis, John Lewis. 1972. *The United States and the Origins of the Cold War, 1941–1947*. New York: Columbia University Press.

———. 2005. *The Cold War: A New History*. New York: Penguin Press.

Galambos, Louis. 1989. *The Papers of Dwight David Eisenhower*. Vol. 12, *NATO and the Campaign of 1952*. London: Johns Hopkins.

Galison, Peter. 2004. "Removing Knowledge." *Critical Inquiry* 31 (1): 229–43.

Galison, Peter, and Baron Bernstein. 1989. "In Any Light: Scientists and the Decision to Build the Superbomb, 1942–1954." *Historical Studies in the Physical and Biological Sciences* 19: 267–347.

Gallois, Pierre-Marie. 1960. *Stratégie de l'âge nucléaire*. Paris: Calmann-Levy.

Garrett, Geoffrey, and Barry Weingast. 1993. "Ideas, Interests, and Institutions: Constructing the European Community's Internal Market." In *Ideas and Foreign Policy: Beliefs, Institutions, and Political Change*, edited by J. Goldstein and R. O. Keohane, 173–206. Ithaca, NY: Cornell University Press.

Gharmari-Tabrizi, Sharon. 2005. *The Worlds of Herman Kahn: The Intuitive Science of Thermonuclear War*. Cambridge, MA: Harvard University Press.

Gibson, David. 2011a. "Avoiding Catastrophe: The Interactional Production of Possibility during the Cuban Missile Crisis." *American Journal of Sociology* 117 (2): 361–419.

———. 2011b. *Talk at the Brink: Deliberation and Decision during the Cuban Missile Crisis*. Princeton, NJ: Princeton University Press.

Gilman, Nils. 2003. *Mandarins of the Future: Modernization Theory in Cold War America*. Baltimore: Johns Hopkins University Press.

Gilpin, Robert. 1962. *American Scientists and Nuclear Weapons Policy*. Princeton, NJ: Princeton University Press.

Goldschmidt, Bertrand. 1982. *The Atomic Complex: A Worldwide Political History of Nuclear Energy*. LaGrange, IL: American Nuclear Society Press.

Goldstone, Jack. 1998. "Initial Conditions, General Laws, Path Dependence, and Explanation in Historical Sociology." *American Journal of Sociology* 104: 829–45.

Gordin, Michael. 2007. *Five Days in August: How World War II Became a Nuclear War*. Princeton, NJ: Princeton University Press.

Greene, Benjamin P. 2007. *Eisenhower, Science Advice and the Nuclear Test-Ban Debate, 1945–1963*. Stanford, CA: Stanford University Press.

Grodzins, M., and E. Rabinowitch. 1963. *The Atomic Age: Scientists in National and World Affairs*. New York: Basic Books.

Guilhot, Nicolas. 2008. "The Realist Gambit: Postwar American Political Science and the Birth of IR Theory." *International Political Sociology* 2 (4): 281–304.

Gusterson, Hugh. 1996. *Nuclear Rites: A Weapons Laboratory at the End of the Cold War*. Berkeley: University of California Press.

———. 2004. *People of the Bomb: Portraits of America's Nuclear Complex*. Minneapolis: University of Minnesota Press.

Haas, Ernest. 1968. *The Uniting of Europe: Political, Social, and Economic Forces, 1950–1957*. Notre Dame, IN: University of Notre Dame Press.

Haas, Peter. 1992 (Winter). "Introduction: Epistemic Communities and International Policy Coordination." "Knowledge, Power, and International Policy Coordination." Special issue, *International Organization* 46 (1): 1–35.

Habermas, Jürgen. 1990. *Moral Consciousness and Communicative Action*. Translated by Christian Lenhardt and Shierry Weber Nicholsen. Cambridge, MA: MIT Press.

———. 1991. *The Structural Transformation of the Public Sphere: An Inquiry into a Category of Bourgeois Society*. Cambridge, MA: MIT Press.

———. 2001. *The Postnational Constellation: Political Essays*. Cambridge, MA: MIT Press.

Hagan, John. 2003. *Justice in the Balkans: Prosecuting War Crimes in the Hague Tribunal*. Chicago: University of Chicago Press.

Halberstam, Daniel. 2010. "Local, Global and Plural Constitutionalism: Europe Meets the World." In *The Worlds of European Constitutionalism*, edited by Grainne De Burca and Joseph Weiler, 150–202. Cambridge: Cambridge University Press.

Hall, Peter A. 1989. Introduction to *The Political Power of Economic Ideas: Keynesianism across Nations*. Edited by Peter A. Hall. Princeton, NJ: Princeton University Press.

Halliday, Terence. 2009. "Recursivity of Global Normmaking: A Sociological Agenda." *Annual Review of Sociology* 5: 263–89.

Halliday, Terence C., and Bruce G. Carruthers. 2007. "The Recursivity of Law: Global Norm Making and National Lawmaking in the Globalization of Corporate Insolvency Regimes." *American Journal of Sociology* 112 (4): 1135–1202.

———. 2009. *Bankrupt: Global Lawmaking and Systemic Financial Crisis*. Stanford, CA: Stanford University Press.

Hecht, Gabrielle. 1998. *The Radiance of France: Nuclear Power and National Identity after World War II*. Cambridge, MA: MIT Press.

———. 2006. "Negotiating Global Nuclearities: Apartheid, Decolonization, and the Cold War in the Making of the IAEA." *Osiris* 21: 25–48.

———. 2010. "The Power of Nuclear Things." *Technology and Culture* 51 (1): 1–30.

———. 2012. *Being Nuclear: Africans and the Global Uranium Trade*. Cambridge, MA: MIT Press.

Hemmer, Christopher, and Peter J. Katzenstein. 2002 (Summer). "Why Is There No NATO in Asia? Collective Identity, Regionalism, and the Origins of Multilateralism." *International Organization* 56 (3): 575–607.

Herken, Gregg. 1985. *Counsels of War*. New York: Knopf.

Hersh, Seymour. 1991. *The Samson Option: Israel's Nuclear Arsenal and American Foreign Policy*. New York: Random House.

Hershberg, James G. 1993. *James B. Conant: Harvard to Hiroshima and the Making of the Nuclear Age*. New York: Knopf.

Herter, Christian. 1963. *Toward an Atlantic Community*. Evanston, IL: Harper and Row for the Council on Foreign Relations.

Hewlett, Richard G., and Oscar E. Anderson Jr. 1962. *History of the United States Atomic Energy Commission*. Vol. 1, *The New World, 1939–1946*. University Park: Pennsylvania State University Press.

Hogan, Michael J. 1998. *A Cross of Iron: Harry S. Truman and the Origins of the National Security State, 1945–1954*. Cambridge: Cambridge University Press.

Hollinger, David. 1998. *Science, Jews, and Secular Culture: Studies in Mid-Twentieth-Century American Intellectual History*. Princeton, NJ: Princeton University Press.

———. 2008 (January 24). "Separation Anxiety." *London Review of Books*, 15–18.

Holloway, David. 1994. *Stalin and the Bomb: The Soviet Union and Atomic Energy, 1939–1956*. New Haven, CT: Yale University Press.

Hooghe, Liesbet, and Gary Marks. 2001. *Multi-level Governance and European Integration*. New York: Rowman and Littlefield.

Hosmer, Craig. 1964 (January 4). "Problems of Proliferation." *Washington Report* 65 (1): 1–4.

Howlett, Darryl A. 1990. *Euratom and Nuclear Safeguards.* London: Macmillan Press.

Hurd, Ian. 2007. *After Anarchy: Legitimacy and Power at the UN Security Council.* Princeton, NJ: Princeton University Press.

International Law Commission (ILC). 2006. *Fragmentation of International Law: Difficulties Arising from the Diversification and Expansion of International Law.* Report of the Study Group of the ILC. Accessed November 2, 2013. http://www.un.org/ga/search/view_doc.asp?symbol=A/CN.4/L.702.

Isaacson, Walter, and Evan Thomas. 1986. *The Wise Men: Six Men and the World They Made—Acheson, Bohlen, Harriman, Kennan, Lovett, McCloy.* New York: Simon and Schuster.

Janis, Irving. 1972. *Victims of Groupthink: A Psychological Study of Foreign Policymaking Decisions and Fiascoes.* Boston: Houghton Mifflin.

Jasper, James M. 1990. *Nuclear Politics: Energy and the State in the United States, Sweden and France.* Princeton, NJ: Princeton University Press.

Jay, Martin. 2010. *The Virtues of Mendacity: On Lying in Politics.* Charlottesville: University of Virginia Press.

Jervis, Robert. 1976. *Perception and Misperception in International Politics.* Princeton, NJ: Princeton University Press.

———. 1983. "Security Regimes." In *International Regimes*, edited by Stephen Krasner, 173–94. Ithaca, NY: Cornell University Press.

Joxe, Alain. 1990. *Le cycle de la dissuasion, 1945–1990.* Paris: Editions La Découverte.

Judt, Tony. 2006. *Postwar: A History of Europe since 1945.* New York: Penguin Books.

Kahn, Herman. 1961. *On Thermonuclear War.* Princeton, NJ: Princeton University Press.

Kahneman, Daniel, and Amos Tversky. 1984. "Choices, Values, and Frames." *American Psychologist* 39 (4): 341–50.

Kaiser, David. 2005. "The Atomic Secret in Red Hands? American Suspicions of Theoretical Physicists during the Early Cold War." *Representations* 90 (1): 28–60.

Kaplan, Fred. 1983. *The Wizards of Armageddon.* New York: Simon and Schuster.

Karpik, Lucien. 2007. *L'économie des singularités.* Paris: Gallimard.

Katzenstein, Peter J., ed. 1996. *The Culture of National Security: Norms and Identity in World Politics.* New York: Columbia University Press.

Kaufman, William W., and Albert Wohlstetter, eds. 1956. *Military Policy and National Security.* Princeton, NJ: Princeton University Press.

Kennedy, David. 2006. "One, Two, Three, Many Legal Orders: Legal Pluralism and the Cosmopolitan Dream." Speech delivered at the International Law Association. http://www.law.harvard.edu/faculty/dkennedy/speeches/LegalOrders.pdf.

Kennedy, Robert. 1969. *Thirteen Days: A Memoir of the Cuban Crisis.* New York: Norton.

Keohane, Robert O. 1983. "The Demand for International Regimes." In *International Regimes*, edited by Stephen Krasner, 141–72. Ithaca, NY: Cornell University Press.

———. 1984. *After Hegemony: Cooperation and Discord in the World Political Economy.* Princeton, NJ: Princeton University Press.

Keohane, Robert, Stephen Macedo, and Andrew Moravcsik. 2009. "Democracy-Enhancing Multilateralism." *International Organization* 63 (4): 1–31.

Keohane, Robert O., and Joseph S. Nye, eds. 1971. *Transnational Relations and World Politics.* Cambridge, MA: Harvard University Press.

Kevles, Daniel. 1978. *The Physicists: The History of a Scientific Community in Modern America.* New York: Knopf.

Killian, James. 1977. *Sputnik, Scientists, and Eisenhower: A Memoir of the First Special Assistant to the President for Science and Technology*. Cambridge, MA: MIT Press.

Kissinger, Henry A. 1958. *Nuclear Weapons and Foreign Policy*. New York: Anchor Books.

———. 1984. *Diplomacy*. New York: Random House.

Klabbers, Jan. 2011. "The Validity of EU Norms Conflicting with International Obligations." In *International Law as Law of the European Union*, edited by Enzo Cannizaaro, Paolo Palchetti, and Ramses Wessel, 110–31. Leiden: Nijhoff Publishers.

Knorr Cetina, Karin. 1999. *Epistemic Cultures: How the Sciences Make Knowledge*. Cambridge, MA: Harvard University Press.

Kohl, Wilfrid. 1971. *French Nuclear Diplomacy*. Princeton, NJ: Princeton University Press.

Koskenniemi, Martti. 2001. *The Gentle Civilizer of Nations: The Rise and Fall of International Law, 1870–1960*. Cambridge: Cambridge University Press.

———. 2002. "Fragmentation of International Law: Postmodern Anxieties." *Leiden Journal of International Law* 15: 552–79.

———. 2007. "Constitutionalism as Mindset: Reflections on Kantian Themes about International Law and Globalization." *Theoretical Inquiries in Law* 8 (1): 9–36.

Kramish, Arnold. 1967. "The Watched and the Unwatched: Inspection in the Nonproliferation Treaty." *Adelphi Papers* 36. London: Institute for Strategic Studies.

Krasner, Stephen D. 1983. "Structural Causes and Regime Consequences: Regimes as Intervening Variables." In *International Regimes*, edited by Stephen Krasner, 1–21. Ithaca, NY: Cornell University Press.

———. 1999. *Sovereignty: Organized Hypocrisy*. Princeton, NJ: Princeton University Press.

Kratochwil, Friedrich V. 1989. *Rules, Norms and Decisions: On the Conditions of Practical and Legal Reasoning in International Relations and Domestic Society*. Cambridge: Cambridge University Press, 1989.

Krause, Keith. 1994. "The Evolution of Arms Control in the Middle East." In *Confidence Building Measures in the Middle East*, edited by Gabriel Ben Dor and David Dewitt, 267–90. Boulder, CO: Westview Press.

Krige, John. 2006a. "Atoms for Peace, Scientific Internationalism and Scientific Intelligence." In *Global Power Knowledge: Science, Technology and International Affairs*, edited by J. Krige and Kai-Henrik Barth, 161–81. *Osiris*, University of Chicago Press Journals.

———. 2006b. *American Hegemony and the Postwar Reconstruction of Science in Europe*. Cambridge, MA: MIT Press.

———. 2008. "The Peaceful Atom as Political Weapon: Euratom and American Foreign Policy." *Historical Studies in the Natural Sciences* 38 (1): 9–48.

Kroenig, Matthew. 2010. *Exporting the Bomb: Technology Transfer and the Spread of Nuclear Weapons*. Ithaca, NY: Cornell University Press.

Kubbig, B. W. 1996. *Communicators in the Cold War: The Pugwash Conferences, the US-Soviet Study Group and the ABM Treaty*. PRIF report no. 44. Frankfurt, Germany: Peace Research Institute Frankfurt.

Kuklick, Bruce. 2006. *Blind Oracles: Intellectuals and War from Kennan to Kissinger*. Princeton, NJ: Princeton University Press.

Latour, Bruno. 1987. *Science in Action: How to Follow Scientists and Engineers through Society*. Cambridge, MA: Harvard University Press.

———. 2002. *La fabrique du droit: Une ethnographie du Conseil d'Etat*. Paris: La Découverte.

———. 2009. *The Making of Law: An Ethnography of the Conseil d'Etat*. New York: Polity Press.

Lebow, Richard Ned. 1983. "The Cuban Missile Crisis: Reading the Lessons Correctly." *Political Science Quarterly* 98 (3): 431–58.

Lebow, Richard Ned, and Janice Gross Stein. 1995. *We All Lost the Cold War*. Princeton, NJ: Princeton University Press.

Levy, Adrian, and Catherine Scott-Clark. 2008. *Deception: Pakistan, the United States and the Secret Trade in Nuclear Weapons*. New York: Bloomsberry.

Licklider, Roy E. 1971. *The Private Nuclear Strategists*. Cleveland: Ohio University Press.

Lilienthal, David. 1946. "How Can Atomic Energy Be Controlled?" *Bulletin of the Atomic Scientists* 8: 13–15.

———. 1949. "The Fellowship Program." *Bulletin of the Atomic Scientists* 35 (3): 166–72.

———. 1963a. *The Journals of David E. Lilienthal*, vol. 1.2. New York: Harper and Row.

———. 1963b. *Change, Hope and the Bomb*. Princeton, NJ: Princeton University Press.

Lindseth, Peter. 2010. *Power and Legitimacy: Reconciling Europe and the Nation-State*. Oxford: Oxford University Press.

Loewenstein, Karl. 1955. "The Bonn Constitution and the European Defense Community Treaties: A Study in Judicial Frustration." *Yale Law Journal* 64 (6): 805–39.

Machiavelli, Niccolò. (1532) 1988. *The Prince*. Edited by Quentin Skinner. Cambridge: Cambridge University Press.

Maddock, Shane Joseph. 1997. "The Nth Country Conundrum: The American and Soviet Quest for Nuclear Nonproliferation, 1945–1970." PhD diss., University of Connecticut.

Madsen, Mikael Rask. 2010. *La genèse de l'Europe des droits de l'homme: Enjeux juridiques et stratégies d'État (France, Grande-Bretagne et pays scandinaves, 1945–1970)*. Strasbourg: Presses Universitaires de Strasbourg.

Majone, Giandomenico. 1993. "The European Community between Social Policy and Social Regulation." *Journal of Common Market Studies* 31 (2): 153–70.

Mallard, Grégoire. 2006. "Quand l'expertise se heurte au pouvoir souverain: La nation américaine face à la prolifération nucléaire, 1945–1953." *Sociologie du Travail* 48 (3): 367–89.

———. 2008a. "Can the Euratom Treaty Inspire the Middle East? The Promises of Nuclear Regional Authorities." *Nonproliferation Review* 15 (3): 459–77.

———. 2008b. "Who Shall Keep Humanity's 'Sacred Trust'? International Liberals, Cosmopolitans, and the Problem of Nuclear Proliferation." In *Global Science and National Sovereignty*, edited by Grégoire Mallard, Catherine Paradeise, and Ashveen Peerbaye, 82–120. New York: Routledge.

———. 2009. "L'Europe puissance nucléaire, cet obscur objet du désir." *Critique internationale* 42.

———. 2012. "From Europe's Past to the Middle East's Future: The Constitutive Purpose of Forward Analogies in International Security." Paper presented at the conference on Predictions in International Security. Paris: SciencesPo.

———. 2014. "Crafting the Nuclear Regime Complex (1950–1975): Dynamics of Harmonization of Opaque Treaty Rules." *European Journal of International Law* 25 (3).

Mallard, Grégoire, and Martial Foucault. 2011. "The Fractal Process of European Integration: A Formal Theory of Recursivity in the Field of European Security." *French Politics, Culture and Society* 29 (3): 68–89.

Mallard, Grégoire, and Andrew Lakoff. 2011. "Knowing the Future to Understand the Present: The Techniques of Prospection in National Security Planning." In *Social Sciences in the Making*, edited by Charles Camic, Michèle Lamont, and Neil Gross, 339–77. Chicago: University of Chicago Press.

Malye, François, and Benjamin Stora. 2012. *François Mitterrand et la guerre d'Algérie*. Paris: Fayard.

May, Andrew. 1998. *The Rand Corporation and the Dynamics of American Strategic Thought, 1946–1962.* Emory University, Department of History.

May, Ernest R., and Philip Zelikow, eds. 1997. *The Kennedy Tapes: Inside the White House during the Cuban Missile Crisis.* Cambridge, MA: Harvard University Press.

Mazower, Mark. 2010. *No Enchanted Palace: The End of Empire and the Ideological Origins of the United Nations.* Princeton, NJ: Princeton University Press.

McCloy, John. 1969. *The Atlantic Alliance: Its Origins and Its Future.* New York: Columbia University Press.

Mearsheimer, John. 1990. "Back to the Future: Instability in Europe after the Cold War." *International Security* 15 (4): 5–56.

———. 2011. *Why Leaders Lie: The Truth about Lying in International Politics.* Oxford: Oxford University Press.

Mérand, Frédéric. 2008. *European Defense Policy.* Oxford: Oxford University Press.

Mérand, Frédéric, and Vincent Pouliot. 2008. "Le monde de Pierre Bourdieu: Éléments pour une théorie sociale des relations internationales." *Canadian Journal of Political Science* 41 (3): 603–25.

Merritt, Richard, and Donald Puchala, eds. 1968. *Western European Perspectives on International Affairs.* New York: Praeger.

Meyer, John W., John Boli, George M. Thomas, and Francisco O. Ramirez. 1997. "World Society and the Nation State." *American Journal of Sociology* 103 (1): 144–81.

Mian, Zia, and M. V. Ramana. 2006. "Wrong Ends, Means and Needs: Behind the U.S. Nuclear Deal with India." *Arms Control Today* (January–February): 11–17.

Milward, Alan. 1992. *The European Rescue of the Nation-State.* London: Routledge.

———. 2002. *The Rise and Fall of a National Strategy, 1945–1963.* London: Whitehall History Publishing.

Mirowski, Philip. 2002. *Machine Dreams: How Economics Became a Cyborg Science.* Cambridge, MA: MIT Press.

Monnet, Jean. 1976. *Mémoires.* Paris: Fayard.

Moore, Kelly. 2008. *Disrupting Science: Social Movements, American Scientists, and the Politics of the Military, 1945–1975.* Princeton, NJ: Princeton University Press.

Moravcsik, Andrew. 1993. "Preferences and Power in the European Community: A Liberal Intergovernmental Approach." *Journal of Common Market Studies* 33: 611–28.

———. 1998. *The Choice for Europe: Social Purpose and State Power from Messina to Maastricht.* Ithaca, NY: Cornell University Press.

———. 2000. "The Origins of Human Rights Regimes: Democratic Delegation in Postwar Europe." *International Organization* 54 (2): 217–52.

Morgenthau, Hans J. 1960. *Politics among Nations.* 3rd ed. New York: Knopf.

Murphy, Cornelius F. 1985. *The Search for World Order: A Study of Thought and Action.* Dordrecht: Martinus Nijhoff Publishers.

Neustadt, Richard E. 1970. *Alliance Politics.* New York: Columbia University Press.

Neustadt, Richard E., and Ernest May. 1986. *Thinking in Time: The Uses of History for Decision-Makers.* New York: Free Press.

Newhouse, John. 1964. "An Appraisal of the MLF." *Bulletin of the Atomic Scientists* 20 (9): 13–18.

Norris, Robert S. 2003. *Racing for the Bomb: General Leslie R. Groves, the Manhattan Project's Indispensable Man.* New York: Steerforth.

Nye, Joseph S. 1971. *Peace in Parts: Integration and Conflict in Regional Organization.* Boston: Little, Brown.

———. 1980. *The International Nonproliferation Regime*. Muscatine, IA: Stanley Foundation.

———. 1981. "Maintaining the Non-proliferation Regime." *International Organization* 35 (1): 15–38.

Nys, Ernest. 1909. *Les Etats-Unis et le droit des gens*. Brussels: Presses de l'Université libre de Bruxelles.

Obama, Barack. 2007. *The Audacity of Hope: Thoughts on Reclaiming the American Dream*. New York: Canongate.

Oppenheimer, J. Robert. 1947. "Functions of the International Agency in Research and Development." *Bulletin of the Atomic Scientists* 16: 173–75.

Parsons, Craig. 2002. "Showing Ideas as Causes: The Origins of the European Union." *International Organization* 56 (1): 47–84.

Paul, T. V. 2003. "Chinese-Pakistani Nuclear/Missile Ties and Balance of Power Politics." *Non-proliferation Review* 10 (2): 21–29.

Péan, Pierre. 1981. *Les deux Bombes*. Paris: Fayard.

Perkovich, George. 1999. *India's Nuclear Bomb: The Impact on Global Proliferation*. Berkeley: University of California Press.

Perkovich, George, Jessica T. Mathews, Joseph Cirincione, Rose Gottemoeller, and Jon B. Wolfsthal. 2007. *Universal Compliance: A Strategy for Nuclear Security*. Washington, DC: Carnegie Endowment for International Peace. http://carnegieendowment.org/files/univ_comp_rpt07_final1.pdf.

Peyrefitte, Alain. 1994. *C'était de Gaulle*. Paris: Gallimard.

Philpott, Daniel. 2001. *Revolutions in Sovereignty: How Ideas Shaped Modern International Relations*. Princeton, NJ: Princeton University Press.

Picciotto, Sol. 2011. "International Transformations of the Capitalist State." *Antipode* 43 (1): 87–107.

Polakow-Suransky, Sasha. 2010. *The Unspoken Alliance: Israel's Secret Relationship with South Africa*. New York: Pantheon.

Polanyi, Michael. 1949. "The Case for Individualism." *Bulletin of the Atomic Scientists* 35: 19–21.

———. 1952. "Some British Experience." *Bulletin of the Atomic Scientists* 8 (7): 223–33.

Posen, Barry R. 1984. *The Sources of Military Doctrine: France, Great Britain and Germany between the World Wars*. Ithaca, NY: Cornell University Press.

Price, Matt. 1995. "Roots of Dissent: The Chicago Met Lab and the Origins of the Franck Report." *Isis* 86 (2): 222–44.

Puchala, Donald J., and Raymond Hopkins. 1983. "International Regimes: Lessons from Inductive Analysis." In *International Regimes*, edited by Stephen Krasner, 61–92. Ithaca, NY: Cornell University Press.

Ranganathan, Surabhi. 2010. "Conflict and Accommodation: The India-US Nuclear Deal and the Nuclear Governance Regime." Paper presented to the SIAS Meetings on Comparative Federalism. Michigan Law School, Ann Arbor.

———. 2011. "Visions of International Law: Lessons from the 123 Agreement." *Indian Journal of International Law* 51 (2): 146–97.

Reich, Bernard. 1994. "The United States and the Arab-Israeli Peace Process." In *Confidence Building Measures in the Middle East*, edited by Gabriel Ben Dor and David Dewitt, 221–48. Boulder, CO: Westview Press.

Rhodes, Richard. 1986. *The Making of the Atomic Bomb*. New York: Touchstone.

Riles, Anneline. 1999 (October). "Models and Documents: Artefacts of International Legal Knowledge." *International and Comparative Law Quarterly* 48: 805–25.

Risse, Thomas, and Kathryn Sikkink. 1999. "The Socialization of International Human Rights Norms into Domestic Practices: Introduction." In *The Power of Human Rights: International Norms and Domestic Change*, edited by Thomas Risse, Stephen C. Ropp, and Kathryn Sikkink, 1–38. New York: Cambridge University Press.

Risse-Kappen, Thomas. 1995. *Cooperation among Democracies: The European Influence on US Foreign Policy*. Princeton, NJ: Princeton University Press.

Rosenberg, David A. 1983. "The Origins of Overkill: Nuclear Weapons and American Strategy, 1945–1960." *International Security* 7 (4): 3–71.

Roth, Etienne. 1994. "Jules Guéron (1907–1990)." In *Les Professeurs du Conservatoire national des Arts et Métiers: Dictionnaire biographique, 1794–1955*, edited by Claudine Fontanon and André Grelon, 596–608. Paris: Institut national de recherche pédagogique du CNAM.

Rydell, Randy J. 1991. "Opaque Proliferation and the Public Agenda." In *Opaque Nuclear Proliferation: Methodological and Policy Implications*, edited by Benjamin Frankel, 125–51. New York: Routledge.

Sagan, Scott D. 1994 (Spring). "The Perils of Proliferation: Organization Theory, Deterrence Theory and the Spread of Nuclear Weapons." *International Security* 18 (4): 66–107.

———. 1996 (Winter). "Why Do States Build Nuclear Weapons? Three Models in Search for a Bomb." *International Security* 21 (3): 54–86.

Saito, Hiro. 2006. "Reiterated Commemoration: Hiroshima as National Trauma." *Sociological Theory* 24 (4): 353–76.

Scharpf, Fritz. 1999. *Governing in Europe: Effective and Democratic?* Oxford: Oxford University Press.

Scheinman, Lawrence. 1966. *Atomic Energy Policy in France under the Fourth Republic*. Princeton, NJ: Princeton University Press.

———. 1967. *Euratom: Nuclear Integration in Europe*. New York: Carnegie Endowment for International Peace.

———. 1987. *The International Atomic Energy Agency and World Nuclear Order*. Washington, DC: Resources for the Future.

Schelling, Thomas. 1960. *The Strategy of Conflicts*. Cambridge, MA: Harvard University Press.

Scheppele, Kim Lane. 2004. "Law in a Time of Emergency: States of Exception and the Temptations of 9/11." *University of Pennsylvania Journal of Constitutional Law* 6 (5): 1001–83.

———. 2006. "The Migration of Anti-constitutional Ideas: The Post-9/11 Globalization of Public Law and the International State of Emergency." In *The Migration of Constitutional Ideas*, edited by Sujit Choudhry. Cambridge: Cambridge University Press.

———. Unpublished. "Counter-constitutions: Creating a Constitutional Nation in Post-communist Hungary."

Schlesinger, Arthur. 1978. *A Thousand Days: John F. Kennedy in the White House*. New York: Mariner Books.

Schmitt, Carl. (1932) 1996. *The Concept of the Political*. Chicago: University of Chicago Press.

———. (1950) 2003. *The Nomos of the Earth in the International Law of the Jus Publicum Europeam*. New York: Telos Press Publishing.

Schrafstetter, Susanna, and Stephen Twigge. 2004. *Avoiding Armageddon: Europe, the United States and the Struggle for Nuclear Nonproliferation, 1945–1970*. London: Praeger.

Schwartz, Hans-Peter. 1992. "Adenauer, le nucléaire et la France." *Revue d'histoire diplomatique* 4: 34–56.

Schwartz, Thomas Alan. 2003. *Lyndon Johnson and Europe: In the Shadow of Vietnam*. Cambridge, MA: Harvard University Press.

Scott, Len, and Steve Smith. 1994. "Lessons of October: Historians, Political Scientists, Policy-Makers and the Cuban Missile Crisis." *International Affairs* 70 (4): 659–84.

Scott, Shirley V. 2004. *International Law in World Politics*. Boulder, CO: Lynne Rienner Publishers.

Seaborg, Glenn, with Benjamin Loeb. 1971. *Kennedy, Khrushchev, and the Test Ban*. Berkeley: University of California Press.

———. 1987. *Stemming the Tide: Arms Control in the Johnson Years*. Lexington, MA: Heath and Company.

Shaffer, Gregory, and Mark Pollack. 2010. "Hard vs. Soft Law: Alternatives, Complements and Antagonists in International Governance." *Minnesota Law Review* 94: 706–97.

———. 2011. "Hard versus Soft Law in International Security." *Boston College Law Review* 52: 1147–1241.

Shaker, Mohammed Ibrahim. 1976. *The Nuclear Non-proliferation Treaty*. New York: Oceana Publications.

Shepard, Todd. 2008. *1962: Comment l'indépendance algérienne a transformé la France*. Paris: Payot.

Shils, Edward. 1946. "Some Political Implications of the State Department Report." *Bulletin of the Atomic Scientists* 4: 7–12.

———. 1952. "America's Paper Curtain." *Bulletin of the Atomic Scientists* 8 (7): 210–17.

Shotwell, James T. 1925. *Plans and Protocols to End War: Historical Outline and Guide*. New York: Carnegie Endowment for International Peace.

Silard, John. 1964. "The Case against the MLF." *Bulletin of the Atomic Scientists* 20 (9): 18–20.

Silbey, Susan, and Austin Sarat. 1987. "Critical Traditions in Law and Society Research." *Law and Society Review* 21 (1): 165–74.

Skogmar, Gunnar. 2004. *The United States and the Nuclear Dimension of European Integration*. London: Palgrave Macmillan.

Slaughter, Anne Marie. 2004. *A New World Order*. Princeton, NJ: Princeton University Press.

Smith, Gerard, and Helena Cobban. 1989. "A Blind Eye to Nuclear Proliferation." *Foreign Affairs* (Summer): 53–70.

Snead David L. 1999. *The Gaither Committee, Eisenhower, and the Cold War*. Columbus: Ohio State University Press.

Sokolski, Henry D. 2001 *Best of Intentions: America's Campaign against Strategic Weapons Proliferation*. Westport, CT: Praeger.

Solingen, Etel. 2000. "The Multilateral Arab-Israeli Negotiations: Genesis, Institutionalization, Pause, Future." *Journal of Peace Research* 37 (2): 167–87.

———. 2007. *Nuclear Logics: Contrasting Path in East Asia*. Princeton, NJ: Princeton University Press.

Soustelle, Jacques. 1965. *A New Road for France*. New York: Robert Speller and Sons.

Soutou, George Henri. 1994. "La politique nucléaire de Pierre Mendès France." In *La France et l'atome: Etudes d'histoire nucléaire*, edited by Maurice Vaïsse, 83–101. Brussels: Bruylant.

———. 1996. *L'alliance incertaine: Les rapports politico-stratégiques franco-allemands, 1954–1996*. Paris: Fayard.

Stein, Arthur A. 1983. "Coordination and Collaboration: Regimes in an Anarchic World." In *International Regimes*, edited by Stephen Krasner, 115–40. Ithaca, NY: Cornell University Press.

Steinmetz, George. 2007. *The Devil's Handwriting: Precoloniality and the German Colonial State in Qingdao, Samoa, and Southwest Africa*. Chicago: University of Chicago Press.

Stirk, Peter M. R., and David Weigall, eds. 1999. *The Origins and Development of European Integration: A Reader and Commentary*. London: Pinter.

Strange, Susan. 1983. "*Cave! hic dragones*: A Critique of Regime Analysis." In *International Regimes*, edited by Stephen Krasner, 337–53. Ithaca, NY: Cornell University Press.

Strauss, Frantz Josef. 1965. *The Grand Design: A European Solution to German Reunification*. New York: Praeger.

Stromseth, Jane. 1988. *The Origins of Flexible Response: NATO's Debates over Strategy*. New York: Saint Martin's Press.

Szilard, Leo. 1949. "Shall We Yield or Fight?" *Bulletin of the Atomic Scientists* 35 (3): 177–79.

———. 1960 (March). "To Stop or Not to Stop." *Bulletin of the Atomic Scientists* 16 (3): 82–84.

Tallberg, Jonas. 2002. "Paths to Compliance: Enforcement, Management, and the European Union." *International Organization* 56 (3): 609–43.

Tannenwald, Nina. 2007. *The Nuclear Taboo: The United States and the Non-use of Nuclear Weapons since 1945*. Cambridge: Cambridge University Press.

Tate, Trevor McMorris. 1990. "Regime-Building in the Non-proliferation System." *Journal of Peace Research* 27 (4): 399–414.

Teller, Edward. 1946. "Commentary on the *Acheson-Lilienthal Report*." *Bulletin of the Atomic Scientists* 10: 3–5.

Tertrais, Bruno. 2004. "Destruction Assurée: The Origins and Development of French Nuclear Strategy (1940–1981)." In *Getting MAD: Nuclear Mutual Assured Destruction, Its Origins and Practice*, edited by Henry Sokolski, 51–122. Strategic Studies Institute. Accessed November 25, 2013. http://www.strategicstudiesinstitute.army.mil/pdffiles/pub585.pdf.

Trachtenberg, Marc. 1999. *A Constructed Peace: The Making of the European Settlement*. Princeton, NJ: Princeton University Press.

United Nations, Commission on Atomic Energy. 1947. "Working Papers." *Bulletin of the Atomic Scientists* 13: 276–77.

Urey, Harold C. 1946. "Atomic Energy and World Peace." *Bulletin of the Atomic Scientists* 9: 2–4.

Vaïsse, Maurice. 1994. "Le choix atomique de la France, 1948–1956." In *La France et l'atome: Etudes d'histoire nucléaire*, edited by Maurice Vaïsse, 41–123. Brussels: Bruylant.

Viner, Jacob. 1946. "The Implications of Atomic Energy for International Relations." *Proceedings of the American Philosophical Society* 90 (1): 56.

Wallace, H., 1946. "Letter to the President." *Bulletin of the Atomic Scientists* 6: 2–4.

Walt, Stephen. 1988. "Testing Theories of Alliance Formation: The Case of Southwest Asia." *International Organization* 42 (2): 275–316.

Waltz, Kenneth N. 1981. *The Spread of Nuclear Weapons: More May Be Better*. London: International Institute for Strategic Studies.

———. 2008. "Reflections on *Theory of International Politics*: A Response to My Critics." In *Realism and International Relations*, 19–27. New York: Routledge.

Wang, Jessica. 2002. "Scientists and the Problem of the Public in Cold War America, 1945–1960." *Osiris* (17): 323–47.

Weiss, Louise. 1968. *Mémoires d'une Européenne*, vol. 2. Paris: Payot.

Williams, Robert Chadwell. 1987. *Klaus Fuchs: Atom Spy*. Cambridge, MA: Harvard University Press.

Wilson, Ward. 2008. "The Myth of Nuclear Deterrence." *Nonproliferation Review* 15 (3): 421–39.

Winand, Pascaline. 1996. *Eisenhower, Kennedy, and the United States of Europe.* New York: Palgrave Macmillan.

Wittner, Lawrence S. 1993. *The Struggle against the Bomb.* Vol. 1, *One World or None: A History of the World Nuclear Disarmament Movement through 1953.* Stanford, CA: Stanford University Press.

———. 1997. *The Struggle against the Bomb.* Vol. 2, *Resisting the Bomb: A History of the World Nuclear Disarmament Movement, 1954–1970.* Stanford, CA: Stanford University Press.

Wohlstetter, Albert. 1958 (November 6). "The Delicate Balance of Terror." http://www.rand.org/about/history/wohlstetter/P1472/P1472.html.

———. 1959. "The Delicate Balance of Terror." *Foreign Affairs* 37 (2): 211–34.

Wohlstetter, Albert, and Roberta Wohlstetter. 1965. "Controlling the Risks in Cuba." Adelphi Paper 17. London: International Institute for Strategic Studies.

Yergin, Daniel. 1977. *Shattered Peace: The Origins of the Cold War and the National Security Peace.* Princeton, NJ: Princeton University Press.

Yondorf, Walter. 1965. "Monnet and the Action Committee: The Formative Period of the European Communities." *International Organization* 19 (4): 885–912.

Young, Oran R. 1983. "Regime Dynamics: The Rise and Fall of International Regimes." In *International Regimes,* edited by Stephen Krasner, 61–92. Ithaca, NY: Cornell University Press.

INDEX

Page numbers for tables are followed by *t*.